Machiavelli's Liberal Republican Legacy

The significance of Machiavelli's political thinking for the development of modern republicanism is a matter of great controversy. In this volume, a distinguished team of political theorists and historians reassesses the evidence, examining the character of Machiavelli's own republicanism and charting his influence on Marchamont Nedham, James Harrington, John Locke, Algernon Sidney, John Trenchard, Thomas Gordon, David Hume, the baron de Montesquieu, Benjamin Franklin, George Washington, John Adams, Thomas Jefferson, James Madison, and Alexander Hamilton. This work argues that although Machiavelli himself was not liberal, he did set the stage for the emergence of liberal republicanism in England. To the exponents of commercial society, he provided the foundations for a moderation of commonwealth ideology, and he exercised considerable, if circumscribed, influence on the statesmen who founded the American Republic. *Machiavelli's Liberal Republican Legacy* will be of great interest to political theorists, early modern historians, and students of the American political tradition.

Paul A. Rahe is Jay P. Walker Professor of American History at the University of Tulsa. His first book, *Republics Ancient and Modern: Classical Republicanism and the American Revolution* (1992), was an alternative selection of the History Book Club and was reissued in a three-volume paperback edition in 1994. He coedited *Montesquieu's Science of Politics: Essays on the Spirit of Laws* (2001) and has published chapters in numerous other edited works as well as articles in journals such as *The American Journal of Philology, The American Historical Review, The Review of Politics, The Journal of the Historical Society, The American Spectator,* and *The Wilson Quarterly.* He is the recipient of a Rhodes scholarship and other research fellowships.

Machiavelli's Liberal Republican Legacy

Edited by

PAUL A. RAHE

University of Tulsa

CAMBRIDGE
UNIVERSITY PRESS

CAMBRIDGE UNIVERSITY PRESS
Cambridge, New York, Melbourne, Madrid, Cape Town, Singapore, São Paulo

Cambridge University Press
40 West 20th Street, New York, NY 10011-4211, USA

www.cambridge.org
Information on this title: www.cambridge.org/9780521851879

First published 2006

Printed in the United States of America

A catalog record for this publication is available from the British Library.

Library of Congress Cataloging in Publication Data

Machiavelli's liberal republican legacy / edited by Paul A. Rahe.
    p.   cm.
Includes bibliographical references and index.
ISBN 0-521-85187-4 (hardback : alk. paper)
1. Machiavelli, Niccolò, 1469–1527 – Influence.   2. Republicanism – History.
I. Rahe, Paul Anthony.   II. Title.
JC143.M4M323   2005
321.8′6–dc22   2005008121

ISBN-13   978-0-521-85187-9 hardback
ISBN-10   0-521-85187-4 hardback

For Harvey C. Mansfield

Contents

Contributors

Paul Carrese is Professor of Political Science at the U.S. Air Force Academy and Director of its Honors Program. He coedited John Marshall's *The Life of George Washington: Special Edition for Schools* (2001) and is author of *The Cloaking of Power: Montesquieu, Blackstone, and the Rise of Judicial Activism* (2003) and articles on political philosophy, constitutional law, the American founding, and George Washington.

John W. Danford, Professor of Political Science at Loyola University Chicago, is author of *Wittgenstein and Political Philosophy* (1978), *David Hume and the Problem of Reason* (1990), and *Roots of Freedom* (2000, 2004). He has also published articles and book chapters on Thomas Hobbes, Adam Smith, and the Scottish Enlightenment.

Markus Fischer, Assistant Professor in the Department of Liberal Studies at California State University, Fullerton, is author of *Well-Ordered License: On the Unity of Machiavelli's Thought* (2000), "Machiavelli's Political Psychology" (*Review of Politics* 1997), and "Machiavelli's Theory of Foreign Politics" (*Security Studies* 1995/96). He has also published on the international relations of feudal Europe and the role of culture in foreign affairs.

Steven Forde, Professor of Political Science at the University of North Texas, is author of *The Ambition to Rule: Alcibiades and the Politics of Imperialism in Thucydides* (1987). He has also published articles on classical and modern political thought, international ethics, and the American founding.

Paul A. Rahe, Jay P. Walker Professor of History at the University of Tulsa, is author of *Republics Ancient and Modern: Classical Republicanism and the American Revolution* (1992) and coeditor of *Montesquieu's Science of Politics: Essays on the Spirit of Laws* (2001). He has published numerous articles and book chapters on the history of self-government.

Gary Rosen is the managing editor of *Commentary*, the author of *American Compact: James Madison and the Problem of Founding* (1999), and the editor the *The Right War? The Conservative Debate on Iraq* (2005). He holds a Ph.D. in political science from Harvard University.

Margaret Michelle Barnes Smith, Instructor of Politics at Oglethorpe University, is a graduate student at Michigan State University. Her contribution to this book is her first publication.

Matthew Spalding, Director of the B. Kenneth Simon Center for American Studies at The Heritage Foundation, is coauthor of *A Sacred Union of Citizens: Washington's Farewell Address and the American Character* (1996) and co-editor of *Patriot Sage: George Washington and the American Political Tradition* (1999). He writes mostly on American political history and constitutionalism.

Vickie B. Sullivan, Associate Professor of Political Science at Tufts University, is the author of *Machiavelli, Hobbes, and the Formation of a Liberal Republicanism in England* (2004) and of *Machiavelli's Three Romes: Religion, Human Liberty, and Politics Reformed* (1996), the editor of *The Comedy and Tragedy of Machiavelli: Essays on the Literary Works* (2000), and coeditor of *Shakespeare's Political Pageant: Essays in Politics and Literature* (1996). She has published articles in *American Political Science Review*, *History of Political Thought*, *Political Theory*, and *Polity*.

C. Bradley Thompson, BB&T Research Professor at Clemson University, is author of the award-winning *John Adams and the Spirit of Liberty* (1998) and editor of *The Revolutionary Writings of John Adams* (2000) and *Antislavery Political Writings, 1833–1860: A Reader* (2003).

Karl-Friedrich Walling, Associate Professor of Strategy at the United States Naval War College, is the author of *Republican Empire: Alexander Hamilton on War and Free Government* (1999) and coeditor with Bradford Lee of *Strategic Logic and Political Rationality* (2003).

Acknowledgments

The project that eventuated in this book began a bit more than ten years ago in early September 1994, when three of the contributors – the authors of Chapters 8, 9, and 11 – appeared together on a panel at the annual meeting of the American Political Science Association. The papers they drafted for that gathering were eventually published together under the title "American Faces of Machiavelli" in *The Review of Politics* 57:3 (Summer 1995): 389–481, and are reprinted here in revised form with the permission of that journal's editor.

Chapter 1 is adapted in part from Paul A. Rahe's "An Inky Wretch: The Outrageous Genius of Marchamont Nedham," *National Interest* 70 (Winter 2002–3): 55–64. That article is reprinted here in revised form with the permission of that journal's editor. It is adapted in part from *Republics Ancient and Modern: Classical Republicanism and the American Revolution* by Paul A. Rahe (Chapel Hill, NC: University of North Carolina Press, 1992), and is used here by permission of the publisher.

Chapter 3 is adapted from Vickie B. Sullivan's, *Machiavelli, Hobbes, and the Formation of a Liberal Republicanism in England* (New York: Cambridge University Press, 2004), and is used here by permission of the publisher. Parts of Chapter 10 were first published in *American Compact: James Madison and the Problem of Founding* by Gary Rosen (Laurence, KS: University Press of Kansas, 1999), and are used here with the publisher's permission.

Abbreviations and Brief Titles

In the footnotes, we have adopted the standard abbreviations for classical texts and inscriptions and for books of the Bible provided in *The Oxford Classical Dictionary*, 3rd edition revised, ed. Simon Hornblower and Antony Spawforth (Oxford, UK: Oxford University Press, 2003), and in *The Chicago Manual of Style*, 15th edition (Chicago: University of Chicago Press, 2003), 15.50–3. Where possible, the ancient texts and medieval and modern works of similar stature are cited by the divisions and subdivisions employed by the author or introduced by subsequent editors (that is, by book, part, chapter, section number, paragraph, act, scene, line, Stephanus page, or page and line number). In some cases, where further specification is needed to help the reader to locate a particular passage, we have included as the last element in a particular citation the page or pages of the pertinent volume of the edition used. Although, for the convenience of those who do not know Italian, we cite recent English translations of Machiavelli's works, we have on occasion altered the translation in light of the Italian original. For modern works and for journals frequently cited, the following abbreviations and short titles have been employed:

ABF	*The Autobiography of Benjamin Franklin*, ed. Leonard W. Labaree et al. (New Haven, CT: Yale University Press, 1964).
AH	Alexander Hamilton.
AJL	*The Adams–Jefferson Letters: The Complete Correspondence between Thomas Jefferson and Abigail and John Adams*, ed. Lester J. Cappon (Chapel Hill, NC: University of North Carolina Press, 1959).
APSR	*The American Political Science Review*.
CJL	*The Correspondence of John Locke*, ed. Esmond S. de Beer (Oxford, UK: Clarendon Press, 1976–89).
CL	John Trenchard and Thomas Gordon, *Cato's Letters: or, Essays on Liberty, Civil and Religious, and Other*

	Important Subjects, ed. Ronald Hamowy (Indianapolis, IN: Liberty Classics, 1995).
Descartes, *DM*	René Descartes, *Discours de la méthode*, in René Descartes, *Oeuvres et lettres*, ed. André Bridoux (Paris: Bibliothéque de la Pléiade, 1953), 125–79.
Fed.	Alexander Hamilton, James Madison, and John Jay, *The Federalist*, ed. Jacob E. Cooke (Middletown, CT: Wesleyan University Press, 1961).
GW	George Washington.
GWC	*George Washington: A Collection*, ed. W. B. Allen (Indianapolis, IN: Liberty Classics, 1988).
Hobbes, *Behemoth*	Thomas Hobbes, *Behemoth, or The Long Parliament*, 2nd edition, ed. Ferdinand Tönnies (New York: Cass, 1969).
———, *Dialogue*	Thomas Hobbes, *A Dialogue between a Philosopher and a Student of the Common Laws of England*, ed. Joseph Cropsey (Chicago: University of Chicago Press, 1971).
———, *Elements*	Thomas Hobbes, *The Elements of Law Natural and Politic*, 2nd edition, ed. Ferdinand Tönnies (London: Cass, 1969).
———, *EW*	*The English Works of Thomas Hobbes of Malmesbury*, ed. Sir William Molesworth (London: J. Bohn, 1839–45).
———, *Leviathan*	Thomas Hobbes, *Leviathan: With Selected Variants from the Latin Edition of 1688* [1651], ed. Edwin Curley (Indianapolis, IN: Hackett, 1994).
———, *Phil. Rud.*	Thomas Hobbes, *Philosophicall Rudiments Concerning Government and Society*, in Hobbes, *De Cive: The English Version*, ed. Howard Warrender (Oxford, UK: Clarendon Press, 1983).
HPT	*History of Political Thought*.
Hume, *EHU*	David Hume, *An Enquiry Concerning Human Understanding*, in David Hume, *Enquiries Concerning the Human Understanding and Concerning the Principles of Morals*, 3rd edition, ed. L. A. Selby-Bigge with text revised and notes by P. H. Nidditch (Oxford, UK: Clarendon Press, 1975), 5–165.
———, *EMPL*	David Hume, *Essays Moral, Political, and Literary*, ed. Eugene F. Miller (Indianapolis, IN: Liberty Classics, 1985).
———, *EPM*	*An Enquiry Concerning the Principles of Morals*, in David Hume, *Enquiries Concerning the Human Understanding and Concerning the Principles of Morals*, 3rd edition, ed. L. A. Selby-Bigge with text

	revised and notes by P. H. Nidditch (Oxford, UK: Clarendon Press, 1975), 169–343.
———, *HE*	David Hume, *The History of England* (Indianapolis, IN: Liberty Classics, 1983).
———, *THN*	David Hume, *A Treatise of Human Nature*, ed. L. A. Selby-Bigge (Oxford, UK: Clarendon Press, 1888).
JA	John Adams.
Jefferson, *NSV*	Thomas Jefferson, *Notes on the State of Virginia*, ed. William Peden (Chapel Hill, NC: University of North Carolina Press, 1954).
JHO	*James Harrington's Oceana*, ed. S. B. Liljegren (Heidelberg: C. Winter, 1924).
JM	James Madison.
Locke, *ECHU*	John Locke, *An Essay Concerning Human Understanding*, ed. Peter H. Nidditch (Oxford, UK: Clarendon Press, 1979).
———, *LCT*	John Locke, *A Letter Concerning Toleration*, ed. James Tully (Indianapolis, IN: Hackett, 1983).
———, *STCE*	John Locke, *Some Thoughts Concerning Education*, ed. John W. Yolton and Jean S. Yolton (Oxford, UK: Clarendon Press, 1989).
———, *TTG*	John Locke, *Two Treatises of Government: A Critical Edition with an Introduction and Apparatus Criticus*, 2nd edition, ed. Peter Laslett (Cambridge, UK: Cambridge University Press, 1970), as corrected by Nathan Tarcov, *Locke's Education for Liberty* (Chicago: University of Chicago Press, 1984), 229–30 n. 324, 253–4 n. 187.
Madison, *MF*	*The Mind of the Founder: Sources of the Political Thought of James Madison*, revised edition, ed. Marvin Meyers (Hanover, NH: University Press of New England, 1981).
Montesquieu, *EL*	Charles de Secondat, baron de La Brède et de Montesquieu, *De l'esprit des lois*, in *WoM* 2:225–995.
———, *LP*	Charles de Secondat, baron de La Brède et de Montesquieu, *Lettres persanes*, in *WoM* 1:129–373.
———, *Rom.*	Charles de Secondat, baron de La Brède et de Montesquieu, *Considérations sur les causes de la grandeur des Romains et de leur décadence*, in *WoM* 2:69–209.
Nedham, *EFS*	Marchamont Nedham, *The Excellencie of a Free State* (1656), ed. Richard Baron (London: A. Millar and T. Cadell, 1767).
NM	Niccolò Machiavelli.

———, *AW*   Niccolò Machiavelli, *Art of War*, ed. and tr. Christopher
               Lynch (Chicago: University of Chicago Press, 2003).
———, *D*   Niccolò Machiavelli, *Discourses on Livy*, ed. and tr.
               Harvey C. Mansfield and Nathan Tarcov (Chicago:
               University of Chicago Press, 1996).
———, *FH*   Niccolò Machiavelli, *Florentine Histories*, ed. and tr.
               Laura F. Banfield and Harvey C. Mansfield (Princeton,
               NJ: Princeton University Press, 1988).
———, *O*   Niccolò Machiavelli, *Tutte le opere*, ed. Mario Martelli
               (Florence: G. C. Sansoni, 1971).
———, *P*   Niccolò Machiavelli, *The Prince*, tr. Harvey C.
               Mansfield (Chicago: University of Chicago Press, 1985).
PAH   *The Papers of Alexander Hamilton*, ed. Harold C. Syrett
               (New York: Columbia University Press, 1961–79).
PBF   *The Papers of Benjamin Franklin*, ed. Leonard W.
               Labaree et al. (New Haven, CT: Yale University Press,
               1959–2003).
PGM   *The Papers of George Mason*, ed. Robert A. Rutland
               (Chapel Hill, NC: University of North Carolina Press,
               1970).
PJA   *Papers of John Adams*, ed. Robert J. Taylor (Cambridge,
               MA: Harvard University Press, 1977–2000).
PJAM   *Papers of John Adams*, Microfilm, Massachusetts
               Historical Society.
PJM   *The Papers of James Madison*, ed. William T.
               Hutchinson, William M. E. Rachal, et al. (Chicago:
               University of Chicago Press, 1962–77; Charlottesville,
               VA: University Press of Virginia, 1977–).
PTJ   *The Papers of Thomas Jefferson*, ed. Julian P. Boyd
               (Princeton, NJ: Princeton University Press, 1950–).
PWoJH   *The Political Works of James Harrington*, ed. J. G. A.
               Pocock (Cambridge, UK: Cambridge University Press,
               1977).
RFC   *The Records of the Federal Convention of 1787*, ed.
               Max Farrand (New Haven, CT: Yale University Press,
               1911–37).
RP   *Review of Politics*.
Sidney, *CM*   Algernon Sidney, *Court Maxims*, ed. Hans W. Blom,
               Eco Haitsma Mulier, and Ronald Janse (Cambridge,
               UK: Cambridge University Press, 1996).
———, *DCG*   Algernon Sidney, *Discourses Concerning Government*,
               ed. Thomas G. West (Indianapolis, IN: Liberty Classics,
               1990).
TJ   Thomas Jefferson.
WMQ   *William and Mary Quarterly*, 3rd series.

WoFB	*The Works of Francis Bacon*, ed. James Spedding, Robert Leslie Ellis, and Douglas Denon Heath (London: Longman, 1857–74).
WoJA	*The Works of John Adams*, ed. Charles Francis Adams (Boston: Little, Brown, 1850–6).
WoJH	James Harrington, *Works: The Oceana and Other Works of James Harrington*, ed. John Toland (London: T. Becket, T. Cadell, and T. Evans, 1771).
WoJL	*The Works of John Locke* (London: T. Tegg, 1823).
WoLB	*The Works of Lord Bolingbroke, with a Life Prepared Expressly for this Edition, Containing Information Relative to His Personal and Public Character* (Philadelphia, PA: Carey and Hart, 1841).
WoM	Charles de Secondat, baron de La Brède et de Montesquieu, *Oeuvres complètes de Montesquieu*, ed. Roger Caillois (Paris: Bibliothèque de la Pléiade, 1949–51).
WoTJ	*The Works of Thomas Jefferson*, ed. Paul Leicester Ford (New York: G. P. Putnam's Sons, 1904–5).
WrBF	Benjamin Franklin, *Writings*, ed. J. A. Leo Lemacy (New York: Library of America, 1987).
WrGW	*The Writings of George Washington*, ed. John C. Fitzpatrick (Washington, DC: United States Government Printing Office, 1931–44).
WrTJ (ed. Ford)	*The Writings of Thomas Jefferson*, ed. Paul Leicester Ford (New York: G. P. Putnam's Sons, 1892–9).
WrTJ (ed. Lipscomb and Bergh)	*The Writings of Thomas Jefferson*, ed. Andrew A. Lipscomb and Albert Ellery Bergh (Washington, DC: Thomas Jefferson Memorial Association, 1903).
WrTJ (ed. Peterson)	Thomas Jefferson, *Writings*, ed. Merrill D. Peterson (New York: Library of America, 1984).
WrTJ (ed. Washington)	*The Writings of Thomas Jefferson*, ed. H. A. Washington (New York: Taylor & Maury, 1853–5).

Introduction

Machiavelli's Liberal Republican Legacy

Paul A. Rahe

The contributors to this volume are debtors. They work in a field that others opened up, cleared, and to a certain extent tilled before most of them even came on the scholarly scene. Their creditors in this particular regard are, as one would expect, numerous – but five of these stand out.

The first is a scholar named Zera Fink. Some sixty years ago, in 1945, as the Second World War came to an end, he published a slender volume entitled *The Classical Republicans: An Essay in the Recovery of a Pattern of Thought in Seventeenth-Century England*, which he characterized as "a chapter in the history of ideas."[1] Fink's book was a pioneering work aimed at establishing the Machiavellian character of much of the thinking inspired by England's abortive republican experiment and at clarifying its overall significance.

Fourteen years after the appearance of Fink's work, Caroline Robbins brought out *The Eighteenth-Century Commonwealthman: Studies in the Transmission, Development and Circumstance of English Liberal Thought from the Restoration of Charles II until the War with the Thirteen Colonies*, a no less seminal book that took up the story of English radicalism at almost precisely the point where Fink left off.[2] Eight years later, Bernard Bailyn presented to the world *The Ideological Origins of the American Revolution*, a work of comparable significance, which traced the influence on the American colonists of the 1760s and 1770s of the thinking of Fink's seventeenth-century classical republicans and Robbins's eighteenth-century commonwealthmen.[3] Then,

---

[1] See Zera S. Fink, *The Classical Republicans: An Essay in the Recovery of a Pattern of Thought in Seventeenth-Century England*, 2nd edition (Evanston, IL: Northwestern University Press, 1962), vii. I cite the preface to the first edition, which was published in 1945.

[2] See Caroline Robbins, *The Eighteenth-Century Commonwealthman: Studies in the Transmission, Development and Circumstance of English Liberal Thought from the Restoration of Charles II until the War with the Thirteen Colonies* (Cambridge, MA: Harvard University Press, 1959).

[3] See Bernard Bailyn, *The Ideological Origins of the American Revolution* (Cambridge, MA: Harvard University Press, 1967).

two years later, Gordon Wood brought out *The Creation of the American Republic, 1776–1787*, which explored the manner in which the tradition of thinking investigated by Fink, Robbins, and Bailyn influenced those who framed governments for the various states within the new American union in the years following the Declaration of Independence as well as those who framed the federal constitution in the summer of 1787.[4]

Finally, in 1974, J. G. A. Pocock published *The Machiavellian Moment: Florentine Political Thought and the Atlantic Republican Tradition*.[5] Drawing on the work of Fink, Robbins, Bailyn, Wood, and others, Pocock articulated a grand synthesis suggesting an essential continuity in republican thought, stretching from Aristotle to Machiavelli, from Machiavelli to James Harrington, and from Harrington to Thomas Jefferson.

Pocock's work was greeted with great applause – in part because it confirmed and strengthened a fashion then already gaining sway among historians and political scientists, who were increasingly inclined to contrast the public-spirited "republicanism" of America's founders with the tawdry "liberalism" of their successors.[6] The book's authority was great and its influence immense. Within the scholarly world, however, many believed that the author of *The Machiavellian Moment* was inclined on occasion to lump where he should have split, and a considerable literature emerged challenging his argument in one or another particular. In 1992, the editor of this volume published a weighty tome – entitled *Republics Ancient and Modern: Classical Republicanism and the American Revolution* – arguing that Pocock had it almost entirely wrong: that the republicanism of the American founders was in most regards a liberal republicanism and that they were the heirs of a series of revolutions in political thought that set Machiavelli at odds with Aristotle and classical republicanism, Harrington at odds with Machiavelli, and Jefferson at odds with Harrington.[7]

If, however, it no longer seems obvious that "liberalism" and the species of "republicanism" embraced by the English republicans, their radical Whig successors, and the American founders are as such incompatible, it is by no means

---

[4] See Gordon S. Wood, *The Creation of the American Republic, 1776–1787* (Chapel Hill, NC: University of North Carolina Press, 1969).

[5] See J. G. A. Pocock, *The Machiavellian Moment: Florentine Political Thought and the Atlantic Republican Tradition* (Princeton, NJ: Princeton University Press, 1974).

[6] See, for example, Robert E. Shalhope, "Toward a Republican Synthesis: The Emergence of an Understanding of Republicanism in American Historiography," *WMQ* 29:1 (January 1972): 49–80. See also Shalhope, "Republicanism and Early American Historiography," *WMQ* 39:2 (April 1982): 334–56. Pocock's earlier work, in anticipating the themes of his *Machiavellian Moment*, had done much to inspire this fashion: See J. G. A. Pocock, "Machiavelli, Harrington, and English Political Ideologies," *WMQ* 22:4 (October 1965): 549–83. See also J. G. A. Pocock, "Civic Humanism and Its Role in Anglo-American Thought," in Pocock, *Politics, Language, and Time: Essays on Political Thought and History* (New York: Atheneum, 1971), 80–103.

[7] See Paul A. Rahe, *Republics Ancient and Modern: Classical Republicanism and the American Revolution* (Chapel Hill, NC: University of North Carolina Press, 1992), which cites much, if not quite all, of the prior secondary literature in favor of and against the Pocockian synthesis.

clear what it was, if anything, that Machiavelli contributed to the development of self-government in modern times. The essays in this volume constitute a series of discrete but closely interrelated attempts to throw light on this matter. They examine with care the argument presented by Machiavelli in his *Discourses on Livy*, and they explore the manner in which the most important of the figures discussed by Fink, Robbins, Bailyn, Wood, and Pocock came to grips with, developed, and adapted the Florentine's argument.

The contributors to this book have much in common. They agree with Pocock that Machiavelli's influence was considerable – that many of the English republicans of the seventeenth century, the English commonwealthmen of the eighteenth century, and the leading figures of the Enlightenment in France and Scotland, as well as some of the American revolutionaries, learned a great deal from reading the *Discourses on Livy* or the works of those who restated its argument in whole or in part. They are united as well in regarding Pocock's depiction of Machiavelli's understanding of republicanism as highly misleading, and they are persuaded that Marchamont Nedham, James Harrington, John Locke, Algernon Sidney, John Trenchard, Thomas Gordon, David Hume, the baron de Montesquieu, George Washington, Benjamin Franklin, John Adams, Thomas Jefferson, James Madison, and Alexander Hamilton – all of whom Machiavelli influenced in one fashion or another – should be read not as semi-conscious speakers of a common political "language" unable to say or think what cannot be expressed in their inherited tongue but as fully conscious agents: liberated from intellectual servitude by their familiarity with a variety of ways of thinking about politics, inclined to judge what they read in light of their own considerable experience in the larger world, and wholly capable of thinking for themselves and of fashioning language with which to express their convictions, however unorthodox. One consequence is that the contributors to this book are convinced that Machiavelli's republican legacy is, while vital for under-standing the origins of modern liberal democracy, nonetheless quite complex and diverse. Their goal has been to do justice to that complexity and diversity while pointing, at the same time, to common threads. As will become clear, in receiving Machiavelli, the English commonwealthmen, their successors in the moderate Enlightenment, and the American founders adapted his teaching to their own needs, rejected it in part, and on occasion followed through on its underlying logic in a fashion that Machiavelli chose not to do.

Machiavelli's Modern Populism

In the prologue, Markus Fischer sets the stage. He begins by examining the civic humanist context within which Machiavelli composed his *Discourses on Livy* – outlining the character of the republicanism found in ancient Greece and Rome; touching on its analysis in the works of Aristotle, Cicero, Polybius, Livy, and Sallust; tracing the revival of civic aspirations in the late Middle Ages and among the humanists of the Renaissance; and demonstrating that Machiavelli, in full consciousness, repudiated his classical republican and civic humanist heritage.

In its stead, as Professor Fischer shows in detail, Machiavelli advocates a new species of republicanism, liberated from the moral restraints promoted by the ancients and their scholastic and humanist admirers. The tradition of natural law the Florentine pointedly ignores; justice he treats as purely instrumental. The notion that an education in moral virtue can be relied on he debunks; and, in its place, he promotes institutions bolstered by a peculiar mixture of savagery, ambition, and dread, which he calls *virtù*. Where the ancients thought concord the bulwark of a republic, Machiavelli favors tumults, seeing them as conducive not only to the defense of liberty but also to the acquisition of empire. That private interests will be pursued in and socioeconomic conflicts will impinge on the public arena he regards as both inevitable and good.

The management of affairs Machiavelli leaves to those whom he terms "princes." To found a republic, fashion its institutions, and make use of superstition to instill in the people that love of the fatherland and devotion to its defense and expansion that constitutes popular *virtù* takes the cunning and ruthlessness of a "new prince," endowed with a species of ambition and a virtuosity that the people can never attain. Moreover, in the absence of leaders constrained to some degree by tumults, inspired by a love of glory, and endowed with princely *virtù*, such a republic cannot be sustained, for it requires frequent refounding through exemplary punishments and deeds aimed at restoring the sense of dread that underpins popular *virtù*. Spirited execution is a *sine qua non* that takes precedence over justice itself.

Such a polity is distinguished from tyranny by the fact that it serves what Machiavelli calls "the common good." In using this term, the Florentine has in mind war, conquest, and empire aimed at satisfying at the expense of outsiders the ambition of the citizens and their longing for glory, power, and wealth. His republicanism inflames appetite; it sanctions and encourages licentiousness; and then, by means of laws and practices, especially those which institutionalize class conflict, it orders and channels appetite in such a way as to sustain liberty and promote expansion. In the end, Machiavelli's rapacious republic is held together by fear and by greed. A republic bereft of threatening enemies and of occasions for the exploitation of outsiders cannot, he believes, be maintained. When it exhausts both by conquering the world, as Rome did in time, it is doomed.

The English Commonwealthmen

Given the rapacious character of Machiavelli's republicanism and its repudiation of moral virtue, I argue in the preface to the book's first part that it is by no means strange that his republicanism encountered resistance – especially since circumstances in the sixteenth century were unfriendly to republics. It took an extraordinary event to make men receptive to the Florentine's blandishments, and the execution of Charles I on 30 January 1649 and the subsequent establishment of the English republic constituted just such an event, opening the way for a widespread consideration of what practical men intent on the preservation of liberty and the well-being of a commonwealth could learn of use from studying the *Discourses on Livy*. This event marked the first stage in the reception of Machiavelli's republican teaching, its adaptation and partial reorientation in light of persistent English concerns, which is the subject of the first three chapters in this book.

As I seek to make clear in this book's initial chapter, the first to distill the fruits of such study was the journalist Marchamont Nedham, who adapted Machiavelli's teaching to English tastes for English use and propagated a species of Machiavellian republicanism initially in the pages of the weekly gazette *Mercurius Politicus* in the period stretching from September 1651 to August 1652 and then in a book entitled *The Excellencie of a Free State*, which he published late in the spring of 1656. James Harrington followed suit with his *Commonwealth of Oceana* late that fall. Nedham emphasized Machiavelli's populism, praising with some reservations his defense of tumults and insisting, above all else, on the need for frequent elections, while Harrington sought to eliminate class conflict and tumults by designing institutions capable of sustaining themselves without princely and popular *virtù* as an auxiliary support. In the process of restating and refining Machiavelli's republicanism, both sought to tone it down and draw out the logic of the Florentine's populism in such a way as to subordinate honor and glory to the more prosaic concern with the protection of personal rights and property that animated the majority of those within the political nation.

Nedham and Harrington may have been the first Englishmen to exploit the tension in Machiavelli's republicanism between his aristocratic taste for grandeur and the populism he espouses. They were by no means the last. As Margaret Michelle Barnes Smith suggests in the second chapter of this book, John Locke followed much the same path, using Machiavelli's debunking of aristocratic virtue against Machiavelli's endorsement of glory to forge an understanding of liberty subordinated to the protection of personal rights and property. In their writings, Nedham and Harrington addressed, first and foremost, the small band of committed republicans who had favored England's republican experiment. Locke's intended audience was much larger and more diverse. In consequence, where these republicans acknowledged, at least in part, the debt they owed Machiavelli and Thomas Hobbes, Locke presented himself as a disciple of the venerable Anglican divine Richard Hooker and mentioned neither the Monster of Malmesbury nor the Florentine said to have given to the devil his moniker "Old Nick."[8]

That Locke read Machiavelli with great care seems, despite his reticence, quite clear. As Smith notes, he was an avid collector of the Florentine's writings, and he uses as the epigraph to his *Two Treatises of Government* a passage from Livy that Machiavelli repeatedly, in crucial passages, quotes. Both are, she contends, committed to a project aimed at liberating human beings from a tyranny grounded in what Hobbes called *Aristotelity*. They share a loathing of

---

[8] See Samuel Butler, *Hudibras*, ed. John Wilders (Oxford, UK: Clarendon Press, 1967), 3.1.1313–16.

what Harrington was the first to call "priestcraft," and they embrace political liberty and acquisitiveness as a solvent. Their methods are not precisely the same, but their goal is quite similar. Where Machiavelli aims at ousting ambitious prelates from the public sphere, Locke seeks to prevent those who enter the public sphere from addressing what he defines as a private concern. Where Machiavelli favors acquisition by martial means, Locke prefers acquisition by trade. Both wish to free politics from religious and clerical influence; both cast doubt on the providential goodness of the Christian God and the natural order; both recognize Aristotelian teleology as an obstacle and seek to debunk it; both treat the common good as a sum of individual, ineluctably private interests; neither argues on behalf of moral virtue as such; and both champion appetite and promote a species of rapacity. The chief difference is twofold: Locke has in mind the conquest of nature and not the acquisition of foreign peoples and lands, and, while encouraging a Machiavellian vigilance on the part of the people and a readiness on their part to resist oppression, like Nedham, he stops just short of embracing, as an ordinary mode of governance, institutionalized class conflict and tumults.

In this book's third chapter, Vickie B. Sullivan picks up the question of liberalism's debt to Machiavelli precisely where Smith leaves off. Professor Sullivan begins by noting that America's founders seemed blissfully unaware of the distinction between "liberalism" and "republicanism" that so occupied scholars in the late twentieth century. Where the latter tended to juxtapose and contrast the "liberalism" of Locke's *Two Treatises of Government* with the "republicanism" purportedly evident in Algernon Sidney's *Discourses Concerning Government* and in the newspaper series entitled *Cato's Letters*, which John Trenchard and Thomas Gordon penned early in the eighteenth century, these early Americans presumed that the political teaching of all three was in essence the same.

In the first half of her contribution, Professor Sullivan explores Sidney's debt to Machiavelli, showing that it was much more profound than is normally supposed; that the English republican plays a sly game of bait and switch, shifting quickly, effortlessly, and for the most part without acknowledgment from the respectable, rational Aristotelian republicanism evident in the early chapters of his *Discourses Concerning Government* to a rapacious republicanism rooted in an unleashing of the passions quite like that espoused in the *Discourses on Livy* – seeming to distance himself from the notorious Florentine while mimicking his subversive rhetoric, following his argument in some detail, and leading his readers step by step toward embracing tumults and acknowledging the necessity of war. In the end, Sidney differs with Machiavelli only where Locke and Nedham do – in subordinating rapacity to rights – and he differs with Locke chiefly in scorning trade and thinking tumults a necessity.

Where Sidney's Machiavellianism is muted but profound, Professor Sullivan argues in the second half of the third chapter, that of Trenchard and Gordon is manifest but comparatively shallow. *Cato's Letters* originated in 1720 as a plea for the imposition of exemplary punishments along Machiavellian lines on the malefactors responsible for the financial crisis known as the South Sea

Bubble, and it quickly turned into an analytical account of the principles of free government. Its authors broadcast their admiration for the Florentine, illustrating their critique of corruption at court with examples freely drawn from the *Discourses on Livy*, subordinating Machiavellian rapacity to the protection of rights and property in the fashion of Sidney, whom they frequently cite, and promoting aggrandizement through trade and technological progress rather than war in the manner favored by Locke.

The Moderate Enlightenment

A commitment to commerce and technology also distinguishes the three representatives of the moderate Enlightenment considered in the second part of the book – David Hume, the baron de Montesquieu, and Benjamin Franklin – and they display as well an aversion to war and a politics oriented by the pursuit of glory. They are, as I suggest in the preface to this book's second part, heirs to the Glorious Revolution, critics of the doctrinaire politics espoused by the radical Whigs, friends of civilized monarchy in a fashion that Machiavelli seems to sanction, and proponents of a species of moderation that owes more to a sober, muted, but nonetheless Machiavellian appreciation of the dictates of material self-interest than to the high-mindedness of the ancient Romans and Greeks. They have much in common with James Harrington, the odd man out in the age of the English republicans and the radical Whigs. Their Machiavellianism is highly qualified, as was his: They bridle at the prospect of tumults, and they prefer to rely on the quiet operation of institutions. Moreover, in all but the most extreme of circumstances, they prefer gradual reform to violent revolution. Their debt to Machiavelli is nonetheless considerable.

Hume is a case in point. To grasp what the Scot took from the Florentine, John Danford indicates in the fourth chapter of this book, one must first take a detour, noting Machiavelli's insistence that in the world of politics and morals nothing is quite as it seems and charting, if only briefly, the considerable debt owed Machiavelli by Sir Francis Bacon, René Descartes, and the other founders of modern science who applied to the natural world the skepticism and distrust he articulated first in the moral and political sphere. Like all the figures thus far considered, Hume took as his starting point Machiavelli's lowering of sights. In doing so, like Locke and the authors of *Cato's Letters*, he followed through on the logic of the Florentine's understanding in a way that set him at odds with the republicanism espoused in the *Discourses on Livy* and yet in a fashion that Machiavelli himself, at times, seems to sanction. Not only did Hume relegate the cultivation of moral virtue and the salvation of souls to the private sphere, he rejected the notion that free governments should seek to instill in their citizens moral and political virtue. Ancient policy he openly rejected as violent. Trade and manufactures he ostentatiously embraced, welcoming both not only because of the prosperity they bring and the appetites they satisfy but also for their political consequences – for the manner in which they promote negotiation, a peaceful adjustment of interests, and a self-interested civility as opposed to savagery. At the same time, Hume rejected social contract theory as likely to inflame the passions and embraced an account of the sentiments that left space for moral virtue of a sort, if only within the private sphere. Machiavelli's claim "that every man must be supposed a knave" Hume endorsed as a just political maxim, even though he regarded it as an inadequate account of man's moral capacities as an individual. He preferred political architecture of the sort devised by Harrington to the tumults recommended by their common Florentine mentor.

As Paul Carrese explains in the fifth chapter, Montesquieu's Machiavellianism is mitigated in a similar fashion. That Montesquieu read Machiavelli with inordinate care is obvious on every page of his "Dissertation on the Policy of the Romans in Religion" (1716), and the same can be said for his *Considerations on the Causes of the Greatness of the Romans and Their Decline* (1734), though he never cites the *Discourses on Livy* or mentions its author in either work. In *The Spirit of Laws* (1748), he is less reticent, citing the Florentine on four separate occasions, but these brief references greatly understate his debt.

Though it is abundantly clear that Montesquieu agrees with Machiavelli, Locke, Harrington, and Sidney in repudiating the ancient rejection of faction, he shies away from Machiavellian ferocity. Already in the *Persian Letters* (1721), he indicated a preference for governments that attain their goals with a minimum of friction. Moderation is for him, as it was for Hume, a watchword. In his *Considerations on the Causes of the Greatness of the Romans and Their Decline*, he accepts in nearly all regards Machiavelli's analysis of republican Roman politics, denounces ancient Rome as cruel and inhumane, and spells out the manner in which that city's success destroyed its liberty. In *The Spirit of Laws*, he celebrates the fact that the growth of commerce and the invention of the letter of exchange had begun to cure the world of Machiavellism and to encourage "more moderation in councils" by rendering "great acts of authority" and "coups d'état" counterproductive. Like Hume, Montesquieu is persuaded that commerce softens mores, promotes civility, and turns men away from a harmful and self-destructive pursuit of glory in war to the salutary, peaceful pursuit of wealth. Interest thereby checks passion. Both Montesquieu and Hume learned from Machiavelli that, in politics, moral virtue is a weak reed. Moderation in politics arises from institutions of the sort that Harrington had aimed at, not from moderation in the soul. With the separation of powers and the constitutionalization of factions associated with the executive and legislative power, Montesquieu sought to achieve an equilibrium conducive to the security and tranquillity of the individual. Crucial to this task, as Professor Carrese makes clear, is the judicial power – exemplified by the parlements of France, which had been singled out as a bulwark of effective government by no less an authority than Machiavelli not only in his *Discourses on Livy* but in *The Prince* as well.

Like Hume and Montesquieu, Steven Forde argues in the sixth chapter of this book, Benjamin Franklin shied away from Machiavelli's endorsement of tumults and war while nonetheless embracing his critique of the high-mindedness of the ancients and their Christian successors, adopting his conviction that it is interest that makes the world go round, promoting a redirection of the rapacity the Florentine favored from the conquest of men to that of nature, encouraging restraints on religious enthusiasm and zealotry, and substituting for moral fervor a general ethos of civility. He, too, was a proponent of what Hume and Montesquieu called "moderation," grounding it, as they did, in the silent operation of well-designed institutions and in a constant calculation of petty interests on the part of the citizenry of a sort quite effectively encouraged by conditions within commercial societies. That Franklin was the most reluctant of the American revolutionaries should come as no surprise.

The American Founding

The five figures discussed in the third part of this book have one thing in common: They were not first and foremost theorists; they were practitioners. They were statesmen, and they were founders. As such, they were saddled with a responsibility not only for the welfare of their contemporaries but also for that of succeeding generations. Justice was, in consequence, their prime concern, and this fact inevitably set them at odds with the author of *The Prince* and the *Discourses on Livy*, who owed his fame in large part to the scandal aroused by his resolute refusal to dignify the question of justice by addressing it. As I point out in the preface to this book's third part, this ruled out on the part of the American founders a wholesale adoption of Machiavelli's republican teaching, but it did not prevent them from finding useful on occasion the devices of Machiavellian statecraft.

Early in his chapter on George Washington, Matthew Spalding issues a salutary warning that should serve as an introduction to each and every one of the chapters that follow – noting that, for all of its purported "realism," Machiavelli's account of politics abstracts quite radically from the actual horizon of politics, which is constituted by the principles and purposes guiding human action, especially the action of statesmen entrusted with the well-being of their political communities. He then goes on to show that any attempt to depict Washington as a Machiavellian prince must fail to do justice to the man, to his self-understanding, to the qualities of character – qualities recognized and celebrated by the most discerning of his contemporaries – that inspired trust and respect and made him simply indispensable, and to his convictions regarding the significance of national character for the future independence, prosperity, and greatness of the country he helped found. As Dr. Spalding remarks, the "connection" that Washington drew "between private morality and national character, between virtue and happiness, hardly seems Machiavellian."

Any such warning that applies to George Washington must almost inevitably apply as well to those who admired his character and regarded it as politically indispensable. This does not mean, however, that John Adams, Thomas Jefferson, James Madison, and Alexander Hamilton owed nothing at all to Machiavelli. It does mean, however, that their use of Machiavelli was circumscribed and constrained – that their understanding of ends was not in accord with his and that they adopted his means only where they deemed it unavoidable.

John Adams is a case in point. As C. Bradley Thompson makes clear in his contribution to this book, Adams read Machiavelli and took him quite seriously. In his *Defence of the Constitutions of the United States of America*, he quoted extensively from the Florentine and openly acknowledged his debt to the man, and he drew heavily on the work of Machiavelli's disciples among the English commonwealthmen. In the first part of his chapter, Professor Thompson shows that Adams is indebted to Machiavelli's *Discourses on Livy* for the political epistemology underpinning his *Defence* and his *Discourses on Davila* and for the empirical method he follows throughout. In the second part, he presents Adams's critique of Machiavelli's constitutionalism, showing that the American statesman believed that, in his *Florentine Histories*, Machiavelli had failed to isolate the crucial defect in the Florentine constitution that had left it so vulnerable to a crippling internecine disorder. Like Harrington and Montesquieu, Adams believed that a well-balanced constitution can greatly reduce the dangers attendant on faction. He departed from Machiavelli altogether when he joined his fellow founders in asserting and demonstrating by example that it was possible to form a constitution on the basis of popular reflection and choice as opposed to force and fraud.

In contrast to John Adams, Thomas Jefferson left behind very little direct evidence that he had grappled with Machiavelli's political teaching. And yet, as I attempt to demonstrate in the ninth chapter, Jefferson's commitment to limited government, his advocacy of a politics of distrust, his eager embrace of a species of modern populism, his ultimate understanding of the executive power, and the intention guiding the comprehensive legislative program that he devised for Virginia make sense only when understood in terms of the new science of republican politics articulated in the *Discourses on Livy*. In reading the chapters in this book on Adams and Jefferson, one can easily discern what it was in their thinking that eventually led the two friends to quarrel.

Like his friend and neighbor Thomas Jefferson, James Madison had next to nothing to say concerning Machiavelli. There are, however, as Gary Rosen points out in Chapter 10, "certain obvious affinities" linking the two. One cannot read Madison on the role played by faction and party in government, on the inadequacy of moral and religious motives as a check on the propensity for factions to oppress those whom they exclude, on the necessity for popular vigilance in a republic, and on liberty's dependence on the rivalry of the ambitious without thinking of *The Prince* and the *Discourses on Livy*. The proximate source for Madison's sensitivity in these regards is, however, more likely to have been the Florentine's disciples Hume, Montesquieu, Locke, and Sidney than Machiavelli himself.

On one question, however, Dr. Rosen argues, there is reason to think that the Virginian went directly to the source, for his understanding of the quite different roles assigned the few and the many, the great and the common, princes and peoples in the founding and sustaining of republics more closely resembles Machiavelli's own than that of anyone else. Put bluntly, Madison shared the Florentine's conviction that it takes a prince to recognize and seize upon an *occasione* as an opportunity for founding and his belief that the people, once the proper institutions are in place, are the best guardians of liberty.

Madison's account differed from Machiavelli's, however, in one particular: His assessment of the princes and of the people was more positive than that of the Florentine. He did not regard the former as "amoral seekers of glory and dominion, indifferent to the needs and claims of the many." At least in America, he initially thought, they were genuinely committed to the republican project. And he did not think it requisite, if the people were to play their proper role, that class conflict and tumults be institutionalized. Nor did he share Machiavelli's conviction that, in all regimes, it is the few who rule. To the American people, as Dr. Rosen puts it, he attributed "a spirited – one might even say a princely – determination to govern themselves."

In time, Madison came to distrust the motives of some of those who had joined him in seizing the *occasione* afforded America's princes by the crisis of the 1780s; and by fostering something like a republican civil religion, in which the Constitution would be honored in the manner of Holy Writ, he sought to rally the *popolo* against the threat he believed America's *grandi* posed. It is only, then, appropriate that the republican prince whom he most feared should form the subject of the final chapter in this volume.

If Karl-Friedrich Walling is correct, however, James Madison misjudged his former colleague Alexander Hamilton, who harbored deep misgivings with regard to the sort of politics we tend to label Machiavellian. Hamilton did have one thing in common with the Florentine, and it distinguished him from his American critics and helps explain the quarrels in which he became enmeshed: He believed it inevitable that the nation be entangled in wars, and he paid extremely close attention to the necessities thereby imposed and to the difficulties that a self-governing people face when confronted with the clash of arms. One consequence of his conviction that war could not simply be sidestepped is that, in the course of the Revolutionary War and its aftermath, Hamilton came to believe that, to be viable in modern times, a republic must be led by an energetic, unitary executive – a veritable republican prince – charged with organizing and conducting the national defense.

Hamilton was equally concerned, however, with avoiding the dangers to republicanism attendant on such a concentration of power. If he favored a national bank, it was because he was intent on providing for the funding of war without resort to pillage and theft. His famous *Report on Manufactures* was written in response to a congressional request that America be made self-sufficient with regard to the technology requisite for war. For similar reasons, Hamilton advocated in wartime a draft and in peacetime the maintenance of a small professional force insufficient in size to be a threat to the polity, equal to the minor emergencies that so frequently arise, and able on short notice, when armed conflict looms, to train a much larger army of citizen soldiers.

The Roman and Spartan models Hamilton thought neither desirable nor practicable. For all of his interest in war, he was, like Hume, a commercial and not a martial republican. As a consequence, he advocated the establishment of a sizeable navy capable of projecting power abroad without threatening the integrity of republican forms at home. In revolutionary France, with its *levée en masse* and its wars of conquest ravaging Europe, he recognized a regime of Machiavellian force and fraud attempting to revive the violent and barbaric policy of ancient Rome. To such rapacity, Hamilton preferred the restraints of the just-war doctrine of the Christian church.

The figures considered in this volume responded to Machiavelli in various ways. None adopted his teaching without reservations. All but George Washington sought to enlist his overall argument in support of ends Machiavelli thought secondary at best, and even Washington – by endorsing the institutional precautions embedded in the American Constitution and praising *The Federalist* – tacitly acknowledged that the Florentine's critique of the virtuous republicanism of the ancients had some force. If one cannot speak of Machiavelli as the father or even the grandfather of the species of republicanism eventually adopted in the United States of America, one can hardly deny that the American founders and those who subsequently took heart from their example owed the Florentine a very great debt.

Prologue

Machiavelli's Rapacious Republicanism

Markus Fischer

Living in Florence at the height of the Italian Renaissance, Niccolò Machiavelli wanted to do for politics what others had done for the arts and letters, namely to have "recourse to the examples of the ancients" (*D* 1.pref.2) in order to recover their greatness – which, to him, meant above all to imitate the institutions and policies of the Roman republic. In the *Discourses on Livy* (ca. 1518), he analyzed the orders and laws of the Romans to teach the youths of Italy the "true way to make a republic great and to acquire empire"; in the *Art of War* (1521), he proposed a reform of the military practices of his age along the lines of Roman military orders; and in the *Florentine Histories* (1525), he contrasted the excellence of the citizens of Rome with the corruption of the inhabitants of Florence. This concern with republics went hand in hand with Machiavelli's tenure as secretary of the Second Chancery of the Florentine republic from 1498 to 1512, and – after the republic had fallen and he had lost his post – with his subsequent visits to the Oricellari Gardens, where young patricians discussed the fate of republics, in particular their rise to greatness, the maintenance of their liberty, their inevitable corruption, and their eventual collapse. Since these discussions were informed by the civic strand of Renaissance humanism, which had abandoned the medieval longing for universal empire and returned to the ancient republicanism celebrated in Aristotle, Cicero, Polybius, Livy, and Sallust, it can be said that civic humanism in particular and the classical republican tradition in general formed the intellectual context of Machiavelli's republican thought.[1]

---

[1] This biographical point has been made by a number of scholars, who claim in addition that civic humanism formed not only the context of Machiavelli's republican thought but shaped its very substance. In their view, Machiavelli's republican writings are thus an integral part of the classical republican tradition. See Rudolf von Albertini, *Das Florentinische Staatsbewusstsein im Übergang von der Republik zum Prinzipat* (Bern: Francke, 1955), 53–74; Hans Baron, "Machiavelli: The Republican Citizen and the Author of 'The Prince,'" *English Historical Review* 76:299 (April 1961): 217–53, esp. 247–53; J. G. A. Pocock, *The Machiavellian Moment: Florentine Political Thought and the Atlantic Republican Tradition* (Princeton, NJ: Princeton University Press,

Classical republicanism belongs to the communitarian strand of political thought, since it conceives republics – modeled after the Greek *pólis* and the Roman *res publica* – as moral communities of men indissolubly joined by a shared way of life. While this concept was already current in Greek city-states during the fifth century B.C., it was Aristotle who gave it a lasting theoretical form. To live the "good life *(eu zên)*" through the collective exercise of rational speech *(lógos)* and other intrinsically worthwhile activities, it was thought that human beings need to be joined to a self-sufficient community that seeks to make them good and just. For such a community to maintain its unity, its citizens must share a deeply felt consensus – called *homonoía* or "like-mindedness" in Greek and *concordia* or "common-heartedness" in Latin – with regard to the beliefs, virtues, and customs that shape their particular way of life. To sustain this agreement, the citizens must create networks of friendship *(philía, amicitia)* that consist not only of exchanges for pleasure and utility but, more importantly, of the mutual recognition of virtue. In addition, such communities should limit their size so that the citizens can know each other's character and deliberate in assembly, they should control foreign contacts to keep out unwholesome ideas and practices, and they need to provide an education *(paideía, disciplina)* that develops specific virtues in the citizens by means of instruction, legal constraint, and habituation. In particular, men ought to be shown how to cultivate prudence in order to rule well, justice in order to give to each what he deserves, courage in order to fight well in defense of the city, moderation in order to demand no more than their share, friendship in order to exchange goods and services and generate concord, generosity in order to contribute funds to public projects, magnanimity in order to take the lead in great undertakings, mildness in order to avoid quarrels, truthfulness in order to be correctly known by their fellows, and piety in order to obey the laws from fear of divine punishment. In this way, classical republicanism sought to bring out the best in man and to perfect his nature as a political animal.[2]

While ethically homogeneous, a classical republic is nonetheless differentiated by the functions that the citizens need to perform in order to make it self-sufficient. Ideally, these functions are organized in the form of a mixed regime, which seeks to combine the distinctive excellences of the simple, unmixed regimes, promoting affective ties between ruler and ruled as in a monarchy, wisdom among the rulers as in an aristocracy, and the liberty of all as in popular

---

1975), vii–viii, 86, 117, 154–218; Quentin Skinner, *The Foundations of Modern Political Thought I: The Renaissance* (Cambridge, UK: Cambridge University Press, 1978), xiv, 45, 47–8, 116, 118–38, 152–89; Maurizio Viroli, "Machiavelli and the Republican Idea of Politics," in *Machiavelli and Republicanism*, ed. Gisela Bock, Quentin Skinner, and Maurizio Viroli (Cambridge, UK: Cambridge University Press, 1990), 143–71.

[2] See Paul A. Rahe, *Republics Ancient and Modern: Classical Republicanism and the American Revolution* (Chapel Hill, NC: University of North Carolina Press, 1992), 15–229; Claude Nicolet, *The World of the Citizen in Republican Rome*, tr. S. Falla (Berkeley, CA: University of California Press, 1980); Ronald C. Wilson, *Ancient Republicanism: Its Struggle for Liberty against Corruption* (New York: Lang, 1989).

government, while preventing the vices characteristic of these regimes: despotism, oligarchic oppression, and the licentious rule of the mob. To this end, authority is distributed among separate offices that hold each other in check. The function of governing is entrusted to elected magistrates whose powers are circumscribed by laws that are ratified by the whole body of citizens. This body, in turn, is divided into two naturally opposed parts: a council of nobles, which debates affairs of state, drafts laws, and advises the magistrates, and an assembly of commoners, which elects the magistrates and ratifies the laws. Such an arrangement encourages longevity because both the rich and the poor have a share in authority and are less likely to desire change; it is conducive to virtue because it promotes the growth of a middle class free from the arrogance of the nobles and the slavishness of the poor; and it preserves liberty, that is, the collective capacity of citizens to rule themselves, because it prevents any part of the city from dominating the whole.

This republican ideal fell into abeyance during the Roman Empire initially as a result of its increasingly autocratic rule and later as a consequence of the rise of Christianity, which directed people's longings to the afterlife rather than to civic life. During the feudal era, the organization of political authority in accordance with the Germanic principle of personal fealty between lord and vassal made institutionalized self-rule a conceptual impossibility. Thus, it was not until the eleventh and twelfth centuries that rudiments of republican government were revived in the independent communes of northern Italy, where memories of ancient republicanism had been preserved. Subsequently, writers such as Bartolus of Saxoferrato, Marsilius of Padua, John of Viterbo, and Brunetto Latini, who sought to legitimize the independence of their native cities from both emperor and pope, praised once more the communal way of life for its liberty and greatness, separated secular from religious government, argued for laws that treated men equally, and called for elected magistrates who upheld justice and citizens who maintained concord and fostered the common good.[3]

Full recovery was not achieved until the fifteenth century, when writers of the so-called civic strand of Renaissance humanism, above all Colluccio Salutati, Leonardo Bruni, Poggio Bracciolini, and Leon Battista Alberti, exhumed the republican works of antiquity and incorporated them into their own treatises on the subject. Rejecting a life devoted to the contemplation of God, they recast the Aristotelian and Ciceronian notion of citizenship as the concept of *vivere*

---

[3] On medieval republicanism, see Quentin Skinner, "The Rediscovery of Republican Values," in Skinner, *Visions of Politics II: Renaissance Virtues* (Cambridge, UK: Cambridge University Press, 2002), 10–38. See also Hans Baron, "Cicero and the Roman Civic Spirit in the Middle Ages and Early Renaissance," *Bulletin of the John Rylands Library* 22 (1938): 72–97; Ronald Witt, "The Rebirth of the Concept of Republican Liberty in Italy," in *Renaissance: Studies in Honor of Hans Baron*, ed. Anthony Molho and John Tedeschi (Florence: Sansoni, 1970), 173–99; Skinner, *The Renaissance*, 3–65; Skinner, "Machiavelli's *Discorsi* and the Pre-Humanist Origins of Republican Ideas," in *Machiavelli and Republicanism*, 121–41; Maurizio Viroli, *From Politics to Reason of State: The Acquisition and Transformation of the Language of Politics 1250–1600* (Cambridge, UK: Cambridge University Press, 1992), 11–70.

civile or *vivere politico*, the civil or political way of life, whereby citizens rule themselves through laws, participate in public deliberation, fill the offices of a mixed regime, develop their virtues, and maintain lasting concord. In embracing the *vivere civile*, these writers supposed, such citizens will come face to face with the whims of Fortune, the allegorical figure that mars the designs of men through unforeseeable calamities but also provides them with opportunities to succeed. To be up to this task, men were thought to be in need of a humanistic education that combines jurisprudence and rhetoric with philosophy, for only those who are practically skilled can realize theoretical ideals – advancing the common good but also gaining personal glory – under the considerable contingency of the human condition.[4]

Machiavelli's Break with Classical Republicanism

It is clear that Machiavelli drew extensively on the rich store of terms, tropes, arguments, and metaphors of both the ancient and humanist strands of classical republicanism. In particular, he used the term *vivere civile* to frame his discussion of republican institutions, taking it to denote a mixed regime ordered by laws and based on a measure of equality. To maintain such a civil way of life, he supposed, the citizens need to possess "virtue," a quality closely linked to "good customs," whose lack spells "corruption." Machiavelli praised republican liberty, elevated greatness as the highest good, and exalted self-sacrificing love of fatherland. The founding of such an order he described in Aristotelian terms as giving form to human matter.

But let us not be misled by this semantic continuity. In substance, a sharp break begins with Machiavelli's famous declaration that he intended to "go directly to the effectual truth of the thing rather than to the imagination of it" (*P* 15), by means of which he rejects the teleological account of man so fundamental to classical theorizing about politics. From Aristotle to Cicero, Aquinas, and beyond, classical thinkers assumed that human beings have a natural capacity for the good, which they can develop by cultivating the virtues, and that the best regime is therefore a realistic goal for political action. To Machiavelli's mind, such an approach is idealistic speculation, for

many have imagined republics and principalities that have never been seen or known to exist in truth; for it is so far from how one lives to how one should live that he who lets go what is done for what should be done learns his ruin rather than his preservation. For a man who wants to make a profession of good in all regards must come to ruin among so many who are not good.   (*P* 15)

---

4 See Hans Baron, *The Crisis of the Early Italian Renaissance: Civic Humanism and Republican Liberty in an Age of Classicism and Tyranny*, 2nd edition (Princeton, NJ: Princeton University Press, 1966), and *From Petrarch to Leonardo Bruni: Studies in Humanistic and Political Literature* (Chicago: University of Chicago Press, 1968); Eugenio Garin, *Italian Humanism, Philosophy and Civic Life in the Renaissance*, tr. Peter Munz (New York: Harper and Row, 1965); Pocock, *The Machiavellian Moment*, vii, 3, 49–80; Skinner, *The Renaissance*, 69–112, 139–44, 152–80; Viroli, *From Politics to Reason of State*, 71–125.

If we want to survive and prosper, he argued, we must construct and maintain political order with a view to what men really are, namely, "ungrateful, fickle, pretenders and dissemblers, evaders of danger, eager for gain" – in short, "wicked" (*P* 17). More precisely, we must take into account the fact that human beings are by nature self-regarding individuals who desire the goods of Fortune and Venus – preservation, glory, power, wealth, and sexual pleasure – and whose minds are limited to serving these desires with ingenuity and to stimulating them to grow through the imagination of ever greater delights, all of which results in a ceaseless ambition that drives men in a limitless struggle for preeminence.[5] If we acknowledge this, we will realize that success in politics and carnal love does not accrue to the virtuous but to shrewd manipulators willing to violate the traditional rules of morality for the purpose of attaining the desired consequences – such as princes who do "not depart from good, when possible, but know how to enter into evil, when forced by necessity" (*P* 18).

This anthropological and ethical pessimism undergirds not only the bleak world of Machiavelli's *Prince* but also the seemingly brighter realm of republics described in his *Discourses on Livy*.[6]

> As all those demonstrate who reason on a civil way of life *(vivere civile)*, and as every history is full of examples, it is necessary to whoever disposes a republic and orders laws in it to presuppose that all men are bad, and that they always have to use the malignity of their spirit whenever they have a free opportunity for it.... Men never work any good unless through necessity, but where choice abounds and one can make use of license, at once everything is full of confusion and disorder. (*D* 1.3.1–2)

Moreover, though habituation to orders and laws can mitigate the deleterious effects of man's fundamental wickedness, it cannot eliminate this wickedness entirely. The practices that Machiavelli calls "good customs" do not perfect a nature already virtuous in its potential and become thereby permanent features of the citizen's character, as the classical view held; "good customs" serve only to oppose a nature that tends to ambitious license. More precisely, since the mind and the desires work their corrupting effects *necessarily*, whereas good customs exist only *contingently*, ambition will eventually dissolve good customs.[7]

Machiavelli's repudiation of the classical tradition had three immediate effects on the history of ideas. First, it issued a fundamental challenge to

---

[5] See Markus Fischer, "Machiavelli's Political Psychology," *RP* 59:4 (Fall 1997): 789–829.

[6] For a systematic account of the manner in which Machiavelli's maxims regarding both principalities and republics flow coherently from a single set of premises, see Markus Fischer, *Well-Ordered License: On the Unity of Machiavelli's Thought* (Lanham, MD: Lexington Press, 2000).

[7] Thus, Pocock, *The Machiavellian Moment*, 184, is profoundly mistaken when he attributes the following to the citizens of Machiavelli's republic:

> ...the experience of citizenship – of what Guicciardini called *partizipazione* – had changed their natures in a way that mere custom could not. Custom at most could affect men's second or acquired natures, but if it was the end of man to be a citizen or political animal, it was his original nature or *prima forma* that was developed, and developed irreversibly, by the experience of a *vivere civile*.

Christianity by repudiating the Pauline principle that "evil must not be done that good may come" (Rom. 3:8), by omitting the soul and natural law, and by claiming that "our religion . . . has rendered the world weak and given it in prey to criminal men" (*D* 2.2.2). Thus, it was not entirely without reason that Cardinal Pole declared in 1539 that the *Prince* had been "written by the hand of Satan."[8] Nor should it seem strange that Machiavelli's works should enjoy a prominent place on the papal index of prohibited books from 1557 to 1890.

Second, Machiavelli's turn toward the "effectual truth" gave an important impulse to the modern scientific project, which renounced final causes for the sake of efficient ones and required that propositions be corroborated by experience. This was acknowledged by Francis Bacon, the first founder of modern science, who wrote in his *Advancement of Learning* (II.xxi.9) in 1605 that "we are much beholden to Machiavel and others, that write what men do, and not what they ought to do" (*WoFB* 3:430).[9]

Third, Machiavelli's consequentialist approach to the good made him the founder of the modern tradition of political realism – variously known as the doctrine of *raison d'état* or reason of state, as *Realpolitik*, or, indeed, as Machiavellism – which holds that politics is fundamentally a matter of promoting the security and greatness of the state by whatever means necessary, including deceit and unjust violence.

Machiavelli believed that most of the ancient writers had known this stark truth but had chosen to express it only surreptitiously. After alluding to the distinction that Cicero (*Off.* 1.11) drew between discussion and force as the human and beastly means of resolving conflict, Machiavelli asserted that what he elsewhere called "the effectual truth of the matter" was

> taught *covertly* to princes by ancient writers, who wrote that Achilles, and many other princes, were given to Chiron the centaur to be raised, so that he would look after them with his discipline. To have as teacher a half-beast, half-man means nothing other than that a prince needs to know how to use both natures.   (*P* 18, emphasis added)

Even the authors of the Bible are said to have practiced this deception when discussing the establishment of lasting institutions, for "whoever reads the Bible *judiciously* will see that since he wished his laws and his orders to go forward, Moses was forced to kill infinite men who, moved by nothing other than envy, were opposed to his plans" (*D* 3.30.1, emphasis added). In other words,

---

[8] *Apologia ad Carolum Quintum* (1539), in *Epistolarum Reginaldi Poli S. R. E. Cardinalis et aliorum ad ipsum collectio*, ed. Angelo M. Quirini (Brescia: J. M. Rizzardi, 1744–57), 1:66–172 (at 137).

[9] Note, however, that Machiavelli's own approach to political knowledge was prudential rather than scientific. Deeply impressed by the contingency of human affairs, he considered his propositions to be maxims of practical reason that hold under most circumstances but not universally (as the scientific method demands). On contingency and prudential knowledge in Machiavelli's thought, see also Eugene Garver, *Machiavelli and the History of Prudence* (Madison, WI: University of Wisconsin Press, 1987).

according to Machiavelli, the story of the golden calf (Exod. 32:25–8) only seems to teach that those who oppose God's will shall justly be punished; in truth, its author meant to suggest that those who found political and religious orders are permitted to murder those who disagree with their vision.

Having made this assumption concerning the ancient writers, Machiavelli deliberately read – or, better, misread – the classics of ancient republicanism in its light. For instance, when alluding to the manner in which Cicero contrasts human laws with beastly force, Machiavelli completely ignores the fact that the Roman moralist argued that a resort to force is neither necessary nor permitted unless a just cause is present, such as a prior injury committed by the other side. Livy – whose history of Rome forms the stated subject of Machiavelli's *Discourses on Livy* – fares no better. In an important passage, Machiavelli claims that Romulus murdered his brother Remus and consented to the murder of Titus Tatius in order to be a more effective founder (*D* 1.9.1–2). But Livy (1.7, 1.13–14) merely reports that Romulus killed Remus either from "jealousy and ambition" or a "fit of rage" about a perceived slight, and writes with regard to Titus Tatius that "Romulus is said to have felt less distress at his death than was strictly proper: possibly the joint reign was not, in fact, entirely harmonious; possibly he felt that Tatius deserved what he got" after having provoked a riot by dispensing justice in favor of his kinsmen.[10] Likewise, when telling the story of the Caudine Forks, where the Romans reneged on a peace guarantee to the Samnites on the dubious ground that neither the Senate nor the people of Rome were bound by agreements made by their consuls in the field, Livy (9.4–15) stresses the Romans' effort to demonstrate that they acted justly; Machiavelli, in contrast, concludes from this event that "it is not shameful not to observe the promises that you have been made to promise by force" (*D* 3.42). Similarly, Machiavelli rips Sallust's famous claim (*Cat.* 7) about the salutary effect of glory – that republics rise to greatness because they allow men to win glory and thus motivate them to work for the common good – from its context, which speaks of concord and justice (*Cat.* 6, 8–9), and turns it into another maxim of expediency: Republics are better at providing for the common good, he contends, because the majority can easily "crush" the minority, regardless of the fact that "it may turn out to harm this or that private individual" (*D* 2.2.1). Where Sallust deplores the conspiracy of Catiline as an instance of Roman moral corruption (*Cat.* 31), Machiavelli cites Catiline's brazen appearance before the Senate after his conspiracy had been exposed as evidence of how much less dangerous it is to conspire against republics than to do so against princes (*D* 3.6.19).

What enabled Machiavelli to break out of the classical context that continued to constrain his contemporaries? Equipped with a penetrating mind and a cynical temper, he looked more to what men do than to what they ought to, as

---

[10] In citing Livy, I use the following translations: *The Early History of Rome*, tr. Aubrey de Sélincourt (London: Penguin, 1960), and *Rome and Italy*, tr. Betty Radice (London: Penguin, 1982).

Bacon would subsequently note. In doing so, he generalized the brutal practices of Renaissance politics into a set of maxims, which he believed he had found in the ancient writings as well, and he therefore took them to explain political life at all times and in all places. Many of the observations and arguments about contemporary affairs that Machiavelli made in his familiar letters and reports to the Florentine government subsequently found their way into the *Prince* and *Discourses on Livy* in virtually unaltered form.[11] For instance, the maxim that the founders of political orders must be armed was probably suggested to Machiavelli in 1498 by the fiery death of Girolamo Savonarola, the Dominican friar who had led the Florentines in founding a republic, for he wrote in 1513 that "Moses, Cyrus, Theseus, and Romulus would not have been able to make their peoples observe their constitutions for long if they had been unarmed, as happened in our times to Brother Girolamo Savonarola" (*P* 6). Likewise, Machiavelli's realization that republican institutions must at times be defended by extralegal force probably arose from the downfall of Piero Soderini, the chief magistrate of the Florentine republic since 1502, who believed that he "could extinguish ill humors with patience and goodness," and therefore failed to "take up extraordinary authority and break up civil equality together with the laws" when it was necessary to do so in order to crush the enemies of the republic (*D* 3.3), who overthrew it in 1512.

Of course, this is not to suggest that the practice of Renaissance politics should replace the discourse of civic humanism as the context to which Machiavelli's thought should be reduced. After all, his contemporaries experienced the same events but did not understand them in a way that would have prompted them to break with the classical tradition. Rather, it took a thinker of Machiavelli's daring or, perhaps, recklessness to transcend the horizon that had safely circumscribed Western political thought since Plato and Aristotle – namely, the assumption that the universe is ethically ordered and that virtue must, therefore, ultimately be compatible with political life.

The Civil Way of Life: Orders and Laws

Machiavelli frequently refers to *vivere civile* and *vivere politico* and to their synonyms, "civility *(civiltà)*" and "free way of life *(vivere libero)*." To the humanists, as we saw previously, *vivere civile* meant a life devoted to the development of man's natural capacity for virtue through participation in political authority. In Machiavelli's narrower and more instrumental understanding, *vivere civile* referred to a political process that unfolds through laws and institutional orders and gives every major group a share.

To begin with, a civil way of life means that the citizens assert claims and resolve conflicts through laws *(leggi)*, rather than by means of threats, riots, or factional violence. Thus, the Florentine magistrates once admonished the leaders of rebellious guilds "to ask for [something new] with civility and not

---

[11] See Quentin Skinner, *Machiavelli* (New York: Hill and Wang, 1981), 9.

with tumults and arms" (*FH* 3.11), and Machiavelli asserts that for cities to order "themselves so that they may be able to live civilly and quietly" is to find "good laws for maintaining themselves free" (*D* 1.49.2). But merely to seek one's advantage by means of laws rather than force is not enough: The laws must also be designed and applied in such a way that they do not unfairly disadvantage any of the city's major groups. The Romans observed this maxim well, since "after some differences, they would come together to create a law whereby the people would be satisfied and the nobles retain their dignities"; in contrast:

the people of Florence fought to be alone in the government without the participation of the nobles . . . so that the nobility readied greater forces for its own defense; and that is why it came to the blood and exile of citizens, and the laws that were made afterwards were not for the common utility but were all ordered in favor of the conqueror.

(*FH* 3.1)

In addition to laws, Machiavelli defines the *vivere civile* in terms of "orders" *(ordini)*, which determine where political authority resides and how it can be exercised – in, for example, the making of the laws. Accordingly, orders are wider in compass and more enduring than laws. In Rome, for instance,

there was the order of the government, or truly of the state, and afterwards the laws, which together with the magistrates checked the citizens. The order of the state was the authority of the people, of the Senate, of the tribunes, of the consuls; the mode of soliciting and creating the magistrates; and the mode of making the laws.   (*D* 1.18.2)

In a civil way of life, authority is institutionalized. Obedience is owed not to concrete persons but to holders of public office, who execute laws that have been ratified by a public assembly. Machiavelli was clearly aware of the advantages of such an arrangement when he wrote:

[I]n a republic, one would not wish anything ever to happen that has to be governed with extraordinary modes [i.e., outside established orders]. For although the extraordinary mode may do good then, nonetheless, the example does ill; for if one sets up a habit of breaking the orders for the sake of good, then later, under that coloring, they are broken for ill.   (*D* 1.34.3)

Most importantly, the orders of a civil way of life check the licentious ambitions of men. In Rome, for instance, the great authority given to the office of *dictator* was limited by his inability to alter the other offices of the state, so that giving dictatorial power to individuals in emergencies proved beneficial rather than harmful; in contrast, the Decemvirate, in which ten men had been authorized to collect and edit the laws, led to tyranny precisely because all other orders had been suspended:

When the dictator was created, the tribunes, consuls, and Senate remained with their authority; nor was the dictator able to take it away from them. If he had been able to deprive one of them of the consulate, one of the Senate, he could not annul the senatorial order and make new laws. So the Senate, the consuls, the tribunes, remaining in their authority, came to be like a guard on him to make him not depart from the right way. But in the creation of the Ten it happened all the contrary; for they annulled the consuls and the tribunes; they gave them authority to make laws and do any other thing, like the Roman people.   (D 1.35)

Indeed, Machiavelli seems to show an incipient appreciation for the importance of due process when he asserts that the "authority to shed blood against its own citizens...was well ordered in Rome because one could appeal to the people ordinarily," that is, through established orders (D 1.49.3). In particular, public accusations differ from calumnies in that the former "have need of true corroborations and of circumstances that show the truth of the accusation" (D 1.8.2).

Machiavelli understood both orders and laws as humanly created means for maintaining effective authority under the changing exigencies of political life. In their original condition, men were thus "reduced to making laws and ordering punishments for whoever acted against them: hence came the knowledge of justice" (D 1.2.3). Thereafter, some cities "were given laws by one alone and at a stroke...like those that were given by Lycurgus to the Spartans; some had them by chance and at many different times, and according to accidents, as had Rome" (D 1.2.1), where a "tribune, or any other citizen whatever, could propose a law to the people, on which every citizen was able to speak, either in favor or against, before it was decided" (D 1.18.3). Likewise, "new necessities in managing that city were always discovered, and it was necessary to create new orders, as happened when they created the censors" as "arbiters of the customs of Rome" (D 1.49.1). That Machiavelli had a positivist notion of orders and laws is further evident from the fact that he never mentioned natural law – a divinely willed, universal standard of right that could be discerned by all rational beings – though he was surely aware that it was the principal concept governing the manner in which men of letters inquired into politics at the time.

This denial of natural law goes hand in hand with Machiavelli's belief that, as a rule, regimes that are shaped by pragmatic responses to changing circumstances are better at preserving their independence and at attaining greatness and empire than those that are rigidly drawn up in accordance with even the best theoretical principles. At Sparta, Lycurgus created a highly artificial order – enforced equality of belongings, lifelong military service, prohibition of immigration and foreign exchange – that was perfectly adapted to preserving Lacedaemon as a small city-state within a system of city-states. Indeed, its cohesion and prudence enabled it to ward off the existential threat posed by Athens' aggression during the Peloponnesian War (432–404 B.C.). But then, having defeated Athens and attained hegemony over all of Greece, Sparta's isolationist regime failed at the novel task of maintaining that hegemony. In Machiavelli's words, "Sparta...after it had subjected almost all of Greece to itself, showed its weak foundation upon one slightest accident; for when other cities rebelled, following the rebellion of Thebes..., that republic was altogether ruined" (*D* 1.6.4). The contingency of human affairs is such that orders conceived by abstract reason eventually find themselves confronted with unforeseen challenges in the face of which they fail catastrophically, due to their inability to deviate from the model believed to be superior. In contrast, orders that evolve over time by way of institutional solutions to concrete problems are shaped by the very contingency that they have to contend with and thus are better at changing as demanded by the exigencies of the moment. For "all things of men are in motion and cannot stay steady . . . and to many things that reason does not bring you, necessity brings you" (*D* 1.7.4). Thus, the Romans, who had their laws "by chance and at many different times, and according to accidents," were able to keep what they acquired after defeating the existential threat posed by Carthage and attain an imperial grandeur hitherto unprecedented. Where ancient writers sought for the single best regime under all circumstances, Machiavelli realized that for a republic to take the contingent challenges of history in stride, it must itself be highly contingent.[12]

Finally, Machiavelli's statement that "in a republic one would not wish anything ever to happen that has to be governed with extraordinary modes" should not be taken to imply that he entertained a precocious admiration for constitutional government and the rule of law. First, his idea of orderly procedures allows for injury to innocents: Every republic should have public accusations by which the ill humors that grow up in cities against certain individuals can be vented, he asserts, for "if a citizen is crushed ordinarily, there follows little or no disorder in the republic, even though he has been done a wrong" (*D* 1.7.2). Second, in cases where observing its orders and laws is not sufficient to avert danger from the state, he believes that its orders and laws should be disregarded. Such a case occurred in the Florentine republic during Machiavelli's tenure in the government of Piero Soderini, who should have summarily executed those in favor of a return to the princely regime of the Medici but abstained because he did not want to "take up extraordinary authority and break up civil equality together with the laws" (*D* 3.3). In this he grievously erred, according to Machiavelli, for one "should never allow an evil to run loose out of respect for a good, when that good could be easily crushed by that evil" (*D* 3.3), as indeed happened shortly thereafter when the republic was overthrown, the Medici returned, Soderini had to flee for his life, and Machiavelli was imprisoned. In sum, one who has not only a positivist conception of orders and laws but sees all of political life through the lens of "the effectual truth," as Machiavelli does, is bound to understand orders and laws as mere means conducive to the stability and prosperity of the whole and thus to conclude that they should allow for meting out expedient injustices to individuals and for their own suspension in cases where their observance would be detrimental to public order.

---

[12] In the metaphysical terms employed by Miguel E. Vatter, *Between Form and Event: Machiavelli's Theory of Political Freedom* (Boston: Kluwer, 2000), to whom this paragraph owes its inspiration, republics ought to remain in the realm of "event" rather than trying to enter into the domain of "form."

Necessary Evil

As we saw previously, Machiavelli holds that those who order republics must assume that all men are wicked and ready to lapse into license unless constrained by necessity. In the preceding paragraph, we had a first glimpse of this necessity: It will repeatedly be necessary to do wrong to individuals and even to suspend the laws for the purpose of maintaining public order. Let us adduce further examples to show clearly that Machiavelli's infamous claim that rulers must "know how to enter into evil, when forced by necessity" (*P* 18) applies not only to the autocratic regimes discussed in *The Prince* but also to the *vivere civile* enjoyed by republics.

According to Machiavelli, "he who wishes to make a republic where there are very many gentlemen" – that is, feudal lords who live idly from their possessions and command from castles – "cannot do it unless he first eliminates all of them" (*D* 1.55.5). Republics can execute policies more effectively than principalities because the majority can easily crush the minority, "although it may turn out to harm this or that private individual" (*D* 2.2.1). To forestall corruption, the magistrates should frequently impose "excessive and notable" punishments on subversive elements in order to put "terror" into the minds of the citizens (*D* 3.1.3). For instance, when the Roman grain merchant Spurius Maelius gained the favor of the plebs by distributing free grain to them during a famine, the Senate, fearing he could use his popular support to usurp public authority, "created a dictator over him and had him killed," even though his actions, as Machiavelli acknowledges, could not "reasonably be condemned" since they appeared public-spirited and violated no laws (*D* 3.28).

In the foreign realm, as we shall see in greater detail, republics are constrained to wage aggressive wars because the citizens need to vent their natural rapacity abroad so that they can live by laws at home, and because security generally rests on striking first and acquiring empire – with the result that "the end of the republic is to enervate and to weaken all other bodies so as to increase its own body" (*D* 2.3.4). Finally, once a civil life has collapsed from the wholesale corruption of the citizens, an autocrat must use "extreme force" to renew their good customs and to cause the republic to be "reborn with many dangers and much blood" (*D* 1.17.3). In sum, for the sake of the republic, one should do whatever it takes, regardless of moral considerations, for "where one deliberates entirely on the safety of his fatherland, there ought not to enter any consideration of either just or unjust, merciful or cruel, praiseworthy or ignominious; indeed every other concern put aside, one ought to follow entirely the policy that saves its life and maintains its liberty" (*D* 3.41). Clearly, necessary evil belongs to the effectual truth of *vivere civile*, the civil way of life. Principalities as well as republics fall under the doctrine of *raison d'état*, which holds that rulers must commit deeds that violate traditional morality for the purpose of providing such political goods as security, prosperity, empire, and greatness.

As this formulation suggests, Machiavelli does not reject traditional morality altogether, for he continues to describe morally wrong but politically expedient acts as "evil," rather than turning them into a new kind of good. Thus, he argues that cruelties "can be called well used (if it is permissible to speak well of evil)" when they "are done at a stroke, out of the necessity to secure oneself" (*P* 10), and he writes, with regard to the founder's need to kill for the purpose of being alone in authority, that it is "very suitable that when the deed accuses him the effect excuses him; and when the effect is good, as was that of Romulus, it will always excuse the deed" (*D* 1.9.2). An excuse implies an admission of fault, whereas a justification implies a denial of fault and an assertion of innocence.[13] Had Machiavelli written that the end justifies the means – voicing an opinion that is often but erroneously attributed to him – he would have argued that the good of the effect canceled the wickedness of the deed and made the doer innocent of crime. But, in implying that the wicked deeds required of princes have to be called evil and that those required of the founders of a *vivere civile* can be excused, he retained traditional morality as a point of reference, and his consequentialism remained limited, therefore, to providing a warrant for the use of evil means and fell short of requiring a wholesale moral revaluation.

Machiavelli was by no means the first one to sanction a violation of moral rules for the sake of the good of the whole. The classical tradition acknowledged the existence of "cases of dire necessity *(casus dirae necessitatis)*" and justified breaches of the moral rules in such cases on the assumption that the need for such deeds arose only under exceptional circumstances and that these violations could be subsumed under the virtues, especially that of prudence, and thus be reconciled with the corresponding moral order.[14] More precisely, medieval theologians argued that men get entangled in cases of dire necessity only because they committed prior sins and now have to face their consequences. As Thomas Aquinas put it, there can be ethical perplexity *secundum quid* (after something) but not *simpliciter* (simply).[15] Thus, the world is assumed to be ethically coherent: People who act virtuously will normally not find themselves in situations where they must commit one wrong in order to avoid another.

This reassuring belief was severely challenged by Machiavelli's claim that in political life, "something appears to be virtue, which if pursued would be one's ruin, and something else appears to be vice, which if pursued results in one's security and well-being" (*P* 15), and, moreover, that the consequent need to enter into vice is a "natural and ordinary necessity" (*P* 3). For it implies an unbridgeable gap between what is ethically true and what is politically effective under normal circumstances. Machiavelli directly refers to this gap when writing that war is an "art by means of which men cannot live honestly in every

---

[13] See Michael Walzer, "Political Action: The Problem of Dirty Hands," *Philosophy and Public Affairs* 2:2 (Winter 1973): 160–80, esp. 170, 175–6; J. L. Austin, "A Plea for Excuses," in *Philosophical Papers*, ed. J. O. Urmson and G. J. Warnock (Oxford, UK: Oxford University Press, 1961), 123–52.

[14] See Kurt Kluxen, *Politik und menschliche Existenz bei Machiavelli: Dargestellt am Begriff der Necessità* (Stuttgart: W. Kohlhammer, 1967), 28–9; Gaines Post, *Studies in Medieval Legal Thought: Public Law and the State, 1100–1322* (Princeton, NJ: Princeton University Press, 1964), 251, 306.

[15] Thomas Aquinas, *Summa Theologiae*, tr. Fathers of the English Dominican Province (New York: Benziger Brothers, 1947), I–II, 19, 6 ad 3; II–II, 62, 2 obj. 2; III, 64, 6 ad 3.

time" (*AW* 1.51), and, especially, when describing the methods by which a new prince should make everything anew, for instance, by moving people around like cattle:

These modes are very cruel, and enemies to every way of life, not only Christian but human; and any man whatever should flee them and wish to live in private rather than as king with so much ruin to men. Nonetheless, he who does not wish to take this first way of the good must enter into this evil one if he wishes to maintain himself.

(*D* 1.26)

One can either be an excellent ruler or a morally good man, but not both, for it is in the nature of politics that such goods as order and prosperity cannot be secured without unjustly injuring a great many individuals not only as a matter of exception but on a recurrent basis.

The historical contingency that subverts the rationally conceived political form and privileges regimes with a built-in capacity for confronting contingency thus finds its metaphysical equivalent in the ethical domain. Just as the classical tradition went wrong in assuming that the wise man could design a single regime that would be best under all circumstances, so it erred in believing in a single ethical principle that could guide our actions under all circumstances, for there are at least two ultimate ends for man – the political good and the moral good – and he cannot escape situations where the pursuit of one undermines the attainment of another.[16]

With regard to Machiavelli's use of the word "virtue," this conclusion implies that he recovered the essentially political meaning it had among the Greeks and Romans before the Socratics, Stoics, and Christians it turned into a primarily ethical category. The pre-Socratic Greeks took *arete* to mean military and political excellence, while the pagan Romans understood *virtus*, which literally meant "manliness," to denote the qualities required of a Roman male in his functions as a citizen, soldier, and patriarch. Thus, Machiavelli speaks of the "virtue" of princes and citizens as the quality that makes for success in political life, which includes the ability to proceed with violence and cunning.[17]

The Mixed Regime

According to Machiavelli, a civil way of life can be organized as either a republic or a kingdom. In a kingdom, authority is concentrated in a line of hereditary

---

[16] For the seminal article on this feature of Machiavelli's thought, see Isaiah Berlin, "The Originality of Machiavelli," in *Studies on Machiavelli*, ed. Myron Gilmore (Florence: Sansoni, 1972), 147–206 (at 194–6).

[17] There are, however, two places (*P* 15–16) where Machiavelli speaks of "virtue" in contrast to the necessities of political life and thus refers to moral excellence. To introduce clarity where Machiavelli invites ambiguity, I will from now on use the Italian noun *virtù*, as well as the adjective *virtuoso* and the adverb *virtuosamente*, when referring to political excellence in Machiavelli's sense, and reserve the word "virtue" for moral excellence. Also, when quoting translations that replace *virtù* and its cognates with English words, I will restore the Italian terms without further notice.

princes who govern in accordance with established laws and customs. In a republic, by contrast, authority is distributed among a number of offices that represent different groups within society and check one another's power. In other words, Machiavelli follows the classical tradition in conceiving of the republic as a mixed regime.

This tradition elevated the mixed regime to the best practical regime on the grounds of longevity, liberty, and virtue. Machiavelli believes in its longevity as well – for, as he explains in his *Discourse Concerning Florentine Affairs after the Death of Lorenzo de' Medici the Younger*, one cannot "believe that republic to be lasting, where those humors are not satisfied, which, if not satisfied, ruin republics" (O 24). By "humors," he refers to groups of men united by common temperaments, outlooks, and interests, above all, the great *(li grandi)* or nobles, united by their "great desire to command and oppress," and the common people *(il populo)*, who "desire neither to be commanded nor oppressed" (P 9). This theory of humors goes back to the ancient physician Galen, who taught that the health of the human body depended on the proper balance among four fluids or "humors" – blood, choler, phlegm, and black bile – which made a person's temper correspondingly sanguine, choleric, phlegmatic, and melancholic. Applied to the body politic, this theory meant that a city would stay healthy as long as its humors participated in government in the right proportion.[18]

Accordingly, in his *Discourse Concerning Florentine Affairs*, Machiavelli criticizes the short-lived republics of Florence on the grounds that their humors were not properly mixed. In the republic that lasted from 1393 to 1434, he observes, the magistrate "had little reputation and too much authority," and "the people did not have its part in it" (O 24). The republic that existed from 1494 to 1512 failed to adopt a "mode that would be durable because the orders did not satisfy all the humors of the citizens" (O 25). To improve matters, Machiavelli suggests a regime that mixes three humors, "the first, the middling, and the last" (O 27). To satisfy the first and most ambitious group, sixty-five citizens of gravity and influence should be appointed for life to fill the offices of the *Signoria* or magistracy on a rotating basis; men of the middling sort should be appointed for life to a Council of the Two Hundred to advise the *Signoria*; and the last humor, that is, the common people, should elect a Council of the Thousand and be given officials with the authority to veto the decisions of the *Signoria* and the Two Hundred and appeal them to the Thousand (O 27–9). This imaginary arrangement bears an obvious resemblance to the mixed regime of Rome, which had its first beginning in the kingship of Romulus, who gave a share in authority to the nobility by appointing the heads of the leading families to a "Senate with which he took counsel and by whose opinion he decided" (D 1.9.2). When the city became a republic in 510 B.C., the powers of the king were vested in a magistracy, headed by two consuls who were elected annually by the people from among the nobles. The popular element was introduced in 494 B.C. when the Roman plebs, under arms, threatened to secede from the city,

---

[18] In this connection, see Anthony J. Parel, *The Machiavellian Cosmos* (New Haven, CT: Yale University Press, 1992), 101–12.

and the Senate, alarmed by the possibility of losing military manpower, granted the plebs the right to elect their own representatives, the tribunes of the plebs, who were inviolable and had the authority to intercede with magisterial action in order to protect the people from transgression. As a result, "the state of that republic came to be more stabilized, since all three kinds of government there had their part"; and "remaining mixed" in this fashion for centuries, Rome "made a perfect republic" (D 1.2.7).

But longevity is not an end in itself for Machiavelli. He esteems the stability of the mixed regime because it allows for freedom: "The common utility that is drawn from a free way of life . . . is being able to enjoy one's things freely, without suspicion, not fearing for the honor of wives and that of children, not to be afraid for oneself" (D 1.16.3). A man who lives in a well-ordered republic "does not fear that his patrimony will be taken away, and he knows not only that [his children] are born free and not slaves, but that they can, through their *virtù*, become princes. Riches are seen to multiply there in large number. . . . For each willingly multiplies that thing and seeks to acquire those goods he believes he can enjoy once acquired" (D 2.2.3). To protect these liberties, every republic requires a "guard of freedom" (D 1.5.1), that is, an office that acts forcefully against individuals or groups that seek to usurp public authority. Since the people's humor tends toward not being oppressed, whereas the nobles want to oppress, the people should elect holders of this office (D 1.5.2) – as was the case in Rome after the establishment of the tribunes of the plebs.

While freedom is a good treasured by Machiavelli, he seems to love greatness or glory even more. For he states with approval that the pagans "placed the highest good *(sommo bene)*" in the "honor of the world" (D 2.2.2), he directs his analysis in the *Discourses on Livy* to those cities that attained greatness on account of their free origin (D 1.1.3–4), and he eulogizes Roman policies as "the true way to make a republic great and to acquire empire" (D 2.19.1). Above all, he links republican freedom with imperial greatness in such a way that the former is revealed as a means to the latter: "it is an easy thing to know whence arises among peoples this affection for the free way of life, for it is seen through experience that cities have never expanded either in dominion or in riches if they have not been in freedom" (D 2.2.1).

The classical republican writers believed that the various parts of a mixed regime ought to be held together by concord and friendship. But there was little concord in Rome, with "the people together crying out against the Senate, the Senate against the people, running tumultuously through the streets, closing shop, the whole plebs leaving Rome" (D 1.4.1). The ancients regarded these conflicts as major defects in the Roman regime. But, according to Machiavelli, these critics "blame those things that were the first cause of keeping Rome free, and . . . consider the noises and the cries that would arise in such tumults more than the good effects they engendered," for "every city ought to have its modes with which the people can vent their ambition, and especially those cities that wish to avail themselves of the people in important things" (D 1.4.1). More precisely, the Romans armed the plebs in order to use their superior numbers to conquer a great empire; consequently, their regime had to accept tumults as expressions of popular grievances (*D* 1.6.3–4). Regarding the other virtues, Machiavelli affirms moderation when he praises the Romans for the fact that "after some differences, they would come together to create a law whereby the people would be satisfied and the nobles retain their dignities" (*FH* 3.1). But his praise of piety, as when he writes that "republics that wish to maintain themselves uncorrupt have above everything else to maintain the ceremonies of their religion uncorrupt and hold them always in veneration" (*D* 1.12.1), falls short of an affirmation of virtue because he understands religion as a fraud used to manipulate the common people. Likewise, Machiavelli's ascription of prudence to the nobility, as when he writes that "there is more foresight and astuteness in the great" (*P* 9), is undermined by the fact that he directs these qualities to the attainment of good ends by evil means.

The Elite and the Multitude

In a mixed regime, the magistrates are generally appointed by a popular assembly that judges the candidates on grounds of their reputation, with regard to both their character and their accomplishments, such as "winning a battle, acquiring a town, carrying out a mission with care and prudence, advising the republic wisely and prosperously" (*FH* 7.1). Machiavelli believes that the common people are quite capable of judging "particular things concerning distributions of ranks and dignities" of precisely this sort (*D* 1.47.3). In fact, the people "are ... seen in their choices of magistrates to make a better choice by far than a prince" (*D* 1.58.3). Of the Roman people, he writes, "in so many hundred years, in so many choices of consuls and tribunes, it did not make four choices of which it might have to repent" (*D* 1.58.3).

This popular sagacity is, however, contingent upon an important fact: that the republic remain at war and in danger from foreign enemies, for "it has always been, and will always be, that great and rare men are neglected in a republic in peaceful times" (*D* 3.16.1). For instance, after the Romans had subdued all the major powers of the Mediterranean world, "they became secure in their freedom," which "made the Roman people no longer regard *virtù* but favor in bestowing the consulate, lifting to that rank those who knew better how to entertain men rather than ... conquer enemies. Afterward, from those who had more favor, they descended to giving it to those who had more power" (*D* 1.18.3).

In addition to choosing leaders, the people can be entrusted with the right to accuse particular persons: "an orderer of a republic should order that every citizen in it can accuse without any fear or without any respect" (*D* 1.8.2), that is, without any concern for the political rank or social status of the accused. In this connection, Machiavelli also approves of the Roman practice of holding all capital trials before the assembly of the people, based on the legal right of *provocatio* or appeal to the people, for "the judges need to be very many because the few always behave in the mode of the few" (*D* 1.7.4).

Again, Machiavelli trusts the judgment of the people with regard to particular things, namely whether individuals are guilty of specific crimes.

While the people of a warlike republic will choose their leaders and adjudicate crimes sensibly, they will not be able to draw up good laws and devise effective policies, for such matters require a wider and more abstract knowledge of the world and the people are "very much deceived in general things" (*D* 1.47.1). To correct this intellectual shortcoming, Machiavelli at first glance seems to affirm Cicero's suggestion (*Amic.* 25.95) that the people can grasp the truth when counseled by a wise man. "If [popular] opinions are false," he writes, "there is for them the remedy of assemblies, where some good man gets up who in orating demonstrates to them how they deceive themselves; and though peoples, as [Cicero] says, are ignorant, they are capable of truth and easily yield when the truth is told them by a man worthy of faith" (*D* 1.4.1). But since men who are "very much deceived in general things" are unlikely to grasp arguments based on general principles, their yielding to the truth will mostly be a matter of having faith in the orator's veracity, just as "nothing is so apt to check an excited multitude as is the reverence for some grave man of authority who puts himself against it" (*D* 1.54). As a result, nefarious rhetoric readily trumps honest argument in popular assemblies:

When gain is seen in the things that are put before the people, even though there is loss concealed underneath, and when it appears spirited, even though there is the ruin of the republic concealed underneath, it will always be easy to persuade the multitude of it; and likewise it may always be difficult to persuade it of these policies if either cowardice or loss might appear, even though safety and gain might be concealed underneath.

(*D* 1.53.2)

For instance, "in the city of Athens, Nicias, a very grave and prudent man, was never able to persuade that people that it might not be good to go to assault Sicily; so when that decision was taken against the wish of the wise, the entire ruin of Athens followed from it" (*D* 1.53.4). In short, the problem of demagogy means that the mental shortcomings of the multitude cannot be mended by deliberation and wise counsel in assembly, at least when it comes to making laws and deciding policies. Direct democracy – as the Athenian experience shows – is a ruinous regime.

Thus, we have arrived at another significant reason for the superiority of the mixed regime: It accords to the multitude that share of authority that it can exercise with competence, namely choosing among candidates for office and adjudicating crimes. At the same time, the tasks of conceiving orders and laws and governing the city are placed in the hands of an elite composed of the heads of the noble families and of men elected to public office. Since many of these elected offices will be won by individuals from the ranks of the great, who possess not only more ambition to command but have the wealth, influence, and reputation to stand out in the public eye, this elite consists by and large of the humor of the great. This fact is beneficial to republics since the great possess "*virtù* in arms and the generosity of spirit" (*FH* 3.1) and are "more prudent and more knowing of natural things" (D 1.12.1). Nonetheless, it is quite possible for men of humble origin to possess enough *virtù* to become capable leaders as well. Michele di Lando, for instance, was a lowly wool carder when a rebellious mob made him chief magistrate of Florence; yet he "deserves to be numbered among the few who have benefited their fatherland" on account of his "spirit, prudence, and goodness" (FH 3.17). Likewise, the fact that the Romans "went to find *virtù* in whatever house it inhabited" and that "the way to any rank whatever and to any honor whatever was not prevented... because of poverty" greatly contributed to the strength of their republic (D 3.25). Indeed, "as men of the people could be placed in the administration of the magistracies, the armies, and the posts of empire together with the nobles, they were filled with the same *virtù* as the nobles, and [Rome], by growing in *virtù*, grew in power" (FH 3.1). In this fashion, Machiavelli anticipates the modern preference for a career open to talent *(une carrière ouverte aux talents)* – for, in consequence of his devotion to the effectual truth, he wants the rulers of republics to be selected according to their abilities and to form an elite that is functional rather than hereditary.

How does the republican elite make itself obeyed by the multitude? Since the minds of the latter cannot grasp policies productive of good over the long term that require sacrifices in the present, informed consent is not a reliable means for securing compliance. Revered leaders can use their *gravitas* to persuade the many, but such a reliance on charisma carries the inherent risk that demagogues will outshine good men. What remains, therefore, as the means necessary for securing popular compliance are force and fraud.

As in any other state, the magistrates of Machiavelli's republic use violence or the threat of violence to compel people to obey the laws and their commands. Should such enforcement prove inadequate because the transgressors are too many, because time is too pressing, because the case is exceptional, or because the people sitting in judgment are "blinded by a species of false good" (D 3.28), the leaders can appoint a dictator with the authority "to decide by himself regarding remedies for that urgent danger, and to do everything without consultation, and to punish everyone without appeal" (D 1.34.2). But even a dictator will be unable to maintain order if the majority of the people are opposed to the government, especially when they have been armed for war. At this point, wise men resort to fraud.

On the simplest level, leaders can promise benefits to the people and then delay their fulfillment, as the Roman elite did when the plebeians demanded that they be made eligible for the consulate. "It was fitting at an early hour that the plebs have hope of gaining the consulate," Machiavelli explains, and so the plebs were "fed a bit with this hope without having it; then the hope was not enough and it was fitting that it come to the effect" (D 1.60). Next, there is electoral fraud and manipulation, of which Machiavelli reports three kinds. Strategic placement of candidates was practiced by the Roman elite when it "corrupted some vile and very ignoble plebeian who, mixed with the plebeians of better quality who ordinarily asked for [the office], also asked them for it," which "made the plebs ashamed to give it" to one of their own (D 1.48). Manipulation of the voting system was practiced by Quintus Fabius, who, in his official capacity as censor, "put all these new men from whom this disorder derived under four tribes, so that by being shut in such small spaces they could not corrupt all Rome" (D 3.49.4), for voting took place by tribe so that the votes of individuals had less weight when the members of the tribe were more numerous. Outright fabrication of results was recommended by Machiavelli in the *Discourse Concerning Florentine Affairs*, which he wrote to suggest to Pope Leo X that a new constitution be drafted for Florence. "Your Holiness," he wrote, "is to select eight couplers, who, remaining in secrecy, can declare elected whomever they wish, and can deny election to anyone" (O 29).

But by far the most reliable means of fraud is religion, which enables the elite to control the many by the threat of divine punishment. "Wise men...have recourse to God," Machiavelli explains, because a "prudent individual knows many goods that do not have in themselves reasons with which one can persuade others" (D 1.11.3). At Rome, religion was introduced by Numa Pompilius, who "pretended to be intimate with a nymph who counseled him on what he had to counsel the people" (D 1.11.2), with the result that "there was never so much fear of God as in that republic, which made easier whatever enterprise the Senate or the great men of Rome might plan to make" (D 1.11.1).

In pagan times, the chief instruments of religious fraud were oaths, promises that call on a god to impose punishment in case of noncompliance, and omens, unusual events that reveal the will of the gods and portend the future. When religious belief is strong, oaths assume a quasi-objective reality, as among the early Romans, who "feared to break an oath much more than the laws, like those who esteemed the power of God more than that of men" (D 1.11.1). For instance, the Roman plebs, who had sworn an oath to obey the consul for the sake of a military enterprise, afterward obeyed his successor, even though he led them to war to prevent them from thinking about a certain law, for from "fear of religion the plebs wished rather to obey the consul than to believe the tribunes" (D 1.13.2). The usefulness of omens lies in the fact that they can be interpreted in favor of the interests of the state. After the Roman people had elected mostly plebeians to the tribuneship with consular power, a plague and a famine struck and a number of prodigies were reported – fires blazing in the sky, the earth trembling, cows talking, and the like. Promptly, the "nobles used the opportunity in the next creation of tribunes to say that the gods were angry because Rome had used the majesty of its [consular power] badly, and that there was no remedy for placating the gods other than to return the election of tribunes to its place." In the next election, "the plebs, terrified by this religion, created as tribunes all nobles" (D 1.13.1). Indeed, the possibilities of interpretation are such that "when reason showed [the Roman leaders] a thing they ought to do – notwithstanding that the auspices had been adverse – they did it in any mode. But they turned it around with means and modes so aptly that it did not appear that they had done it with disdain for religion" (D 1.14.1).

But if the leading men of Machiavelli's republic can so readily manipulate the multitude, to what extent is it really a mixed regime in which the people have a share in authority and are able to check the tyrannical ambitions of the nobles? Machiavelli's answer to this important question is twofold. First, the people's ability to choose good leaders applies equally to those who are entrusted with the "guard of freedom," such as the tribunes of the plebs at Rome. And since their political success depends on pursuing the popular interest, the people thereby gain a measure of protection. Second, although the people cannot fathom a universe without divine agency, they can see through religious fraud that benefits particular individuals or groups. For when the ancient oracles "began to speak in the mode of the powerful, and as that falsity was exposed among the peoples, men became incredulous and apt to disturb every good order" (D 1.12.1). Likewise, when Pope Boniface VIII (1294–1303) excommunicated his personal enemies and declared a crusade against them, the "arms which had been used *virtuosamente* for the love of faith, when used for his own ambition against Christians, began not to cut" (FH 1.25).

Founding, Good Customs, Corruption, and Return to Beginnings

Without "ordered government," human beings exist by nature in a condition of "ambitious license" (D 1.47.3), where "everything is full of confusion and disorder" (D 1.3.2). To escape this natural condition, they need to be constrained by a "new prince" who comes to power by the ruthless use of force. Once the new prince has secured his hold over the population, he faces a choice: either to indulge in the pleasures of tyranny – wielding power arbitrarily, depriving his subjects of their possessions, abusing their women, and the like – or to use his coercive power to found civil institutions. Sadly, "deceived by a false good and a false glory, almost all let themselves go, either voluntarily or ignorantly, into the ranks of those" who "turn to tyranny" – even "though, to their perpetual honor, they are able to make a republic or kingdom" (D 1.10.1). The reason for this rarity of a founding is not only that most people prefer immediate pleasure to remote honor, but that the enterprise of founding a civil life in the natural condition of license comes up against the inherent tension between pursuing a good end and doing evil deeds. "Because the reordering of a city for a political way of life presupposes a good man," Machiavelli observes, "and becoming prince of a republic by violence presupposes a bad man, one will find that it very rarely happens that someone good wishes to become prince by bad ways, even though his end be good." Conversely, it very rarely happens "that it will ever occur" to "someone wicked, having become prince," to "use well the authority that he has acquired badly" (D 1.18.4). Thus, Machiavelli realized, at least on the personal level, that the doctrine of *raison d'état* suffers from an inherent contradiction between the goodness of the end and the wickedness of the means. But he accepted it as part of a fragmented reality in which "one never seeks to avoid one inconvenience without running into another," and in which "prudence consists in knowing how to recognize the qualities of inconveniences, and in picking the less bad as good" (*P* 21).

At any rate, an autocratic founding is necessary because the "many are not capable of ordering a thing because they do not know its good, which is because of the diverse opinions among them" (*D* 1.9.2). On the other hand, for a civil way of life to last, it must have the support of the people. "If one individual is capable of ordering, the thing itself is ordered to last long not if it remains on the shoulders of one individual but rather if it remains in the care of many and its maintenance stays with many," for "when they have come to know it, they do not agree to abandon it" (*D* 1.9.2). However, the people do not cling to the civil way of life because they understand in principle why it is better to live under orders and laws, for, as we know, they are incapable of grasping such general ideas. Instead, they defend it against usurpers because they are "accustomed to living by their own laws and in liberty" (*P* 5). In general, "laws have need of good customs so as to be observed" (*D* 1.18.1).

The customs that matter most to a *vivere civile* concern military service, consumption, and religious belief. The Romans "were accustomed to serve in the military on their own" expense (*D* 1.51), and even "did not esteem it a dishonorable thing to obey now one whom they had commanded at another time . . . a custom contrary to the opinions, orders, and modes of citizens in our times" (*D* 1.36). People need to be "content with those goods, to live by those foods, to dress with those woolens that the country provides," as the Germans still do, whereas the "French or Spanish or Italian customs" are "the corruption of the world" (*D* 1.55.3). In the cities of Italy "both sexes at every age are full of foul customs, for which good laws, because they are spoiled by wicked use, are no remedy" (*FH* 3.5). Florence, in particular, is "full of courtly delicacies and customs, contrary to all well-ordered civility" (*FH* 7.28). "Every religion has the foundation of its life on some principal order of its own," which consists of "ceremonies, sacrifices, and rites" (*D* 1.12.1). In pagan religion, "the action of the sacrifice, full of blood and ferocity" offered a sight that, "being terrible, rendered men similar to itself" (*D* 2.2.2). In short, it is such good customs that constitute the *virtù* or goodness of citizens, enabling them to maintain the orders and laws of a civil way of life.

People acquire their customs under the constraint of the founder, who habituates them to living by orders and laws through punishment – just as parents do with their children. In so doing, founders who work with rustic peoples, whose licentiousness arises only from their first nature, have an easier task than those who must reform corrupt city-dwellers, whose original tendency to license has been reinforced by foul customs. Romulus, Numa, Lycurgus, and Solon "could easily impress any new form whatever" on their matter since the "men with whom they had to labor were crude," just as a "sculptor will get a beautiful statue more easily from coarse marble than from one badly blocked out by another" (*D* 1.11.3).

Since habits are merely acquired whereas the human tendency to ambitious license is innate, good customs are subject to corruption as soon as the founder's constraint has been lifted and citizens begin to rule themselves. This explains why men of tyrannical ambition came to power in Rome a mere sixty years after its founding: "One also notes in the matter of the Decemvirate [rule of ten] how easily men are corrupted...and how Quintus Fabius,...blinded by a little ambition and persuaded by the malignity of Appius, changed his good customs to the worst, and became like him" (D 1.42).

To prevent such corruption from spreading throughout a republic, "it is necessary to draw it back often toward its beginning" (D 3.1.title), that is, to renew the customs that prevailed at the founding by putting a comparable dread in the minds of men. For when a certain amount of "time is past, men begin to vary in their customs and to transgress the laws" unless "something arises by which punishment is brought back to their memory and fear is renewed in their spirits" (D 3.1.3). This salutary fear can arise from an "external beating," such as the sack of Rome by the Gauls in 395 B.C., which shocked the Romans into restoring the customary piety and law-abidingness that supported their civil way of life (D 3.1.2). But such events are obviously too accidental and dangerous to serve as a reliable remedy for corruption that "of necessity" spreads "little by little and from generation to generation" (D 3.8.2). Instead, fear-based renewal of good customs should be institutionalized in the manner of "the orders that drew the Roman republic back toward its beginning," which were "the tribunes of the plebs, the censors, and all the other laws that went against the ambition and the insolence of men." More concretely, transgressors need to be punished in "excessive and notable" ways (D 3.1.3), so that the mere thought of emulating them fills everyone with dread. For instance, when the sons of Brutus conspired to overthrow the young Roman republic, they were put to death by their own father in his capacity as chief magistrate, which, according to Machiavelli, was "an example rare in all memories of things" (D 1.3.3). In the case of Maelius the grain dealer, who fed the plebs and was put to death on the mere suspicion of conspiring against the republic, the excess arose from the fact that his work appeared "merciful" and could not "reasonably be condemned" (D 3.28). The punishment of Manlius Capitolinus, sentenced to death for agitating the plebs and planning revolution, was notable in that he had once been celebrated as a hero for retaking the Capitoline hill but now "was without any respect for his merits thrown headlong" from the very rock that he had once saved "with so much glory for himself" (D 1.24.2). And Manlius Torquatus became famous for his severity when, as commander of the Roman army, he had his own son decapitated for disobeying the order not to engage the enemy, even though the young man had been provoked and returned victorious (D 2.16.1, 3.1.3, 22.4, 34.2).

In addition to fear, good customs can be renewed by the exemplary deeds of virtuoso individuals who "are of such reputation and so much example that good men desire to imitate them and the wicked are ashamed to hold to a life contrary to theirs. In Rome, those who particularly produced these good effects were Horatius Cocles, Scaevola, Fabricius, the two Decii, Regulus Attilius, and some others" (D 3.1.3). Horatius Cocles, for instance, single-handedly held off an entire Etruscan army to shield the retreat of his comrades; Mutius Scaevola thrust his hand into fire to show the enemy king what kind of men he was dealing with in making war on the Romans; and Regulus Attilius, having been released by the Carthaginians on the condition that he return with a Roman offer of peace, showed that a Roman values his word more than his life, for even though the Senate had declined peace, he returned to Carthage and was tortured to death. That such heroic actions had indeed a salutary effect on the customs of the Romans is attested by Livy (2.14), who wrote that "the public recognition of Mucius [Scaevola]'s heroism inspired even the women of Rome to emulate him."

For corruption to be held at bay, such returns to the beginnings must recur at certain intervals. In the first chapter of the third book of the *Discourses on Livy*, where Machiavelli discusses returns to beginnings at length, he puts this interval at ten years: "If the executions written above, together with these particular examples, had continued at least every ten years in that city, it follows of necessity that it would never have been corrupt" (D 3.1.3). However, in the last chapter of the third book, he writes that "a republic has need of new acts of foresight every day if one wishes to maintain it free" (D 3.49.title), and he cites as exemplary a series of punishments that seem as excessive and notable as the ones mentioned previously: putting to death the Roman matrons who had conspired to poison their senatorial husbands; summarily executing thousands suspected of participating in the obscene and subversive rites of Bacchus; sentencing to death an entire legion or city; "decimating" entire armies for cowardice, that is, executing every tenth man regardless of individual guilt (D 3.49.1–3). By asserting the necessity that there be a daily return to beginnings at the end of a book that he had begun with the suggestion that a decennial return to beginnings would suffice, Machiavelli intimates that sustained reflection on the topic – such as the ruminations he engaged in while writing the third book of his *Discourses on Livy* – leads one to conclude that excessive and notable punishments must occur every day if good customs are to be maintained.

But this conclusion casts serious doubt on the effectiveness of good customs as a cause for compliance, for they were supposed to make the citizens obey the orders and laws of the civil way of life in the absence of punishment by an autocrat. To resolve this issue, we need to make an analytical distinction between the citizens who administer the daily punishments and all the others who experience their salutary dread. For then we realize that good customs are needed to motivate the enforcers who cannot be governed by fear of punishment themselves. In Machiavelli's opinion, "the orders that drew the Roman republic back to its beginnings... have need of being brought to life by the *virtù* of a citizen who rushes spiritedly to execute them against the power of those who transgress them" (D 3.1.3), and this *virtù*, as we have seen, is a matter of good customs. In other words, Machiavelli seeks to prevent the natural ambition of human beings from destroying the civil way of life by means of institutions as well as character. The holders of public office are charged with excessively and notably punishing transgressors every day so as to make all others observe the orders and laws from fear. But since institutions do not work by themselves but must be made effective by the actions of human beings, he hopes that the latter can be moved to do their duty from a customary sense of allegiance to the regime.

But human affairs are inescapably contingent. Thus, it will eventually happen that transgressions go unpunished with the result that more citizens lose their good customs: "When [excessive and notable punishments] began to be more rare, they also began to give more space to men to corrupt themselves and to behave with greater danger and more tumult," and "soon so many delinquents join together that they can no longer be punished without danger" (*D* 3.1.3). Hence, the theoretical possibility of making a republic last forever by continuously returning its citizens to the beginnings cannot be realized; in practice, "it is impossible to order a perpetual republic, because its ruin is caused through a thousand unexpected ways" (*D* 3.17). Ultimately, even the mixed regime cannot escape the cycle of generation and corruption that plagues simple regimes. For, although different humors can be made to check each other's ambitions, the fact that all of them tend by nature to ambitious license remains.

Once corruption has spread to most citizens, the civil way of life collapses. In Rome, this terminal phase "arose from the corruption which the Marian parties had put in the people" at the beginning of the first century B.C., so that in 42 B.C., at the battle of Philippi, "the authority and severity of Brutus, together with all the eastern legions, were not enough" to defend republican liberty against the usurper Mark Anthony, who had taken up Caesar's mantle (*D* 1.17.1). At this point, another founder is needed who acts autocratically, outside the law and without respect for any of the institutions, in order to create new ones. In Machiavelli's words, "neither laws nor orders can be found that are enough to check a universal corruption... but it is necessary to go to the extraordinary, such as violence and arms, and before everything else become prince of that city, able to dispose it in one's own mode" (*D* 1.18.1, 18.4). Just as at the beginning of the civil way of life, this autocrat needs to habituate men to the new orders and laws: "where [the matter] is corrupt, well-ordered laws" must be "put in motion by one individual who with an extreme force ensures their observance so that the matter becomes good" (*D* 1.17.3). However, additional difficulties arise from the fact that this would-be founder faces a people quite unlike the unspoiled rustics of the original founding, a people whose licentious nature has been aggravated by bad habits. "There cannot be one man of such long life as to have enough time to inure to good a city that has been inured to bad for a long time," for "as soon as such a one is dead, it returns to its early habit" (*D* 1.17.3). Given the persistence of licentious habits on top of a licentious nature, the only solution is for a new generation to grow up under the new order and for the current generation to pass away, either by natural causes or at the murderous hands of the founder. "If one individual of very long life or two *virtuoso* ones continued in succession do not arrange" the city, "it is ruined, unless indeed he makes it be reborn with many dangers and much blood" (*D* 1.17.3).

In sum, corruption of good customs can be violently countered in two ways: As long as corruption remains within certain limits, it suffices that magistrates and concerned citizens punish transgressors within the institutional framework of the civil way of life by means of the law; when corruption has become universal, however, autocrats must use massive coercion outside any existing orders to establish new ones – that is, they must undertake another founding. Machiavelli makes this distinction most explicit when he claims in reference to institutional renovation that those republics have "longer life that *by means of their orders can often be renewed*" (*D* 3.1.1, emphasis added), and when he states with regard to renewed founding that "it never or rarely happens that any republic or kingdom is ordered well from the beginning or *reformed altogether anew outside its old orders* unless it is ordered by one individual" (*D* 1.9.2, emphasis added). This distinction is crucial for understanding the institutional character of Machiavelli's republican thought. Otherwise, we might take the fact that excessive violence is used in both cases to suggest that institutional renovation on a daily basis should be combined with the autocratic aspect of renewed founding, and thus follow Leo Strauss in his erroneous conclusion that Machiavelli's republic is at bottom a tyranny on the part of its leading men.[19] But as we have seen, daily returns to the beginnings occur within the orders and laws of the civil way of life and are typically executed by holders of public office. True, their actions often involve necessary evil – for instance, when they execute men without a trial or decimate armies – but they are consistently carried out in defense of the laws and institutions of the republic. Hence, Machiavelli's republic remains an institutional regime, although one that readily commits injustice for the purpose of maintaining itself.

War and Empire

According to Machiavelli, human beings have a natural desire for glory, power, and wealth. Unconstrained pursuit of these goods, or "license," leads to conflict because they are exclusive or at least relative: The wealth possessed by one cannot be enjoyed by another; the power held by one must be measured in relation to that of others; the more glory shines on one, the less it falls on others. By allowing discord, Machiavelli's conception of the civil way of life also permits citizens to come into conflict over these goods, as long as they do so without violence. However, the natural tendency of human ambition to grow without limits implies that the glory, power, and wealth that can be had within the boundaries of the city will quickly become insufficient to satisfy the

---

[19] See Leo Strauss, *Thoughts on Machiavelli* (Chicago: University of Chicago Press, 1958), 44, 166–7, 228–31, 274, 278, where Strauss makes this point in rather oblique fashion; Harvey C. Mansfield and Nathan Tarcov make it more clearly in Mansfield and Tarcov, "Introduction," in NM, *D* xvii–xliv, at xxv–xxvi.

competing individuals and humors. As their dissatisfaction increases, it becomes harder and harder for the magistrates to defend the institutional order against ambitious transgressors. To maintain their civil way of life, republics are thus constrained to vent their citizens' ambitions abroad, that is, to lead wars that bring greatness, empire, and wealth. In his poem "Of Ambition," Machiavelli describes this outward deflection of human desire in language that is especially evocative:

Ambition uses against exterior people that fury which neither the law nor the king consent to using inside; wherefore one's own evil almost always ceases; but she is sure to keep disturbing the sheepfolds of others, where that fury of hers puts down the banner.

(O 985)

Conversely, a shared threat from abroad helps the great and the people to resolve their conflicts through laws rather than arms. When the Senate and the plebs were once at loggerheads and two foreign powers attacked Rome in the hope of exploiting their quarrel, "the Romans from being disunited became united and, coming to fight, broke them and won" (D 2.25.1). In general, it can thus be said that "the cause of the disunion of republics is usually idleness and peace; the cause of union is fear and war" (D 2.25.1).

It is for these reasons that republics are much more warlike than principalities. Princes can plunder their own subjects to satisfy their desires, but citizens must exploit foreigners to maintain their civil way of life. Princes come to power by usurpation or succession; the magistrates of republics are elected by people who need foreign threats to make good choices. In principalities, fear of the prince prevents the natural discord between the nobles and the people from turning violent; in republics, this discord needs to be constrained by fear of a foreign enemy. As a result, "of all hard servitudes, that is hardest that submits you to a republic . . . because the end of the republic is to enervate and to weaken all other bodies so as to increase its own body"; in contrast, "a prince who makes you submit does not do this, if that prince is not some barbarian prince" (D 2.2.4).

But republics are constrained to wage war not only on these domestic grounds but also because they have to preempt foreign threats. Machiavelli comes to this conclusion when asking hypothetically whether a republic could escape war altogether by withdrawing behind natural defenses, limiting the ambition of its citizens, and, above all, by being strong enough to deter aggression but not so powerful as to provoke attacks from fear:

I would well believe that to make a republic that would last a long time, the mode would be to order it within like Sparta or like Venice; to settle it in a strong place of such power that nobody would believe he could crush it at once. On the other hand, it would not be so great as to be formidable to its neighbors; and so it could enjoy its state at length. For war is made on a republic for two causes: one, to become master of it; the other, for fear lest it seize you. . . . If it stays within its limits, and it is seen by experience that there is no ambition in it, it will never occur that one will make war for fear of it; and so much the more would this be if there were in it a constitution and laws to prohibit it from expanding. Without doubt I believe that if the thing could be held balanced in this mode, it would be the true political way of life and the true quiet of a city.

(*D* 1.6.4)

Strikingly similar in its logic to a passage in Aristotle (*Pol.* 1267a21–7), this picture of the "true political way of life" clearly draws on the classical ideal of the self-sufficient city that remains small, limits desires, and minimizes foreign contact.

Unfortunately, the effectual truth of the thing differs once more from its classical imagination. First, the sheer contingency of human affairs makes it impossible to strike an exact balance between inviting aggression from weakness and provoking war through excessive strength. In Machiavelli's words, "all things of men are in motion and cannot stay steady, they must either rise or fall" (*D* 1.6.4); hence, "one cannot . . . balance this thing, nor maintain this middle way exactly"; even though a republic "will not molest others, it will be molested, and from being molested will arise the wish and the necessity to acquire" empire (*D* 2.19.1). Second, even if a city were fortunate enough not to be "molested" while trying to follow this middle way, the very absence of war would accelerate the corruption of its citizens and lead to a loss of military prowess or, worse, civil strife, thus making the city easy prey to foreign powers: "if heaven were so kind that it did not have to make war, from that would arise the idleness to make it either effeminate or divided; these two things together, or each by itself, would be the cause of its ruin" (*D* 1.6.4). Third, cities cannot avoid being drawn into the wars of others by staying neutral, for, as Machiavelli observed in a letter he addressed to his friend Francesco Vettori on 10 December 1514, "he who stays neutral is sure to be hated by him who loses, and despised by him who wins"; being "esteemed a useless friend and unformidable enemy, he needs to fear that every injury will be done to him and every ruin planned for him" (*O* 1184). In sum, no republic can lastingly escape the state of war that characterizes the foreign condition.

The inference that Machiavelli draws from this fact is ruthlessly logical: Since war cannot be avoided, it must be won by striking first: "The Romans, seeing inconveniences from afar, always found remedies for them and never allowed them to continue so as to escape a war, because they knew war may not be avoided but is deferred to the advantage of others" (*P* 3).

But simply to defeat another city in the field will bring only temporary relief, as the city will rearm in short order. To gain lasting security, one must eliminate the capabilities that generated the threat or bring them under one's control. Thus, in antiquity, "men conquered in war were either killed or remained in perpetual slavery . . . conquered towns were either dissolved or, their goods taken, the inhabitants were driven out and sent dispersed throughout the world" (*AW* 2.305). But while cities can be razed and people killed, enslaved, and dispersed, territory cannot so readily be destroyed. It needs to be added to one's own dominion in order to prevent others from using it as an asset. Accordingly, Machiavelli concludes his inquiry into the middle way constituting the "true political way of life" – that is, classical republicanism – with the following maxim: "In ordering a republic there is need...to order it in a mode that if indeed necessity brings it to expand, it can keep what it has seized"; hence, "it is necessary to follow the Roman order and not that of the other republics," such as Sparta and Venice (*D* 1.6.4). And the Roman order is the "true way to make a republic great and to acquire empire" (*D* 2.19.2).

In sum, there are two necessities that drive republics to make war on foreigners and to seek to acquire empire: First and particular to republics, they must satisfy their citizens' ambitions abroad and maintain a shared sense of outside threat in order to sustain a nonviolent civil way of life at home; second, like any other political community, republics are constrained to take the offensive because standing on the defensive can preserve a city only for so long.

To go forth and conquer, a republic must increase the number of citizens and arm them in order to achieve numerical superiority on the battlefield. Rome conquered the Mediterranean world because it "could already put in arms two hundred eighty thousand men, [whereas] Sparta and Athens never passed beyond twenty thousand each" (*D* 2.3). The Romans generated this manpower in two ways. After defeating cities in war, they often made them into partners *(socii)*, who could keep their own laws but had to supply troops to the Romans (*D* 2.4.1, 23.2). Further, they encouraged foreigners to take residence in their city and liberally admitted them to citizenship (*D* 2.3) – contrary to the classical maxim of limiting citizenship to men of good breeding and honorable occupation for the sake of concord, friendship, and virtue.

Plato (*Rep.* 415c–417b, 422a–423d; *Leg.* 742a–b) had argued that the virtue that a city attains from limiting its size and inhibiting foreign commerce would always suffice to vanquish large and open cities in war. This claim may have seemed plausible at the time, for aristocratic and isolationist Sparta had just defeated the populous and innovative city of Athens in the Peloponnesian War (432–404 B.C.). But it was shown to be wrong when Rome acquired its empire on account of superior numbers drawn from plebeians and *socii* as well as its inventiveness in warfare. Hence, Machiavelli was right when he argued that the foreign aspect of the human condition makes the classical conception of a small and virtuous republic nonviable.

Well-Ordered License

Committed to the effectual truth, Machiavelli does not consider human beings in terms of what they could be at their ethical best but in terms of what they happen to be: self-regarding individuals whose minds are as incapable of ruling their desires as they are given to serving them with ingenuity and inflaming them with imagination. Rejecting the classical definition of nature as the fully developed form reached by the best, he anticipates Thomas Hobbes in advancing the modern understanding of nature as the primitive beginning shared by all: "all men, having had the same beginning, are equally ancient and have been made by nature in one mode" (*FH* 3.13). The few are not superior to the many, as "all men particularly, and especially princes, can be accused of that defect of which the [ancient] writers accuse the multitude" (D 1.58.2), and, therefore, as Machiavelli puts it in his play *Mandragola* (3.4, in O 879), "good is what does good to most, and with which most are contented." It is no accident that Machiavelli's image of man closely resembles Aristotle's description of the many *(hoi polloí)*, who seek "wealth, goods, power, reputation, and all such things ... to excess without limit" (*Pol.* 1323a36–7).

Accordingly, the orders and laws of Machiavelli's republic no longer seek to make men virtuous: It is sufficient that they be satisfied. More precisely, the purpose of the civil way of life is to coordinate men's efforts at gratifying their desires in such a way that they generate far more glory, power, freedom, and wealth by acting in concert, than they could have gotten from proceeding individually. In Aristotle's terms (*Pol.* 1280b5–1281a3), Machiavelli's republic is a mere "alliance *(summachía)*," that is, a "partnership in location and for the sake of not committing injustice against each other and of transacting business." It is not a "partnership in living well *(eu zên koinonía)*" whose laws are designed to "make the citizens good and just." Instead of canceling their efforts by fighting each other, Machiavelli's men are organized by orders and laws to combine their energies in the joint exploitation of others. Thus, the charge that Machiavelli's republic is a tyranny turns out to be true after all. However, it is not a tyranny of the few over the many; it is a tyranny of citizens over foreigners.

Machiavelli's Project

Taking men as they happen to be, denying the classical distinction between the few and the many, and understanding the city as a means to the satisfaction of men's conflicting ambitions are characteristically modern ideas. But was it Machiavelli's intention to bring about an entirely new kind of political life? It may seem so according to the first paragraph of the *Discourses on Livy*, where Machiavelli states that he has found "new modes and orders" like the great discoverers of his age who had reached "unknown waters and lands," and thus claims to have taken a "path as yet untrodden by anyone" (D 1.pref.1). But in the next paragraph, we find that Machiavelli elaborates this claim to novelty as doing for politics what other Renaissance men had done for the arts and letters, namely recovering and imitating the superior ways of the ancients: "Considering thus how much honor is awarded to antiquity ... and seeing on the other hand, that the most *virtuoso* works the histories show us, which have been done by ancient kingdoms and republics, by kings, captains, citizens, legislators, and others who have labored for their fatherland, are admired rather than imitated ... I can do no other than marvel and grieve." This grievous failure to imitate ancient political life has been caused to some extent by "the weakness into which the present religion [i.e., Christianity] has led the world," but, more importantly, it results from "not having a true knowledge of histories, through not getting from reading them that sense nor tasting that flavor that they have in themselves." To mend this shortcoming is the avowed purpose of Machiavelli's

Discourses on Livy: "Wishing, therefore, to turn men from this error, I have judged it necessary to write on all those books of Titus Livy . . . whatever I shall judge necessary for their greater understanding, according to knowledge of ancient and modern things" (*D* 1.pref.2).

But what precisely did Machiavelli mean by the "true knowledge" and the "greater understanding" of the ancient histories and the "sense" and "flavor" that they have in themselves"? None other than what is implied by his reading the Bible, Cicero, Sallust, and Livy "judiciously," by which he revealed what was taught covertly to princes by ancient writers: namely, that necessary evil in the pursuit of the natural desires for security, glory, dominion, liberty, and riches constitutes the effective truth of political life – princely as well as republican. Conversely, we gain a false understanding of history by reading the ancient authors in the manner of the humanists, who took their affirmations of virtue at face value and then brought their cities to ruin by governing accordingly. According to Felix Gilbert, this became clear to Machiavelli and his friends when the leading men of Florence – who anchored their political claims in the moral teachings that the humanists had derived from their study of the classical world – failed to defend the city against the superior force of the French and Spanish invaders of Italy.[20] In Machiavelli's words, "before they tasted the blows of ultramontane war," Italy's leaders believed "that it was enough for a prince to know how to think of a sharp response in his studies, to write a beautiful letter, to show wit and quickness in his deeds and words, to know how to weave a fraud, to be ornamented by gems and gold," from which "arose in 1494 great terrors, sudden flights, and miraculous losses" (*AW* 7.236–7). Hence, the "path as yet untrodden by anyone," which Machiavelli blazes in the *Discourses on Livy*, leads in the same direction as the intention he broadcasts in *The Prince* when he says that he departs "from the orders of others": namely, it leads directly to the "effectual truth" of political life, rather than to the imagination of "republics and principalities that have never been seen or known to exist in truth" (*P* 15).

Hence, Machiavelli helped to bring about modernity by his effort to uncover the timeless truth about politics, which he had generalized from the practices of his contemporaries and believed to have read between the lines of the ancients. Accordingly, he did not wittingly attempt a revaluation of all values in the Nietzschean sense, whereby human beings understand themselves and construct their reality in a fundamentally new way. Indeed, Machiavelli's view of history did not allow him even to conceive of such an endeavor, for he assumed that the basic order of things remains forever the same. Thus, he chides his contemporaries for "judging that imitation [of the ancients] is not only difficult but impossible – as if heaven, sun, elements, men had varied in motion, order, and power from what they were in antiquity" (*D* 1.pref.2), declaring instead that "I judge the world always to have been in the same mode" (*D* 2.pref.2). Change,

---

[20] Felix Gilbert, *Machiavelli and Guicciardini: Politics and History in Sixteenth Century Florence* (New York: W. W. Norton, 1984), esp. 79–80, 117–39, 150–2, 243–54.

wrought aplenty by Fortune, is constrained by the cyclical order assumed by the ancients. A different way of thinking about the world – what Machiavelli calls an "education" – can at most change the amount of *virtù* with which people face the perils of their existence:

All worldly things in every time have their own counterpart in ancient times. That arises because these are the work of men, who always have and always had the same passions, and they must of necessity result in the same effect. It is true that their works are more *virtuoso* now in this province than in that, and in that more than this, according to the form of education in which those people have taken their mode of life. (D 3.43)

Since *virtù* refers to the ability to create and maintain political order, understanding history as a variation of *virtù* leads to seeing it in terms of the successive generation and fragmentation of empire. This can be clearly

seen by one who has knowledge of those ancient kingdoms, which varied from one to another because of the variation of customs, though the world remained the same. There was this difference only: that where [the world] had first placed its *virtù* in Assyria, it put it in Media, then in Persia, until it came to be in Italy and Rome. And if no empire followed after the Roman Empire that might have endured and in which the world might have kept its *virtù* together, it is seen nonetheless to be scattered in many nations where they lived *virtuosamente*, such as the kingdom of the Franks, the kingdom of the Turks, that of the sultan, and the peoples of Germany today. (D 2.pref.2)

To demonstrate how the Romans can be imitated in acquiring an empire that would bring the world's scattered *virtù* together again is Machiavelli's daring political project. In closing the *Art of War*, he admits this ambition rather openly:

I assert to you that whichever of those who today keep states in Italy first enters by this way [of reorganizing the military], he will be lord of this province before anyone else. And it will happen to his state as to the kingdom of the Macedonians. Coming under Philip, who had learned the mode of ordering armies from the Theban Epaminondas – and since the rest of Greece was in idleness and attended to the performance of comedies – it became so powerful with this order and these armies that he could in a few years occupy all of [Greece], [and] leave to his son [Alexander the Great] such a foundation that he was able to make himself prince of all the world. (AW 7.243)

After all, the exaltation of the founder is second only to that of the gods, and, as Machiavelli observes in his *Discourse Concerning Florentine Affairs*, founding has been "esteemed so much by men, who have sought nothing other than glory, that when unable to make a republic in action, they made one in writing, like Aristotle, Plato, and many others" (O 30–1). Where Aristotle and Plato had fashioned republics in writing that could never exist in reality, Machiavelli would fashion one that could master the world.

PART I

THE ENGLISH COMMONWEALTHMEN

For more than a century subsequent to his death in 1527, Niccolò Machiavelli was known to the larger world as a counselor of princes, as an enemy to morality and the Christian religion, and as an inspiration to the advocates of *raison d'état*. It was not until after the execution of Charles I in January 1649 that he would become almost equally famous also as an advocate for republican rule.

There is no great mystery in this. Machiavelli's *Prince* is, at least on the surface, a much more accessible book than his *Discourses on Livy*. It is shorter, pithier, and more vigorous, and it enjoyed a *grand succès de scandale* from the very first. In contrast, the *Discourses on Livy* is long, subtle, complex, and difficult to decipher. In short, the work in which republicanism looms large is as unattractive to the casual reader as *The Prince* is alluring. Even now, the longer book is much more rarely read.

Of course, from the outset, there were those who argued that Machiavelli revealed his true opinions only in his *Discourses on Livy*. Within six years of the appearance of the Florentine's two great masterpieces in printed form, an inquisitive and well-connected English visitor to Florence named Reginald Pole was told by one or more of Machiavelli's compatriots that the author of the *Discourses on Livy* had written *The Prince* solely in order to trip up the Medici and bring about their demise. Machiavelli had purportedly acknowledged as much himself. Although Pole was not himself inclined to entertain this claim,[1] others who learned of the report were perfectly prepared to do so,[2] and the

---

[1] See the report in his *Apologia ad Carolum Quintum* (1539), in *Epistolarum Reginaldi Poli S. R. E. Cardinalis et aliorum ad ipsum collectio*, ed. Angelo M. Quirini (Brescia: J. M. Rizzardi, 1744–57), 1:66–171 (esp. 151–2), where Pole refers to a visit to Florence that took place in the winter of 1538.

[2] See, for example, Giovanni Matteo Toscano, *Peplus Italiae* (Paris: Morelli, 1578), 52; André Rossant, *Les meurs, humeurs et comportemens de Henry de Valois* (Paris: P. Mercier, 1589), 11. Cf., however, Thomas Fitzherbert, *The First Part of a Treatise Concerning Policy and Religion* (Douai: L. Kellam, 1606), 412. Although Pole's *Apologia ad Carolum Quintum* was not published

tendency for students of the subject to discount *The Prince* on one ground or another and to treat the *Discourses on Livy* as representative of Machiavelli's real thinking has had adherents ever since – especially in the English-speaking world, where in some quarters Machiavelli's apparent espousal of republican-ism has long inspired admiration.[3]

Alberico Gentili is a case in point. In a scholarly volume on the conduct of embassies, which he dedicated to Sir Philip Sidney and published in 1585, not long before he was created Regius Professor of Civil Law at Oxford University, Gentili singled out as "precious" the *Discourses on Livy*, described their author as "*Democratiae laudator et assertor*," termed him "a very great enemy to tyranny," and claimed that he had written *The Prince* not "to instruct the tyrant but to expose openly his secret deeds and exhibit him naked and clearly recognizable to the wretched peoples" of the world. "It was," he explained, "the strategy of this most prudent of all men to educate the people on the pretext of educating the prince."[4]

Some of the most enthusiastic seventeenth-century admirers of Machiavelli's republican reflections thought this sort of special pleading preposterous. Henry Neville was one such. After the Restoration, James Harrington's longtime friend and associate published an English translation of Machiavelli's works, to which he contributed a preface. Included in his preface was a letter purportedly by Machiavelli himself, describing *The Prince* as "both a Satyr against" tyrants "and a true Character of them." To this letter, which was to mislead unsuspect-ing readers from the late seventeenth well into the nineteenth century, Neville puckishly assigned the date 1 April 1537 – which was April Fool's Day, some ten years after its putative author's death.[5]

Neville's gentle mockery of those who could not stomach *The Prince* should serve as a warning to us all, for Machiavelli's republican book is by no means as unfriendly to principality as one might suppose. In fact, the author of the *Discourses on Livy* appears to have been no less willing than the author of *The Prince* to dispense his advice indiscriminately – not just to republics and their citizens, but to princes, to aspirants to one-man rule, and even to those

in printed form until the eighteenth century, what he said therein almost immediately found its way into diplomatic reports: See *Letters and Papers (Foreign and Domestic) of the Reign of Henry VIII*, ed. J. W. Brewer, James Gairdner, and R. H. Brodie (London: Longman, 1862–1910), 14:1, no. 200.

3 For an analysis and critique of the most influential recent attempt to drive a wedge between *The Prince* and the *Discourses on Livy* and to justify giving precedence to the latter, see Paul A. Rahe, "Situating Machiavelli," in *Renaissance Civic Humanism: Reappraisals and Reflections*, ed. James Hankins (Cambridge, UK: Cambridge University Press, 2000), 270–308.

4 Alberico Gentili, *De legationibus libri tres* (London: Thomas Vautrollerius, 1585), 3.9 (Sig. oiii). Traiano Boccalini's satirical account of his contemporaries' response to Machiavelli points in the direction of Gentili's conclusions: See *De'ragguagli di Parnaso* (Venice: P. Farri, 1612–15), 1.89.

5 See *The Works of the Famous Nicholas Machiavel, Citizen and Secretary of Florence* (London: John Starkey, 1675), sig. (***3) v.

whom he unashamedly singles out as tyrants.[6] His *Discourses* are addressed neither to the citizens of republics as such nor even to "those who are princes" already, but rather to "those who, for their infinite good parts, deserve to be" princes – for, in a republic, individual citizens may "by means of their *virtù* become princes," as happened, he expressly notes, in the case of Hiero of Syracuse.[7] It is no wonder that readers have always tended to give priority to Machiavelli's counsel concerning the acquisition and retention of political power.

Bad timing no doubt contributed as well to the eclipse of Machiavelli's republican teaching. The Florentine composed *The Prince* and his *Discourses on Livy* in the second decade of the sixteenth century after the collapse of the Florentine republic and the reestablishment of Medici rule. The two works circulated widely in manuscript for some time thereafter, both in Florence and abroad; and, within five years of their author's death in 1527, they were published in Rome under the imprimatur of Machiavelli's patron Clement VII, the second of the two Medici popes.[8] The Florentine's two most important books could not have appeared at a moment less favorable to the republican cause. In the century that followed, everything conspired to strengthen the executive power.

The military revolution, to which Machiavelli had contributed much, restored infantry to the supremacy that it had enjoyed in classical times,[9] but in the process it eliminated the usefulness of the feudal levy and thereby undermined the contractual foundations of limited kingship. The consequence was not a revival of the citizen militia along the lines that had sustained the republics of classical antiquity. Nor did this revolution eventuate in the arrangement Machiavelli had himself championed: the establishment of conscript armies drawn promiscuously from the various polities' citizen and subject populations.[10] The infantry's new-found primacy contributed, instead, to the predominance of professional armies, the traditional tool of absolute rulers. To make matters worse, in the very same years in which the military revolution began to reshape the conditions of political rule, the Reformation shattered the unity of Christendom and gave rise to civil strife and war in central and western Europe on a scale hitherto unknown. In this environment, with rare exceptions, such as

---

[6] See NM, *D* 1.16.3–5, 19, 21, 25–7, 30, 32, 33.5, 40–3, 45.3, 51, 55.5, 2.12–14, 18.5, 20, 23.3, 24, 27–8, 31, 3.3–6, 8, 11, 15, 22–3, 26.2, 27, 29–30, 34.3, 38, 42–4.

[7] See NM, *D* Ep. Ded., 2.2.3, which should be read in light of *P* 1, 6–14 (esp. 6 and 13).

[8] For the prepublication and publication history of Machiavelli's works, see Adolph Gerber, *Niccolò Machiavelli: Die Handschriften, Ausgaben und Übersetzungen seiner Werke im 16. und 17. Jahrhundert* (Turin: Bottega d'Erasmo, 1962). It was under the commission of Clement VII that Machiavelli composed the *Florentine Histories*.

[9] See Geoffrey Parker, *The Military Revolution: Military Innovation and the Rise of the West, 1500–1800* (Cambridge, UK: Cambridge University Press, 1988).

[10] Machiavelli did not, as is often suggested, link arms-bearing with citizenship per se: Note *P* 12–13, 20; *D* 1.21, 2.10, 12.4, 13.2, 20, 24, 30, 3.24; see *AW* 1.128–96. For further discussion, see Chapter 1.

Venice, Genoa, and Lucca, civic republics became principalities,[11] and, in principalities, representative assemblies ceased to meet. The formalities associated with securing consent count for little when disorder looms and life becomes increasingly nasty, brutish, and short. In times of anarchy, for the sake of peace and protection, most men will sacrifice everything else.

Of course, England was to some extent an exception to the rule, and Englishmen were acutely sensitive to this fact.[12] Prior to the 1640s, England managed to escape the sort of disorder that had paralyzed France in the late sixteenth century, and its parliament not only continued to meet throughout this period, it gained in strength, influence, and assertiveness,[13] while local self-government flourished in the parishes, boroughs, and shires.[14] This caused some of the English Crown's subjects to think of themselves as citizens and even to conceive of England as a republic of sorts,[15] and it occasioned on the part of many of the better educated a keen interest in the political institutions, practices, and ethos of the ancient commonwealths and a curiosity concerning the sources of

[11] For the fate of republican theorizing in Italy in the wake of this development, see Vittor Ivo Comparato, "From the Crisis of Civil Culture to the Neapolitan Republic of 1647: Republicanism in Italy between the Sixteenth and Seventeenth Centuries," in *Republicanism: A Shared Heritage I: Republicanism and Constitutionalism in Early Modern Europe*, ed. Martin van Gelderen and Quentin Skinner (Cambridge, UK: Cambridge University Press, 2002), 169–93.

[12] See William E. Klein, "Parliament, Liberty and the Continent in the Early Seventeenth Century: The Perception," *Parliamentary History* 6 (1987): 209–20; Robert Zaller, "Parliament and the Crisis of European Liberty," in *Parliament and Liberty: From the Reign of Elizabeth to the English Civil War*, ed. J. H. Hexter (Stanford, CA: Stanford University Press, 1992), 201–24.

[13] Cf. Wallace Notestein, "The Winning of the Initiative by the House of Commons," *Proceedings of the British Proceedings* 2 (1924–5): 125–75, with G. R. Elton, "A High Road to Civil War?" in *From the Renaissance to the Counter-Reformation: Essays in Honor of Garrett Mattingly*, ed. Charles H. Carter (New York: Random House, 1965), 325–47, and see J. H. Hexter, "The Apology," in *For Veronica Wedgwood These: Studies in Seventeenth-Century History*, ed. Richard Ollard and Pamela Tudor-Craig (London: Collins, 1986), 13–44. Then, cf. J. E. Neale, *The Elizabethan House of Commons* (London: J. Cape, 1949), *Elizabeth I and Her Parliaments, 1559–1581* (London: J. Cape, 1953), and *Elizabeth I and Her Parliaments, 1584–1601* (London: J. Cape, 1957), with G. R. Elton, *The Parliament of England, 1559–1581* (Cambridge, UK: Cambridge University Press, 1986), and see Patrick Collinson, "Puritans, Men of Business and Elizabethan Parliaments," in Collinson, *Elizabethan Essays* (London: Hambledon Press, 1994), 59–86. Then, consider J. H. Hexter, "Parliament, Liberty, and Freedom of Elections"; Johann P. Sommerville, "Parliament, Privilege, and the Liberties of the Subject"; David Harris Sacks, "Parliament, Liberty, and the Commonweal"; Clive Holmes, "Parliament, Liberty, Taxation, and Property"; Charles M. Gray, "Parliament, Liberty, and the Law"; Thomas Cogswell, "War and the Liberties of the Subject," in *Parliament and Liberty*, 1–200, 225–51.

[14] See Mark Goldie, "The Unacknowledged Republic: Officeholding in Early Modern England," in *The Politics of the Excluded, ca. 1500–1850*, ed. Tim Harris (Houndsmills, UK: Palgrave, 2001), 153–94.

[15] See Patrick Collinson, "The Monarchical Republic of Queen Elizabeth I," *Bulletin of the John Rylands University Library of Manchester* 69 (1987): 394–424; Markku Peltonen, "Citizenship and Republicanism in Elizabethan England," in *Republicanism and Constitutionalism in Early Modern Europe*, 85–106.

Venice's undoubted success.[16] Playwrights, such as William Shakespeare and Ben Jonson, seized upon this fashion as an opportunity for the exploration of republican themes. In England, a handful of would-be statesmen even turned to the *Discourses on Livy* for enlightenment concerning their country's aptitude for imperial grandeur.[17] By and large, however, interest in the ancients and in Machiavelli remained speculative: it did not, at that time, eventuate in a concrete program of reform, much less a political movement aimed at the establishment of a republic on English soil.[18]

In the Elizabethan and Jacobean periods, most Englishmen took it for granted that their king governed by divine right.[19] Most understood their rights and responsibilities in terms of prescription under the common law as a matter of tradition made rational by a process of trial and error and sanctioned by time out of mind.[20] Some were inclined to think all government contractual, to treat the king's coronation oath as confirmation of this fact, and even to envisage their monarchy as some sort of mixed regime,[21] but republicans they were not. When Thomas Hobbes (*Leviathan* II.xxi.8–9; *Behemoth* 158) blamed the English civil war on the fact that so many of his countrymen were well read in the classics, he greatly exaggerated the importance of the phenomenon.[22]

[16] See Markku Peltonen, *Classical Humanism and Republicanism in English Political Thought, 1570–1640* (Cambridge, UK: Cambridge University Press, 1995).

[17] Cf. Mario Praz, "Machiavelli and the Elizabethans," *Proceedings of the British Academy* 14 (1928): 49–97, and Christopher Morris, "Machiavelli's Reputation in Tudor England," *Il Pensiero Politico* 2 (1969): 416–33, with Sydney Anglo, "The Reception of Machiavelli in Tudor England: A Reassessment," *Il Politico* 31 (1966): 127–38, and see Peltonen, *Classical Humanism and Republicanism in English Political Thought*, 73–102, 190–270, 302–4, 310–12. For particular examples, see Sydney Anglo, "A Machiavellian Solution to the Irish Problem: Richard Beacon's *Solon His Follie* (1594)," in *England and the Continental Renaissance: Essays in Honour of J. B. Trapp*, ed. Edward Chaney and Peter Mack (Woodbridge, UK: Boydell Press, 1990), 153–64, and Markku Peltonen, "Classical Republicanism in England: The Case of Richard Beacon's *Solon His Follie*," HPT 15:4 (Winter 1994): 469–503; Anne Jacobson Shutte, "An Early Stuart Critique of Machiavelli as Historiographer: Thomas Jackson and the Discorsi," *Albion* 15 (1983): 1–18; Michael Mendle, "A Machiavellian in the Long Parliament before the Civil War," *Parliamentary History* 8 (1989): 116–24.

[18] An exception to the rule was Thomas Starkey, who privately urged just such a program on Henry VIII in the 1530s – but to no avail: See Thomas F. Mayer, *Thomas Starkey and the Commonweal: Humanist Politics and Religion in the Reign of Henry VIII* (Cambridge, UK: Cambridge University Press, 1989).

[19] See J. P. Sommerville, *Royalists and Patriots: Politics and Ideology in England, 1603–1640* (London: Longman, 1999), 9–54.

[20] Cf. J. G. A. Pocock, *The Ancient Constitution and the Feudal Law: A Study of English Historical Thought in the Seventeenth Century: A Reissue with a Retrospect* (Cambridge, UK: Cambridge University Press, 1987), with Glenn Burgess, *The Politics of the Ancient Constitution: An Introduction to English Political Thought, 1603–1642* (University Park, PA: Pennsylvania State University Press, 1993), and see Sommerville, *Royalists and Patriots*, 81–104.

[21] See Sommerville, *Royalists and Patriots*, 55–80; Peltonen, *Classical Humanism and Republicanism in English Political Thought*, 47–51, 91–8, 106–8, 112–13, 119–89, 229–70, 304, 309.

[22] Cf. David Norbrook, *Writing the English Republic: Poetry, Rhetoric and Politics, 1627–1660* (Cambridge, UK: Cambridge University Press, 1999), with Blair Worden, "Republicanism,

Sir Philip Sidney came closer to the truth in his *Arcadia* when he treated the late Elizabethan enthusiasm for republicanism on the model of Athens, Sparta, and Rome as an academic concern, "a matter more in imagination than practice" appealing solely to "the discoursing sort of men."[23]

It is no surprise, then, that, in England as well as on the continent, Machiavelli was at first valued almost solely for the advice that he gave to princes, their ministers, and aspirants to princely rule on matters of state.[24] In fact, given the unfavorable character of the circumstances in which his books became available to the larger world, the only real ground for astonishment is that the Florentine ever came to be widely appreciated for his republicanism at all. In England, it took a revolution to force a reassessment of the *Discourses on Livy*, and even then there were serious obstacles standing in the way.

After all, the trial and execution of Charles I were not a part of anyone's plan. When the Long Parliament was elected late in October 1640, its members were chosen for the purpose of achieving a redress of grievances. Apart, perhaps, from Henry Marten,[25] no one at the time was intent on overthrowing England's ancient constitution: Their goal was to save it. No one else even imagined that their attempt at a redress of grievances would eventuate in civil war, the beheading of a king, the abolition of the monarchy and House of Lords, and the establishment of a republic on English soil. Had anyone even suggested the possibility, nearly all of those then elected would have recoiled in horror.[26]

Regicide and Republic: The English Experience," in *Republicanism and Constitutionalism in Early Modern Europe*, 307–27.

[23] Sir Philip Sidney, *The Countess of Pembroke's Arcadia (The Old Arcadia)*, ed. Jean Robertson (Oxford, UK: Clarendon Press, 1973), 320–1. See Blair Worden, *The Sound of Virtue: Philip Sidney's Arcadia and Elizabethan Politics* (New Haven, CT: Yale University Press, 1997), esp. 209–94, and consider Worden, "Classical Republicanism and the Puritan Revolution," in *History and Imagination: Essays in Honour of H. R. Trevor-Roper*, ed. Hugh Lloyd-Jones, Valerie Pearl, and Blair Worden (London: Duckworth, 1981), 182–200.

[24] See Felix Raab, *The English Face of Machiavelli: A Changing Interpretation, 1500–1700* (London: Routledge and Kegan Paul, 1964), 30–117; Victoria Kahn, *Machiavellian Rhetoric: From the Counter-Reformation to Milton* (Princeton, NJ: Princeton University Press, 1994), 85–148; Peltonen, *Classical Humanism and Republicanism in English Political Thought*, 73–102, 190–270.

[25] See Edward Hyde, earl of Clarendon, *The Life of Edward Earl of Clarendon* (Oxford, UK: Oxford University Press, 1857), 1.91. In this connection, see also Edward Hyde, earl of Clarendon, *The History of the Rebellion and Civil Wars in England*, ed. W. Dunn Macray (Oxford, UK: Clarendon Press, 1888), 5.280. On Marten more generally, see C. M. Williams, "The Anatomy of a Radical Gentleman: Henry Marten," in *Puritans and Revolutionaries: Essays in Seventeenth-Century History Presented to Christopher Hill*, ed. Donald Pennington and Keith Thomas (Oxford, UK: Clarendon Press, 1978), 118–38; Sarah Barber, *A Revolutionary Rogue: Henry Marten and the English Republic* (Phoenix Mill: Sutton Publishing, 2000).

[26] See Margaret Atwood Judson, *The Crisis of the Constitution: An Essay in Constitutional and Political Thought in England, 1603–1645* (New Brunswick, NJ: Rutgers University Press, 1949). Note also Hugh R. Trevor-Roper, "Oliver Cromwell and his Parliaments," *The Seventeenth Century: Religion Reformation, and Social Change* (New York: Harper & Row, 1968), 345–91 (esp. 345–55).

Of course, when the civil war began in earnest, as it did late in 1642, a few bold speculators did think their way through the logic then unfolding.[27] In Parliament, from that time on, Marten, Sir Peter Wentworth, and the handful of radicals under their sway exploited the conflict mercilessly, seizing on every opportunity to attack royal authority, to intensify the antagonisms occasioned by bloodshed, and to subvert the awe and reverence then still almost universally accorded the king.[28] Their efforts, however, were largely wasted, for all but a tiny minority of their colleagues did, in fact, recoil in horror in December 1648 and January 1649, when the erstwhile adherents of the parliamentary cause found themselves forced to choose between the unpalatable alternatives of regicide and a compromise with Charles that was tantamount to an abandonment of nearly everything for which they had fought.[29] There can be little doubt as to the revulsion provoked by this unprecedented, revolutionary act.[30] Within the first year of its appearance in the immediate aftermath of Charles's beheading, the royalist tract *Eikon Basilikē: The Portraiture of His Sacred Majesty in His Solitude and Sufferings* went through thirty-five editions in London and twenty-five more in Ireland and elsewhere.[31] By the dark deed that gave it birth, the English republic was arguably doomed from the start.

The recognition of their isolation to a very considerable degree paralyzed the Rump Parliament that governed England after Colonel Thomas Pride's purge of the Long Parliament on 6 December 1648.[32] It was not until 19 May 1649, more than four months after the execution of the king, that this assembly even managed formally to declare England "a Commonwealth and Free State . . . henceforth to be governed . . . by the supreme authority of this nation, the representatives of the people in Parliament, . . . and that without any king or House of Lords."[33] The knowledge, however, that the regicide republicans were

---

[27] See David Wootton, "From Rebellion to Revolution: The Crisis of the Winter of 1642/43 and the Origins of Civil War Radicalism," *English Historical Review* 105:416 (July 1990): 654–69.

[28] Begin with C. M. Williams, "Extremist Tactics in the Long Parliament, 1642–1643," *Historical Studies* 15 (1971): 136–50; then see Sarah Barber, *Regicide and Republicanism: Politics and Ethics in the English Revolution* (Edinburgh, UK: Edinburgh University Press, 1998), 1–146, and *A Revolutionary Rogue*, 1–24.

[29] See David Underdown, *Pride's Purge: Politics in the Puritan Revolution* (Oxford, UK: Clarendon Press, 1971), 7–256; Barber, *Regicide and Republicanism*, 121–46.

[30] See Underdown, *Pride's Purge*, 260–1, 297–335.

[31] See Merritt Y. Hughes, "Introduction," in *Complete Prose Works of John Milton*, ed. Don M. Wolfe (New Haven, CT: Yale University Press, 1953–82), 3:150. See, as well, Hugh Trevor-Roper, "'Eikon Basilikē:' The Problem of the King's Book," in *Historical Essays* (New York: Harper & Row, 1957), 211–20; Kevin Sharpe, "The King's Writ: Royal Authors and Royal Authority in Early Modern England," in *Culture and Politics in Early Stuart England*, ed. Kevin Sharpe and Peter Lake (Stanford, CA: Stanford University Press, 1993), 117–38.

[32] See Underdown, *Pride's Purge*, 258–96; Blair Worden, *The Rump Parliament, 1648–1653* (Cambridge, UK: Cambridge University Press, 1974); Barber, *Regicide and Republicanism*, 147–201. See also Worden, "Republicanism, Regicide and Republic," 316–27.

[33] "An Act Declaring England to be a Commonwealth," 19 May 1649, in *The Constitutional Documents of the Puritan Revolution, 1625–1660*, 3rd edition, ed. Samuel Rawson Gardiner (Oxford, UK: Clarendon Press, 1906), 388.

a small and insular minority did not deter the handful of men in Parliament who had already demonstrated, in the crisis of this time, the extraordinary resolution requisite if they were to follow through on the logic of what they had almost all so innocently and unheedingly begun more than eight years before. If anything, their sense of isolation made these men all the more resolute – all the more insistent on defending the propriety of all that they had done, all the more intent on asserting the dignity and legitimacy of the new regime, and all the more eager to prove it a success in its endeavors both at home and abroad.[34]

It was among this select group and the small proportion of those within the populace as a whole who admired their courage and determination that we find those who set out to rethink English politics from the ground up in light of the new species of republicanism championed by Niccolò Machiavelli. These were, however, exceedingly few in number, for most of their fellow republicans were Puritans, and for understandable reasons, devout Christians tended to balk at the prospect of embracing a thinker said to have given to the devil his English moniker "Old Nick."[35] In no way, however, as we shall soon see, did such concerns act as a restraint upon Marchamont Nedham or James Harrington.

[34] Cf. Barber, *Regicide and Republicanism*, 1–146, with 147–201, and see Sean Kelsey, *Inventing a Republic: The Political Culture of the English Commonwealth, 1649–1653* (Stanford, CA: Stanford University Press, 1997); Norbrook, *Writing the English Republic*, 192–242.

[35] See Samuel Butler, *Hudibras*, ed. John Wilders (Oxford, UK: Clarendon Press, 1967), 3.1.1313–16.

I

Machiavelli in the English Revolution

Paul A. Rahe

Marchamont Nedham was a journalist, one of the very first and most distinguished members of a breed in his day entirely new to the world. He was born in August 1620 at Burford in Gloucestershire into a genteel family of modest means. He studied at All Souls College and took his B.A. from the University of Oxford in 1637. That year or the next, he accepted a position as an usher at Merchant Taylor's School in London, and in 1640 he successfully sought better remunerated employment as an underclerk at Gray's Inn. Three years thereafter, as internecine strife tore England apart and effective censorship fell into abeyance, Nedham discovered his true métier. He was, then, barely twenty-three years of age.[1]

Nedham was an entertainer of sorts and a time-server – "a jack of all sides," as one contemporary critic put it, "transcendently gifted in opprobrious and treasonable Droll."[2] In the course of a long and checkered career – stretching from early in the English civil war in 1643 to a time shortly before his death in

---

[1] For the details, see Joseph Frank, *Cromwell's Press Agent: A Critical Biography of Marchamont Nedham, 1620–1678* (Lanham, MD: University Press of America, 1980). For a more penetrating analysis, see Blair Worden, "'Wit in a Roundhead': The Dilemma of Marchamont Nedham," in *Political Culture and Cultural Politics in Early Modern England: Essays Presented to David Underdown*, ed. Susan D. Amussen and Mark A. Kishlansky (Manchester, UK: Manchester University Press, 1995), 301–37; "Milton and Marchamont Nedham," in *Milton and Republicanism*, ed. David Armitage, Armand Himy, and Quentin Skinner (Cambridge, UK: Cambridge University Press, 1995), 156–80, along with Joad Raymond "The Cracking of the Republican Spokes," *Prose Studies* 19 (1996): 255–74, and "'A Mercury with a Winged Conscience': Marchamont Nedham, Monopoly and Censorship," *Media History* 4:1 (1998): 7–18.

[2] See James Heath, *A Brief Chronicle of the Late Intestine War: The Second Impression Greatly Enlarged*: (London: [s.n.]., 1663), 492.

Much of the material in this chapter is adapted from Paul A. Rahe, "An Inky Wretch: The Outrageous Genius of Marchamont Nedham," *National Interest* 70 (Winter 2002–3): 55–64, and *Republics Ancient and Modern: Classical Republicanism and the American Revolution* (Chapel Hill, NC: University of North Carolina Press, 1992), 409–26, and reprinted with permission. All translations are my own.

1678, when the Exclusion Crisis was just getting under way – he displayed a political and moral flexibility and a lust for lucre exceeded only by his talent. He began as a fierce defender of the parliamentary cause, switched in 1647 to the side of the king, and then, some nine months after his royal patron's demise, while on the lam from Newgate Jail, he wrote to offer his services to the presiding officer of the regicide court.[3]

Nedham's was not a costive muse. In the course of his career, he published more than thirty-four pamphlets and books.[4] In addition, he composed most of the copy that appeared in the Roundhead newsbook *Mercurius Britanicus*, then edited the Cavalier newsbook *Mercurius Pragmaticus*; and then he edited the newsbook *Mercurius Politicus* – in turn for the Rump, for the Nominated Parliament, for the Protectorate, and for the Rump twice again, celebrating the coups d'état that overthrew each and, in the end, even hailing the return of the king. On the eve of the Restoration, after publishing a brief but bitter satire warning the Roundheads of vengeance to come,[5] he prudently withdrew into exile. But soon he managed to purchase for himself a personal pardon; and, while many of his erstwhile associates suffered execution, imprisonment, or exile, he ended his days writing pamphlets for Charles II, the earl of Danby, and their Tory allies against the Exclusion Whigs and their leader, the first earl of Shaftesbury, whom Nedham had the effrontery to denounce not just as "*a man of . . . dapper Conscience, and dexterity, that can dance through a Hoop; or that can be a Tambler through Parties, or a small Teazer of Religions, and Tonzer of Factions,*" but also as "*a Pettifogger of Politicks*" ever ready "*to shift Principles like Shirts*; and *quit an unlucky Side in a fright at the noise of a New Prevailing Party,*" and even as "*a Will-with-a-Wisp, that uses to lead Men out of the way; then leaves them at last in a Ditch and Darkness, and nimbly retreats for Self-security.*"[6]

Nedham knew whereof he wrote. He, too, was a man of dapper conscience and dexterity; he had a well-earned reputation for shifting principles like shirts; and he was certainly a "Will-with-a-Wisp," possessed of what one contemporary described as "a dextrous faculty of creeping into the breech of every Rising Power."[7] What he lacked in integrity, this inky wretch made up for in audacity.

---

3 See Letters from Marchamont Nedham to Henry Oxinden, 8 and 19 November 1649, in *The Oxinden and Peyton Letters, 1642–1670*, ed. Dorothy Gardiner (London: Sheldon Press, 1937), 160–1; and for the terms of the deal, see Anthony à Wood, *Athenæ Oxonienses* (London: F. C. & J. Rivington, 1813–20), 3:1180–90 (at 1181).

4 See Frank, *Cromwell's Press Agent*, 196–9, whose list is undoubtedly incomplete.

5 See [Marchamont Nedham], *Newes from Brussels, in a Letter from a Neer Attendant on His Maiesties Person. To a Person of Honour Here, Which Casually Became Thus Publique* (London: Livewell Chapman, 1660).

6 See [Marchamont Nedham], *A Pacquet of Advices and Animadversions, Sent from London to the Men of Shaftesbury* (London: [s.n.], 1676), 2, 30, which was written in response to Shaftesbury's *Letter from a Person of Quality to His Friend in the Country* (1675), reprinted in WoJL 10:200–46. Nedham's reply is thought to have been exceedingly effective: See K. H. D. Haley, *The First Earl of Shaftesbury* (Oxford, UK: Clarendon Press, 1968), 414–15.

7 See *Fanatique Queries Propos'd to the Present Assertors of the Good Old Cause* (London: Printed for Praise-God-Barebones, the Rumps Leatherfeller, 1660), 4.

His own virtuosity as a flack invited on the part of his critics flights of fancy not unlike his own in Shaftesbury's case. On the eve of the Restoration, an opponent described him as "a Mercury with a winged conscience, the Skip-Jack of all fortunes, that like a Shittle-cock drive him which way you will, falls still with the cork end forwards."[8] In a satirical pamphlet published early in 1660, the editor of *Mercurius Politicus* is represented as taking leave of his regicide associates with the following words: "for now [that] the *scæne's* alter'd, *I* must go change my habit; if ever the times turn, you shall find me as faithful as *I* was before."[9] Another critic predicted at that time that Nedham would soon be writing for the Cavaliers. "He is like a Catt," he wrote, "that (throw him which way you will) still light[s] on his feet."[10]

In fact, as the Royalist penman Roger L'Estrange readily conceded, Marchamont Nedham was "the *Golia[t]h* of the *Philistines*," and his "pen was in comparison of others like a Weavers beam." It is, L'Estrange added, "incredible what influence" his weekly newsbooks "had upon numbers of inconsidering persons." Nedham had "with so much malice calumniated his Sovereign, so scurrilously abused the Nobility, so impudently blasphemed the Church, and so industriously poysoned the people with dangerous principles," that, had "the Devil himself (the Father of Lies)" held this particular journalist's "office, he could not have exceeded him."[11]

It seems only fitting, then, that this same diabolical colossus it was who first deployed in the public prints Niccolò Machiavelli's reflections on the rise and fall of republics, doing so in a systematic effort to sort out the practical exigencies of England's republican experiment. Nedham had, in fact, never been averse to the Florentine, and from quite early on he had brazenly championed *raison d'état* as preached by the Duc de Rohan, arguing that it is material interest, not justice, honor, or religion, that makes the world go round.[12] In *The Case of the Kingdom Stated, According to the Proper Interest of the Severall Parties Ingaged*, the first tract that Nedham wrote in any way sympathetic to the Royalist cause, he first cited this renowned Huguenot grandee, then analyzed in coldblooded terms the interests of England's various contending parties, and ultimately advised patience on the part of the king, arguing that

---

[8] [Samuel Butler], *The Character of the Rump* (London: [s.n.], 1660), 3.

[9] See *The Private Debates, Conferences and Resolutions, of the Late Rump* (London: [s.n.], 1660), 30.

[10] *A Word for All: Or, the Rumps Funeral Sermon: Held Forth by Mr. Feak to a Conventicle of Fanatiques at Bedlam upon the Last Dissolution of the Half Quarter Parliament* (London: [s.n.], 1660). Raymond, "The Cracking of the Republican Spokes," 257–8, gives reason for assigning this work to Samuel Butler.

[11] See [Roger L'Estrange], *A Rope for Pol, or, a Hue and Cry after Marchemont Nedham* (London: [s.n.], 1660), Advertisement to the Reader.

[12] In this connection, see Felix Raab, *The English Face of Machiavelli: A Changing Interpretation, 1500–1700* (London: Routledge and Kegan Paul, 1964), 159–63, 228–30; J. A. W. Gunn, *Politics and the Public Interest in the Seventeenth Century* (London: Routledge and Kegan Paul, 1969), 33–5, 43–4, 52. Note Worden, "'Wit in a Roundhead,'" 317–19. For Nedham's most elaborate statement along these lines, see Marchamont Nedham, *Interest Will Not Lie* (London: Tho. Newcomb, 1659).

Charles could profit from the quarrel then emerging between the Presbyterians and Independents if he tarried until the moment when it would be "his only Interest . . . , to close with that Party which gives most hope of Indulgence to his Prerogative, and greatest probability of favour to his Friends." The policy of divide and rule is, he explained, "what *Machiavell* sets downe as a sure *Principle* toward the purchase of *Empire*."[13]

Of course, when the rhetorical situation required it, Nedham could pass himself off as a believing Christian and frequently did so, and he was perfectly capable of speaking in the familiar accents of moral rectitude, denouncing one side or the other for an addiction to hypocrisy, blasphemy, and vice. But nearly as often, especially when the opportunity for candor presented itself, he displayed an outright contempt for high-mindedness of virtually every kind. "Interest," he insisted, "is the true *Zenith* of every State and Person, according to which they may certainly be understood, though cloathed never so much with the most specious disguise of Religion, Justice and Necessity."[14]

Nedham's skepticism in matters religious and moral, his propensity for scoffing, and his fascination with Machiavelli may, in fact, be the key to understanding his astonishing trajectory. He was venal and mercenary but not lacking in courage. In that unstable age, he accommodated every twist and turn in the course of events without betraying the slightest sign of any discomfort or shame, and he served each and every one of his masters with vigor and panache, displaying a gift for invective and a literary virtuosity that made him one of the minor wonders of the age.[15]

The Excellencie of a Free State

Some months after Marchamont Nedham offered his services to the English republic, he made good on his promise to write on its behalf by publishing a tract, entitled *The Case of the Commonwealth Stated*, arguing on quasi-Hobbesian grounds that it was both proper and prudent that the various groups that had opposed the execution of the king and the institution of the republic now lend their support to what had become an established and settled regime. For almost a year, starting in September 1650, Nedham reprinted in *Mercurius*

---

[13] See [Marchamont Nedham], *The Case of the Kingdom Stated* (London: n.p., 1647), 1–6.

[14] See A Friend to This Commonwealth [Marchamont Nedham], *The Case Stated between England and the United Provinces, in this Present Juncture* (London: Thomas Newcomb, 1652), 23.

[15] Much can be learned from Blair Worden's various attempts to come to grips with the significance of what Nedham did and said; see the works cited in footnote 1, and "Marchamont Nedham and the Beginnings of English Republicanism, 1649–1656," in *Republicanism, Liberty, and Commercial Society, 1649–1776*, ed. David Wootton (Stanford, CA: Stanford University Press, 1994), 45–81. I have profited also from Perez Zagorin, *A History of Political Thought in the English Revolution* (London: Routledge and Paul, 1954), 121–7; Philip A. Knachel, "Introduction," in *The Case of the Commonwealth of England, Stated* (1650), ed. Philip A. Knachel (Charlottesville, VA: University Press of Virginia, 1969), ix–xlii; Vickie B. Sullivan, *Machiavelli, Hobbes, and the Formation of a Liberal Republicanism in England* (New York: Cambridge University Press, 2004), 113–43.

Politicus excerpts from this tract.[16] Then, soon after the New Model Army's
decisive victory at the battle of Worcester on 3 September 1651 put paid to
Royalist hopes, brought an end to the emergency, and opened up the possibility
that there would soon be a general constitutional settlement, Nedham reversed
this procedure, gradually elaborating in newsbook editorials published in the
period stretching from 9 October 1651 to 12 August 1652 much of the argument
that would make up *The Excellencie of a Free State*, which he published as a
book in June 1656.[17]

In this later work, Nedham explicitly embraces modern populism on the
precise terms in which it was espoused by Machiavelli. After remarking that
"if liberty is the most precious jewel under the sun, then when it is once in
possession, it requires more than an ordinary art and industry to preserve it"
(*EFS* xiv), he goes on to identify the crucial element in the requisite art by reiter-
ating the Florentine's controversial claim (*D* 1.5) that liberty can be preserved
only "by placing the guardianship in the hands of the people" (*EFS* xiv, 2,
18–19).

In this connection, to be sure, Nedham is prepared to quote Cicero on man's
capacity to rule, and he argues "that by the light of nature people are taught to be
their own carvers and contrivers, in the framing of that government under which
they mean to live." In the same context, he asserts that the people are "the only
proper judges of the convenience or inconvenience of a government when it is
erected, and of the behaviour of governors after they are chosen." He celebrates
the fact "that in the people's form, men have liberty to make use of that reason
and understanding God hath given them, in chusing of governors, and providing for their safety in government" (*EFS* 33–5). He even remarks, in a manner
suggestive of Aristotle's discussion of man's nature as a political animal (*Pol.*
1252b27–1253a39, 1278b15–30, 1280a25–1281a10, 1283b42–1284a3), that,
where the people are denied this prerogative, the course followed is "destructive to the reason, common interest, and majesty of that noble creature, called
man," serving "no other end, but to transform men into beasts" (*EFS* 35). This
brief disquisition in praise of man's rational capacities might be taken as an
indication that, like his friend John Milton, Nedham embraced the theory of
differential moral and political rationality that underpinned the republicanism
of ancient Greece and Rome,[18] but it is, in fact, no more than a passing rhetorical flourish, conferring a certain specious dignity on a populist argument that
is otherwise Machiavellian through and through. Like his Florentine mentor,
Nedham rejected the classical notion that man is a political animal endowed
with a rational capacity enabling him, if given the proper civic education and
in no way otherwise impaired, to deliberate in common with others of a similar
character concerning the advantageous, the just, and the good; and, like him

[16] For a list of the passages reprinted, see Frank, *Cromwell's Press Agent*, 182–5.
[17] See ibid., 93–101. For a list of the editorials that Nedham recycled, see ibid., 182–5.
[18] See Paul A. Rahe, "The Classical Republicanism of John Milton," *HPT* 25:2 (Summer 2004):
243–75.

as well, he thought it essential for the success of his modern republican project that it be disguised as a return to classical norms.[19]

Nowhere, to be sure, does Marchamont Nedham in his *Excellencie of a Free State* quote verbatim Machiavelli's claim (*D* 1.3.1) that it is incumbent on anyone intent on setting up a republic and ordaining its laws to presuppose that "all men are wicked and that they will make use of the malignity of their spirit whenever they are free and have occasion to do so." But he does ground his defense of the guardianship of the people on the Machiavellian assertion (*D* 1.4–5, 16.5) that ordinary folk possess a defect in appetite, being "bounded within a more lowly pitch of desire and imagination" than the grandees (*EFS* 21–2), and he defends the people against the charge of "inconstancy" in good Machiavellian fashion (*D* 1.58) by insisting that they are far less inconstant than "standing powers," who generally run "into all the extremes of inconstancy, upon every new project, petty humour, and occasion that" seems "favourable for effecting of their by-designs." Nedham does not, however, attribute the constancy of the people to their moral superiority. Here, too, he follows the Florentine (*D* 1.2.3, 44, 54, 57–8). If "in the framing of laws," he writes, the "aim" of the people "was ever at the general good," it is simply and solely because the general good is, in fact, indistinguishable from "their own interest." Such a coincidence of their own self–interest and the good of the whole cannot be attributed to the grandees (*EFS* 78–80).

In consequence, "extreme jealousy" is Nedham's watchword. "The interest of freedom is," he insists, "a virgin that every one seeks to deflour; and like a virgin, it must be kept from any other form, or else (so great is the lust of mankind after dominion) there follows a rape upon the first opportunity." Frequent popular elections and a "succession of powers and persons" are, in fact, "the only remedy against self-seeking, with all the powerful temptations and charms of self-interest" (*EFS* xii–xiii, 8–9, 18–19, 81).

In Nedham's judgment, it was Solon of Athens and not one of Machiavelli's Romans who left "the only pattern of a free-state fit for all the world to follow," for the Athenian lawgiver placed "the power of legislation, or law-making, in a successive course of people's assemblies," and he avoided thereby the Roman dilemma: "kingly tyranny on the one side, and senatical incroachments on the other" (*EFS* xvi–xvii). Every "standing senate" will be, Nedham warns with Roman history in mind, "more studious of their own, than the common good." Indeed, no matter how "good a patriot" a particular individual may be, "yet if his power be prolonged, he will find it hard to keep self from creeping in upon him, and prompting him to some extravagancies for his own private benefit." The only safe reliance is, then, self-interest, for moral virtue is generally a sham and always a weak reed. If a man "be shortly to return to a condition common

---

[19] For Machiavelli's repudiation of the presumptions concerning human rationality that under-pinned classical practice, see Paul A. Rahe, "Situating Machiavelli," in *Renaissance Civic Humanism: Reappraisals and Reflections*, ed. James Hankins (Cambridge, UK: Cambridge University Press, 2000), 270–308, and the prologue to this book.

with the rest of his brethren, self-interest binds him to do nothing but what is just and equal; he himself being to reap the good or evil of what is done, as well as the meanest of the people" (*EFS* 9, 12).

The Spirit of Popular Distrust

Thus, when Nedham sets out to catalogue "the errors of government" and to list the "rules of policy," the spirit of political distrust is his primary theme. If he is willing to condemn popular ingratitude to the benefactors of the commonwealth, he nonetheless takes this as an occasion to remind his readers that "it concerns them, for the public peace and security, not to impose a trust in the hands of any person or persons, further than as they may take it back again at pleasure." Honors, he warns in this context, "change 'men's manners;' accessions, and continuations of power and greatness, expose the mind to temptations: they are sails too big for any bulk of mortality to steer an even course by." A great many "free-states and commonwealths" have,

by trusting their own servants too far,... been forced, in the end, to receive them for their masters. Nor is it to be wondered at by any, considering that immoderate power soon lets in high and ambitious thoughts; and where they are once admitted, no design [is] so absurd, or contrary to a man's principles, but he rusheth into it, without the least remorse or consideration: for the spirit of ambition is a spirit of giddiness; it foxes men that receive it, and makes them more drunk than the spirit of wine.

"Without question," Nedham concludes, "it highly concerns a people that have redeemed and rescued their liberties out of the hands of tyranny, and are declared a free-state, so to regulate their affairs, that all temptations, and opportunities of ambition, may be removed out of the way: or else there follows a necessity of tumult and civil dissension, the common consequence whereof hath ever been a ruin of the public freedom" (*EFS* 134–5).

As this suggests, Nedham envisages elections as a salutary alternative to tumults. They are, he intimates, a far better remedy than the one devised by Machiavelli (*D* 1.1–6), for they accomplish Machiavelli's end without occasioning genuine disorder. They are, in fact, the perfect substitute for a risky venture that, in Nedham's opinion, should always be a last resort, reserved for those rare occasions when no other expedient will serve. By reining in the magistrates and putting them to the test, by suspending for a brief moment all governance and reminding the rulers and the ruled of the former's subjection to and dependence on the latter, by ritually re-enacting government's emergence from the consent of the governed, such elections force at frequent and regular intervals a chastening return to the republic's *principii* – its origins in the primordial fear that dispels every form of inequality and inspires in men of all humors a profound longing for security and well-being (cf. *EFS* 64–70, 135 with NM, *D* 3.1, 22.3).

To check temptation and restrain ambition, Nedham advocated a separation of powers as well. Nedham was a close student of Machiavellian statecraft.

He acknowledged the Tacitean distinction that the Florentine's admirers drew between *"acta imperii*, and *arcana imperii*: that is, acts of state, and secrets of state," and he asserted that the former properly belonged to "the legislative power" while reserving the latter for "the executive part of government" since the *arcana imperii* are "of a nature remote from ordinary apprehensions, and such as necessarily require prudence, time, and experience, to fit men for management" (*EFS* 60–1).[20] He reluctantly conceded that "much in reason may be said, and must be granted, for the continuation of such trusts in the same hands, as relate to matter of counsel, or administration of justice, more or less, according to their good or ill-behaviour," and he was therefore willing to allow "a prudential continuation of these . . . upon discretion," since if those exercising the executive power "do amiss, they are easily accountable to the people's assemblies." But he was not willing to countenance a similar "continuation" for the members of Parliament (*EFS* 61–4), and he insisted that the legislative and executive functions and those exercising them remain distinct.

Where "the legislative and executive powers of a state" are allowed "to rest in one and the same hands and persons," Nedham warned, "unlimited arbitrary power" is always the result. It follows, then, that in keeping "these two powers distinct, following in distinct channels, so that they may never meet in one, save upon some short extraordinary occasion, consists the safety of a state." The "reason" is, Nedham insists, perfectly "evident." Where "the lawmakers (who ever have the supreme power) should be also the constant administrators and dispensers of law and justice, then (by consequence) the people would be left without remedy, in case of injustice, since no appeal can lie under heaven against such as have the supremacy." A combination of these powers is "inconsistent with the very intent and natural import of true policy: which ever supposeth that men in power may be unrighteous." One must always, he adds, presume "the worst" (*EFS* 147–54 [esp. 147–9]).

For similar reasons, Nedham observes, one must constitute "authority" in such a manner "that it shall be rather a burthen than benefit to those that undertake it; and be qualified with such slender advantages of profit or pleasure, that men shall reap little by the enjoyment." Only in this fashion can one guarantee that "none but honest, generous, and public spirits" will "desire to be in authority, and that only for the common good" (*EFS* 3). To achieve this end, Nedham follows Machiavelli (*D* 1.7–8) in advocating public accusations. "All powers," he says, must be made "accountable for misdemeanors in government." When "he that ere-while was a governor" is "reduced to the condition of a subject" and "lies open to the force of the laws," he "may with ease be brought to punishment for his offence." Others, then, who "succeed will become the less daring to offend, or to abuse their trust in authority, to an oppression of the

---

[20] Cf. Tac. *Ann.* 2.36.2 (along with 1.6.6, 2.59.4) and *Hist.* 1.4.2. In this connection, note Malcolm Smuts, "Court-Centred Politics and the Uses of Roman Historians, c. 1590–1630," in *Culture and Politics in Early Stuart England*, ed. Kevin Sharpe and Peter Lake (Stanford, CA: Stanford University Press, 1993), 21–43 (esp. 28–9).

people." In the absence of such an institution, Nedham insists, there will be "no security of life and estate, liberty and property." A "liberty of accusation by the people, before their supreme assemblies," he adds, "cuts the very throat of all tyranny; and doth not only root it up when at full growth, but crusheth the cockatrice in the egg, destroys it in the feed, in the principle, and in the very possibilities of its being for ever after" (*EFS* 42, 72–6).

The capstone of this edifice was to be the militia. Machiavelli is sometimes depicted as a proponent of arms-bearing citizenship.[21] In fact, he did praise the Romans for admitting those whom they conquered into *societas* and even for extending to some of them *civitas sine suffragio* and *civitas optimo iure*, and this he did with an eye to their deployment of these *socii* and newly made citizens on the field of the sword.[22] But the Florentine never contended that arms-bearing should depend on citizenship or vice versa. In *The Prince* and in his *Discourses on Livy*, he criticized mercenary forces as unreliable; and, in both, he insisted that a prince and a republic alike need their own arms.[23] To this end, in his *Art of War*, he championed the creation of a popular militia – but this was to be drawn not only or even primarily from the citizens of Florence but also from the subject population inhabiting the *contado* lying outside that city's walls (*AW* 1.128–96). "One's own arms," as he explained in *The Prince*, "are those which are composed either of subjects (*sudditi*) or of citizens or of creatures that are your own (*creati tuoi*)" (*p* 13).

Machiavelli's concern throughout was simply that one's military manpower be plentiful and that one's arms be really and truly at one's beck and call. With regard to the bearing of arms, everything that he recommended, whether to a prince or a republic, was instrumental to ensuring the fidelity of a sufficiently large, well-trained armed force. The first modern political theorist to insist, as the ancients had done, that in a republic the citizens must be soldiers and all the soldiers citizens so that citizenship and the bearing of arms should be inextricably linked was Marchamont Nedham, and it is telling that he cites not Machiavelli but Aristotle (*Pol.* 1297b1–27) to bolster his case (*EFS* 114–19).[24]

Political participation as such was not Nedham's primary concern. Like Machiavelli, he was simply persuaded that, to be viable, a polity must rely on its own arms. To this observation, however, he added a corollary never explicitly mentioned by the Florentine sage: that "the sword, and sovereignty, ever walk hand in hand." If "the people be continually trained up in the exercise of arms," he contended, and if "the militia [be] lodged only in the people's

---

[21] The *locus classicus* is J. G. A. Pocock, *The Machiavellian Moment: Florentine Political Thought and the Atlantic Republican Tradition* (Princeton, NJ: Princeton University Press, 1975), 194–218 (esp. 199–203, 208–14), 384–6. See also Pocock, "Introduction," in *PWoJH* 18–19, 43–4.

[22] Consider NM, *D* 2.3–4, 13.2, 23, in light of *D* 3.49.4. In this connection, see also *D* 2.21. Machiavelli speaks of the Roman practice of founding colonies on the territory of those conquered with the same concern in mind: Consider *D* 2.6–7 in light of 2.30.3–4.

[23] See NM, *P* 12–13, 20, and *D* 1.21, 2.10, 12.4, 13.2, 20, 24, 30, 3.31.4, which should be read in light of *D* 3.24.

[24] In this connection, see Rahe, *Republics Ancient and Modern*, 28–135.

hands," then "nothing" can "at any time be imposed upon the people, but by their consent; that is, by the consent of themselves; or of such as were by them instrusted." Among the ancient Romans, he explained, "a general exercise of the best part of the people in the use of arms" was regarded as "the only bulwark of their liberty: this was reckoned the surest way to preserve it both at home, and abroad; the majesty of the people being secured thereby, as well against domestic affronts from any of their own citizens, as against the foreign invasions of bad neighbours." It was only when "necessity constrained" the Romans "to erect a continued stipendiary soldiery (abroad in foreign parts) either for the holding, or winning of provinces," that, "luxury increasing with dominion, the strict rule and discipline of freedom was . . . quitted," and stipendiary "forces were kept up at home" as well. It was then that liberty was lost (*EFS* 114–19).

Of course, when Nedham speaks of "the people," he does not have everyone in mind. In his discussion of the militia, when he suggests that the militia be lodged in the people's hands, he indicates that it suffices that it be lodged in the hands of "that part of them, which are most firm to the interest of liberty." Later, when he describes the practice of the ancient Romans in this regard, he observes with impressive accuracy that early on

their arms were never lodged in the hands of any, but such as had an interest in the public; such as were acted by that interest, not drawn only by pay; such as thought themselves well paid, in repelling invaders, that they might with freedom return to their affairs: for, the truth is, so long as Rome acted by the pure principles of a free-state, it used no arms to defend itself, but, such as we call, sufficient men; such, as for the most part were men of estate, masters of families, that took arms (only upon occasion) *pro aris et focis*, for their wives, their children, and their country.

In the time immediately following the expulsion of the Tarquins, Nedham pointedly adds, "the milita was lodged and exercised," as it was in his own day, "in the hands of that party, which was firm to the 'interest of freedom'" (*EFS* 114–16).

Elsewhere Nedham acknowledges as well that, in the aftermath of a civil war, such as the one in England so recently fought, "there ought to be an especial care had to the composure and complexion" of the public assemblies, "where it is ever to be supposed, there will be many discontented humours a-working, and labouring to insinuate themselves into the body of the people, to undermine the settlement and security of the commonwealth, that by gaining an interest and share with the better sort, in the supreme authority, they may attain those corrupt ends of policy, which were lost by power." For this reason, he excludes from political participation those, such as the Royalists, the Presbyterians, the malignants, and the neuters, "who have forfeited their rights by delinquency, neutrality, or apostacy, &c. in relation to the divided state of any nation" (*EFS* 38, 56–60, 172–6).

Nedham is not even willing to go as far as the Levellers. He begins by conceding the democratic principle: that, in "a commonwealth in its settled and composed state, when all men within it are presumed to be its friends, questionless, a right to chuse and to be chosen, is then to be allowed the people, (without distinction) in as great a latitude, as may stand with right reason and convenience, for managing a matter of so high consequence as their supreme assemblies." But he then goes on to emphasize the role left to "human prudence" in discerning the dictates of "right reason and convenience" and in determining thereby "the latitude . . . to be admitted more or less, according to the nature, circumstances, and necessities" of the nation and the times, and he elsewhere specifies that in his own country it would be appropriate to exclude from the ranks of those choosing and chosen "the confused promiscuous body of the people" (*EFS* 38, 56). Moreover, he considers an enforced "equality" of the sort purportedly espoused by the Levellers to be "irrational and odious," and he prefers the establishment of what he calls "an equability of condition among all the members" of the commonwealth "so that no particular man or men shall be permitted to grow over-great in power; nor any rank of men be allowed above the ordinary standard, to assume unto themselves the state and title of nobility" (*EFS* 39).

The End of Government

Although hostile to the claims of a titled nobility, Nedham was no more averse to the spirit of honor, dominion, glory, and renown than was his Florentine mentor. He delighted in the fact that "in this form of government by the people, the door of dignity stands open to all (without exception) that ascend thither by the steps of worth and virtue," and he believed that "the consideration whereof hath this noble effect in free states, that it edges mens spirits with an active emulation, and raiseth them to a lofty pitch of design and action." In this regard, Rome was the exemplar. When it became a free state, the "thoughts and power" of the people

began to exceed the bounds of Italy, and aspire towards that prodigious empire. For while the road of preferment lay plain to every man, no public work was done, nor any conquest made; but every man thought he did and conquered all for himself, as long as he remained valiant and virtuous: it was not alliance, nor friendship, nor faction, nor riches, that could advance men; but knowledge, valour, and virtuous poverty, was preferred above them all.   (*EFS* 14–15)

Honor, dominion, glory, and renown did not, however, constitute Nedham's primary theme; and, in this important particular, he really did differ from the author of the *Discourses on Livy*. Marchamont Nedham seems, in fact, to have been the very first to have recognized and realized the bourgeois potential inherent in Machiavelli's argument.

As Markus Fischer points out in the prologue to this book, the Florentine had placed great emphasis on "the popular desire . . . to be free," but he had also insisted that only "a very small part" of the people "desire to be free in order to command; all the others, who are infinite in number, desire liberty in order to live securely." As he conceded, "the common utility" that ordinary men draw "from a free way of life *(vivere libero)*" is extremely prosaic: "being able to possess one's things freely without any suspicion, not having grounds for doubting the honor of women and of children, not fearing for oneself" (D 1.16.3–5). Nedham followed through on the logic of Machiavelli's modern populism in a fashion that the Florentine had not done by grounding the polity exclusively on the desire of the people for security while subordinating to that desire quite systematically the vain aspirations of the grandees for honor, glory, conquest, and command.

"The end of all government is (or ought to be)," Nedham wrote, "the good and ease of the people, in a secure enjoyment of their rights, without pressure and oppression." This he took to be a sufficient justification for popular government, for "the people" are "most sensible of their own burthens," and "being once put into a capacity and freedom of acting, are the most likely to provide remedies for their own relief." After all, they alone

know where the shoe wrings, what grievances are most heavy, and what future fences they stand in need of, to shelter them from the injurious assaults of those powers that are above them: And therefore it is but reason, they should see that none be interested in the supreme authority, but persons of their own election, and such as must in a short time return again into the same condition with themselves, to reap the same benefit or burthen, by the laws enacted, that befals the rest of the people. Then the issue of such a constitution must needs be this, that no load shall be laid upon any, but what is common to all, and that always by common consent; not to serve the lusts of any, but only to supply the necessities of their country.   (EFS 11)

In drawing out, elaborating, and extending the prosaic, bourgeois element within Machiavelli's spirited republican teaching, Nedham sought to forge a workable compromise between the modern populism championed by the Florentine and the traditional, English parliamentary concern with the safeguarding of rights, the protection of persons and property, and the redress of grievances.

In one other telling regard, Nedham seems to shy away from Machiavelli's argument. He had long championed *raison d'état*, as we have seen, and there is no reason to suppose that the future author of *Interest Will Not Lie* had altered his outlook in this regard. But he apparently calculated that it was one thing to persuade the supporters of the commonwealth to embrace the surface teaching of the *Discourses on Livy* and another to convince them to adopt that of *The Prince*. Not for the first or the last time in his life Nedham opted for obfuscation, insisting that his free state reject "that reason of state which is the statesman's reason, or rather his will and lust, when he admits ambition to be a reason, preferment, power, profit, revenge, and opportunity, to be reason, sufficient to put him upon any design of action that may tend to the present advantage; though contrary to the law of God, or the law of common honesty and nations." In "opposition to this sandy foundation of policy, called 'reason of state,'" he urged in good Puritan fashion "a simple reliance upon God in the vigorous and present actings of all righteousness," and he rejected as "an impiety that ought to be exploded out of all nations, that bear the name of Christians," the "violation of faith, principles, promises, and engagements, upon every turn of time, and advantage."

Of course, immediately after denouncing the time-serving and the chicanery that he had so long and so skillfully practiced himself, Nedham acknowledged the force of the argument, "exprest in Machiavel," that because "the greatest part of the world" is "wicked, unjust, deceitful, full of treachery and circumvention, there is a necessity that those which are downright, and confine themselves to the strict rule of honesty, must ever look to be over-reached by the knavery of others." To be sure, he then treats as "a sad inference, and fit only for the practice of Italy," the Florentine's contention that, "because some men are wicked and perfidious, I must be so too"; and he does insist, as is only just, that "the ancient Heathen would have loathed" Machiavelli's argument. But Nedham then suddenly reverses course by slyly adopting the teaching of "that unworthy book of his, entitled '*The Prince*,'" and he turns this teaching to the advantage of the distrustful modern populism pioneered by the very same author in his *Discourses on Livy*. To this end, Nedham quotes at considerable length from "that unworthy" tract lest his compatriots fail to recognize what he calls "the old court Gospel," and he warns them against neglecting to keep watch on "the great ones of the world," who tend, he says, to be quite attached to the "doctrine" preached in *The Prince*. "If the right of laws be the way of men," Nedham observes, and if "force [be that] of beasts and great ones, then it concerns any nation or people to secure themselves, and keep great men from degenerating into beasts, by holding up of law, liberty, privilege, birth-right, elective power, against the ignoble beastly way of powerful domination." If the people are to be proper guardians for their liberty, he concludes, they must be alert to the machinations of those who "sometimes resemble the lion, and sometimes the fox," and they must "cage the lion, and unkennel the fox, and never leave till they have stript the one, and unraised the other" (cf. *EFS* 141–7, 163–72, with NM, *P* 15–18).

To Machiavelli's republican legacy, Marchamont Nedham made two profound contributions that would be taken up by John Locke and the radical Whigs and passed on to their admirers in England's colonies in the New World. He subordinated Machiavellian ferocity to the traditional English insistence on the individual's right to life, liberty, and property, and he thereby transformed what was in the Florentine first and foremost a matter of class resentment into a spirit of vigilance aimed at restraining those entrusted with governance, as, in subsequent chapters, we shall see.[25] His contemporary James Harrington followed a different course, taking to heart Thomas Hobbes's trenchant critique of the Florentine and proposing a republicanism devoid of tumults, free from the need for popular vigilance, and reliant, instead, on institutional restraints.

[25] See Chapters 2 and 3. In this connection, note John P. McCormick, "Machiavellian Democracy: Controlling Elites with Ferocious Populism," *APSR* 95:2 (June 2001): 297–313.

It, too, would have a profound impact on subsequent Whig thinking, and, as we shall also see, it would stimulate on the part of figures such as David Hume, the baron de Montesquieu, and the framers of the American Constitution sustained meditation on the political architecture best suited to the constitution of liberty.[26]

The Commonwealth of Oceana

As a landed gentleman and a private scholar, James Harrington was everything that Marchamont Nedham was not. Because he possessed a competence, he was independent, and his pen was always his own. Prior to November 1656, however, he had no public profile. Had he not then published *The Common-wealth of Oceana*, close students of Charles I's experience in captivity might be aware that an individual with his name had been appointed gentleman of the bedchamber to the king less than two years before the Stuart monarch's execution, and they might be vaguely aware that this individual was subsequently barred from further attendance on the king by the commissioners in charge for being too partial to Charles.[27]

Almost six years subsequent to the execution of Charles I – after Oliver Cromwell had put an end to the sitting of the Rump, at a time when the Lord Protector of the Commonwealth of England, Ireland, and Scotland had dismissed a number of officers found to be "murmuring" against the new regime with the quip that they knew "not what they meant" when they spoke of a commonwealth – Harrington was putatively approached by "some sober men" who told him that, "if any man in *England* could show what a Commonwealth was, it was" he.[28] Two years later, some five months after the appearance of Marchamont Nedham's *Excellencie of a Free State*, there was an advertisement in *Mercurius Politicus* offering for sale Harrington's *Commonwealth of Oceana*.[29]

The books and pamphlets that poured forth at a furious rate from Harrington's pen in the three years that followed are quite easily misunderstood. In them, he presents himself as a determined opponent of what he calls "modern prudence." He has ransacked "the *Archives of ancient prudence*" (*JHO* 59) in search of evidence and arguments with which "to vindicate the reason of popular government" (*PWoJH* 390), and he takes every available opportunity

---

[26] See Chapters 4 and 5 and 8 through 11.

[27] For a brief summary of what the surviving sources have to say, see Pocock, "Introduction," in *PWoJH* 1–5.

[28] Cf. *The Examination of James Harrington* (1662–77), in *PWoJH* 859, with *JHO* 125–6, where Harrington deploys Cromwell's phrase in mocking the Lord Protector; see Pocock, "Introduction," in *PWoJH* 6–14, who identifies Harrington's murmuring officers with the authors of *The Humble Petition of Several Colonels of the Army*, which appeared in October 1654; and consider Barbara Taft, "The Humble Petition of Several Colonels of the Army: Causes, Character, and Results of Military Opposition to Cromwell's Protectorate," *Huntington Library Quarterly* 42:1 (1978): 15–41.

[29] See S. B. Liljegren, "Introduction," in *JHO* xi.

to advertise the admiration that he harbors for ancient Athens, Sparta, and Rome. In his eagerness to adorn his own project with the authority of antiquity, he virtually wraps himself in a toga. One can hardly fault scholars for jumping to the conclusion that, at heart, the man was a classical republican.[30] Like Machiavelli and Nedham, Harrington actively courted such a misreading himself.[31]

In *The Commonwealth of Oceana* and in his other writings, he consistently used ancient and modern prudence as a way of distinguishing the arguments from expediency that had traditionally been deployed in favor of purely popular government from those used to defend a regulated monarchy composed of king, lords, and commons (*WoJH* 221). As a consequence, like Nedham, Harrington found it expedient to paper over the chasm separating Machiavelli from Thucydides, Xenophon, Plato, Aristotle, Polybius, Cicero, Livy, Tacitus, Plutarch, and the like; and, in similar fashion, he neglected the degree to which contemporary defenders of England's mixed monarchy had rested their case almost entirely on Polybius' analysis and defense of the mixed regime.[32] He, too, wanted to acquire for his modern republican project the authority of classical Greece and Rome.

The classical elements within Harrington's discussion are many and obtrusive,[33] but they are, in fact, peripheral to his overall scheme. Thus, for example, though he often cites Aristotle in support of his argument,[34] the English republican never once alludes to the crucial passage – singled out repeatedly

---

[30] To Zera S. Fink and J. G. A. Pocock, whom I cite in *Republics Ancient and Modern*, 991, n. 57, I can now add the following: Blair Worden, "James Harrington and *The Commonwealth of Oceana*, 1656," and "Harrington's *Oceana*: Origins and Aftermath, 1651–1660," in *Republicanism, Liberty, and Commercial Society*, 82–138; Arihiro Fukuda, *Sovereignty and the Sword: Harrington, Hobbes, and Mixed Government in the English Civil Wars* (Oxford, UK: Clarendon Press, 1997).

[31] Doubts have been cast on the classical character of Harrington's thought by the scholars listed in *Republics Ancient and Modern*, 991, n. 58, and by the following: Jonathan Scott, "The Rapture of Motion: James Harrington's Republicanism," in *Political Discourse in Early Modern Britain*, ed. Nicholas Phillipson and Quentin Skinner (Cambridge, UK: Cambridge University Press, 1993), 139–63; Gary Remer, "James Harrington's New Deliberative Rhetoric: Reflections of an Anticlassical Republican," *HPT* 16:4 (Winter 1995): 532–57, and Sullivan, *Machiavelli, Hobbes, and the Formation of a Liberal Republicanism in England*, 144–73. I have profited as well from the work of the scholars mentioned in *Republics Ancient and Modern*, 991, n. 58, and from the works listed in footnote 30 of this chapter.

[32] Cf. *His Majesty's Answer to the Nineteen Propositions of Both Houses of Parliament*, 18 June 1642, in *The Stuart Constitution, 1603–1688: Documents and Commentary*, ed. J. P. Kenyon (Cambridge, UK: Cambridge University Press, 1966), 21–3, with Polyb. 6.3.5–10.14. For the determinative influence exercised by the document cited, see Corinne Comstock Weston, *English Constitutional Theory and the House of Lords, 1556–1832* (New York: Columbia University Press, 1965).

[33] See Charles Blitzer, *An Immortal Commonwealth: The Political Thought of James Harrington* (New Haven, CT: Yale University Press, 1960), 283–93; Eric Nelson, *The Greek Tradition in Republican Thought* (Cambridge, UK: Cambridge University Press, 2004), 114–21.

[34] See *JHO* 10, 12–13, 17, 21, 29, 57, 87, 90–1, 123, 136, 142; *WoJH* 219, 224–5, 232, 271–2, 275, 281–4, 319, 324, 338, 342, 366, 381, 405, 464, 528, 535–7, 539, 543, 548, 552, 554, 561, 585.

for attack by his chosen antagonist Thomas Hobbes – in which the peripatetic articulates the premise that serves as the foundation for classical republicanism: that man is by nature a political animal endowed with a capacity for *lógos*, enabling him to distinguish and make clear to others what is advantageous, just, and good.[35] Nor does he echo any of the passages asserting the primacy of politics that one finds scattered through the works of the other ancient writers he cites.[36] James Harrington is, in fact, a modern populist on the Machiavellian model.[37] Like Hobbes and Nedham, he rejects the classical principle of differential moral and political rationality, and like the latter, he explicitly endorses the notion that the multitude is wiser and more constant than any prince can ever be, and he even quotes Machiavelli (*D* 1.58) to this effect. The "reason or interest" of an aristocracy "when they are all together . . . is," he contends, "but that of a party." That of "the people taken apart" may be "but so many private interests," but, when "you take them together, they are the publick interest" (*JHO* 141–2).

The one thing that Harrington does do in the classical vein is to challenge his contemporaries to rise to the occasion. "If we have any thing of Piety or of prudence," he writes in his *Commonwealth of Oceana*, "let us raise our selves out of the mire of private interest, unto the contemplation of Virtue, and put an hand unto the removal of *this Evil from under the Sun*; this evil against which no Government that is not secured, can be good; this evill from which the Government that is secure, must be perfect" (*JHO* 20–1). Otherwise, however, he is almost entirely silent on the subject of virtue, and in the course of his argument, he makes it abundantly clear that the perfection belonging to a government that is genuinely secure presupposes a reliance on the distribution of property and on private interest and precludes any dependence on the personal qualities of the citizens. Like Thomas Hobbes, James Harrington was a modern Platonist – convinced that institutional arrangements can achieve what education can never guarantee: the coincidence of wisdom and virtue with rule.[38]

Harrington's silence with regard to the principal themes of ancient republican politics is not an oversight. Like Machiavelli, Nedham, and Hobbes, he was steeped in the classics; and when it suits his turn, he is more than prepared to

---

[35] Cf. Hobbes, *Phil. Rud.* II.vi.9, with Arist. *Pol.* 1252b27–1253a39, and see Hobbes, *Leviathan* I.v.3. Consider Hobbes, *Elements* II.i.10, *Phil. Rud.* pref. [8], II.xii.1, *Leviathan* IV.xlvi.11, 13, 31–2, and then see *Elements* II.x.8, *Phil. Rud.* II.vi.13, III.xvii.12, and *Dialogue* 67. Note Sheldon Wolin, *Politics and Vision: Continuity and Innovation in Western Political Thought* (Boston: Little Brown, 1960), 253–60.

[36] See Paul A. Rahe, "The Primacy of Politics in Classical Greece," *American Historical Review* 89:2 (April 1984): 265–93.

[37] See Rahe, "Situating Machiavelli," 270–308.

[38] Consider *JHO* 20, 34, in light of Hobbes, *Leviathan* II.xxxi.41, and see *JHO* 29–30, 53–4, 56, 84–5, 104, 119–20. Cf. Nelson, *The Greek Tradition in Republican Thought*, 87–126, and Alan Cromartie, "Harringtonian Virtue: Harrington, Machiavelli, and the Method of the Moment," *Historical Journal* 41:4 (December 1998): 987–1009, who misapprehend the character of Harrington's debt to Plato and his successors.

borrow an argument from Thucydides, Plato, Aristotle, Cicero, and the like. But the "ancient prudence" that really interests him is neither the teaching concerning moral virtue laid out by Aristotle in his *Nicomachean Ethics* and passed on to the modern West by Cicero and the Stoics nor the doctrine of regime *(politeía)* found in the writings of the ancient political scientists and historians; it is, rather, the institutional teaching articulated by the ancients' "learned Disciple *Machiavill*" – whom he variously terms "the onely Polititian of later Ages," "the sole retreiver of this *ancient Prudence*," "the greatest Artist in the modern World," "the Prince of Polititians," and the "incomparable Patron of the people" (*JHO* 13, 30, 118, 135). Indeed, if truth be told, James Harrington owes far, far less to the many thinkers of classical antiquity than to Thomas Hobbes, whom he judges in most things, apart from his monarchist bias, "the best writer, at this day, in the world." If he "oppos'd the politics of Mr. Hobbs," he readily confesses, it was merely "to shew him what he taught me" (*WoJH* 241). Accordingly, though Harrington elects "to follow the Ancients" in some respects, he nevertheless intends, as he openly admits, "[t]o go mine own way" (*JHO* 14).

What Harrington means by asserting that he intends "[t]o go mine own way, and yet to follow the Ancients," is nowhere more evident than in his typology of regimes. At first glance, he seems intent on resurrecting a distinction asserted by Plato, Aristotle, and Polybius, tacitly abandoned by Machiavelli, and openly repudiated by Hobbes: that between monarchy and tyranny, between aristocracy and oligarchy, and between well-ordered popular government and the regime variously called democracy, anarchy, or mob rule. In resurrecting this scheme of classification, however, Harrington follows not its ancient proponents but their modern critics, for he jettisons the moral argument that had made the classical distinction intelligible in the first place, and he nowhere acknowledges that the distribution of offices and honors *(táxis tôn archôn)* within a given community determines the education *(paideía)* that shapes the character of its citizens and defines it as a regime.[39] If he seems to restore the traditional typology, it is because he retains the familiar names to camouflage what is, in fact, a new typology grounded on a material and institutional rather than a moral and educational foundation.

In the original conception, monarchy, aristocracy, and the well-ordered popular regime had been the lawful rule of the one, the wealthy few, and the impoverished many over willing subjects in the interest of those ruled, while tyranny, oligarchy, and the disorderly popular regime had been the lawless rule of each of the same three elements over unwilling subjects solely in the interest of the rulers themselves. Each of the correct regimes was deemed to exhibit and foster its own peculiar virtue, but – given human weakness – it was thought also to evidence a pronounced tendency to degenerate into its generic opposite. The mixed regime, as outlined by Polybius, was designed to combine the virtues of

[39] For a detailed discussion contrasting the traditional with the modern typology, see Rahe, *Republics Ancient and Modern*, 17–27.

the various correct regimes while checking their propensity for corruption.[40] This is the species of political analysis that Machiavelli and Hobbes abandoned, and they did so on the supposition that it is naive to think that the dominant element within any polity would ever rule in anyone's interest other than its own.[41]

Harrington shared the conviction of Machiavelli (*D* 1.5, 37, 2.pref.) and Hobbes (*Leviathan* I.viii.14–16, xi.1–2, xii.2–6) that human desire is insatiate and that reason is therefore enslaved to the passions. With regard to the Malmesbury philosopher's "treatises of human nature, and of liberty and necessity" (*EW* 4:1–76, 229–78), he wrote, "they are the greatest of new lights, and those which I have follow'd, and shall follow" (*WoJH* 241).[42] Consequently, he joined the Florentine sage and the English philosopher in concluding that self–interested rule is what the former had dubbed "the effectual truth of the matter" (*P* 15). He reiterates Machiavelli's contention (*D* 1.3.1) that "*it is the duty of a* Legislator *to presume all men to be wicked*" (*JHO* 152, 155). He quotes with approval Hobbes's dictum (*EW* 4:xiii; see *Leviathan* I.xi.21) that "*as often as reason is against a man, so often will a man be against reason.*" Moreover, he concedes that, in practice, "*reason is nothing but interest*"; and he concludes that "there be divers *interests*, and so divers *reasons*" (*JHO* 22). In short, Harrington accepts Machiavelli's critique of moral reason and the moral imagination.[43] If he never asserts that man is by nature a political animal, and if he never explores the manner in which the ordering of public offices and honors constitutes a species of civic moral education, it is because he has tacitly joined Hobbes in rejecting as practically untenable Aristotle's conviction that man's capacity for *lógos* makes it possible for him to ascend from a calculation of his own immediate, material advantage to a concern with what is truly just and good. As he puts it in dismissing the self-styled "saints" who advocate godly rule, "*Give us good men and they will make us good Lawes* is the *Maxime* of a *Demagogue*, and (through the alteration which is commonly perceivable in men, when they have power to work their own wills) exceedingly *fallible*" (*JHO* 56).

In place of this hoary dictum, Harrington embraces the thoroughly modern principles of "the greatest Artist in the modern World." And so he suggests

[40] Cf. Polyb. 6.3.5–10.14 with Pl. *Pol.* 291d–303b, *Laws* 3.689e–702d, 4.712c–715d, 8.832b–d; Arist. *Eth. Nic.* 1160a31–1161b10, *Pol.* 1278b30–1280a5, 1295a7–24, *Rhet.* 1365b21–1366a22; see Pl. *Laws* 6.756e–758a; Arist. *Pol.* 1281b22–38 (esp. 28–31), 1295a25–1297a12 (esp. 1296b14–16), 1297b1–27, 1329a2–17, 1332b12–41. Note, in this connection, Pind. *Pyth.* 2.86–8; Hdt. 3.80–3; Thuc. 8.97.2. In Harrington's day, the pertinent passages of Cicero's *Republic* (1.20.33–2.44.70, 3.13.23, 25.37–35.48) were as yet undiscovered.

[41] See NM, *D* 1.2–8 (which should be read in light of Harvey C. Mansfield, *Machiavelli's New Modes and Orders: A Study of the Discourses on Livy* [Ithaca, NY: Cornell University Press, 1979], 32–62); Hobbes, *Elements* II.i.3, *Phil. Rud.* II.vii.1–17, x.2, *Leviathan* II.xix.1–2.

[42] In the treatise on human nature, which forms the first part of his *Elements of Law Natural and Politic*, Hobbes articulates the political psychology that provides the foundation for the overall argument presented first in *The Elements of Law*, then in *De cive*, and finally in *Leviathan*.

[43] Consider NM, *D* 1.6, 2.pref. in light of *P* 15, and see Rahe, "Situating Machiavelli," 270–308.

that "*give us good orders, and they will make us good men* is the *Maxime* of a *Legislator* and the most *infallible* in the *Politickes*" (*JHO* 56). Thus, in the English republican's estimation, "the perfection of Government lyeth upon such a libration in the frame of it, that no man or men, in or under it, can have the interest; or having the interest, can have the power to disturb it with sedition" (*JHO* 30). While at Rome, he remarks, he once saw a pageant

which represented a kitchen, with all the proper utensils in use and action. The cooks were all cats and kitlings, set in such frames, so try'd and so ordered, that the poor creatures could make no motion to get loose, but the same caused one to turn the spit, another to baste the meat, a third to scim the pot and a fourth to make green-sauce. If the frame of your commonwealth be no such, as causeth everyone to perform his certain function as necessarily as this did the cat to make green-sauce, it is not right.

(*WoJH* 573–4)

Harrington's ultimate purpose is precisely that of Hobbes: to "put such principles down for a foundation, as passion, not mistrusting, may not seek to displace" (*EW* 4:xiii).[44] The "superstructures" of the well-ordered commonwealth are intended to be substitutes for the moral and political virtue that no man can be supposed to possess (*JHO* 32–3, *WoJH* 271–2, 469, 579). In a regime such as Oceana, which pursues what Machiavelli had pointedly termed "the common benefit of each" (*D* 1.pref.), by fitting "privat to public" and "even public to privat utility," no one, says Harrington, not even a "*nobleman*," need "*own a shame for preferring his own interest before that of a whole nation*" (*WoJH* 277–8).

In presenting his new typology of regimes, Harrington stresses the central importance of a single institution: the distribution of land. To institute a monarchy, an aristocracy, or a democracy, he contends, a legislator "must either frame the Government unto the foundation, or the foundation unto the Government." Thus, a legislator can set up a workable monarchy only "[i]f one man be sole Landlord of a territory, or overballance the people, for example, three parts in four." He can effectively establish the aristocratic rule embodied in the "mixed *Monarchy*" favored by proponents of "the *Gothick* ballance" only if "the Few or a Nobility, or a Nobility with the Clergy be Landlords or overballance the people unto like proportion." And he can institute a stable commonwealth only "[i]f the whole people be Landlords, or hold the lands so divided among them, that no one man, or number of men, within the compass of the *Few* or *Aristocracy*, overballance them." Harrington takes it for granted that it is impossible for a government to maintain an adequate standing army on the basis of its tax revenues alone. He therefore believes that whoever controls a nation's farms and feeds its militia can, if he wishes, control that militia. And he concludes that whoever is able in this fashion to control the militia will be forced

---

[44] Cf. *JHO* 30–2, 56, 185, and *WoJH* 242–6, 403–4, 468–9, 483, 567–74 (esp. 573–4), and see NM, *D* 1.4. The passages cited from Harrington are hard to reconcile with his contention that "in the politics there is nothing mechanic, or like it." See *WoJH* 247.

eventually, in defense of his own interests, to seize control of the government as well. Thus, where a legislator frames "the Government not according unto the ballance," its rule will be inherently unstable and therefore "not natural but violent." In short, tyranny will supplant monarchy; oligarchy, aristocracy; and anarchy, well-ordered popular rule (*JHO* 14–15).[45] By distinguishing between correct and incorrect regimes in this fashion, Harrington indicates his acceptance of Hobbes's contention (*Leviathan* II.xxix.4) that one must judge political arrangements solely with regard to "the difference of Convenience, or Aptitude to produce the Peace, and Security of the people."

It is on this basis that Harrington defends republicanism. He denies that an aristocracy is capable of ruling on its own; and for "the Gothic balance" and the feudal system on which it is grounded he has little use. The mixed regime is a halfway house between monarchy and republic; and, as Hobbes had already pointed out, it is inherently unstable as such. This "*Master-piece of Moderne Prudence* hath beene cry'd up to the *Skyes*, as the only invention, whereby at once to maintain the soveraignty of a *Prince*, and the liberty of the *people*," Harrington writes, but the history of Europe proves that, even where mixed monarchy accords with "the ballance" of property, "it hath been no other than a wrestling match" between the nobility and their king.[46] In his judgment, the real contest of regimes is between absolute monarchy, as exemplified by the Ottoman Empire, and the species of republicanism he defends himself. The former is grounded on the Sultan's ownership of the land and his ability to assign allotments to individual timariots in return for their service; and to it, the English republican is prepared to concede a great deal. But he hastens to add that the Ottoman regime has one, apparently insuperable defect: Absolute monarchy requires, for its own defense, a praetorian guard. More often than not, the Ottoman Sultan is the creature of the janissaries who serve him in that capacity; and even when this is not the case, they "have frequent interest and perpetual power to raise *sedition*, and to tear the *Magistrate*, even the *Prince* himself, in pieces" (*JHO* 31–2, 40–1; *WoJH* 248–9, 368). It is the burden of Harrington's argument to show that republicanism can be purged of comparable defects.

To this end, he advanced two arguments. The first was comparatively simple to make. Against those, such as Machiavelli, who draw attention to the civil disorders occasioned at Rome by disputes over the distribution of land, he asserts that, in England, where the "wrestling match" between the monarch and the nobility has resulted in there being a relatively egalitarian distribution of such property, it would be easy and painless to establish and maintain the requisite "ballance." One need only pass and enforce an agrarian law

---

[45] Note *WoJH* 226–32. Those "black maxims, set down by some politicians, particularly MACHIAVEL in his *prince*" have their natural home where there is "CORRUPTION in government," that is, in "anarchy, oligarchy, or tyranny." See *WoJH* 482.

[46] Cf. *JHO* 47–8 with Hobbes, *Elements* II.i.15–17, *Phil. Rud.* II.vii.4, *Leviathan* II.xix.4. Also note *WoJH* 368–9, 481.

restricting dowries, setting a limit to the amount of land one can acquire, and denying those possessed of property greatly in excess of that limit the right to leave a disproportionate amount to any one child (*JHO* 9–10, 15–16, 47–56, 85–99).[47]

The second argument was more complex. Against those, such as Hobbes, who point to the inherent contentiousness of republican politics, Harrington articulates new modes and orders designed to achieve within a republican framework what the author of *Leviathan* believed could best be accomplished in an absolute monarchy: the containment, reduction, and virtual elimination of politics itself.

A Republic Tongue-Ty'd

Like Hobbes, Harrington was acutely aware that political "ambition" can easily undermine the stability of a republican regime. When he cites Aristotle's contention (*Pol.* 1292b25–30, 1318b6–1319a39) that the best democracy is predominantly agricultural, he emphasizes that "such an one" is "the most obstinate assertresse of her liberty, and the least subject unto innovation or turbulency." This is the balance that he wants to achieve. But he recognizes that commonwealths, such as Athens, where "the City life hath had the stronger influence," have, in fact, "seldome or never been quiet, but at the best are found to have injured their own businesse by overdoing it." Apart from communities much like Venice, where the bulk of the populace is excluded from power, "a Commonwealth consisting but of one City, would doubtlesse be stormy, in regard that ambition would be every mans trade" (*JHO* 10, 169).

If, like Hobbes, Harrington looked askance at city life, it was largely because, again like Hobbes, he greatly feared public debate.[48] "Consider," he exhorted his readers, "how we have been tossed with every wind of Doctrine, lost by the glib tongues of your Demagogs and Grandees in our Havens." He had read Thucydides, he had studied the history of the ancient republics, and when he reviewed all that can take place in the political sphere, he could think of "nothing more dangerous" than "debate in a crowd," for "such sport is debate in a Popular Assembly as ... was the destruction of Athens." A commonwealth "where the People is talkative in their political capacity" will inevitably be "carried away by Vain-glorious Men" and "Swim down the sink." It is not, then, surprising that Harrington chose to adapt to the needs of a commonwealth situated on a large territory the one set of republican regulations that had earned the full approval of that form of government's most severe and exacting critic. Like the philosopher of Malmesbury, he found in the modes and orders

---

[47] In this connection, see *WoJH* 242–8, 269–81, 367.

[48] Consider Hobbes, "The Answer of Mr. Hobbes to Sir William Davenant's Preface before Gondibert," in *EW* 4:443–4, in light of *Elements* II.ii.5, v.3–8. See *Phil. Rud.* II.x.6–7, 11, *Leviathan* II.xix.5–9. See also "Of the Life and History of Thucydides," in *EW* 8:xv–xviii.

employed by the serene Republic of Venice an antidote for "the overflowing and boundless passions" of the "multitude."[49]

"The tongue of man is," Thomas Hobbes once observed, "a trumpet of warre and sedition" (*Phil. Rud.* II.v.5). To silence that trumpet, Harrington makes of his *Oceana* a republic "tongue-ty'd." Except behind closed doors, within the narrow confines of its Senate and the various councils drawn from the members of that body, debate and discussion are strictly forbidden. When a law has been promulgated and is soon to be voted on in Oceana's more popular house, the magistrates are to see to it *"that there be no laying of heads together; Conventicles, or Canvassing to carry on, or to oppose any thing."* To the same end, the deputies elected to the lower house are required to take an oath that *"they will neither introduce, cause, nor to their power suffer debate to be introduced into any popular Assembly of this Government, but to their utmost be ayding and assisting to seize and deliver any Person or Persons in that way offending and striking at the Root of this Commonwealth unto the Councill of War."* It would be an error to underestimate the importance that Harrington attached to the prohibition of canvassing and public debate. To render political maneuvering ineffective, the fundamental orders of Oceana dictate the use of the secret ballot in legislative assemblies. To deter discussion, they solemnly stipulate that anyone who tries to introduce debate within a popular assembly be executed.[50] With Harrington, for the first time, in a definitive way, popular consent has replaced public deliberation as the fundamental principle of republican politics (*JHO* 142–44, 205–6; *WoJH* 277).

The suppression of public discussion and public voting was one way in which the author of *Oceana* sought through republican orders to eliminate the "middle ground" that had been the central feature of self-government in ancient times.[51] There were others as well. Thus, for example, Harrington thought it necessary to bar from his legislative assemblies the entire profession of lawyers with "their incurable run upon their own narrow bias," "their perpetuall invectives against *Machiavill*," and their propensity, as "Tradesmen," for a "knitting of Nets" when there should be a "making of Lawes." Harrington was similarly suspicious of divines, who were "neither to be allow'd Synods nor Assemblies" nor to be "suffred to meddle with affaires of State" (*JHO* 118, 163–4, 172–4), for he was no less acutely aware than Hobbes of the manner in which the marriage of Athens and Jerusalem had allowed the bitter politics of the ancient Greek *ekklēsía* to survive within the Christian church.[52] This worried him less

---

49 Cf. *JHO* 123–9 (esp. 125–8), with Hobbes, *Elements* II.v.8, *Phil. Rud.* II.x.15; and see *WoJH* 573–4. Later he added, "debate in the people makes anarchy." See *WoJH* 286. See also *WoJH* 418, 570.

50 See *JHO* 80, 99–102, 109, 115–17, 127–8, 142; *WoJH* 417–19, 487–8, 503. In this connection, note *JHO* 99–105.

51 See Rahe, "The Primacy of Politics in Classical Greece," 265–93.

52 See Hobbes, *Dialogue* 122–32 (esp. 123–6), and "An Historical Narration Concerning Heresy and the Punishment Thereof," in *EW* 4:387–408. See also *Elements* II.vii.9; *Concerning Body* Ep. Ded., in *EW* 1:ix–xi; *Leviathan* IV.xliv.2, xlvi–xlvii; *Behemoth* 8–20; Samuel I. Mintz,

than it did his infamous countryman, for he deemed it impossible "that mens animosityes should over ballance their Interest, for any [great] time," and he was therefore persuaded that a "sound and steddy" government that "taketh in all *interests*" could easily eliminate "the animosity" and the "triviall" divisions to which "parties that are *Spiritual*" so often give rise (*JHO* 55–6, 209, 217). Nonetheless, like Marchamont Nedham, he regarded civil liberty and the liberty of conscience as inseparable, and so he took considerable care to defuse the situation and eliminate every occasion for the exercise of what he was the first to dub "priest craft." To this end, he excluded ministers of the Gospel from holding public office in Oceana; he established religious freedom for all Christian sects not owing allegiance to a foreign power; and he provided for strict civilian control of the established church – chiefly, by authorizing the local parish congregation to select its own parson but also by empowering the Senate's council of religion to supervise the activities of the nation's clergy. Mindful of the manner in which his contemporaries had been "tossed with every wind of Doctrine," Harrington sought to bridle the "glib tongues" of the nation's priests. "If you know not how to rule your Clergy," his Lord Archon warns, "you will most certainly be like a man that cannot rule his Wife," having "neither quiet at home, nor honour abroad."[53]

The English republican was no less fully persuaded than Hobbes (*Leviathan* II.xviii) that "the soverain power" within a state must be "entire and absolute" (*WoJH* 404, 478–9). But while he considered the full concentration of power "necessary," he thought it "*a formidable creature*" as well, and he compared it to "*the Powder, which (as you are Soldiers) is at once your safety and danger*" (*JHO* 84–5), for he feared the *libido dominandi* of the few (*WoJH* 469). Consequently, he tried to suppress or at least contain the ambition for office, for power, and for political glory. To this end, he introduced two institutions: rotation, and what he called "the Venetian ballot." Rotation ensures that all who govern are governed in turn: Members of Parliament serve for three years and are ineligible for that office for three years thereafter; other officials must similarly vacate any magistracy they have held for a period equal to, if not double, the length of their term in office.

The Venetian ballot has a number of provisions. To begin with, it guarantees that all of the magistrates owe their status to the people: The freeholders of the parish over thirty years of age elect parish officials at an assembly held each year; deputies whom they select from among their number gather annually to choose the justices of the peace and the other magistrates of the district, the tribal officeholders, and the tribe's representatives to Parliament. Moreover, since the ballot is in every case secret and therefore private, Oceana's citizens, their deputies, and their representatives in Parliament can ignore the contentious questions of justice and the transcendent good and vote their own

"Hobbes on the Law of Heresy: A New Manuscript," *Journal of the History of Ideas* 29:3 (July–September 1968): 409–14.
[53] See *JHO* 37–8, 69–70, 109–10, 125, 169–73; *WoJH* 474–6, 484, 519, 530, 572–4.

interests without fear or shame. Finally, the arrangements effectively preclude campaigning for office and thereby contribute further to the suppression of the public deliberation that had been the very soul of classical politics: As in Venice, an individual is chosen by lot and authorized to nominate candidates for the position soon to be vacant, and no one of these can be elected who has not been approved by a majority of those present and eligible to vote.[54]

Rotation and the Venetian ballot enable the citizens of Oceana to ignore public opinion, to consult their interests in private, and to select reasonably able men for high office; and, most important of all, they prevent the emergence of a narrow political class and give minimal scope to the great longing "to be first and superior to all others" that had crippled the mythical Achaean army of Homer's *Iliad* and plagued the tumultuous *póleis* of ancient Greece.

An Immortal Commonwealth

To disprove Hobbes's contention that civil disorder is endemic within republics and to construct an "*immortal Commonwealth*" utterly free from every "*internall cause of Commotion*," Harrington had to do more than restrict public debate, rein in the lawyers, frustrate priestcraft, quell political ambition, and emancipate self-interest (*JHO* 61, 84, 135). He was, in fact, caught in a quandary. He thought it preposterous to suppose that the fear of death or even the fear of God would reconcile ordinary men with severe oppression. In one passage, he wrote, "A People when they are reduced unto misery and despair, become their own Polititians." In another, he added, "Take the bread out of the peoples mouthes, as did the *Roman Patricians*, and you are sure enough of a war" (*JHO* 138, 156).[55] In short, the only way to prevent the civil strife synonymous with the people's eruption into the political arena is to safeguard their interests. That is, however, inordinately difficult to accomplish: Harrington doubted that a monarchy or oligarchy would ever be solicitous of the interests of ordinary men, and he was painfully aware that the people can never effectively function as "their own polititians." They may be able to "feel," but they "cannot see" (*JHO* 118; *WoJH* 404, 483, 489).

Where Machiavelli and Hobbes had distinguished between "princes" driven by the desire for dominion and the lust for more, and "the people" fearful of being dominated and intent on retaining what they have,[56] their English disciple spoke of "the natural aristocracy" and "the natural democracy." Like Hobbes, he identified the former with those among the wealthy who are the most learned, and he appears to have taken it for granted that their superior intelligence derives from the overriding passion for power, riches, knowledge,

---

[54] See *JHO* 33, 66–8, 71–82, 99–108; *WoJH* 282–300, 369–70, 419, 504.

[55] See *JHO* 129–33; *WoJH* 242–3.

[56] Cf. NM, *D* 1.5, 37, 2.pref. with *P* Ep. Ded., 9, and see Hobbes, *Elements* I.xiv.3, *Phil. Rud.* I.i.4, *Leviathan* I.xiii.2–8, with "The Answer of Mr. Hobbes to Sir William Davenant's Preface before Gondibert," in *EW* 4:443–4; *Leviathan* II.xxx.6.

and honor instilled in them by nature and their upbringing.[57] Harrington was persuaded that initiative in government invariably falls to members of this "natural aristocracy" and that, if allowed to do so, those who have seized or been entrusted with the initiative will inevitably betray the public trust. "[A] man doth not look upon *reason* as it is *right* or *wrong* in it *self*," he insisted, "but as it makes for him or against him." Consequently, he added,

unlesse you can shew such *orders* of a *Government*, as like those of *God* in *nature* shall be able to constrain this or that *creature* to shake off that *inclination* which is more peculiar unto it, and take up that which regards the *common good* or *interest*; all this is to no more end, then to perswade every man in a *popular Government*, not to carve himself of that which he desires most, but to be mannerly at the publick Table, and give the best from himself unto decency and the *common interest*. (*JHO* 23)

Harrington's subsequent fame stems largely from the fact that he was the first proponent of self-government to construct republican orders independent of the fundamental premise of classical republicanism that one can inculcate civic virtue and public-spiritedness through education. Mindful of "the effectual truth of the matter," he sought to devise institutions that would not just compensate for the defects arising from man's troublesome faculty of speech but actually elicit pursuit of what Machiavelli had termed "the common benefit of each" from man's natural, ineradicable, and utterly selfish "*inclination* . . . to carve himself of that which he desires most." It was with this in mind that he considered the Florentine's controversial account of the contribution made to Rome's greatness by the struggle between the Senate and the people of republican Rome.

Where the ancients had been obsessed with communal solidarity,[58] Harrington's Florentine mentor was fascinated by political conflict. He reveled in it, and he found virtue in the very party and class divisions that the ancients and their subsequent admirers regarded as the supreme political malady. In his *Discourses on Livy*, as Markus Fischer has pointed out in the prologue to this book, Machiavelli made the unprecedented assertion that it was the institutionalization of just such a conflict that accounted for the greatness of Rome and its superiority to Sparta and the other ancient polities. There are circumstances, he implied, in which certain types of political struggle can be rendered if not quite compatible with stability, then conducive to vitality and long-term prosperity, for the right sort of intestine strife gives rise to the dikes, embankments, and canals of *virtù* that enable a polity to withstand fortune's flood (cf. *D* 1.2–8 with *P* 25). Harrington thought that he could improve on the man's argument. "There is not a more noble, or usefull question in the Politicks," he

---

[57] Consider *JHO* 23–25, 117–24 (esp. 119, 123), 145–6, 174–5, and *WoJH* 215, 236–8, in light of Hobbes, *Leviathan* I.viii.14–16. See *Behemoth* 159–60. Note that while men may be more or less equal in their capacity to kill one another and with respect to what they call wisdom, they are by no means equal in their capacity for science: *Leviathan* I.xiii.1–3. See also *Elements* I.x.1–5.

[58] See Rahe, *Republics Ancient and Modern*, 55–135.

wrote, "then that which is started by *Machiavil*, Whether means were to be found whereby the Enmity that was between the Senate and the people of *Rome* might have been removed" (*JHO* 133–9).

Harrington's strategy for eliminating this enmity was disarmingly simple. Even *"girles,"* he remarked, know how to guarantee equity in situations where interests are opposed:

For example, two of them have a cake yet undivided, which was given between them, that each of them therefore may have that which is due: Divide, sayes one unto the other, and I will choose; or let me divide, and you shall choose: if this be but once agreed upon, it is enough: for the divident, dividing unequally loses, in regard that the other takes the better half; wherefore she divides equally, and so both have right.

In much the same fashion, Harrington contended, "the whole *Mystery* of a *Common-wealth . . .* lyes only in *dividing and choosing."* One need only assign the right of *"debate"* to "the natural aristocracy" while reserving the right to determine the "result" to "the natural democracy" (*JHO* 23–5, 115–17, 142–4; *WoJH* 235–8).

To finesse the opposition of interests separating the many from the few, Harrington proposed the establishment of a bicameral parliament elected by the people by means of the Venetian ballot, with one house drawn exclusively from the well-to-do and the other predominantly from those with lesser means. Given the natural propensity of mankind to defer to their betters, the handful of men elected to the Senate would inevitably be representative of the nation's "natural aristocracy" – the only group endowed with the education and the leisure for reflection that is prerequisite to political prudence. If allowed to rule on their own, these men would undoubtedly rule in their own interest. There were, however, ways to prevent them from abusing their trust. Harrington was persuaded that *"the many cannot be otherwise represented in a state of liberty, than by so many, and so qualify'd, as may within the compass of that number and nature imbrace the interest of the whole people."* But he did not doubt that it was possible, in an agrarian commonwealth, to constitute a sizeable assembly, elected from constituencies more or less equally populous, "such as can imbibe or contract no other interest than that only of the whole people." To render a Senate drawn from the nation's "natural aristocracy" useful to that commonwealth, one need only empower such a popular assembly with the right to reject or accept by secret ballot whatever this Senate proposes. For, if checked in this fashion, an aristocratic house composed of temporary officeholders would have reason to present no measures but those which, in its wisdom, it deemed best suited to the long-term, public good.[59] Oceana's "natural aristocracy" is to be a modern aristocracy of service; in contrast with the martial aristocracies and urban patriciates of the classical and medieval periods, it is never to rule of right and in its own name.

[59] See *JHO* 80–1, 115–26, 142–4; *WoJH* 215, 236–8, 246–7, 403, 418–19, 487, 570.

In all of this, there is evident a popular bias that might, at first glance, seem incompatible with impartial rule. The "natural aristocracy" is not only checked by the many; it is elected by and, in a sense, submerged in the many (*WoJH* 243). If Oceana eludes the dangers thought by the ancients to be attendant on purely popular government, it is chiefly because "the natural democracy" is instinctively impartial – at least, when liberated from priestcraft, cured of the ambition to which public debate gives rise, and encouraged by the secrecy of the ballot to ignore questions of principle and deliberate in private concerning material interest. In reaching this conclusion, Harrington would appear once again to have had Athens in mind. By ancient standards, that city possessed a remarkably tolerant regime. In fact, it was so tolerant that, in the eyes of the ancient philosophers, democracy hardly qualified as a regime at all. According to one figure in Thucydides (7.69.2), Athens provided "to all an unregulated power over the conduct of life." Democracy confers on the citizens, so Aristotle claims, "the license to do whatever one wants." Plato (*Rep.* 8.557a–558a) compared it with "a many-colored cloak decorated in every hue" because it was "decorated with every disposition" and afforded a welcome "to all sorts of human beings."

To Harrington, unconcerned as he was with the fostering of civic virtue, it mattered little that the ancients thought democracy deficient in the ethos of reverence and friendship required by republican government. He was, in fact, heartened by the prosaic aspirations and narrow, paltry concerns that guide democratic man: after all, as Aristotle had observed, the only thing that ordinary farming people ask is that they not be robbed or prevented from earning their own way.[60] Where such men advocate a redistribution of property, it is solely because they have been denied scope for their own industry: "Men that have equall possessions," Harrington notes, "and the same security of their estates and of their liberties that you have, have the same cause with you to defend." Moreover, given the bright prospects for agricultural improvement, where property is secure and widely distributed, no one willing to work need be in want. This last point needs particular emphasis, for it explains why "the whole spirit of the people, even as to matter of government" is summed up for Harrington in the fact that, even when offended, ordinary human beings are inclined to shrug their shoulders and mutter, "*What care I for him? I can live without him*" (*JHO* 55, 156; *WoJH* 246–7, 471, 580). It is the general indifference of most men and the willingness of those not in desperate straits to mind their own business and to live and let live that makes possible a non-partisan, impartial "*Empire* of *Lawes* and not of *Men*" indistinguishable from "the interest" and therefore the "will" of the people as a whole.

[60] Cf. Arist. *Pol.* 1280a7–1287b35 (esp. 1281a11–38), 1318a11–26 (esp. 17–26), with 1292b25–30, 1297b6–8, 1318b6–1319a39; and see 1295a25–1296b1.

2

The Philosophy of Liberty

Locke's Machiavellian Teaching

Margaret Michelle Barnes Smith

John Locke has been accused of being a Calvinist, a Socinian, an atheist, a Hobbesian, an elitist, a product of his times, and even a neurotic – but never a Machiavellian.[1] On the face of it, this is easy enough to understand. Nowhere does Locke acknowledge any debt to Machiavelli, nor does he leave behind any written expression of admiration for the Florentine thinker. Characteristic Lockeian concepts such as the state of nature do not show up in Machiavelli's writings. In fact, Machiavelli is notable for his silence on natural law, which is a key component of Locke's teaching.[2] Furthermore, common opinions about Machiavelli himself – that he was a Renaissance humanist, an Aristotelian, a patriot, or even a teacher of evil – do not seem to point in Locke's direction.[3]

---

[1] For Locke as a Calvinist and product of his times, see John Dunn, *The Political Thought of John Locke: An Historical Account of the Argument of the Two Treatises* (Cambridge, UK: Cambridge University Press, 1969). Dunn is also notable for his insistence that Locke was not only incoherent, but also a neurotic emotional cripple: See 13, 28–39, 79–83, 164, 193, 256–61. For the argument that Locke was a Hobbesian and an atheist, see Leo Strauss, *Natural Right and History* (Chicago: University of Chicago Press, 1953), 202–51, and "Locke's Doctrine of Natural Law," in Strauss, *What Is Political Philosophy?* (Chicago: University of Chicago Press, 1988), 197–220. C. B. Macpherson, *The Political Theory of Possessive Individualism: Hobbes to Locke* (Oxford, UK: Oxford University Press, 1962), 5–8, 194–262, argues that Locke reflected his historical context in his elitist economic class bias. Richard Ashcraft, *Revolutionary Politics and Locke's Two Treatises of Government* (Princeton, NJ: Princeton University Press, 1986), 3–16, 75–127, argues that Locke's thought must be understood in light of his political loyalties and social context. Locke's contemporary enemies, John Edwards and Edward Stillingfleet, accused him of Socinianism and the promotion of atheism: See Maurice Cranston, *John Locke: A Biography* (London: Longmans Press, 1957), 276, 410, 412–16, 467–8; Neal Wood, *The Politics of Locke's Philosophy: A Social Study of "An Essay Concerning Human Understanding"* (Berkeley, CA: University of California Press, 1983), 53–8.

[2] See the prologue of this book.

[3] See Mark Hulliung, *Citizen Machiavelli* (Princeton, NJ: Princeton University Press, 1983); J. G. A. Pocock, *The Machiavellian Moment: Florentine Political Thought and the Atlantic Republican Tradition* (Princeton, NJ: Princeton University Press, 1975); Quentin Skinner, *Machiavelli* (New York: Hill and Wang, 1981); Leo Strauss, *Thoughts on Machiavelli* (Chicago: University of

John Locke has a reputation for sobriety rather than wickedness, and his position on the brink of the Enlightenment seems far removed from Renaissance Italy.

In spite of the evidence suggesting that there is little reason to make a philosophical connection between the two thinkers, there are details that suggest that Locke was indebted to Machiavelli. The first and most obvious is that Locke was an avid collector of Machiavelli's books, and there is no reason to think that he did not read them.[4] The second and less obvious is a connection between their books. Both the Florentine and the Englishman cite a particular speech from Titus Livy's *History of Rome* (9.1).[5] The speech is given by the general of an enemy of Rome, who charges the Romans with injustice and claims that their conduct justifies his own people's resort to arms against them. Machiavelli and Locke each cite two different sentences from the speech. Locke cites the general's complaint about Roman injustice on the title page of the 1698 edition of the *Two Treatises of Government*, the last edition published during his lifetime.[6] The sentence Locke presents as an epigraph reads as follows:

But if no common justice is left to the weak when dealing with the powerful, I can still turn to the gods who exact vengeance for intolerable pride, and beg them to direct their wrath against those who are satisfied neither by the restoration of their own property nor by its increase from what belongs to other men; whose savage fury will not be sated by the death of the guilty, and surrender of their lifeless bodies, nor by the owners' property following on that surrender, unless we give them our blood to drink and our vitals to tear.[7]

Machiavelli cites from the speech a sentence that immediately follows the one quoted by Locke. In this, the general defends the decision for war by saying, "War is just...when it is necessary, and arms are righteous for those whose only hope remains in arms." Machiavelli quotes this sentence in both *The Prince* (26) and the *Discourses on Livy* (3.12). This is hardly decisive as evidence for a connection. The two do not cite precisely the same text, and it could certainly be

Chicago Press, 1984); Isaiah Berlin, "The Originality of Machiavelli," in *Studies on Machiavelli*, ed. Myron Gilmore (Florence: Sansoni, 1972), 147–206; Maurizio Viroli, *Machiavelli* (Oxford, UK: Oxford University Press, 1998), 148–74; Paul A. Rahe, "Situating Machiavelli," in *Renaissance Civic Humanism: Reappraisals and Reflections*, ed. James Hankins (Cambridge, UK: Cambridge University Press, 2000), 270–308.

[4] John Harrison and Peter Laslett, *The Library of John Locke* (Oxford, UK: Clarendon Press, 1971), 21–3.

[5] See Paul A. Rahe, *Republics Ancient and Modern: Classical Republicanism and the American Revolution* (Chapel Hill, NC: University of North Carolina Press, 1992), 467–72; Thomas L. Pangle, "Executive Energy and Popular Spirit in Lockean Constitutionalism," *Presidential Studies Quarterly* 17:2 (Spring 1987): 253–65.

[6] For a history of the text and its publication, see Peter Laslett, "Introduction," in *TTG* 6–15.

[7] I use the following translation: Titus Livy, *Rome and Italy: Books VI–X of the History of Rome from Its Foundation*, tr. Betty Radice (New York: Penguin, 1982).

coincidental that Machiavelli and Locke deploy this particular passage. Their resort to it does, however, suggest a common interest and spirit.[8]

To be precise, the passage from Livy suggests on the part of both Machiavelli and Locke a concern with resistance to tyranny. A comparison of their writings confirms that they do, indeed, share this concern. In the second of his *Two Treatises of Government* (2.19), for example, Locke justifies violent resistance to oppressive government. In Chapter 26 of *The Prince*, where Machiavelli cites the pertinent passage from Livy, he is exhorting a new prince to rise up and liberate Italy from its slavery. This, again, is hardly decisive as evidence that Locke is in any way philosophically beholden to Machiavelli. While each of the two may advocate resisting certain institutions, their resistance need hardly be theoretically related. Close scrutiny of their works, however, reveals that the two share a concern with liberation that is more than coincidental and transcends the political, although the critique of certain political institutions is very important for both of them. On a deeper level, Locke follows Machiavelli in a project to liberate human beings from what they both considered to be the theological and philosophical origins of tyranny, and, like the Florentine, he takes care to trace the political implications of this liberation.

The Liberation from Heaven

The theological concept that both Machiavelli and Locke reject is, put abstractly, faith in the goodness of the divine. Put concretely, it is the Christian faith that God is just and good. Christianity teaches that, since God uses His power to care for His creatures in a just and wise way, the reasonable course of action is to leave matters in His hands. Jesus teaches his people not to worry about clothing themselves but to trust that their God will clothe them as He clothes the lilies of the field (Matt. 6:28–30, Luke 12:27–28). Machiavelli's most fundamental criticism of this faith becomes manifest when he intimates that God Himself is tyrannical and unjust.[9] This suggestion finds an echo in Locke's doctrine of property. Both Machiavelli and Locke aim at the liberation of the mind from faith in a providential God. As long as human beings continue to acknowledge a dependence on God, they cannot be self-sufficient.[10] To put

---

[8] See Rahe, *Republics Ancient and Modern*, 291–3, 472–9. Laslett, "Introduction," 86–7, claims that while Locke owed nothing to Machiavelli in terms of substance, he could be called "Machiavelli's philosopher" because of a tendency to practicality rather than system. See also 23.

[9] See Strauss, *Thoughts on Machiavelli*, 49; Harvey C. Mansfield, *Machiavelli's New Modes and Orders: A Study of the Discourses on Livy* (Ithaca, NY: Cornell University Press, 1979), 99–100; Harvey C. Mansfield and Nathan Tarcov, "Introduction" in *D* xxxv.

[10] See Nathan Tarcov, "John Locke and the Foundations of Toleration" in *Early Modern Skepticism and the Origins of Toleration*, ed. Alan Levine (Lanham, MD: Lexington, 1999), 179–95. Tarcov argues here that Locke's doctrine of toleration was meant to promote this sort of intellectual independence. Note also Harvey C. Mansfield, "Machiavelli's Virtue," in Mansfield, *Machiavelli's Virtue* (Chicago: University of Chicago Press, 1996), 48, and *Taming the Prince: The Ambivalence of Modern Executive Power* (Baltimore, MD: Johns Hopkins University Press, 1993), 123–4; as well as Rahe, *Republics Ancient and Modern*, 472–9.

one's trust in God, these two writers lead their readers to conclude, is to impose on oneself a punishment undeserved, since relying on God is in practice equivalent to tossing one's fate to the wind. Human beings should, they intimate, cast off the naïve faith that a loving God will reward piety and virtue, and they should take their fates into their own hands.

It is in the *Discourses on Livy* that Machiavelli hints that God is a tyrant (D 1.26). There he says that, if one wishes to establish a new government, one must make everything new. This means that all those ruled by a new prince should be made to see that "there is no rank, no order, no state, no wealth there that he who holds it does not know it as from" the prince. In short, all subjects of such a prince should understand that they are dependent on the prince himself for everything. The means by which a prince accomplishes this are, he admits, "very cruel, and enemies to every way of life, not only Christian but human." Machiavelli asserts that this is the way in which David ordered his kingdom. To illustrate this point, Machiavelli (D 1.26.1) quotes the Magnificat (Luke 1:53), which says of God that He "filled the hungry with good things and sent the rich away empty." Here, as elsewhere (D 3.30.1), the Florentine interprets Scripture "judiciously,"[11] applying the Magnificat's description of God not to God but to David, a king who is said to have reordered his kingdom using the most cruel and tyrannical methods. The implication here is not that David is like God but that God is like David in being both tyrannical and cruel.

In Machiavelli's account, God and David share the same goal: They both wish to make their subjects utterly dependent on them. The Bible makes clear that it is a concern of God to make His creatures realize that they owe everything they have to Him. The story of the Tower of Babel (Gen. 11:1–9) illustrates His intentions in this regard. Its construction begins after the Flood that destroyed all mankind except for Noah and his family. After the Flood, God commanded Noah and his family to "fill the earth" (Gen. 9:1). Instead of fulfilling this command, the generation after the Flood settled in a valley and said to one another, "Let us build us a city, and a tower with its top in the sky, to make a name for ourselves" (Gen. 11:1). The reason for the disobedience of postdiluvian humanity is the desire to make a name for humanity. A tower that reaches into the sky is a demonstration of human power and ingenuity, and the same can be said for the city surrounding the tower. The city is the place where the labor and planning required to build the tower are located. The government of the city must organize resources, human and otherwise, for the sake of the common task. Using the power of the human mind to plan, organize, and engineer and the power of the human body to labor, the city is the place where human beings are most capable of taking full responsibility for their own well-being. The tower is a monument to this power. Indeed, the very image of the tower reaching into the sky suggests human grasping after the power

---

[11] See the prologue of this book.

of God.[12] As a testimony to human power, the tower establishes a name for humanity.

God, however, wants human beings to call on Him by name. Machiavelli hints that their acknowledgment of such a state of dependence brings "ruin to men" (*D* 1.26.1). The cause of their ruin is His need to make all things anew. This is precisely what God does during the Flood itself. He washes away almost all life and leaves a single family that is utterly dependent on Him. Machiavelli can hardly object to God's conduct in this case, since he advises human princes to follow His lead. Believers in God must, of course, object to Machiavelli's interpretation of God's actions because it belies the Biblical claim that God is just and His providential care good for His creatures. It is hard to imagine that methods of ruling that are "enemies of every way of life" could be just and caring. In light of these reflections, it is hardly surprising that the generation after the Flood might be attracted to the thought that human beings should attempt to become self-sufficient. Machiavelli's aim is to attract his readers to this same thought.

Locke, too, subtly undermines the view that God is just and good in providing for His creatures. He approaches this issue in the second of the *Two Treatises* through the idea of property. Specifically, he makes a puzzle of the question of the ownership of individual human beings. In Chapter 2, Locke says that human beings are "all the workmanship of one omnipotent, and infinitely wise maker" and that "they are his property" (*TTG* 2.2.6). In Chapter 5, however, he says the opposite: that "every man has a *property* in his own *person*" (*TTG* 2.5.27). It is possible that Locke thinks that God gave to human beings their bodies as property and that these bodies can at the same time be both His and their own. If so, these two statements would not be contradictory. But Locke's final statement on the distinction between paternal, political, and despotical power makes such a reading difficult to sustain, for there he distinguishes political power, "where men have property in their own disposal," from despotical power, which is power "over such as have no property at all" (*TTG* 2.15.173). Here, of course, property could refer solely to goods such as houses, land, clothing, or food. But if human beings all possess their bodies as property, it is hard to see how anyone could be "such as have no property at all." Yet Locke clearly states that there is such a thing as despotical power and that it is exercised over those without any property whatever. The only human beings to whom Locke refers who lack property altogether are those whose bodies are God's property. If the statement in Chapter 2 that human beings are all God's property is meant to be taken literally, it is Locke's claim that God exercises despotical power over His people. The nature of this despotism is the denial of property in themselves to His people.

---

[12] See Leon Kass, "What's Wrong with Babel?" *American Scholar* 58:1 (Winter 1989): 41–60. Kass argues that the Tower of Babel represents the human impulse that motivates the modern aspiration to self-sufficiency. While the Bible teaches that this impulse is misguided and destructive, it is precisely the faith in human reason and technology, presented in the Babel story, that both Machiavelli and Locke wish to liberate.

Locke's Biblical exegesis in the *First Treatise* supports this reading.[13] Locke asserts that the Bible and reason agree on the subject of property. According to Locke, man's "strong desire of Preserving his Life and Being" has been planted in him by God, as has reason, which is *"the Voice of God in him"* (*TTG* 1.9.86). Reason tells man that he has a "right to make use of those Creatures, which by his Reason or Senses he could discover would be serviceable" to his preservation (*TTG* 1.9.86). As Locke reiterates in the *Second Treatise*, reason and revelation both tell us "that men, being once born, have a right to their preservation, and consequently to meat and drink, and such other things as nature affords for their subsistence" (*TTG* 2.5.25). What reason enables us to discern by inference, revelation is supposed to tell us outright through the recounting of God's grants to Adam and Noah. But, as we shall see, the Biblical accounts of the donations to Adam and Noah do not agree with the teaching that Locke ascribes to reason.

Locke notes in his analysis of the donation to Adam that the creation accounts for three ranks of creatures: They are cattle, wild beasts, and reptiles. In the donation to Adam, God leaves out cattle. This is a conspicuous omission because cattle "were or might be tame, and so [could] be the Private possession of particular Men" (*TTG* 1.4.25). In other words, cattle are the most potentially useful to humanity of the creatures.[14] It is only dominion that Adam is given by God and not property.[15] Adam was a ruler of the inferior animals, but his rule did not give him the right to eat any of his charges. It was Noah who was granted by God the right to eat animals, "which was not allowed to *Adam* in his charter." While Adam was granted dominion over the animals, Noah was granted property in them, "which is a right to destroy any thing by using it" (*TTG* 1.4.39). While Noah was granted the right to eat meat, Adam was not.

Locke hints at the intention of the Biblical God by elaborating on the nature of Adam's dominion. Dominion is that "which a Shepherd may have" as opposed to "full Property as an Owner" (*TTG* 1.4.39). Adam was a kind of shepherd or caretaker of creatures that were owned by someone else, namely God. When Locke calls human beings the property of God in the *Second Treatise*, it is God's status as creator that makes them His property.[16] According to Locke, God owns what He has made, and He has made the world and everything in it. The role of humanity is to shepherd God's creation for His purposes and not their own.[17] In fact, God is, by definition, free to use human

---

[13] For a general comment on Locke's use of Biblical text in the *TTG*, see Rahe, *Republics Ancient and Modern*, 488–93.

[14] See David Foster, "The Bible and Natural Freedom," in *Piety and Humanity: Essays on Religion and Early Modern Political Philosophy*, ed. Douglas Kries (Lanham, MD: Rowman and Littlefield, 1997), 192–3.

[15] See Thomas L. Pangle, *The Spirit of Modern Republicanism: The Moral Vision of the American Founders and the Philosophy of Locke* (Chicago: University of Chicago Press, 1988), 142–3.

[16] Locke (*TTG* 2.2.6) says of human beings that they are God's property because God created them: "they are his property, whose workmanship they are."

[17] See Foster, "The Bible and Natural Freedom," 195.

beings by destroying them because of His property in them. The accounts of the grants given to Adam and Noah, as Locke elucidates them, do not support the conclusions of reason.

An examination by reason of God's dominion over the earth shows that His rule is harsh and tyrannical. In his *First Treatise*, Locke asks whether or not Adam's dominion over the earth conferred on him an "Arbitrary Authority over the Persons of Men." He concludes that a just God would not give such "*Private Dominion*" to a sovereign. This is because "the most specious thing to be said, is, that he that is Proprietor of the Whole World, may deny all the rest of Mankind Food, and so at his pleasure starve them" (*TTG* 1.5.40–1).[18] Locke goes further in finding it unbelievable that God would grant an earthly sovereign "Power to destroy them [human beings] when he pleased." While Locke speaks here of Adam or a hypothetical earthly ruler, the phrase "Proprietor of the Whole World" suggests God, the Creator and Owner of the world (*TTG* 1.4.41). As Locke has pointed out, however, God *does* deny His people food and originally granted humanity "the Herbs but in common with the Beasts" (*TTG* 1.4.39). While this may have been adequate in the Garden of Eden, God does not extend the grant of food to include meat after Adam and Eve are expelled from the Garden. Furthermore, the mention of Noah should remind Locke's readers that God did indeed destroy almost all the human beings on the earth at one time. What Locke finds impossible to believe that God would grant to an earthly ruler to do, God Himself has done. If a just God would not allow an earthly sovereign to starve or destroy humanity, how could it be just of God to do these things Himself?

One might say that the justice of these actions consisted in their being deserved as punishment for sins. Adam and Eve sinned in the Garden, and they deserved the hardship they suffered afterward. Locke grants that Adam and Eve might deserve such treatment, but he denies that God meant to punish their children and descendants for the sins committed by their parents. God speaks to Adam "in the Singular Number" and does not mean to include all humanity in the punishment (*TTG* 1.5.46).[19] Eve's subjection to her husband and pain in childbirth were "a Punishment laid upon *Eve*." In her curse there is "no more Law to oblige a woman to such a Subjection . . . then there is, that she should bring forth her Children in Sorrow and Pain" (*TTG* 1.5.47).[20] To punish all humanity for a crime committed by only two members of the human species would be to punish all the others aside from these two undeservedly.[21] God does not speak to Eve as a representative of women but "foretels what should be the Womans Lot" (*TTG* 1.5.47). Women in general may suffer from the subjection to their husbands and pain in childbirth, but it is not a

---

[18] See ibid., 196–7.
[19] See Pangle, *The Spirit of Modern Republicanism*, 144.
[20] See Strauss, *Natural Right and History*, 215–16.
[21] See Pangle, *The Spirit of Modern Republicanism*, 144–5; Foster, "The Bible and Natural Freedom," 201–4.

punishment they deserve. Similarly, men and human beings in general may suffer from poverty and the necessity to labor, but it is not a punishment they deserve. If human beings do not deserve such suffering, then it cannot be just on God's part to inflict this suffering on them.[22] If undeserved poverty, subjection, and pain are the gifts of God to His people, then God is unjust. He is a tyrant.

The root of this tyranny is the fact that God is indistinguishable from fortune or nature. In the penultimate chapter of *The Prince*, God and fortune are all but explicitly equated, and Machiavelli quickly drops any mention of God in his account of the forces that affect human life (P 25).[23] In the *Second Treatise*, human beings originate not in a Garden of Eden ruled by God, but in a natural state in which the primary law is given to them by nature. Human beings must understand and exert control over nature in order to live well. If they do not, they leave their fates in the hands of dumb luck. The faith that God will clothe His people as He does the lilies of the field is, in the eyes of both Machiavelli and Locke, ruinous naïveté.

The Liberation from Teleology

Such naïveté is not instilled by theology alone. It is also instilled by philosophy. Ancient political philosophy of the Aristotelian variety opens the mind to teachings such as those propagated by Christianity. It is not enough, therefore, to liberate humanity from explicit theological doctrines. The mind must also be liberated from the philosophical culprit that opens it to such doctrines, and this is teleology.[24] As Markus Fischer points out in the prologue to this book, Aristotelian teleology is the teaching that the good is the natural human end or fulfillment. Aristotle claims that man is by nature distinguished from the other beings, living or otherwise, by the possession of the faculty of reason. Mere possession of this faculty is not enough to make a person happy. The faculty of reason must be used. This means that happiness is an activity of the "rational element" or at least one in harmony with it. Furthermore, this activity must be carried on in the proper fashion with a view to excellence (*Eth. Nic.* 1098a). Reason and virtue must be cultivated, and Aristotle recognizes that most human beings do not cultivate either. Most, "living under the sway of emotion," pursue pleasure and avoid pain and "do not even have a notion of what is noble" (*Eth. Nic.* 1179b10–15). Such human beings cannot be persuaded by argument or reason to pursue the noble or virtuous and, therefore, must be educated by

---

[22] Cf. Peter Myers, *Our Only Star and Compass: Locke and the Struggle for Political Rationality* (Lanham, MD: Rowman and Littlefield, 1998), 179–244, who disputes this reading by referring to Locke's particular interpretation of Christianity. This interpretation, however, is not necessarily the same as traditional Christianity. Locke's revised Christianity may provide its believers with a foundation for independence. Locke's criticism of traditional Christianity is that it does not provide such a foundation.

[23] See Strauss, *Thoughts on Machiavelli*, 221; Mansfield, "Introduction," in *P*, xxiii.

[24] See Mansfield, "Machiavelli's Political Science," in *Machiavelli's Virtue*, 279.

habituation (*Eth. Nic.* 1103a25). Observance of good laws provides the habituation needed. The highest function of political life is to provide its participants
with the means to make actual their potential for activity in accordance with
the good. At its best, political life should lead citizens to the achievement of the
excellence of which they are capable (*Eth. Nic.* 1103b).[25]

As Markus Fischer makes clear in the prologue, Machiavelli simply rejects
this idea as a fond dream. Human beings "desire to acquire," and the necessity
of the world in which they find themselves requires it (*P* 4).[26] This Machiavellian
teaching is reflected in Locke's assertion that human beings in their original
state were forced to labor because "the penury of [their] condition required it"
(*TTG* 2.5.32). Human beings were not required to labor for the sake of some
idle philosopher's dream of perfection but for the sake of the acquisition of the
property that would keep them alive. The cold necessities of an uncaring world
drive human beings to appropriate pieces of that world to themselves, and the
process of acquisition does not admit of the leisure to pursue idealistic notions
of nobility.

On the basis of the teaching that the noble is the ground of justice, Machiavelli tells us, thinkers of the past have "imagined republics and principalities
that have never been seen or known to exist." The reason that they have not
existed is that they cannot. The sincere attempt to live a virtuous life is disas-
trously naïve because "it is so far from how one lives to how one should live that
he who lets go of what is done for what should be done learns his ruin rather
than his preservation" (*P* 15).[27] The life of virtue is not, as Aristotle would
have it, the expression of human nature. For Machiavelli, as Markus Fischer
points out in the prologue to this book, human beings are rather as Aristotle
describes the vulgar. They pursue pleasures and the means to pleasures, and
they flee pains. According to Aristotle, this means that they cannot be happy.
According to Machiavelli, they are doing what nature or necessity forces them
to do. Machiavelli drops the notion that there is any end or fulfillment of human
nature at all, much less one that leads to happiness.

Instead, human beings are filled with restless desires, and their "appetites
are insatiable" (*D* 2.pref.3). This is their true nature, for "nature has created
men so that they are able to desire everything" (*D* 1.37.1). Insatiable appetite

---

[25] See, however, Quentin Skinner, "Machiavelli's *Discorsi* and the Pre-Humanist Origins of Republican Ideas"; Maurizio Viroli, "Machiavelli and the Republican Idea of Politics," in *Machiavelli
and Republicanism*, ed. Gisela Bock, Quentin Skinner, and Maurizio Viroli (Cambridge, UK:
Cambridge University Press, 1990), 121–71 (esp. 137, 158–60). For a rebuttal of Skinner's view,
see Rahe, "Situating Machiavelli," 278–92.

[26] See Mansfield, "Machiavelli's Virtue," 13–14, who notes that acquisition is not, as with Aristotle,
for the sake of leisure but for the sake of getting ahead of one's rivals.

[27] See, however, Viroli, "Machiavelli and the Republican Idea of Politics," 166–71; *Machiavelli*,
50–6; Quentin Skinner, *The Foundations of Modern Political Thought I: The Renaissance*
(Cambridge, UK: Cambridge University Press, 1978), 180–9. Viroli argues that the good statesman must be able to be bad but in the service of a good end, namely the common good. See the
following argument on the status of the common good in Machiavelli's thought.

comes from the human ability to foresee loss. Since human beings know that what they have can be lost, they consequently fear to lose what they have. Therefore, they desire the security of present possessions. They do not think, however, that they can have security without further acquisition, for "it does not appear to men that they possess securely what a man has unless he acquires something else new" (*D* 1.5.4). Nothing in the world ever satisfies human appetites fully. Men are driven by nature not toward a final fulfillment, but to constant acquisitive activity.

This picture of human nature is reflected in Locke's account in *An Essay Concerning Human Understanding*. While Locke does speak of human happiness, as does Aristotle, he discusses it in the section of the *Essay* on power and not, as one might expect of an Aristotelian, in the section on reason or virtue. In the former section, he defines happiness as "the utmost Pleasure we are capable of." Happiness is completely marred by pain or uneasiness, and "for as much as whilst we are under any uneasiness, we cannot apprehend ourselves happy," our first actions "will always be the removing of pain." We human beings cannot be happy until we are free from pains and uneasiness, but "in the multitude of wants, and desires, we are beset with in this imperfect State," we are "not like ever to be freed" from discomfort of this sort. This constant goading by nature will not "leave us free to the attraction of remoter absent good," such as our ultimate fulfillment might be (*ECHU* 2.21.36, 42, 45). If a final fulfillment of human nature did exist, human beings would not have the leisure to pursue it.

Nature's constant goading, however, is an indication that, in fact, there really is no such fulfillment. Nature moves different individuals in different ways, and there is no one satisfaction for them all so that "you will as fruitlessly endeavor to delight all Men with Riches or Glory, as you would to satisfy all Men's Hunger with Cheese or Lobsters." It is just as fruitless for philosophers such as Aristotle to ask "whether *Summum Bonum* [greatest good] consisted in Riches, or bodily Delights, or Virtue, or Contemplation." Human beings all choose different ends, but they "all chuse right" (*ECHU* 2.21.55).[28] There is no one true end in contrast to many wrong ones. There are many "ends" of human nature because there are many passions. Such passions come and go, and individuals seek to satisfy them as they arise. Locke's description of human nature directly reflects the Machiavellian image of restless humanity seeking to avoid pain through continual acquisition.[29]

---

[28] See Rahe, *Republics Ancient and Modern*, 293–8.

[29] Hence Strauss, *Natural Right and History*, 251, characterizes the life depicted by Locke as "the joyless quest for joy." In *Our Only Star and Compass* (esp. 137–72), Myers argues that Strauss's characterization here is exaggerated. There is a rational content to Locke's understanding of human happiness in that human happiness consists of rationally forming a life plan. Since reason does play a decisive part in happiness and thus virtue, rationality in others forms a potential basis for mutual admiration and true friendship. This subtler presentation of happiness softens Locke's critique of teleology and its political implications, but it does not undo them.

If human nature has no one fulfillment, then the lives of individual human beings cannot be united by one common good. Locke suggests that there may be an infinite variety of ends that individuals pursue. It is not immediately evident from his discussion of human nature that their ends might not be compatible. This conclusion seems to be contradicted by Machiavelli's statement about the common good in republics. He says in the *Discourses* that the "common good is not observed if not in republics," and that "it is not the particular good but the common good that makes cities great" (*D* 2.2.1). What he means by the common good, however, is not the same as what Aristotle means. As Markus Fischer shows us in the prologue to this book, Machiavellian republics achieve their good by crushing the few (*D* 2.2.1). In Machiavelli's account, the pursuit of the common good may be good for most but bad for others.

This understanding of the common good violates the Aristotelian notion of distributive justice. In other words, the pursuit of the common good as Machiavelli describes it is not just. Aristotle clearly identifies distributive justice as justice in distributing rewards and punishments. Those who deserve rewards should receive them, while those who deserve punishments should get what they deserve (*Eth. Nic.* 1131a25). It is clear that many of those whom Machiavelli says might be crushed by the republic in its pursuit of the public good are, as Fischer notes in the prologue, innocents. He explicitly says that the justification of the harm done them is not that they deserve it but that a great number of others benefit. Machiavelli's praise of Borgia's execution of his lieutenant, Remirro, nowhere mentions the justice of that punishment (*P* 7). Remirro was to reduce to order a province that was full of violence and crime. While he was cruel in carrying out his orders, it may well be that the criminal inhabitants of the province richly deserved their cruel treatment. In any case, Machiavelli approves of cruelty well used, and Remirro's seems to be a prime example of well-used cruelty (*P* 8). Borgia executed Remirro, not because he was deserving of punishment, but because he was hated. Since that hatred might have extended to Borgia himself, Borgia purged the hatred with a public execution.[30] The execution of Remirro might have been useful, but it was not just.[31]

Machiavelli advocates a distribution of rewards and punishments that is useful to the distributor rather than one that gives to the recipient of the rewards or punishments what he deserves. There is a clear statement of this principle in *The Prince*. Machiavelli advises princes to distribute harm all at once and rewards little bit by little bit. Harm done at a stroke is felt less than drawn out harm. The sufferer can forget about it more quickly. Rewards, however, should

---

[30] See also *D* 1.16.1–6, 3.3.1, where Machiavelli states that a "memorable execution" satiates the desire of the people for revenge.

[31] Markus Fischer points out similar examples; see the prologue. See also Vickie Sullivan's discussion of the role played by ingratitude in *Cato's Letters* in Chapter 3, and John McCormick, "Machiavellian Democracy: Controlling Elites with Ferocious Populism," *APSR* 95:2 (June 2001): 298, where McCormick says that elites must be "cut down to size."

be given in small pieces over a long period of time so that they are appreciated more (*P* 8).[32] As Markus Fischer points out, utility rather than justice is the basis of Machiavelli's advice. Just distribution, according to Aristotle, is consonant with the pursuit of the common good because justice is understood relative to the good pursued. If virtue is the good, then those who are greater in virtue deserve greater reward than do those who are less virtuous. It may be that Machiavelli teaches that utility can provide a similar foundation for justice. Those who, for example, are more useful to the city would be more deserving of good – that is, of useful things – than those who are less useful. If this were the case, the citizens would have a shared interest in pursuing the city's good. Their interests would not be in conflict because the useful citizens could expect reward and the useless no reward or even punishment.

Utility, however, is not this sort of good, according to Machiavelli. Remirro was not punished because he was useless. In fact, his actions were not only useful but also necessary. If utility in the Machiavellian sense were a common good strictly speaking, then Remirro should have been rewarded. He could not be rewarded, however, because his actions, useful and necessary though they may have been, made the people of the province hate him. They could not see that he was benefiting them by reducing the violence in their province. This ignorance or error is useful to no one and so the people themselves seem worthy of punishment on account of their error. Further punishment inflicted by Remirro would probably have only increased the people's hatred, not only of Remirro but also of Borgia. Machiavelli insists that, in general, the hatred of the people is dangerous for the prince (*P* 17). Borgia, therefore, had to kill Remirro in order to purge the hatred the people felt against him. Killing Remirro was useful to Borgia. It was also useful to the people themselves. Since they were awed by the spectacle of Remirro's death, they were more likely to be peaceful among themselves and obedient to their ruler. The stability caused by the execution was good for both prince and people, but it was not good for the person who was executed. Furthermore, the person who was executed died because, while being useful, he engendered hatred. His very usefulness was the cause of his punishment. Remirro's punishment is not only unjust, but it is also a signal example of why utility in the Machiavellian sense cannot be a common good. Remirro's personal interests were incompatible with the interests of the rest of the province. They could have no good in common.

In this respect, Locke seems to differ fundamentally from Machiavelli. He makes the "regulating and preserving of property" the purpose of political power and the common aim of civil society (*TTG* 2.1.3). The protection of property becomes the foundation of justice in his teaching so that wealth shared in common might seem to be the common good. Unlike Machiavelli, Locke offers an account of natural justice in his natural law teaching. Locke speaks of the "public good" and of the right of resistance against tyranny. For these

---

[32] See Strauss, *Thoughts on Machiavelli*, 9.

reasons, it appears as though Locke understands the pursuit of property as a communal effort for the sake of common material benefit.[33]

As he points out, however, property is not something that can be truly shared in common. When he says that God gives the earth and its resources to mankind in common, he says this to indicate a problem (*TTG* 2.5.25). In order for resources to be "at all beneficial to any particular man," individuals must find "*a means to appropriate* them some way or other" (*TTG* 2.5.26). Individuals cannot use a single piece of property at the same time. Imagine two people trying to eat the same apple simultaneously. They may each get part of the apple, which is what is meant when we say that two people share an apple. They cannot each digest the same parts of the apple. Any appropriation of resources by one individual necessarily means the deprivation of another. This is because property is the "right to destroy something by using it" (*TTG* 1.4.39). Property may be a good, but it is not a common good. Furthermore, those who are deprived of a useful resource on account of another's appropriation of it do not necessarily deserve their deprivation any more than those crushed by the Machiavellian republic or principality.

It might be objected that it is Locke's natural law doctrine that splits Locke and Machiavelli decisively on the question of justice. As is pointed out in the prologue to this book, Machiavelli is notably silent concerning natural law, while Locke offers a natural law doctrine. The law of nature is the foundation of natural justice. If Locke offers a doctrine of natural justice, he must surely recognize a common good. This is not the case, however. Locke's natural law doctrine only affirms Locke's kinship with Machiavelli in the matter of justice and the common good.[34]

The law of nature, according to Locke, commands self-preservation first and the preservation of others second (*TTG* 2.2.6). It is permissible, indeed compulsory, to harm another human being if his preservation interferes with one's own self-preservation. In a world in which resources are scarce, conflict over resources would be inevitable because there would not be enough for everyone. Locke indicates that the state of nature is a state of scarcity when he says that human beings were originally required to labor because of the "penury of their condition."[35] The natural human state is one of poverty, and natural law commands human beings to compete for the sake of self-preservation. In Locke's account, natural law is not a foundation for a common good but the

---

[33] See, however, Macpherson, *The Political Theory of Possessive Individualism*, 200–1, who stresses the fact that property right is, for Locke, an individual, not a common, right.

[34] See Harvey C. Mansfield, "Burke and Machiavelli on Principles in Politics," in *Machiavelli's Virtue*, 103–5; J. W. Gough, *John Locke's Political Philosophy: Eight Studies*, 2nd edition (Oxford, UK: Clarendon Press, 1973), 1–26; Laslett, "Introduction," 79–91; Martin Seliger, *The Liberal Politics of John Locke* (London: George Allen and Unwin, 1968), 45–81; Chapter 9 of this book.

[35] *TTG* 2.5.32, 35: "[Man's] wants forced him to *labour*." Pangle, *The Spirit of Modern Republicanism*, 162–3, points out that a rule for the determination of property ownership would be meaningless in conditions of abundance.

motive behind human competitive conflict.[36] The only justice that is possible for humanity becomes possible with the human creation of civil society through the founding compact.

This is not to say that Machiavelli and Locke do not, in fact, part ways on the question of justice. Natural law is the foundation, in Locke's teaching, of the human right to life, liberty, and the pursuit of property. The concept of human rights is a moral one, and there is no corresponding concept in Machiavelli's thought.[37]

According to Machiavelli, human beings desire dominion, but dominion cannot necessarily be pursued while respecting the human right to self-preservation. On the other hand, Locke makes the pursuit of property a central human right, if not *the* human right. Since the law of nature commands self-preservation, it stands to reason that human beings are entitled to the means to their preservation, and that is property.[38]

The pursuit of property through labor in the context of a civil society is not only a right but also a way of satisfying the second command of the law of nature. The second command is that human beings "as much as [they] can... preserve the rest of mankind" (*TTG* 2.4.6). Under conditions of scarcity, as noted, the law of nature brings individuals into conflict. Such conflict is seriously harmful if not deadly. In civil society, however, the pursuit of property need not involve such conflict. Locke repeatedly emphasizes the immense productive power of human labor (*TTG* 2.5.37, 40–3, 50).[39] If the right to the profit of labor rewards human labor, and this is the very task of political power, then human labor can create ever more goods. The more goods there are circulating in an economy, the higher the material well-being of the individuals in that economy is.[40] This is because more goods are available to everyone. Not only

---

[36] See Strauss, *Natural Right and History*, 224.

[37] Judith Best, "The Innocent, the Ignorant, and the Rational: The Content of Lockian Consent," in *The Crisis of Liberal Democracy*, ed. Kenneth L. Deutsch and Walter Soffer (Albany, NY: State University of New York Press, 1987), 174, argues that natural law is, in Locke's teachings, descriptive rather than prescriptive. It is probably more accurate to say that it is both because it prefers one human motivation to another; see my discussion of Locke's suspicion of glory, later in this chapter. See also Strauss, *Natural Right and History*, 203–4, as well as Raymond Polin, "John Locke's Conception of Freedom," in *John Locke: Problems and Perspectives*, ed. John W. Yolton (Cambridge, UK: Cambridge University Press, 1969), 1–18.

[38] See Strauss, *Natural Right and History*, 235.

[39] Note Pangle, *The Spirit of Modern Republicanism*, 166, and see Paul A. Rahe, *Republics Ancient and Modern*, 500–4, and "The Political Needs of a Tool-Making Animal: Madison, Hamilton, Locke and the Question of Property," *Social Philosophy and Policy* 22:1 (Winter 2005): 1–26. David Foster, "The Bible and Natural Freedom in John Locke's Political Thought," 197–201, points out that the emphasis in the *Second Treatise* on the power of human labor indirectly underscores what little God truly gives humanity.

[40] See Macpherson, *The Political Theory of Possessive Individualism*, 211–14, who here explains the Lockeian teaching that unlimited acquisition will benefit all through the rising level of goods in production. The key to the legitimacy of this argument, according to Macpherson, is the assumption that the goods will be distributed to individuals in such quantity as to compensate them for the loss that the ownership of land by others would cause. In other words, it rests on

that, but goods are cheaper where there is abundance since scarcity makes prices go up and abundance makes them drop. Not everyone benefits equally, but the increase in material well-being provided by labor can make competition and the pursuit of property compatible not only with moral rights but also with the means to preserve them.[41] One could thus describe property, in Locke's thought, as an approximation of the common good.

It is important to keep in mind, however, that these moral rights do not rest on an Aristotelian view of justice and the common good. To repeat, Aristotle asserts that the aim of political life is the life of moral virtue. By virtue, Aristotle understands a noble mean between extremes (*Eth. Nic.* 1106a25–1107a25).[42] Furthermore, the virtuous behave virtuously for the sake of virtue itself and not for the sake of reward (*Eth. Nic.* 1099a7–22, 1115b19–24). This understanding of virtue involves the aspiration to rise above limited selfish and particularly physical needs and interests. Virtue can be a common good in the strictest sense because practicing it and sharing it with others (for example, through education) necessitate no loss to the virtuous person in the way that a sharing of status and property would. In rejecting Aristotelian teleology, Machiavelli and Locke adopt the limited goods of status and property and abandon the common good.

Arms of One's Own

Both Machiavelli and Locke abandon the common good for the sake of human liberty. Liberty, however, creates political problems. Individuals at liberty necessarily pursue a variety of ends. Not all human ends are mutually compatible, and individuals pursuing incompatible ends eventually come into conflict with one another. Without any higher principle than self-interest to mediate between conflicting interests, individuals must compete in order to get what they want. Therefore, competition, rather than harmony, characterizes political life. In such political circumstances, individuals must understand that they are free to act on their own behalf. They must, as Machiavelli would say, rely on arms of their own. If they do, political competition can provide goods that satisfy most people most of the time, and this is the best that can be hoped for since a true common good is impossible. The liberation from Christian and Aristotelian ideals that Machiavelli and Locke bring about, therefore, is for the sake of a competitive political life led by individuals who see themselves as self-sufficient.

---

the assumption that everyone will be able to make enough on which to live. Elsewhere (203–11), Macpherson spells out the role of money in overcoming the scarcity of nature. See also Gough, *John Locke's Political Philosophy*, 80–103; Martin Seliger, *The Liberal Politics of John Locke*, 139–208.

[41] See Strauss, *Natural Right and History*, 242–4.

[42] For discussions of the distinction between Machiavellian and Aristotelian virtue, see Richard Cox, "Aristotle and Machiavelli on Liberality," in *The Crisis of Liberal Democracy*, 125–47; Mansfield, "Machiavelli's Virtue," 6–52.

In Machiavelli's account, there are two fundamentally different political interests. The people want to be left alone, while the great want to dominate them. Even competition between these, however, does not have to result in anarchy and misery. If the great are capable of winning empire, then the people are in an enviable situation: They rule over others and enjoy the benefits of the conqueror.[43] If the great are capable of building a lasting empire, then even the conquered peoples may enjoy security just as the people of the Romagna were brought to order and peace under the cruel and tyrannical Remirro. As Markus Fischer points out in the prologue to this book, while it is true that, according to Machiavelli, conquerors are capable of horrible oppression and that republics are the worst oppressors, the Florentine also asserts that it is a good policy for republics to admit their conquered subjects into citizenship for the sake of using them to further their conquests (D 2.3.1). While this is not good for individuals who are unfortunate enough to suffer during a war, it ultimately brings more security to more people than the reign of priests, whose rule never brings security to anyone except themselves (P 9, D 2.2.2).

Competition between the great for acquisition and glory keeps the great busy. If they are struggling with one another for position and for victory, they have little time or attention to devote to dominating the people. Machiavelli introduces the idea that ambition can counteract ambition, but the competition between ambitious people is not necessarily meant to limit them.[44] It is meant to distract them. When the great compete among themselves, they (or the ones who win) secure dominion and glory, and the people are, by and large, left alone. Most of the people, therefore, are satisfied most of the time. Such satisfaction is not a common good, but it could be called an approximation of the common good. Human beings must settle for an approximation of the common good because there is, after all, no greatest good.

The success of Machiavellian political competition depends on the rehabilitation of worldly glory. The aspiration to glory in the Kingdom of God leads only to a surrender of the world to criminal men (D 2.2.2). While Machiavelli wishes to rehabilitate worldly glory, Locke is suspicious of glory as a motive of human behavior.[45] The human desire for glory is "but too keen," he writes (TTG 1.11.106). This "itch after *Honour, Power,* or *Riches*, etc.," is "fantastical" and only adds to the constant uneasiness that necessity already presses on us (ECHU 2.21.45).

Since Locke understands happiness as the diminishment, as far as possible, of uneasiness, fantastical itches only add to the difficulty of the attainment of human happiness. They not only make happiness more difficult to attain for the one who feels them, but they also have "ruin'd Cities, depopulated Countries, and disordered the Peace of the World," so that they shatter the

---

[43] See the prologue of this book, and Viroli, *Machiavelli*, 131–43.

[44] See Mansfield, "Machiavelli's New Regime," in *Machiavelli's Virtue*, 253–4.

[45] See Mansfield, "Machiavelli's Virtue," 28–9, who argues that Machiavelli, in contrast to Locke, leaves room for the aspirations of noble characters to glory.

happiness of those they attack as well (*TTG* 1.11.106). When Locke points to "an Army at the sacking of a Town" and the "Outrages they do" as proof that there are no moral principles innate to the human mind, a man who is much less impressed than Machiavelli with feats of military prowess speaks (*ECHU* 1.3.9).[46]

In Locke's view, therefore, an approximation of the common good is best derived from competition for property. This has been indicated in the preceding discussion of the law of nature. It is important to add to that discussion that Locke sees in the desire for property more than an impulse to self-preservation. While property is certainly useful for self-preservation, human beings ultimately want things in order to feel powerful.[47] Children "shew their love of Dominion" by "their desire to have things be theirs; they would have *Propriety* and Possession, pleasing themselves with the Power which that seems to give" (*STCE* 105).[48] This makes property politically useful in the extreme. Precisely because it is useful, property is a less destructive way of satisfying the human itch after power. The great can become captains of industry rather than captains of armies. Their competition for profits can produce an abundance of useful goods and services. Thus the lust for greatness can be channeled in such a way that it produces material well-being rather than the sorry "*Robberies, Murders, Rapes*" associated with unrestrained soldiery (*ECHU* 1.3.9).

If the great can be distracted by a conquest of scarcity rather than one of provinces, then the common good can be approximated much more closely than it could be otherwise. The people benefit from advancing economic prosperity, and the great command enormous empires of wealth. The great economic empires may be built on the backs of the workers, but the workers not only are not being killed while their wives and daughters are raped by soldiers, but they have opportunities for economic advancement as well.[49] Even if they cannot increase their levels of personal wealth, they have an easier life than those who live in communities that do not recognize the good to be had in the pursuit of wealth. After all, the ordinary English day laborer "is clad, feeds and lodges better than a king in the Americas" (*TTG* 2.5.41).[50] Not everyone can

---

[46] See Pangle, *The Spirit of Modern Republicanism*, 179–81.

[47] Ibid., 180–1.

[48] Nathan Tarcov, *Locke's Education for Liberty* (Chicago: University of Chicago Press, 1984), 130–2, observes that Locke juxtaposes love of dominion with love of liberty. The love of liberty should be encouraged, while the love of dominion should be discouraged. The common root of these two loves might be said to be perception of the necessity to win liberty through the domination of one's surroundings. It seems, therefore, that Locke's answer to the problem of the love of dominion, in the final analysis, is to redirect it. Locke's suspicion of glory and his moral emphasis on human rights is one of the ways in which Locke and Machiavelli truly part ways.

[49] See Pangle, *The Spirit of Modern Republicanism*, 168–9.

[50] Macpherson, *The Political Theory of Possessive Individualism*, 216–20, argues that Locke presumes that all laborers will remain at subsistence wages and that Locke did not understand that the alienation of labor through its sale for wages is equivalent to the loss of life and liberty. Pangle, *The Spirit of Modern Republicanism*, 169, offers a brief rejoinder.

command great riches, but it is possible to attain the small amount necessary
to avoid the uneasiness or fear that is common to all, and that is death. Even
though Locke is suspicious of military dominion and conquest, his political doctrine rests on the Machiavellian idea that competition among self-interested
individuals is better for human life than the collective pursuit of heaven or
virtue.

According to Machiavelli, the aspiration to nobility that is enshrined in
Christianity and ancient philosophy causes more harm than the ambition of
generals, mercenary captains, and princes. These at least are capable of winning
empire. With empire comes as much security for the people as they are likely
to get in this world. In an ecclesiastical principality, they are not defended at
all. Generals, mercenary captains, and princes are motivated to win empire by
a desire for dominion and this – worldly glory. In order to win glory, however,
someone must be admiring of the deeds that are done for the sake of glory.
If most people do not admire great deeds of political and military prowess, as
they do not under Christianity, then all that is left to the great is dominion
(*D* 2.2.2.). Since the people are also taught to endure their sufferings, the great
in Christian nations have more or less free reign. Since they are not well schooled
in the ways of political and military mastery, however, and since the Church
stands in the way of empire in the West, the great are never able to build
lasting political states. Both the people and the great are frustrated in their
desires.

In restoring the status of this-worldly glory, Machiavelli tries to eliminate
what political scientists might call a bad incentive structure. If the possibility
of worldly glory is added to the prizes that the great can hope to win, then
they become, to a certain extent, accountable to the people. This is another
benefit that may come from competition. If the great are to win worldly glory,
they must do things that the people think are glorious. While the people can
certainly be deceived, they are deceived in generalities but not in particulars.
Theology and philosophy are generalities *par excellence* and the truth of either
of these is difficult, if not impossible, for the people to judge. On the other hand,
they can see easily whether or not their leaders win or lose wars (*D* 2.18.3).[51]
Competition by the great for glory gives the people a means to judge their rulers.
Of course, this does not mean that the people have the power to get their way
all the time or to hold their rulers absolutely accountable. If the people are
taught the general rule that they should endure their sufferings and not speak
evil of evil, however, they will judge that they should not strike out against any
of their leaders (*D* 3.1.4). In this case, leaders are not accountable for their
actions at all. Rather than obey their leaders unconditionally, the people would
be best off judging and competing with them.

In the *Discourses*, Machiavelli maintains that the competition between the
Senate and the plebs of Rome was "the first cause of keeping Rome free"

---

[51] Fischer, in this book's prologue, points out that the people are far more likely to judge their
leaders wisely during war than during peace.

(*D* 1.4.1).[52] Even though the spectacle of "the people together crying out against the Senate, the Senate against the people, running tumultuously through the streets, closing shops, the whole plebs leaving Rome," may seem terrifying, such competition is necessary (*D* 1.4.1).[53] The reason for this is that "every city ought to have its modes with which the people can vent its ambition." This is particularly true in cities, such as Rome, that wish to use its people "in important things" such as the acquisition of empire (*D* 1.4.1). In fact, the people vent ambition not only through domestic competition, but also through foreign acquisition. As Markus Fischer points out in the prologue, in Machiavelli's scheme, violent conquest is an outlet for the people and ties them to the republic (*D* 1.43.1).[54]

Not only can the people defend the republic and acquire empire for it, but also the people are better defenders of a free way of life than are the great (*D* 1.4.1).[55] It might seem that the great would be better defenders of freedom because they wish only to maintain what they have. Since the great already have satisfied their desire to acquire, it might seem that they would have no ambition to despoil others or to create disorder for the sake of gain. Machiavelli, however, denies that this is so. Those who wish to maintain what they have are driven to further acquisition, for "the fear of losing generates the same wishes that are in those who desire to acquire" (*D* 1.5.4). The great, since they have a wealth of resources, have more power at their disposal. Therefore, they wish, as the people do, to acquire, but they have more power to create disturbances than the people do, who have little (*D* 1.5.4). Furthermore, the ambitions of the people are better suited to a free life than those of the great (*D* 1.5.2, *P* 9). The great desire dominion, while the people desire not to be ruled. The people desire, in a word, freedom. They rebel because they are "oppressed" or because of "suspicion that they may be oppressed" (*D* 1.4.1). The tumult of the people against the great is, or should be, only really terrifying to the great.

The assertion that the people rise on account of their oppression or of the fear of oppression is echoed in Locke's argument for the toleration of religious dissenters. Such dissenters ought not to be feared as rebels as long as they are left free to worship as they see fit. They do not resort to rebellion because their religious beliefs teach them to do it; rather, "their Sufferings and Oppressions...make them willing to ease themselves" (*LCT* 52). The solution

---

[52] See also Skinner, *The Renaissance*, 180–1.

[53] See John McCormick, "Addressing the Political Exception: Machiavelli's 'Accidents' and the Mixed Regime," *APSR* 87:4 (December 1993): 894, who argues that disunion between the people and the great produces politically healthy *accidenti*. This understanding of the relationship between the people and the great is for the most part in accord with the interpretation offered here, but McCormick also asserts that this teaching does not represent a genuine break with Aristotle. Given the emphasis that Aristotle places on concord, this seems to involve a misreading; see the prologue.

[54] Note also McCormick, "Addressing the Political Exception," 889.

[55] See Skinner, "Machiavelli's *Discorsi* and the Pre-Humanist Origins of Republican Ideas," 139–41; McCormick, "Machiavellian Democracy," 298–9.

to the problem of religious warfare is to leave dissenters free to follow their beliefs. The solution to the problem of political strife is to leave the people free to enjoy their lives, liberty, and property. In the *Second Treatise*, Locke says:

Whenever the legislators endeavour to take away, and destroy the property of the people, or to reduce them to slavery under arbitrary power, they put themselves into a state of war with the people, who are thereupon absolved of any further obedience, and are left to the common refuge, which God hath provided for all men, against force and violence.

(*TTG* 2.19.222)

That refuge is an appeal to heaven (*TTG* 2.3.20).[56]

While it might seem that the words "appeal to heaven" suggest a pious appeal to God for relief from tyranny, this is not the manner in which Locke uses the phrase. In the third chapter of the *Second Treatise*, he denies that to appeal to heaven is to ask God to "decide the controversy." The controversy between Jephtha and the Ammonites was decided by Jephtha leading "his army to battle." To appeal to heaven is only to ask God for justification of the cause as the combatant "will answer it, at the great day, to the supreme judge of all men" (*TTG* 2.3.21). The appeal to heaven is not to have God's power in the decision of victory, because armies and not God win battles.[57] When government puts itself into a state of war with its people through abuse of power, the people should take up their arms. In other words, the appeal to heaven is a euphemism for rebellion.

It is thus in a Machiavellian spirit that Locke recommends to the people that they be vigilant and defend their liberties, even if it requires violence.[58] Human beings cannot rationally consent to their own subjection to an absolute arbitrary power. A sovereign "who has the command of 100,000" men is far more dangerous to an individual than "100,000 single men" (*TTG* 2.11.137). In the state of nature, no individual will have to face one hundred thousand enemies at once. That number of men could not act in concert outside civil society. This is Locke's point. In civil society, one hundred thousand men can act in concert because a sovereign leads them. If the sovereign decides to direct that force against an individual, he is at far less advantage than when facing even ten or twenty enemies in the state of nature. In the state of nature, one has,

[56] See also James Tully, "Locke," in *The Cambridge History of Political Thought: 1450–1700*, ed. J. H. Burns and Mark Goldie (Cambridge, UK: Cambridge University Press, 1991), 622–5.

[57] See Strauss, *Natural Right and History*, 214–15.

[58] See Nathan Tarcov, "Locke's *Second Treatise* and 'the Best Fence against Rebellion,'" *RP* 43:1 (Winter 1981): 198–217; Pangle, "Executive Energy and Popular Spirit in Lockean Constitutionalism," 253–65; Gough, *John Locke's Political Philosophy*, 134–53; Martin Seliger, *The Liberal Politics of John Locke*, 107–38; J. G. A. Pocock, "The Myth of John Locke and the Obsession with Liberalism," in *John Locke: Papers Read at a Clark Library Seminar, 10 December 1977*, ed. J. G. A. Pocock and Richard Ashcraft (Los Angeles: William Andrews Clark Memorial Library, 1980), 3–24; James Tully, "Placing the 'Two Treatises,'" in *Political Discourse in Early Modern Britain*, ed. Nicholas Phillipson and Quentin Skinner (Cambridge, UK: Cambridge University Press, 1993), 253–80; Best, "The Innocent, the Ignorant, and the Rational," 167–8; Rahe, *Republics Ancient and Modern*, 472–9.

at least, a sporting chance. While Locke does not delight in the prospect of civil unrest in the way Machiavelli seems to do, he does not see it as an unmitigated disaster.[59]

Locke's doctrine of rebellion points to what he and Machiavelli both consider to be the heart of the human political problem. This human problem can be understood as necessity or fate. In the penultimate chapter of *The Prince*, Machiavelli presents fate or Fortuna as an essentially hostile force that must be subdued (*P* 25). In the *Discourses*, he says that nature makes human beings want everything but also makes it impossible for them to fulfill their desires (*D* 1.37.1). Cities originate, in his account, either from a collective sense of insecurity or from the migrations of groups expelled from their homeland because there was no longer room for them (*D* 1.1.1–4, 2.8.1–4). In the *Two Treatises*, Locke describes the natural condition of man as one of scarcity and pain. Furthermore, the only law given to natural man leads him to conflict and war. Locke's picture of human nature as ceaselessly desiring reflects Machiavelli's image of man as naturally insatiable. Neither nature nor nature's God have provided well for humanity.

Since neither nature nor God will provide, human beings must provide for themselves. Locke's doctrine of rebellion teaches them to do just that. More importantly, however, Locke's presentation of the origins of political communities reflects the necessity imposed on humanity to care for itself. Man's original condition in the state of nature is hostile to his interests. It is also not a political state (*TTG* 2.9.124–6).[60] Political life is a product of reason's response to the "inconveniencies" of life in the state of nature (*TTG* 2.9.127). Political community is, therefore, a human artifact created by deliberate decision embodied in a social contract designed to provide for the improvement of the natural human condition. The right of rebellion follows logically from this understanding of political life. Human beings create society and government for their own ends and are free to destroy or alter them if they do not achieve the desired ends.[61]

Conclusion

John Locke's philosophy is not simply hidden Machiavellism, and I will not accuse Locke of being a straightforward Machiavellian here. There can, however, be no doubt that he is Machiavelli's philosophical kin. Machiavelli and Locke share a project of liberation from previous moral teachings. These are the teachings of Christianity and Aristotle. In both cases, the general accusation that Machiavelli and Locke level is that too much is being asked of human beings. They necessarily fall short of the unrealistic goals set for them by idle priests

---

[59] See Pangle, *The Spirit of Modern Republicanism*, 259.
[60] See also Hans Aarsleff, "The State of Nature and the Nature of Man in Locke," in *John Locke: Problems and Perspectives*, 99–136.
[61] See Mansfield, *Taming the Prince*, 187.

and philosophers, and, in the process, they become both weak and needlessly cruel.[62] The unavoidable outcome of this is pointless suffering.

Machiavelli is no moralist. The reason for this must be, at least in part, his view that morality causes pointless suffering. In his rejection of high ideals, he hopes to improve human life. Locke is not as sanguine as Machiavelli about the possibility of such improvement in the absence of a moral order, but the purpose of the order that he has in mind is largely utilitarian. The law of nature gives the people a standard to which to appeal when they resist tyrannical government. Consideration of this purpose points to a question as yet unanswered. If Machiavelli and Locke were so eager to jettison a demanding moral order, why did they, in their desire to overcome Christian cruelty, so insistently demand a manifestly moral goal?

---

[62] See ibid., 123–31.

3

Muted and Manifest English Machiavellianism

The Reconciliation of Machiavellian Republicanism with Liberalism in Sidney's Discourses Concerning Government *and Trenchard's and Gordon's* Cato's Letters

Vickie B. Sullivan

When selecting the curriculum for the university that he had founded, Thomas Jefferson identified the sources from which he believed the American principles of government derived. The minutes of the 4 March 1825 meeting of the Board of Visitors for the University of Virginia report the following resolution: "it is the opinion of this Board that as to the general principles of liberty and the rights of man, in nature and in society, the doctrines of Locke, in his 'Essay concerning the true original extent and end of civil government,' and of Sidney in his 'Discourses on government,' may be considered as those generally approved by our fellow citizens of this, and the United States" (*WrTJ* [ed. Peterson] 479). The Board enjoined its scholars to imbibe the prescribed dose of American liberty directly from its sources in the thought of these two Englishmen.

What was so apparent to Virginia's Board of Visitors is no longer clear to scholars of the American founding. The Board's declaration challenges in at least two fundamental ways the course of several decades of prominent scholarship on the founding. First, it asserts the importance of John Locke; and second, it asserts that the thought of Locke and Algernon Sidney are compatible.

The principles of the American revolutionaries, this scholarship maintains, were republican, inspired by Niccolò Machiavelli, not liberal, inspired by John Locke. In this way, the republican scholarship argues that Locke's thought was largely irrelevant to the work of the American revolutionaries.[1] Not only does

[1] See J. G. A. Pocock, *The Machiavellian Moment: Florentine Political Thought and the Atlantic Republican Tradition* (Princeton, NJ: Princeton University Press, 1975), 545. See also Gordon S. Wood, *The Creation of the American Republic, 1776–1787* (Chapel Hill, NC: University of North Carolina Press, 1969). Although Caroline Robbins' book, *The Eighteenth-Century Commonwealthman: Studies in the Transmission, Development and Circumstance of English Liberal*

I am grateful to Paul A. Rahe and Michael P. Zuckert for their helpful comments on earlier drafts of this chapter. Any errors that remain are my own. My interpretations of Sidney's *Discourses* and of *Cato's Letters* appear in expanded form in Vickie B. Sullivan, *Machiavelli, Hobbes, and the Formation of a Liberal Republicanism in England* (New York: Cambridge University Press, 2004).

this scholarship maintain the existence of two different traditions, it argues that these two traditions, Lockean liberalism and Machiavellian republicanism, offer mutually contradictory alternatives. Machiavelli's thought represents a recourse to a republicanism that derives from Aristotle in placing a premium on a type of political participation characterized by the renunciation of individuals' selfish interests in the name of the public good.[2] Locke, more selfish and more modern, provides an individualistic understanding of the relation between a state and its citizens. In the Lockean view, the role of the state is not to provide fulfillment of a fundamentally political human nature, but merely to protect individuals in their private pursuits. According to the classical republican scholarship, then, because Locke and Machiavelli represent mutually contradictory alternatives, where Lockean elements are present, Machiavellian ones must be absent, and where Machiavellian elements exist, Lockean ones will surely be eschewed. Therefore, Jefferson's linking of Locke and Sidney challenges the scholars who draw a distinction between these two traditions because Sidney clearly draws on the teachings of Machiavelli.[3] According to the republican scholarship, then, Sidney belongs on the other side of the divide, but Jefferson ignores the chasm, finding compatible the theories of Sidney and Locke.

Another approach to assessing the intellectual influences on the founding generation – that is, a survey of reading material available in colonial libraries – underscores Jefferson's claim for the importance of Sidney and Locke, and also introduces a third important influence. John Trenchard's and Thomas Gordon's *Cato's Letters*, Locke's *Second Treatise of Government*, and Sidney's *Discourses Concerning Government* were the English texts most often housed in these libraries.[4] Again, one finds that Locke's thought is prominent. Although the

---

Thought from the Restoration of Charles II until the War with the Thirteen Colonies (Cambridge, MA: Harvard University Press, 1959), is a precursor to the later works of the republican interpretation, it does not exclude John Locke from this commonwealth tradition but notes that "he had no sentimental attachment to Commonwealth experiments" (58–67).

[2] Pocock emphasizes this Aristotelian element in his characterization of "civic humanism" that flowed through Machiavelli to the American founders (*The Machiavellian Moment*, 203). Pocock follows Zera S. Fink, *The Classical Republicans: An Essay in the Recovery of a Pattern of Thought in Seventeenth-Century England* (Evanston, IL: Northwestern University Press, 1945), in portraying Machiavelli and his influence in terms of a recourse to the classical republicanism of Polybius' theory of the mixed regime. For a discussion of Machiavelli's rejection of Polybius, see Harvey C. Mansfield, "Machiavelli and the Idea of Progress," in Mansfield, *Machiavelli's Virtue* (Chicago: University of Chicago Press, 1996), 116–19, and of the classical understanding generally, see Neal Wood, "The Value of Asocial Sociability: Contributions of Machiavelli, Sidney and Montesquieu," in *Machiavelli and the Nature of Political Thought*, ed. Martin Fleisher (New York: Atheneum, 1972), 287–8.

[3] Felix Raab maintains that "Sidney was the 'classical' republican *par excellence*"; see Raab, *The English Face of Machiavelli: A Changing Interpretation, 1500–1700* (London: Routledge and Kegan Paul, 1964), 221.

[4] H. Trevor Colbourn, *The Lamp of Experience: Whig History and the Intellectual Origins of the American Revolution* (Chapel Hill, NC: University of North Carolina Press, 1965), 199–232; Peter Karsten, *Patriot-Heroes in England and America: Political Symbolism and Changing Values over Three Centuries* (Madison, WI: University of Wisconsin Press, 1978), 34–5. See also

declaration of the Board of Virginia presumes that the thought of Locke and Sidney are compatible in their exposition of the principles of liberty, the survey of reading material makes no such presumption. Nevertheless, the popularity of these three particular works indicates that the founding generation was seeking guidance from what contemporary scholarship deems to be distinct and contradictory traditions.

Even in this case, though, the republican interpretation faces the presence or intermingling of purportedly distinct traditions, as in the case of Jefferson's delineating of the sources of American liberty. Not only does Sidney make use of Machiavelli's theories, but Cato is particularly vocal in expressing approval for the ideas of the Florentine. Despite their use of Machiavelli, both Sidney and Cato share important ideas with Locke.[5] Because Sidney and Cato were such popular conveyers of the thought of Machiavelli, they must receive special consideration in any story that traces the influence of Machiavelli on the new world. Moreover, not only were they themselves important resources in American libraries of the revolutionary period, but they were also central in the intellectual formation of Montesquieu, another admirer of Machiavelli.[6] Montesquieu, in turn, provided further inspiration for the Americans.[7] In examining the role of Machiavelli in the writings of Sidney and Cato, a scholar must also confront the question that the resolution of the Board of Visitors for the University of Virginia and the surveys of colonial library holdings raise: What is the relationship between the English admirers of Machiavelli and the teachings of Locke that the Americans also favored? In delineating the manner in which Sidney and Cato appeal to the thought of Machiavelli, this chapter will corroborate Margaret Michelle Barnes Smith's finding in Chapter 2 that some Machiavellian and Lockean elements can coexist harmoniously.[8] In important respects, then, both Sidney and Cato can be termed Machiavellian; nevertheless, the Machiavellianism of each does not signify that they are utterly suspicious

Steven M. Dworetz, *The Unvarnished Doctrine: Locke, Liberalism, and the American Revolution* (Durham, NC: Duke University Press, 1990), 35, 41; Michael P. Zuckert, *Natural Rights and the New Republicanism* (Princeton, NJ: Princeton University Press, 1994), 20.

[5] Ronald Hamowy, "*Cato's Letters*, John Locke, and the Republican Paradigm," *HPT* 11:2 (Summer 1990): 273–94, and Alan Craig Houston, *Algernon Sidney and the Republican Heritage in England and America* (Princeton, NJ: Princeton University Press, 1991), 5–8, 164–5, show the agreement between their respective subjects and the thought of Locke but distance them from Machiavelli in apparent reliance on the classical republican interpretation of Machiavelli.

[6] See Robert Shackleton, "Montesquieu and Machiavelli: A Reappraisal," *Comparative Literature Studies* 1 (1964): 1–13, and Chapter 5 of this book. See also Wood, "The Value of Asocial Sociability," 298–9.

[7] Houston, *Algernon Sidney and the Republican Heritage in England and America*, 258; Donald S. Lutz, "The Relative Influence of European Writers on Late Eighteenth-Century American Political Thought," *APSR* 78:1 (March 1984): 189–97.

[8] See Chapter 2 of this book; Thomas L. Pangle, *The Spirit of Modern Republicanism: The Moral Vision of the American Founders and the Philosophy of Locke* (Chicago: University of Chicago Press, 1988), 30; Paul A. Rahe, *Republics Ancient and Modern: Classical Republicanism and the American Revolution* (Chapel Hill, NC: University of North Carolina Press, 1992), 472–9.

of important doctrines that came to be associated with the liberalism to which Locke gave his name.

Sidney's Muted Machiavellianism

Executed for his involvement in the Rye House Plot during the reign of Charles II, Sidney was both theorist and hero for the Americans. Both roles, intellectual forbear and heroic martyr, are closely intertwined in his reception in America,[9] as well they should be, because the prosecution used his ideas as espoused in his *Discourses Concerning Government* as the second witness necessary for conviction for treason under English law. Surely, the ability of the English Whigs to apotheosize Sidney's memory derives from the manner of his death, but there is also evidence – particularly in America – for an appreciation of Sidney's theory unencumbered by the memory of his heroism, as the declaration of the University of Virginia's Board of Visitors makes clear.

As that declaration indicates, Sidney is an outspoken advocate for liberty. More specifically, he vindicates human liberty by repudiating the doctrines of Robert Filmer, whose *Patriarcha* maintains that nature and God dictate human dependency. Human beings, in Filmer's view, are born subject to a rigidly hierarchical chain of command that passes upward from the father, to the king, and finally to God. On the way to his repudiation of the Filmerian divine right of kings, Sidney produced the diffuse *Discourses Concerning Government*, which, among many other topics, considers the corrupting influence of monarchy, the unreasonable character of inheritance as a claim to rule, and the vigor of republics.

Although scholars have frequently noted a Machiavellian element in his admiration for republics,[10] scholars have not fully explored the extent to which

---

[9] See Houston, *Algernon Sidney and the Republican Heritage in England and America*, 235; Blair Worden, *Roundhead Reputations: The English Civil Wars and the Passions of Posterity* (London: Penguin Press, 2001), 129. For considerations of Sidney's impact in America, see Caroline Robbins, "Algernon Sidney's *Discourses Concerning Government*: Textbook on Revolution," *WMQ* 4:3 (July 1947): 267–96; Bernard Bailyn, *The Ideological Origins of the American Revolution* (Cambridge, MA: Harvard University Press, 1967), 34–5; Karsten, *Patriot-Heroes*, 38–44.

[10] See Fink, *The Classical Republicans*, 155–8; Raab, *The English Face of Machiavelli*, 221–3; Jonathan Scott, *Algernon Sidney and the English Republic, 1623–1677* (Cambridge, UK: Cambridge University Press, 1988), 13, 15, 17–18, 30–3; *Algernon Sidney and the Restoration Crisis, 1677–1683* (Cambridge, UK: Cambridge University Press, 1991), 350, 354, 357–8; Edward G. West, foreword to Algernon Sidney, *Discourses Concerning Government*, (Indianapolis, IN: Liberty Classics, 1990), xxii; Wood, "The Value of Asocial Sociability," 292–9; Worden, *Roundhead Reputations*, 140; Blair Worden, "The Commonwealth Kidney of Algernon Sidney," *Journal of British Studies* 24:1 (January 1985): 18–19; Blair Worden, "Classical Republicanism and the Puritan Revolution" in *History and Imagination: Essays in Honor of H. R. Trevor-Roper*, ed. Hugh Lloyd-Jones, Valerie Pearl, and Blair Worden (New York: Holmes and Meier, 1981), 188. Scott is the only one of these scholars who examines in any extended fashion Sidney's reliance on Machiavelli's thought (*Algernon Sidney and the Restoration Crisis*, 235–7). In contrast, Houston denies that Machiavelli exerted an important influence on Sidney (*Algernon Sidney and the Republican Heritage in England and America*, 164–5).

Sidney follows Machiavelli in both method and substance when he does not explicitly refer to the Florentine. The lack of attention to these passages on the part of those interested in Sidney's Machiavellian origins is far from surprising given that Sidney appears to wish to obscure the source for his ruminations. Although it is easy to dismiss Sidney's *Discourses* as too maddeningly convoluted to contain a method, I shall argue that the development of this work contains two seemingly contradictory purposes: first, to mimic the manner in which his Florentine master presents important arguments; and second, to appear to maintain a respectable distance from that very master. Despite Sidney's best efforts, however, the very rhetoric that seeks to distance itself from Machiavelli actually ties the Englishman more closely to that association he would prefer to avoid. Sidney's rhetorical style is thoroughly Machiavellian.[11]

To assert that Machiavelli's prose style is distinctive is to risk an understatement. Indeed, a recent scholar characterizes Machiavelli's rhetoric as featuring the following elements: a "dichotomizing mode of argument, hyperbolic and theatrical style, apparent contradictions and deliberately failed examples." These elements serve to educate his readers in politics: "Because [Machiavelli's] goal is to make the reader deliberate more effectively about the realm of practical political action, he duplicates on the rhetorical level the practical problem of judgment that the prince will have to face."[12]

Sidney imports this style of argumentation into his own *Discourses*. He follows Machiavelli's rhetoric, for example, when he argues for one of the central points of the Florentine's *Discourses on Livy*: the superiority of bellicose Rome to all other republics. Like Machiavelli, Sidney does not embrace this conclusion without travail, subjecting initial conclusions to fundamental revision. So close

---

[11] Worden explores the possibility that when John Toland edited Sidney's manuscript in the late 1690s, he largely rewrote it (*Roundhead Reputations*, 13, 95–121). Ultimately, however, Worden concludes that "[w]e probably have, in the *Discourses*, more or less the text Sidney wrote" (131–2, see also 144). One particularly interesting aspect of Worden's claim for Toland's editorship of the *Discourses* is that Toland is the known author of *Tetradymus*. In the second part of that work, entitled "Clidophorus, or of the Exoteric and Esoteric Philosophy," Toland argues that ancient and modern authors alike have hidden their true meanings for the sake of self-preservation. The rhetoric of the *Discourses Concerning Government* that obscures Sidney's reliance on Machiavelli's teachings is strikingly akin to the type of dissimulating writing that Toland describes in this work. The question that arises from this recognition is whether Toland might be responsible both for the deep reliance on Machiavelli's teachings in Sidney's *Discourses* as it has come down to us and for the attempt to obscure the depth of that reliance. A comparison of the *Discourses Concerning Government* with the *Court Maxims*, written in the mid-1660s but not discovered until 1976, for which Sidney was almost certainly solely responsible, seems to support Toland's responsibility for the later work, because, although Sidney also makes use of Machiavelli's thought, his attitude toward it is very different. See, for example, Sidney, *CM* 2.13–14; on this point, see also Scott, *Algernon Sidney and the English Republic*, 191. This difference buttresses Worden's suggestion that Toland may have played a significant role in editing Sidney's *Discourses* (*Roundhead Reputations*, 144). Nevertheless, given this uncertainty regarding the authorship of the work, I will refer to its author as Sidney.

[12] See Victoria Kahn, *Machiavellian Rhetoric: From the Counter-Reformation to Milton* (Princeton, NJ: Princeton University Press, 1994), 26, 32.

is Sidney's rhetoric to Machiavelli's that it cannot fail to serve the same end, either through intent or through practical effect, of informing the judgment of his readers. In the end Sidney shows, as does Machiavelli, that that judgment must accept the necessity – indeed, the desirability – of war. These conclusions, in turn, force Sidney to break with the philosophical authority of Aristotle,[13] to whom Sidney often refers and whom he clearly follows early in his *Discourses* when he offers the dictum that *"homo est animal rationale"* (*DCG* 1.18.60; see also 1.16.51). In effect, in the course of his *Discourses*, Sidney moves from espousing the highly respectable republicanism of Aristotle to the belligerent republicanism of Machiavelli. Whereas Aristotle's republicanism endeavors to cultivate the reason of its citizens, Machiavelli's endeavors to unleash their passions. Sidney's desire to dissemble his allegiance to Machiavelli is hardly surprising given the fact that even in the latter part of the seventeenth century, Machiavelli's name carried "pejorative overtones" in England.[14]

Despite relying on Machiavelli's political teachings, Sidney does his utmost to distance himself from Machiavelli. As a consideration of Sidney's use of the Machiavellian principle that endorses a periodic return to first principles will show, Sidney finds reason to dispute his teacher's conclusions even when compelled to acknowledge Machiavelli's tutelage. This dispute notwithstanding, Sidney embraces, with a relish that surpasses even Machiavelli's, the import of this particular lesson of his mentor. Sidney gleefully endorses the necessity of ferocity in punishing wrongdoers. But Sidney applies that Machiavellian ferocity to a liberal purpose, that of punishing a despotic ruler's encroachment on the rights of citizens.[15]

In the entirety of his first chapter, Sidney does not mention Machiavelli's name. The extent of Sidney's deliberate reticence regarding his deep reliance on Machiavelli's thought is revealed by the fact that the Englishman suppresses Machiavelli's name when he agrees with one of his maxims very early in his work, but provides that name, when in the third and last chapter of the work, he mentions the same idea, attributes it to Machiavelli, and disagrees with it. The care that Sidney so evidently takes to distance himself from Machiavelli in each of these two instances allows us to conclude that Sidney's initial silence with regard to Machiavelli is a product of coyness rather than of ignorance.[16]

Sidney borrows from Machiavelli when he declares early in his work that "'tis an eternal truth, that a weak or wicked prince can never have a wise council, nor receive any benefit by one that is imposed upon him, unless they have a power of acting without him, which would render the government in

---

[13] The civic humanist interpretation would not necessarily discern an important difference between a reliance on Machiavelli and one on Aristotle. I address the incompatibility between the two thinkers later in this chapter.

[14] See Raab, *The English Face of Machiavelli*, 183–4, 226.

[15] Cf. Chapter 2, where Smith identifies this Machiavellian spirit in Locke's theory of resistance.

[16] Cf. John Toland's "distinction" between *"the External and Internal Doctrine"*: Toland, *Tetradymus* (London: J. Brotherton and W. Meadows, 1720), 85.

effect aristocratical, and would probably displease our author [Filmer] as much as if it were so in name also" (*DCG* 1.3.14). In Chapter 23 of *The Prince*, Machiavelli broaches this very issue of a deficient prince being advised by an astute subordinate:

> For this is a general rule that never fails: that a prince who is not wise by himself cannot be counseled well, unless indeed by chance he should submit himself to one person alone to govern him in everything, who is a very prudent man. In this case he could well be, but it would not last long because that governor would in a short time take away his state.   (*P* 18)

Sidney agrees with Machiavelli's conclusion that the existence of so clever an advisor will transform the character of the state. Moreover, Sidney is as convinced as is Machiavelli of the veracity of this maxim. Sidney's "eternal truth" is a clear echo of Machiavelli's "general rule that never fails." Nevertheless, Sidney assiduously fails to credit Machiavelli for this idea.

Much later in the *Discourses*, Sidney returns to the same issue. This time he credits Machiavelli with the idea, but disagrees with him: "... tho it were not impossible (as Machiavelli says it is) for a weak prince to receive any benefit from a good council, we may certainly conclude, that a people can never expect any good council chosen by one who is weak or vicious" (*DCG* 3.16.404–5). Sidney seems willing to attribute an idea to Machiavelli, if he disagrees with it explicitly, but when he agrees with the Florentine, he refuses to acknowledge his source; this strategy is consistent throughout the entirety of the work. His Machiavellianism is muted. Sidney's reluctance to identify himself with his teacher almost certainly stems from the disreputable character of Machiavelli's thought. Nevertheless, Sidney's rhetorical style reveals its author to be quite Machiavellian.

Sidney becomes quite Machiavellian when in Chapter 2 he argues for the necessity of war. In making his case, Sidney borrows not only the matter of Machiavelli's arguments but also the manner of their presentation, and he does not bother to cite his source. The passions of human beings demand that states must always maintain a posture of war. War, in turn, dictates that a state that is to persevere in such a hostile environment must cultivate the passions – not the reason – of it citizens. Sidney's ever deepening adherence to Machiavellian necessity impels Sidney to jettison the remainder of his Aristotelian predilections.[17]

Machiavelli is quite outspoken about his own divergence from classical authorities. He announces that he differs from his predecessors in taking as

---

[17] Although the civic humanist interpretation of Machiavelli does not discern this type of incompatibility between Aristotle and Machiavelli, Pocock does recognize that Machiavelli introduces an innovation within the Aristotelian paradigm: Machiavelli's "armed virtù" allows citizens to fulfill their human nature by bearing arms in service of their republic (*The Machiavellian Moment*, 202). For a criticism of Pocock's claim for Aristotle's influence on Machiavelli in this regard, see Vickie B. Sullivan, "Machiavelli's Momentary 'Machiavellian Moment': A Reconsideration of Pocock's Treatment of the *Discourses*," *Political Theory* 20:2 (May 1992): 309–18.

his guide the "effectual truth" because "it is so far from how one lives to how one should live that he who lets go of what is done for what should be done learns his ruin rather than his preservation" (*P* 15). Thus, according to Machiavelli, those who, like Aristotle, had not taken mere preservation as their guide are purveyors of a noxious teaching.[18] Because Sidney wishes to learn the requirements for preservation, he listens to Machiavelli's arguments in favor of Rome and emerges a devoted Machiavellian.

Rome, and therewith Machiavelli's analysis of it, becomes Sidney's focus when Filmer's castigation of Rome's governance under the republic provokes Sidney to defend the honor of the martial republic. Filmer's claim that "Rome began her empire under Kings, and did perfect it under Emperors,"[19] is simply false, avers Sidney (*DCG* 2.12). The opening chapters of Machiavelli's *Discourses on Livy* furnish Sidney with the materials necessary to launch his attack against Filmer.

Sidney sides with Machiavelli on the issue of the merit of republican Rome despite the fact that his Florentine ally initially assumes a defensive position in this work when he reveals that he will use Rome as his exemplary republic. Machiavelli admits that many observers are apt to criticize Rome for the tumults that arose between the plebeians and the patricians, but such critics, he charges, do not realize that the contention between the classes was the very cause of Rome's liberty. As Markus Fischer has shown in the prologue to this volume, Machiavelli maintains that if the plebeians had not had a voice in the city's governance, the patricians' desire to oppress the people would not have been held in check.

Despite the good effects of Rome's tumults, Machiavelli concedes that there are other ways to organize a republic so as to contain domestic turmoil. Venice and Sparta, for example, avoided internal dissension, but they did so in a manner that circumscribed their ability to expand in dominion. The Spartans did not allow foreigners to become citizens, and the Venetians did not make the people soldiers in the city's army. Because the Venetians and Spartans ensured in these ways that the people's numbers and power were limited, they could not field vast armies to conquer and maintain additional possessions. Thus, it appears from Machiavelli's exposition to this point that cities can make a choice between the confusion and military might of Rome on the one hand and the domestic harmony of Sparta and Venice on the other. If the choice is made for expansion, then "it is necessary to order it like Rome and make a place for tumults and universal dissensions... for without a great number of men, and well armed, a republic can never grow, or, if it grows, maintain itself," as Machiavelli explains (*D* 1.6.4).

---

[18] See Harvey C. Mansfield, "Machiavelli's Virtue," in Mansfield, *Machiavelli's Virtue*, 13–16; Clifford Orwin, "Machiavelli's Unchristian Charity," *APSR* 72:4 (December 1978): 1217–28; Rahe, *Republics Ancient and Modern*, 261–7.

[19] See Robert Filmer, *Patriarcha and Other Political Works of Sir Robert Filmer*, ed. Peter Laslett (New York: Garland, 1984), 87.

No sooner does Machiavelli offer the choice between expansion and harmony than he rescinds his offer. As Fischer observes in the prologue to this book, Machiavelli then proceeds in this very same chapter to explain that a republic has no choice but to seek armed expansion:

[A]ll things of men are in motion and cannot stay steady, they must either rise or fall; and to many things that reason does not bring you, necessity brings you. So when a republic that has been ordered so as to be capable of maintaining itself does not expand, and necessity leads it to expand, this would come to take away its foundations and make it come to ruin sooner.

As a result of these necessities, Machiavelli unreservedly embraces Rome: "I believe that it is necessary to follow the Roman order and not that of the other republics" (*D* 1.6.4).

In sections 21–23 of Chapter 2, Sidney agrees with Machiavelli's judgment of Rome's superiority to all other republics, including Sparta. Sidney's rejection of that Spartan alternative will have significant reverberations for his apparent alliance with Aristotle. Merely the titles of these sections reveal the progression of his argument. The title of section 21 proclaims that "Mixed and Popular Governments preserve Peace, and manage Wars, better than Absolute Monarchies" (*DCG* 2.21.195). Whereas Sidney is decidedly in favor of republics, he expresses a degree of impartiality on the question of whether a republic should pursue war or peace. The title of section 23, however, abandons that element of impartiality: "That is the best Government, which best provides for War" (*DCG* 2.23.209).

In section 22, "Commonwealths Seek Peace or War According to the Variety of Their Constitutions," Sidney provides the groundwork for the conclusion he will articulate in the following section by distinguishing among three varieties of republics: those that "have been principally constituted for war"; those that "have as much delighted in peace"; and those that "having taken the middle, and (as some think) the best way, have so moderated their love to peace, as not to suffer the spirits of the people to fall, but kept them in a perpetual readiness to make war when there was occasion." Sidney designates Venice, Florence, Genoa, and Lucca as being pacific and as "aim[ing] at trade" to such a degree that they had to use mercenaries when they went to war. Although he initially groups Rome and Sparta together as cities that "seem to have intended nothing but the just preservation of liberty at home, and making war abroad," later in the section he draws a distinction between the two republics: "some of those that intended war desir'd to enlarge their territories by conquest; others only to preserve their own, and to live with freedom and safety upon them." Rome is of the first sort, and Sparta is of the second. Thus, Sparta, according to Sidney, is of the middle type that some thinkers prefer (*DCG* 2.22.202–4).

Sidney here mimics Machiavelli's manner of describing Sparta. Indeed, Machiavelli uses the term "middle way" when treating those republics that hope to avoid incursion while they shun expansion: "since one cannot, as I believe, balance this thing, nor maintain this middle way exactly, in ordering a republic there is need to think of the more honorable part and to order it so that if indeed necessity brings it to expand, it can conserve what it has seized" (*D* 1.6.4). Machiavelli rejects the "middle way" of Sparta.

Sidney not only borrows Machiavelli's notion of the equation of Sparta with the "middle way," but he will ultimately reject the "middle way" that Sparta represents on Machiavellian grounds. For eight hundred years, Machiavelli (*D* 1.2.6) claimed, the Spartans remained free, and Sidney, who makes this claim his own, explains that when they undertook "such wars as could not be carried on without money, and greater numbers of men than a small city was able to furnish...[they] fell into such straits as were never recovered" (*DCG* 2.22.204). Machiavelli and Sidney agree that Sparta's constitution could not sustain an empire, but whereas Machiavelli, when contemplating Sparta's collapse, implies that expansion is simply a necessity, Sidney here suggests that Sparta's decision to expand was freely chosen. The implication is that if Sparta had not abandoned its long-standing defensive stance, it might have persisted for an even longer period of time. Therefore, Sidney's favorable disposition toward Sparta itself persists as he resists making a decision between Sparta and Rome in this section.

In the very next section, however, Sidney rejects Sparta when he declares the necessity of following the example of Rome. His judgment comes to light when he discusses the best form of government: "that government is evidently the best, which, not relying upon what it does at first enjoy, seeks to increase the number, strength, and riches of the people." The power that Sidney seeks for his best government will be garnered through offensive forays: "when a people multiplies (as they will always do in a good climate under a good government) such an enlargement of territory as is necessary for their subsistence can be acquired only by war."[20] A state must seek such an increase because "[i]f it do not grow, it must pine and perish; for in this world nothing is permanent; that which does not grow better will grow worse" (*DCG* 2.23.209–10). Sidney adheres to Machiavelli's view that "all things of men are in motion and cannot stay steady, they must either rise or fall" (*D* 1.6.4). Sparta made the mistake of seeking permanence in a world that does not permit it. As a result, Sidney rejects the view that Sparta's middle way exemplifies the best form of government. Thus, according to Sidney's Machiavellian ruminations, Roman aggression is the only alternative (cf. *CM* 15–16).

These reflections have taken Sidney much beyond his disagreement with Filmer regarding the issue of whether Rome's empire was acquired under the republic or the emperors. On his way to vindicating the honor of republican Rome, and hence the republican principle, Sidney presents a view of the human situation that demands human preparedness against necessity. Necessity itself dictates the type of political life a state must cultivate. Rather than being organized with a view to peace, a state must be organized with a view to wars of aggrandizement.

---

[20] Cf. West, foreword to *DCG*, xxii.

This view places Sidney very much at odds with Aristotle's claims for political life. Of course, because Aristotle lived before the military achievements of republican Rome, he did not comment on them, but he knew Sparta's constitution well. Although Aristotle maintains in his *Politics* that Sparta is one of the best states that has existed, he finds important deficiencies in its constitution. Whereas Sidney and Machiavelli suggest that Sparta is not warlike enough, Aristotle locates its critical flaw in the fact that the Spartan regime is too focused on war.[21] The Spartan regime aims, he tells us, at inculcating warlike virtue in its citizens with a view to dominating others (*Pol.* 1271b1–2, 1333b4–15). According to Aristotle, because any city exists for the sake of living well, the highest purposes of the city are to be found in the highest faculties of human beings, specifically those required for participation in politics or philosophy. Both activities require the leisure that peace affords. In contrast to the position of Machiavelli and Sidney that war is the end for the best organized city, Aristotle maintains that "war must be for the sake of peace" (*Pol.* 1333a35). Because the Spartan regime promoted war and the martial virtue of courage to such a high degree, the Spartans did not know how to be at leisure. The Spartans, in Aristotle's view, were incapable of pursuing the activities of peace, and hence the true purposes of the city.

In supporting leisure, Aristotle promotes the highest faculties of human beings. Conversely, the passions of human beings find prominence in the thought of Machiavelli and Sidney, who conclude that states cannot seek the leisure that nurtures the application of reason. The passions of human beings dictate a predatory posture for a state; as the examination of Sidney's writing shows, the passions fuel not only the aggressiveness of neighboring states but also that of one's own state as prosperity promotes the desire of citizens for more – a desire that can be satisfied only by aggression against others.

As a result, reason can no longer occupy as prominent a place in the state as Sidney originally advocated.[22] In the first chapter, Sidney expresses admiration for those who "lived private lives, as Plato, Socrates, Epictetus, and others, made it their business to abate men's lusts, by shewing the folly of seeking vain honours, useless riches, or unsatisfying pleasures" (*DCG* 1.19.67). But Sidney has established the need for constant military adventure and praised the Romans for having the people's "spirits raised to delight in conquests" (*DCG* 2.16.170). Given this need, one must wonder whether a state can afford to exalt those who teach through precept and example that the desires for riches and honor should be curbed.[23]

---

[21] See also Rahe, *Republics Ancient and Modern*, 262–3, for a discussion of the implications of Machiavelli's choice of Rome over Sparta.

[22] Cf. West, foreword to *DCG*, xxv.

[23] For further corroboration of Sidney's rejection of peaceful endeavors, see my discussion of his ultimate rejection of Numa, Rome's second king, whom he terms "an unarmed philosopher" (*DCG* 1.16.48; cf. NM, *P* 6), in Sullivan, *Machiavelli, Hobbes, and the Formation of a Liberal Republicanism*, 210–12. His comparison of Romulus and Numa follows that of Machiavelli (*D* 1.19).

As thoroughly Machiavellian as is Sidney's analysis of the necessity of war, the Englishman nevertheless remains reluctant to acknowledge his full debt to Machiavelli as his analysis of the necessity to reduce a state to its first principles, which appears in several places throughout Sidney's work, shows. On this topic, Sidney does credit Machiavelli. It is this fact that accounts for the willingness of scholars to identify Sidney's thought with Machiavelli's. Nevertheless, Sidney still refuses to acknowledge his full debt to Machiavelli. Indeed, in the one place he does point to Machiavelli as the author of the idea, he questions how deeply Machiavelli is committed to his own principle. Sidney is able to quibble with Machiavelli in this way because he seems not to grasp the full implication of Machiavelli's injunction. Sidney mistakenly takes its meaning to be a mere endorsement of returning a state to its original laws and traditions, ignoring Machiavelli's harsher enjoinder to reintroduce to the state the type of fear that existed at its founding. According to Machiavelli, citizens will begin to dare to break the laws, "[u]nless something arises by which punishment is brought back to their memory and fear is renewed in their spirits" (*D* 3.1.3). Elsewhere, however, when Sidney does not explicitly refer to Machiavelli, his use of the idea shows that he not only grasps but readily accepts this harsher meaning with which Machiavelli endows his principle.

Sidney explicitly refers to this Machiavellian principle when, after reflecting that the products of human hands are imperfect and that even natural bodies are in need of "medicines and other occasional helps," he concludes that states require the same remedial action. "Some men observing this, have proposed a necessity of reducing every state once in an age or two, to the integrity of its first principle" (*DCG* 3.25.462). Although Sidney suggests that a number of men make such a claim, one man in particular does, and Sidney acknowledges this fact when he points to Machiavelli's *Discourses on Livy* as the source for this notion.[24]

Sidney thus adheres to Machiavelli's idea regarding the necessity of continuous renovation for a state, but he immediately distances himself from the one whom he has just acknowledged: "but [those who propose this as a necessity] ought to have examined, whether that principle be good or evil." If those who seek to renovate do not examine this question, they will likely "render errors perpetual" and thus deprive "mankind of the benefits of wisdom, industry, experience, and right use of reason" (*DCG* 3.25.462). Sidney thus objects that Machiavelli does not go far enough. If the original foundation is wanting, Sidney advises not renovation but an entirely new basis for the state; one should not unthinkingly adhere to inadequate principles. The dispute that Sidney initiates

---

[24] Although Sidney refers to the second book of Machiavelli's *Discourses on Livy*, the discussion is actually found in 3.1. Because Houston and Raab maintain that Machiavelli was fundamentally influenced by Polybius' pessimistic view of politics expressed in the cycle of regimes, they do not attribute proper credit to Machiavelli for informing Sidney's claim regarding the invigorating power of a return to the beginnings. See Houston, *Algernon Sidney and the Republican Heritage in England and America*, 217–18; Raab, *The English Face of Machiavelli*, 222.

with Machiavelli here obscures his fundamental agreement with Machiavelli on the need for innovation.

Sidney's advocacy of thorough innovation is linked to his promotion of the necessity of progress. Against Filmer, who maintains that any deviation from God's original provision for humankind represents a decline, Sidney insists that people should not be beholden to their ancestors to the extent that they perpetually replicate ancient foibles and misunderstandings. He is fond of saying that people are no more bound to follow the ways of their ancestors than they are "obliged . . . to live upon acorns, or inhabit hollow trees, because their fathers did it when they had no better dwellings, and found no better nourishment in the uncultivated world" (*DCG* 2.8.122). Although he eagerly appeals to the authority of history and Scripture when it serves his point, he baldly states that recourse to such authority is wrongheaded: "We are not therefore so much to inquire after that which is most ancient, as that which is best" (*DCG* 3.25.460). The corollary of Sidney's emphasis on the necessity of human activity in the service of progress is an understanding of nature as radically defective.

Machiavelli would certainly not deny this conclusion of Sidney. In initiating this dispute with Machiavelli, Sidney not only averts his eyes from Machiavelli's endorsement of harsh punishment as a means of returning a state to its beginning, but he also neglects other important aspects of Machiavelli's thought that support Sidney's conclusion regarding the necessity of human activity generally and of the renovation of states specifically. After all, Machiavelli is adamant that human beings rouse themselves from the languor and the reliance on chance that derives from the view that "worldly things are so governed by fortune and by God, that men cannot correct them with their prudence, indeed that they have no remedy at all" (*P* 25). Like Sidney's, Machiavelli's view of the imperfection of the human situation colors his view of politics. Machiavelli prefers Rome – whose founding was incomplete – to Sparta – whose founding was completed at a single stroke by Lycurgus. Although Machiavelli prefers incomplete Rome in part because it was better able to respond to the exigencies that arose to threaten it, he is not reluctant to criticize his model city for not making changes radical enough. He says that Rome, when it became corrupt, should have "changed" its "orders" "together with [its] innovation in laws" (*D* 1.18.2). In Machiavelli's lexicon, a change in "orders" denotes a thoroughgoing innovation equivalent to a new founding. As a result of this failure to innovate at a critical juncture, the republic fell, laments Machiavelli. Thus, Machiavelli initiates a criticism of the Romans for not transforming their foundation, a criticism entirely in keeping with Sidney's concern.[25]

Thus, while using Machiavelli's terminology, Sidney distances himself from his source, but the difference that initiates the quarrel, as we have seen, is superficial rather than substantial. Moreover, Sidney obscures the true meaning, and hence the harshness, of Machiavelli's injunction to restore a state to its origins. Machiavelli introduces this notion with the reflection that although

[25] Cf. Worden, "The Commonwealth Kidney of Algernon Sidney," 18–19.

the things of the world are transient, human intervention can prolong their lives. States are vulnerable to corruption because human beings easily become complacent; it is necessary to rid them of their complacency with a return to the fear coeval with the original founding. Such a return to the beginning can be achieved either through extrinsic or intrinsic causes. As Fischer notes in the prologue to this book, because an extrinsic cause can be as dangerous and unpredictable as the near sacking of a state at the hands of the enemy, Machiavelli indicates that a state should use intrinsic causes for renewal. These causes arise either from the institution of new laws that mitigate "the ambition and the insolence of men" or from rare examples. Among the rare examples Machiavelli furnishes are the execution of those who attempted to overturn the state or of young men who, eager for the fray, merely disobeyed military orders. "Because they were excessive and notable," explains Machiavelli, "such things made men draw back toward the mark whenever one of them arose" (*D* 3.1.3). Machiavelli's return to first principles brings with it frighteningly bloody spectacles.

The excessiveness of Machiavelli's own discussion of the necessity of excessive actions clearly does not repel Sidney. Both before and after he has explicitly referred to and criticized Machiavelli's notion of the need for a return to first principles, Sidney endorses, without attribution, Machiavelli's enjoinder to "reduce [states] to their first principles" (*DCG* 2.30.302; see also 2.31.306, 2.13.150, 3.41.550). Moreover, apparently guided by Machiavelli's provision of the list of Rome's salutary executions, Sidney advocates harsh punishments against those who disregard the laws of the state. He clearly grasps the harshness of Machiavelli's teaching – the very harshness he ignores when he attributes the idea to Machiavelli: "If injustice therefore be evil, and injuries forbidden, they are also to be punished; and the law instituted for their prevention, must necessarily intend the avenging of such as cannot be prevented" (*DCG* 2.24.219). He also follows the Machiavelli of 3.1 in approving of the action that Rome took against Scipio. A commander who had vanquished the great Carthaginian general Hannibal, Scipio was awarded the honorific title of Africanus. Despite his unsurpassed military record, the Romans prosecuted him for a number of crimes. Livy (38.50–6) suggests that those who supported the prosecution were motivated not so much by the belief that he had committed the crimes of which he was accused, but by the fear that Scipio had grown too great to live under republican laws. Like Machiavelli, Sidney sides with Scipio's accusers: "Scipio being the first Roman that thus disdained the power of law, I do not know whether the prejudice brought upon the city by so dangerous an example, did not outweigh all the services he had done" (*DCG* 2.18.179; cf. *D* 1.29). Sidney understands and endorses the spirit in which Machiavelli offers his teaching.

Sidney, however, expends his real ire, not on the insolent young men of a republic, as does Machiavelli, but on wayward monarchs. When it comes to the prospect of punishing kings, Sidney actually surpasses Machiavelli in advocating ferocity. Sidney's principle that allows for the deposition of malevolent rulers marries Machiavellian vengefulness and important principles of liberalism.

Machiavelli seems to recommend his stern regimen with a view to republics in particular, because he draws his examples of such salutary punishment from the history of the Roman Republic. But as 3.1 comes to a close, he turns his attention to monarchies, and broaches a far less violent method of performing "executions" in the context of a discussion of the French monarchy. He comments about the French monarchy that laws and orders "are renewed" whenever the parlement of Paris "makes an execution against a prince of that kingdom and when it condemns the king in its verdicts" (*D* 3.1.5). Sidney follows his source to the extent that he offers reflections akin to those of Machiavelli on the necessity of institutions that restrain a monarch. In speaking of the need to have kings observe the fundamental laws of the state, Sidney states, "Nothing is more essential and fundamental in the constitutions of kingdoms, than that diets, parliaments, and assemblies of estates should see this perform'd" (*DCG* 2.30.296).

But Sidney is not content merely with the benign "executions" against a king that Machiavelli recommends. Sidney says later that "it may well fall out, that the magistrate who will not follow the directive power of the law, may fall under the coercive, and then the fear is turned upon him, with this aggravation, that it is not only actual, but just." Moreover, he observes, not without a degree of satisfaction, that "many emperors and kings of the greatest nations in the world... have been so utterly deprived of all power, that they have been imprisoned, deposed, confined to monasteries, kill'd, drawn through the streets, cut in pieces, thrown into rivers, and indeed suffer'd all that could be suffer'd by the vilest slaves" (*DCG* 3.11.382). In contemplating the violence to which a king may be subject, Sidney bests Machiavelli in bloodthirstiness. Such an action taken against a king must, of course, qualify as a circumstance in which the state is reduced to its first principles. At this point, it becomes evident why Sidney stresses the need for a people to reconsider the foundational principles of the state. It is precisely at such a juncture that a people may well decide to alter the basis of the state by changing a monarchy to a republic.

The people's punishment of a malevolent monarch is justified in Sidney's understanding because political rule originates in a contract. When a population agrees to form political society, it can contract with a king to provide for its welfare, but the people will always remain the judge of that contract. When the monarch, whom the people has established for its benefit, acts contrary to the people's interests, the people have a right to punish his malfeasance.[26]

At this point, Machiavellian ire meets Lockean liberalism in Sidney's writings.[27] Although Locke does not speak of a contract that binds the ruler and ruled, he does find the origin of political society in a contract. According to both

---

[26] See ibid., 16.

[27] It is highly unlikely that Sidney knew of Locke's manuscript given Locke's secrecy regarding it (Peter Laslett, "Introduction," in *TTG* 25–66). Worden's conjecture that Toland later forged portions of Sidney's *Discourses* would explain the almost uncanny anticipation of Locke's thought contained in Sidney's work.

Sidney and Locke, before the people decide to contract to leave the prepolitical condition, they possess an unrestrained liberty. Sidney explains that "universal liberty [is that] which I assert" (*DCG* 1.12.34). In another place, Sidney seems to posit something very close to a Lockean right to liberty: "equality of right and exemption from the domination of any other is called liberty: that he who enjoys it cannot be deprived of it, unless by his own consent, or by force" (*DCG* 2.31.304).

Although Locke and Sidney use the condition of human beings before government to vindicate natural freedom, a notion that has important ramifications for their conceptions of a just government, they both concede that civil society is the remedy for the "Inconveniences" of the prepolitical state (Locke, *TTG* 2.2.13). Sidney observes, "No one man or family is able to provide that which is requisite for their convenience or security, whilst everyone has an equal right to everything, and none acknowledges a superior to determine the controversies, that . . . will probably be so many and great, that mankind cannot bear them" (*DCG* 1.10.30). Although Sidney nowhere speaks of the "state of nature," he does assert, as we have seen, the existence of a prepolitical condition populated by human beings who reside in hollow trees and derive their sustenance from a diet of acorns. Such a condition is unsatisfactory:

The fierce barbarity of a loose multitude, bound by no law, and regulated by no discipline, is wholly repugnant to [the good of ourselves]: Whilst every man fears his neighbour, and has no other defence than his own strength, he must live in that perpetual anxiety which is equally contrary to that happiness, and that sedate temper of mind which is required for the search of it. The first step towards the cure of this pestilent evil, is for many to join in one body, that everyone may be protected by the united force of all.

(*DCG* 2.1.83)

Both Locke and Sidney maintain that after the people have joined together in one body, that body retains the right to judge whether the government that it constituted for its security is actually threatening that security. In this manner, they posit a right of resistance. Locke specifies that the citizens are not rebels because they merely resist those who are properly termed rebels – those who "bring back again the state of War" by the "*endeavour to take away, and destroy the Property of the People*, or to reduce them to Slavery under Arbitrary Power" (*TTG* 2.19.222, 226). Similarly, Sidney insists in the section heading of 3.36 that "The general revolt of a Nation cannot be called a Rebellion." In the body of the section, he explains that the Latin *rebellare* means to renew a war, and thus the word is not applicable to a citizen body that was never at war with its governors: "The whole body therefore of a nation cannot be tied to any other obedience than is consistent with the common good, according to their own judgment: and having never been subdued or brought to terms of peace with their magistrates, they cannot be said to revolt or rebel against them to whom they owe no more than seems good to themselves" (*DCG* 3.36.519).

The difference visible here between the teachings of Sidney and Locke on the right of resistance is negligible: Whereas Locke speaks of a return to war, Sidney does not. This difference derives from the fact that Locke's writings contain a more fully elaborated state of nature, which according to his specification devolves into a state of war before human beings will endeavor to seek refuge in civil society. Perhaps the more fundamental difference between them on the subject of resistance resides in the pleasure, which we have already witnessed, that Sidney derives from the contemplation of the punishment that an errant monarch would receive at the hands of his vengeful subjects.

Sidney must be differentiated in one very important respect from Locke, however. Unlike Locke, Sidney is scornful of republics based on trade rather than on war. And he praises Plato, for example, for not teaching "us how to erect manufactures, and to increase trade or riches; but how magistrates may be helpful to nations" (*DCG* 2.1.83). He prefers, of course, those republics outfitted for acquisitive war.

Conversely, as Smith notes in the second chapter of this book, Locke shuns war. In fact, in the *Second Treatise*, he outlines an understanding of the just rewards of conquest, which, if put into practice, would discourage the ravages of war that remove farmers from the plow and merchants from the scale. First, Locke announces that an aggressor nation that conquers its quarry cannot have a right to the spoils (*TTG* 2.16.176). This position is, of course, far removed from the view that Machiavelli and Sidney articulate, which proclaims that not only is expansion necessary, but is a legitimate way for a nation to benefit its citizens. Moreover, Locke denies that those who are victorious in resisting the incursion of an unjust foe have a right to the spoils. Of course, they have a right to reparations, but even their seemingly just demand to have the cost of their defense repaid must be limited. The wives and children of those who fought on the side of the unjust vanquished do not deserve to lose their estates as a result of an action in which they had no part.

Despite what appears to be a fundamental difference between Locke, on the one hand, and Machiavelli and Sidney, on the other, all three are united in viewing the purpose of government in terms starkly different from those that Aristotle employs. The difference is particularly evident when considering the thought of Sidney and Locke. As a result of their view that politics originates in a contract, they envision the possibility that human beings can exist without a state. In contrast, Aristotle explicitly denies this possibility, declaring that human beings are naturally political and that a being without need of a city is either a beast or a god (*Pol.* 1253a1–19, 29).[28] Additionally, Aristotle explicitly denies that political life can begin in a contract because its end surpasses that which any contract could secure. The purpose of government is not merely to guarantee justice, but to make the citizens good and just, declares Aristotle (*Pol.* 1280b10–4).

Although not a social contract thinker, Machiavelli shares the contractarian view of Sidney and Locke that human beings are not naturally political. Politics does not furnish an arena in which to exercise the highest faculties of human

---

[28] Note Houston, *Algernon Sidney and the Republican Heritage in England and America*, 119.

beings; instead, it provides the means for the satisfaction of individual desires.[29] Sidney expresses this idea in language strikingly similar to that of Locke: The laws are "the best defence of our lives, liberties, and estates" (*DCG* 3.43.558).

In another place, Sidney expresses the basis for his dedication to republics in language similar to that of Machiavelli. In 2.2 of the *Discourses on Livy*, Machiavelli reveals that he favors republics because most people benefit from their rule:

For all towns and provinces that live freely in every part . . . make very great profits. For larger peoples are seen there, because marriages are freer and more desirable to men since each willingly procreates those children he believes he can nourish. He does not fear that his patrimony will be taken away, and he knows not only that they are born free and not slaves, but that they can, through their virtue, become princes.   (*D* 2.2.3)

Sidney concurs with Machiavelli's opinion, declaring that in commonwealths, "[w]hilst the laws, and that discipline which nourishes virtue is in force, men of wisdom and valor are never wanting; and every man desires to give testimony of his virtue when he knows 'twill be rewarded with honour and power" (*DCG* 2.24.248). Therefore, both Machiavelli and Locke would agree with Sidney's declaration that

as the wisdom of a father is seen, not only in providing bread for his family, or increasing his patrimonial estate, but in making all possible provision for the security of it; so that government is evidently the best, which, not relying upon what it does at first enjoy, seeks to increase the number, strength, and riches of the people; and by the best discipline to bring the power so improved into such order as may be of most use to the publick.

(*DCG* 2.23.209)

Whereas Machiavelli would agree with the continuation of Sidney's discussion that legitimizes the pursuit of increase through violence, Locke would not. Nevertheless, all three seek the same end for politics – the attempt to satisfy human desire.

Cato's Manifest Machiavellianism

In some ways, the authors of *Cato's Letters* are more outspokenly Machiavellian than is Sidney. Trenchard and Gordon are more likely to cite the Renaissance writer with approval; they even refer to him as a "great authority" (*CL* 16.121), a public honor that Sidney refuses to accord his master. Like Sidney, Cato adopts Machiavelli's views both that ambitious men must not be trusted and that when they inevitably exceed the bounds they must be punished severely. In making the case for harsh punishments, Cato cites with approval the manner in which the Roman Republic dealt with those of overweening ambition. Cato also joins in Sidney's embrace of Machiavelli's doctrine concerning the necessity of increase, but this point of agreement actually leads to Cato's divergence from Machiavelli

[29] See ibid., 166; Wood, "The Value of Asocial Sociability," 294.

and Sidney. Cato does not share their view that such increase is to be derived from armed competition among states. Although Cato retains the conception of the intransigent selfishness of human nature that causes contention and competition among human beings and makes the pursuit of increase a necessity, he moves the venue of this competition from the blood-stained battlefield to the high seas, where nations struggle to become dominant in trade. Metaphorical wounds are surely inflicted in this contest, but the goal of the struggle is the promotion of commodious living at home. Therefore, whereas Sidney's use of Machiavellian premises far outstrips his acknowledged use of them, Cato's use of Machiavelli, while manifest, is less thoroughgoing than is Sidney's. Despite – or rather because of – these deviations from Machiavellian orthodoxy, Cato is an important Machiavellian, for he illustrates how a Machiavellian sensibility can be made compatible with the peaceful pursuits of a Lockean.

Cato's immediate purpose in writing offered much occasion for the expression of Machiavellian vengeance. Trenchard and Gordon began writing the letters that ran from 1720 to 1723 in the *London Journal* and then in the *British Journal* later in 1723 as a response to the South Sea Bubble. The South Sea Company had been granted a monopoly of trade with the South Seas and South America. The managers of the company had inflated the price of the stock to unsustainable levels. When the bubble burst in 1720, the investors in the company lost their fortunes. Many radical Whigs, Cato among them, saw this financial crisis as an instance in which corrupt public officials and members of the court had conspired with the managers of the company to make their own fortunes at the expense of the public good.

To allow such crimes to go unpunished would be to risk, in Cato's mind, the continued health of the commonwealth. In discussing the appropriate penalty for those who betray their homeland, Cato refers explicitly to Machiavelli's harsh teaching,[30] reminding his readers that the Florentine insists that "a free government is not to be preserved but by destroying Brutus's sons" (*CL* 16.121). Here Cato has recourse to Machiavelli's discussion in the *Discourses on Livy* concerning the immediate aftermath of the expulsion of the kings. Although Brutus had the central role in driving the Tarquins from Rome and establishing the republic, Livy (2.3–5) tells us that his sons resented losing the privileged place that aristocrats such as they had enjoyed in the monarchy. They acted on their resentment by conspiring to reestablish the Tarquins as rulers in Rome; when their conspiracy was discovered, Brutus presided at his sons' trial and was present at their execution. Machiavelli transforms Livy's account of this particular case into a general rule regarding the necessity for republics to take extreme measures for the sake of the preservation of their freedom: "there is no remedy more powerful, nor more valid, more secure, and more necessary, than to kill the sons of Brutus" (*D* 1.16.4, 3.3.1). Cato eagerly applies the harsh maxim that Machiavelli has furnished him, and in a later letter attests to the

---

[30] See Pocock, *The Machiavellian Moment*, 468; Vickie B. Sullivan, "The Civic Humanist Portrait of Machiavelli's English Successors," *HPT* 15:1 (Spring 1994): 73–96.

potency of this remedy in the Roman case and hence suggests its desirability in modern times when he goadingly notes that "[a]fter the death of the sons of Brutus,... we hear no more of any conspirators in Rome to restore the Tarquins" (*CL* 20.142). In this manner, Cato suggests that the country can actually benefit from its current crisis.

In further developing this theme of the benefit to be derived from hardship, Cato has additional occasion in which to draw on other elements of Machiavelli's teaching – elements that furnish Cato both with the proper attitude to the crisis and its method of resolution. Cato enjoins his readers, "Let us make earning of our misfortunes, and accept our calamities as an opportunity thrown into our laps by indulgent providence, to save ourselves" (*CL* 16.121). Cato embraces Machiavelli's teaching that misfortune is actually the *occasione*, which the sagacious will seize in order to magnify their greatness. Machiavelli's four great founders – Moses, Cyrus, Romulus, and Theseus – were able to parlay into great fame the misfortunes into which they were born – fame far greater than they would have garnered had they not been so fortunate in encountering misfortune. If one studies their lives, Machiavelli concludes, "one does not see that they had anything else from fortune than the opportunity (*occasione*)" (*P* 6).

Machiavelli teaches the same lesson in his *Discourses on Livy*, declaring that a great man is fortunate in being confronted by a thoroughly corrupt city, because it affords him the possibility of great fame. He states: "if a prince seeks the glory of the world he ought to desire to possess a corrupt city – not to spoil it entirely... but to reorder it.... And truly the heavens cannot give to men a greater opportunity for glory, nor can men desire any greater" (*D* 1.10.6). Cato follows Machiavelli's lead in a letter addressed to the members of the House of Commons. He insists that the current condition of England affords them the possibility of great fame:

Here is a scene of glory, an opportunity put by gracious heaven into your hands, to exercise your virtues, and to obtain a reputation far above the tinsel triumphs of fabulous and imaginary heroes. Virtuous men could not ask more of providence; nor could providence bestow more upon mortal men, than to set them at the head of a corrupted and almost undone people, and to give them the honour of restoring their power, and reforming their manners.   (*CL* 98.701)

Having been given this opportunity, Cato suggests elsewhere that the solution itself should be Machiavellian: "Machiavelli tells us, that no government can long subsist, but by recurring often to its first principles." Cato displays a partiality for Machiavelli's teaching in the first chapter of the third book of the *Discourses on Livy*, where Machiavelli counsels that complacency in a state can be overcome through public executions, which remind all of their vulnerability. Displaying a particular awareness of the dangers of the complacency of which Machiavelli warns, Cato comments that the most propitious time for a recurrence to first principles is "when men are awakened by misfortunes, and frighted with the approach and near view of present evils; then they will wish for remedies, and their minds are prepared to receive them, to hear reasons, and to fall into measures proposed by wise men for their security" (*CL* 16.121). The punishment of the malefactors responsible for the South Sea Crisis, thus, will demonstrate to all citizens their vulnerability and the need for vigilance.

Although Cato and Sidney share the same regard for Machiavelli's injunction to reduce states to their first principles, the bases for their regard seem to differ. Whereas Sidney appears to have in mind primarily the punishment of a way-ward king and the good effects that such punishment would have on the state either by producing more tractable successors to the throne or by furnishing the occasion for the establishment of a republic, Cato's concern is more psychologi-cal in nature and, at least in this place where he explicitly refers to Machiavelli's principle, relates to the attitude of the governed toward their leaders. During a time of crisis, the people will be more likely to listen to wise men, such as Cato, for example. At other times, when danger does not appear to impinge on them, they will take their own security and wise counsel for granted. It is precisely at such a time that their governors are likely to take advantage of them.

This is not to say, of course, that Cato is unconcerned with setting a fright-ening example for other likely malefactors just as Machiavelli recommends in *Discourses* 3.1 when he comments suggestively with regard to the decline of Rome that "as the memory of that beating is eliminated, men began to dare to try new things and to say evil" (*D* 3.1.3). Indeed, when broaching the fact that in England high status does not protect one from punishment, Cato indicates that he would welcome a spectacle so frightening that the memory of it would furnish a restraint to possible transgressors long into the future:

[Y]ou may, at present, load every gallows in England with directors and stock-jobbers.... A thousand stock-jobbers, well trussed up ... would be one certain expedient to soften the rage of the people; and to convince them that the future direction of their wealth and estates shall be put into the hands of those, who will as effectually study to promote the general benefit and publick good, as others have, lately, most infamously sacrificed both to their private advantage.   (*CL* 2.42)

Given that such favorable results will flow from stern measures, Cato is embold-ened to intone in his most authoritative Machiavellian accent that the opposite tack may occasion harm: "mercy may be cruelty" (*CL* 2.41; *P* 17).[31]

Although Cato's immediate historical circumstances demand this severity, he also offers general reflections on which any free state can draw in order to avoid the danger that its ambitious leaders pose at all times. Two letters of Cato in particular, 118 and 119, devoted to the subject of ingratitude, deal with this subject. He draws heavily on Machiavelli's own section on ingratitude in the *Discourses on Livy*, Chapters 28–32 of the first book. The ostensible purpose of each treatment is to examine the phenomenon of gratitude in a republic: Machiavelli purports to examine why Rome was less ungrateful than Athens, whereas Cato undertakes to defend free states from the charge that they are

---

[31] See ibid., 95–6.

more ungrateful to the men who perform great services for them than are arbitrary states. Because each discussion defends a type of state that the author deems grateful, each appears to presume gratitude to be a virtue for a state – something to be praised rather than blamed. Nevertheless, a strong current in each discussion suggests that an excess of gratitude extended to powerful and talented men can be quite dangerous and that stern punishment is a potent antidote for the nefarious ambition of such men.

Cato begins by treating a phenomenon that all states encounter: Those who perform great services for them rarely think that the rewards conferred on them adequately recompense the services they have performed. As a result, such men, "being neither pleased with the measure nor duration of their power, where it is not boundless and perpetual, are apt to be struggling to make it so, though to the ruin of those who gave it for their own preservation" (*CL* 118.821). When a free people takes measures to protect liberty from the machinations of the ambitious, the people are thus termed ungrateful: "The dearest and most valuable things are most apt to create jealousies and fears about them: and the dearest of all being liberty, as that which produces and secures all the rest, the people's zeal to preserve it has been ever called ingratitude by such as had designs against it" (*CL* 118.824).

Machiavelli too emphasizes the difficulty that states face in rewarding their leading men. In a chapter preceding his section on ingratitude, he provides the following encapsulation of that difficulty: "a free way of life proffers honors and rewards through certain honest and determinate causes, and outside these it neither rewards nor honors anyone; and when one has those honors and those useful things that it appears to him he merits, he does not confess that he has an obligation to those who reward him" (*D* 1.16.3). As a result of this difficulty, a free state has "partisan enemies and not partisan friends." Quite in keeping with the aspect of his thought that Cato finds so appealing, Machiavelli recommends the expedient of "kill[ing] the sons of Brutus" (*D* 1.16.4).

Thus, both Machiavelli and Cato enter their discussions of ingratitude asserting that free states find themselves in a precarious position with respect to their great men. The abilities of talented men are needed to maintain the liberty of their state, but their ambitions are dangerous; too great rewards will make them insolent, too few will make them vengeful. As a result, Machiavelli and Cato concur that a state can never be too suspicious. Cato expresses this sentiment as follows: "Considering what sort of a creature man is, it is scarce possible to put him under too many restraints, when he is possessed of great power" (*CL* 33.234).

Cato's strict reliance on Machiavelli's treatment of ingratitude is evident from the fact that, in accord with Machiavelli's own strategy, he examines in detail, for the purpose of exonerating Rome, the cases of Coriolanus, Camillus, and Scipio. Machiavelli attempts to vitiate the charge of ingratitude that might be lodged against Rome in the cases of Coriolanus and Camillus by noting that these two men "were made exiles for the injuries that both had done to the plebs," thereby suggesting that their deserts were just (*D* 1.29.3).

Cato follows Machiavelli's lead when he finds that they were "guilty of . . . partiality . . . towards the nobles" (*CL* 118.825). In the case of Scipio, however, both Machiavelli and Cato determine that another tack must be taken. Indeed, Machiavelli goes so far in distinguishing this case that he states that there was "no other example [of ingratitude] other than that of Scipio." Nevertheless, Machiavelli excuses Rome even in this case by raising concerns regarding the prominence that the hero had attained: Rome was justified in taking the action against Scipio because "a city could not call itself free where there was a citizen who was feared by the magistrates" (*D* 1.29.3). Similarly, the English Cato, while acknowledging the man's accomplishments, states that the regard that the people had for him set a dangerous precedent. Indeed, it "shook the foundations of Rome, and made way for the violent proceedings and usurpations of Marius, and afterwards of Caesar" (*CL* 118.826). Just as Sidney had done, Cato sides with Machiavelli in condoning Rome's prosecution of Scipio. Therefore, even in the cases of these three prominent soldiers, whose victories proved so beneficial to Rome, Machiavelli and Cato either refuse to admit to instances of ingratitude or offer palliation for such instances.

Cato reveals another aspect of his Machiavellian sensibility in another passage of the same letter. He declares, for instance, that the dictator provided a great service to his city when he sentenced Spurius Melius to death for having endeavored to raise his stature in the state by distributing free corn to the Roman plebeians. Similarly, he commends Rome for throwing Manlius Capitolinus from the Capitol – the very Capitol he had once saved – for becoming discontent with the honors his city had bestowed on him for his valor. Both of these punishments are cited by Machiavelli in *Discourses* 3.1 as examples of executions that brought Rome "back toward its beginning" (*D* 3.1.3).

Cato's high regard for *Discourses* 3.1 surfaces again when he finds irresistible the urge to apply these general reflections to recent events: "Even in England, the hanging of two or three great men among the many guilty, once in a reign or two, would have prevented much evil, and many dangers and oppressions, and saved this nation many millions" (*CL* 119.828). He thus exhorts England to use the remedy that would have prevented, according to Machiavelli's assessment, the collapse of Rome: If stern punishments had "continued at least every ten years in that city, it follows of necessity that it would never have been corrupt" (*D* 3.1.3). According to Cato's assessment, then, a state's expression of gratitude is less a virtue than a vice. He goes so far as to assert that "there is generally more crime and insecurity in not punishing well, than in not paying well; a fault too frequent in free states" (*CL* 118.823–4).

Having so emphasized the notion that gratitude is a dangerous luxury for a free state, Cato appears to have made more difficult the task of arguing his ostensible point that free states are less ungrateful than arbitrary princes. He calls on Machiavelli's help to extricate himself from this difficulty, explicitly deferring to the authority of Machiavelli's discussion of ingratitude in the *Discourses on Livy* for the only time in these two thoroughly Machiavellian letters: "Machiavel . . . says, that a great and successful general, under an arbitrary prince, has but two ways to escape the certain ruin which his glory, services, and renown, will else bring upon him: He must either quit the army, and, retiring from all power, live like a private man; or depose his master, and set up himself: Which last is generally the safer course" (*CL* 120.830; cf. *D* 1.30). Cato's point is that whereas the free state waits for a false step or even the slightest sign of insolence from a glorious victor, such a prince does not; success itself is enough to trigger a prince's wrath. One wonders, however, how Cato can maintain this distinction when he notes elsewhere that the democratic Athenians punished great men "though they could prove no other crime against them but that of being great men" (*CL* 11.92).[32]

Cato's deep concern for constraining the celebrated great originates in his view of human nature. Again, this understanding is linked to Cato's reading of Machiavelli: "Machiavelli tells us, that it is rare to find a man perfectly good or perfectly bad: Men generally swim between the two extremes" (*CL* 80.583; cf. *D* 1.27). Despite this cynicism regarding human nature, he does not despair of great men. Indeed, great men are needed to pursue the end that free states seek: the maintenance of their liberty. Moreover, Cato appears to proffer his praise of the heroes of the past for the purpose of promoting the recurrence of such examples in his own time:

I know that it is exceeding hard and rare, for any man to separate his passions from his own person and interest; but it is certain that there have been such men. Brutus, Cato, Regulus, Timoleon, Dion, and Epaminondas, were such, as were many more ancient Greeks and Romans; and, I hope, England has still some such. And though, in pursuing publick views, men regard themselves and their own advantages; yet if they regard the publick more, or their own in subserviency to the publick, they may justly be esteemed virtuous and good.   (*CL* 39.276–7)

This appeal for selflessness notwithstanding, in the same letter Cato expresses a wariness of those who enjoin others to renounce their selfish passions: "We have, all of us, heard much of the duty of subduing our appetites, and extinguishing our passions, from men, who by these phrases shewed at once their ignorance of human nature, and yet that they aimed at an absolute dominion over it" (*CL* 39.273).[33] Thus, Cato promotes suspicion even of those who preach self-abnegation. Moreover, it is really the latter of the two methods of pursuing the public good mentioned in the preceding block quotation – that of subsuming one's own good in service to the public good – that Cato finds the more effective. This is so because he finds self-interest to be the pervasive motivator of human action. Indeed, at one point he goes so far as to refuse to exclude any human being from this depiction: "I think it impossible for any man to act upon any other motive than his own self-interest" (*CL* 117.815).

---

[32] See Pangle, *The Spirit of Modern Republicanism*, 31.

[33] Cf. Sullivan, "The Civic Humanist Portrait of Machiavelli's English Successors," 89–90 and Dworetz, *The Unvarnished Doctrine*, 100, with Pocock, *The Machiavellian Moment*, 472.

Cato does not find this conclusion disheartening because the recognition of this truth is a step toward improving politics. To this end, he propagates Machiavelli's notion that in making laws it is necessary to presume "all men naturally wicked" (*CL* 31.222; cf. *D* 1.3).[34] And he explains that his "complaints of the crookedness and corruption of human nature are made with no malignant intention to break the bonds of society," but rather "to shew, that as selfishness is the strongest bias of men, every man ought to be upon his guard against another, that he become not the prey of another" (*CL* 40.280). As his declared purpose here suggests, the self-interest that manifests itself both in the desire for security and in the vigilance necessary to avert the depredations of others is a self-interest that a state should encourage. The notion that the all-pervasive and intransigent pursuit of self-interest is at once the great threat for states and the means by which they are to maintain their liberty is one that Cato develops at much greater length. At one point, he describes how the selfish passions can serve to preserve liberty rather than to threaten it:

[W]hilst men are men, ambition, avarice, and vanity, and other passions, will govern their actions; in spite of all equity and reason, they will be ever usurping, or attempting to usurp, upon the liberty and fortunes of one another, and all men will be striving to enlarge their own. Dominion will always desire increase, and property always to preserve itself; and these opposite views and interests will be causing a perpetual struggle: But by this struggle liberty is preserved, as water is kept sweet by motion.   (*CL* 70.504)

In Cato's view, then, when all parts of society act on self-interest and hence contend to increase their share of desired goods, the result can only be favorable for the state.[35] By pursuing their desired goods, the parties will prevent the dangerous aggregation of power in any one portion of society.

The distinctively Machiavellian character of Cato's argument here is unmistakable. Machiavelli defends the tumultuous character of Rome by claiming that the constant clash between the patricians and the plebeians resulted in the liberty of that state. Once attained, that liberty is best maintained by the people, declares Cato: "It is certain, that the whole people . . . are the best judges, whether things go ill or well with the publick." In positing this "doctrine of liberty" (*CL* 13.103), Cato follows the authority of Machiavelli, who recommends the example of republican Rome, which placed the guard of liberty in the hands of the people (*D* 1.5).

Moreover, Machiavelli also distinguishes between two parties in the state: those who desire property and security on the one hand, and those who desire dominion and glory on the other (*D* 1.16; *P* 9). Cato makes use of this distinction in delineating how both the pursuit of property and that of glory can serve to maintain a state's liberty. He specifies in one place that he does not regard the desire for property as an unmitigated evil: "I do not condemn the

---

34 See Rahe, *Republics Ancient and Modern*, 266, 434.
35 See Shelley Burtt, *Virtue Transformed: Political Argument in England, 1688–1740* (Cambridge, UK: Cambridge University Press, 1992), 76.

moderate pursuit of wealth, if we do not buy it too dear, and at the price of our healthier integrity" (*CL* 103.726). Moreover, in another place he declares that the acquisition and the protection of property support the type of government he seeks. He says that "[t]o live securely, happily, and independently, is the end and effect of liberty," and continues that property is the means by which this end is attained: "all men are animated by the passion of acquiring and defending property, because property is the best support of that independency, so passionately desired by all men" (*CL* 68.483). In another place, he describes one of the benefits of liberty as the privilege "of growing as rich as we can, without any other restriction, than that by all this we hurt not the publick, nor one another" (*CL* 62.432).

As for the pursuit of glory, Cato, although thoroughly suspicious of the passions of great men, is also grateful – even greedy – for them; great passions give rise to great accomplishments: "No man can be too ambitious of the glory and security of his country, nor too angry at its misfortunes and ill usage; nor too revengeful against those that abuse and betray it . . ., provided that in doing it he violates not the rights of others." As he expresses suspicion for those who advocate the suppression of the passions, he regrets the loss that such suppression may engender; men "become cowards, by stifling the love of glory" (*CL* 39.277, 275).

As Cato has made abundantly clear, although selfish interests can serve desirable ends, they are also dangerous. To meet this danger, self-interest must be enlightened. This is a difficult task because a "very small part of mankind have capacities large enough to judge the whole of things; but catch at every appearance which promises present benefit, without considering how it will affect their general interest; and so bring misfortunes and lasting misery upon themselves to gratify a present appetite, passion or desire." Cato does not ask for the renunciation of such appetites, but rather a better considered satisfaction of them: "How many are there, who do not prefer a servile office or pension before the general interest of their country, in which their own is involved; and so sacrifice their liberty and the protection which they receive from equal laws, for momentary and precarious advantages?" (*CL* 89.638). Cato advocates a greater, well-considered gain for the individual rather than a smaller, ill-considered one. To this end, he redefines the meaning of self-interest: "*self-interest*, in the ill sense of the word, ought to be new-defined, and made applicable only to those who prefer a small interest to a great one, or to such who take a wrong way to attain that great one" (*CL* 117.816). Therefore, if citizens can be made to understand that their own good results when the whole thrives, then Cato will laud self-interest.

The selfish passions, then, are not to be decried. They are to be channeled to produce good rather than evil results. Therefore, whether the good sought is property or glory, Cato is in complete accord with Machiavelli's declaration that "it is a very natural and ordinary thing to desire to acquire" (*P* 3). Indeed, Cato declares that "it is certainly the interest and duty of states, by all prudent and just methods to increase their wealth and power, and in consequence their security and protection" (*CL* 87.626). Moreover, like Sidney and Machiavelli, Cato is quite forthright in his readiness to augment his own nation's wealth and power at the expense of others. "All the advantage procured by conquest is to secure what we possess ourselves, or to gain the possessions of others, that is, the produce of their country, and the acquisitions of their labour and industry" (*CL* 87.628–9).

Nevertheless, he differs substantially with Machiavelli and Sidney on the means by which such aggrandizement is to be achieved. Admitting that augmentation is to be had "either by arms or trade," he shuns war and seeks the refuge of trade:

The balance of trade will return more clear money from neighbouring countries, than can be forced from them by fleets or armies, and more advantageously than under the odious name of tribute. It enervates rival states by their own consent, and obligates them, whilst it impoverishes and ruins them: It keeps our own people at home employed in arts, manufactures, and husbandry, instead of murdering them in wild, expensive, and hazardous expeditions, to the weakening their own country, and the pillaging and destroying their neighbours, and only for the fruitless and imaginary glory of conquest.
(*CL* 87.628–9)

In this remarkable passage, Cato has managed to combine the Machiavellian passion for the fray – the fray that will eventuate in the exaltation of the winner and the subjugation of the vanquished – with the Lockean sensibility that promotes comfort and peace through the industry of individuals.

It is the Lockean, however, that gains the upper hand in this particular contest for Cato's ultimate allegiance. For example, at other points, Cato allows the competitive edge to his praise of trade to fall away. In these places, he offers his praise of peace in terms of public benefits rather than in those of the belligerent glorification of England (e.g., *CL* 89.639, 86.619). Elsewhere, his Lockean allegiance is particularly evident when he mimics Locke's assertion (*TTG* 2.5.37) regarding the productivity of cultivated land: "One acre of ground well manured, cultivated, and sowed with corn, will produce ten times as much for the sustenance of man, as ten acres not cultivated, or ill cultivated" (*CL* 87.631).[36] Cato goes further than does Locke, asserting in the sequel that a good artisan is ten times more productive even than a farmer.

Laying aside the benefits of peaceful employment, Cato also produces a more principled rejection of war. He declares, for example, that "[c]onquest, or fighting for territory, is, for the most part, the most shameless thing in the world." Moreover, war should not be the method by which the person of the ruler is decided: "in all contests among conquerors about territory, if natural justice and common sense were to decide it, that prince ought to carry it, who can satisfy the people that he will use them best" (*CL* 74.549). Interestingly, here Cato appears to apply more consistently Sidney's own principle. Although it was Sidney's claim that a people has the right to choose its governors, he was

---

[36] See Zuckert, *Natural Rights and the New Republicanism*, 307.

forced to lapse in the application of his own principle when he so pugnaciously favored an aggressive state. Of course, even when the conqueror is a republic, the vanquished have no voice in the choice of their rulers, and, thus, whereas consent may be the basis of rule in the conquering country, it certainly is not in the conquered country. In this manner, Sidney often allowed his cherished principle of consent to be trampled by the intoxicating spirit of war (cf. *DCG* 3.36).

Therefore, it can be said that the Lockean manner in which Cato rejects armed aggression allows for a more universal application of Sidney's own principles. Cato himself recognizes the debt he owes to that most thoroughly Machiavellian of Englishmen. Cato extols Sidney, claiming that he "can never be too much valued or read" because he "has written better upon government than any Englishman, and as well as any foreigner" (*CL* 26.188).

Cato, in fact, endeavors to encourage the reading of Sidney in his own age by filling two of his own letters with extended extracts from Sidney's *Discourses Concerning Government*. The portions of Sidney's work that Cato selects treat the ease by which unscrupulous monarchs can corrupt the populace, using the lure of special favors to transform loyalty to the public to loyalty to their persons. By extensively quoting Sidney, Cato transmits Machiavelli's sentiment that "corruption thus beginning in the head, must necessarily diffuse itself into the members of the commonwealth" (*CL* 26.193–4; cf. *D* 1.17.1). In the second of the two letters devoted to Sidney's writings, Cato defends himself against the charge, occasioned by the first, that he shares Sidney's republican sympathies. Cato proclaims his loyalty to the English constitution when he calls it "the best republick in the world, with a prince at the head of it" (*CL* 37.262).

Aside from the possibility of shared republican sympathies, what Cato shares with Sidney, Cato also shares with Locke.[37] Like his two English predecessors, Cato claims that government is conventional and originates in a contract. Before the institution of government, human beings lived in a state of nature where all were equal in not being subject to any other. "Men are naturally equal, and none ever rose above the rest but by force or consent," states Cato (*CL* 45.306). Because the natural rights of human beings were not secure in the state of nature, human beings established government, "the business and design" of which is "to defend . . . men's natural rights" (*CL* 90.644). Even after the advent of government, the understanding of the natural condition furnishes a standard by which to judge governments. Cato declares that "to know the jurisdiction of governors, and its limits, we must have recourse to the institution of government, and ascertain those limits by the measure of power, which men in the state of nature have over themselves and one another" (*CL* 60.414).

Because government originates in a contract and because the natural condition of human beings furnishes a standard, citizens can withdraw their consent

---

[37] For discussions of the Lockean elements of Cato's thought, see, in particular, Burtt, *Virtue Transformed*, 81; Dworetz, *The Unvarnished Doctrine*, 109; Hamowy, "*Cato's Letters*, John Locke, and the Republican Paradigm," 281–3, 289, 292–4; Rahe, *Republics Ancient and Modern*, 532; Zuckert, *Natural Rights and the New Republicanism*, 300–4.

when the government they have established becomes subversive of the purposes for which they established it. On this basis, Cato's thought also contains a doctrine of resistance: "It is said, that the doctrine of resistance would destroy the peace of the world: But it may be more truly said, that the contrary doctrine would destroy the world itself, as it has already some of the best countries in it" (*CL* 42.292).

Cato thus supports a Lockean understanding of the origin, purpose, and bounds of government. In this manner, the Machiavellian vengeance to which Cato so evidently gives vent, as well as the Machiavellian view of human nature that, in Cato's view, justifies such rancor, serve ends different from the ones Machiavelli envisioned. In Cato, therefore, Machiavelli's bold spirit is housed in a Lockean body.

Conclusion

Algernon Sidney and the authors of *Cato's Letters* are Machiavellians. Although there are significant differences between the manner in which each uses the Florentine, there exist important similarities. For instance, Sidney and Cato share Machiavelli's admiration for the accomplishments of great men. In maintaining that republics are the nursery of virtue, Sidney consistently holds up the example of the leading men of Rome. Cato, who is actually much closer to Machiavelli in his intense suspiciousness of the ambitions of great men, is also close to Machiavelli in admiring the great deeds that those ambitions fueled. Even though Cato renounces the arena in which much of their honor was garnered, he cannot resist the allure of those awesome accomplishments of the ancients.

In another and perhaps more important way, Sidney and Cato, as well as Locke, can be deemed Machiavellians. They are all much beholden to necessity for dictating the ends that they believe a government must pursue. They all concur that necessity demands that governments seek increase. Indeed, all three of the Englishmen can be deemed disciples of the Italian in transmitting Machiavelli's dictum that if a state is not increasing in scope and power, then it is surely declining. Whereas Machiavelli and Sidney encourage armed aggression under the banner of such necessity, Cato and Locke choose the peaceful method of trade and individual industry in pursuit of the same end.

Nevertheless, in so far reconciling Machiavelli and Locke, Cato actually builds on the platform that Sidney had already provided. It was Sidney, after all, who had made Machiavelli's understanding compatible with the notions of consent and of natural rights. And it was Sidney's and Cato's spirited defense – a largely Machiavellian spirit – of those principles that so aroused the admiration of the Americans.

PART II

THE MODERATE ENLIGHTENMENT

E vents are sometimes dispositive – even with regard to political thought. On 13 August 1704, just such an event took place, one little remembered today, and less often discussed – though it signaled a political and an ideological transformation that was arguably no less significant than the one marked in our own time by the fall of the Berlin Wall and the dismemberment of the Soviet Union.

In the late spring and summer of that fateful year, two armies made their way from western to central Europe. The first, led by the comte de Tallard, marshal of France, aimed at upsetting the balance of power in Europe; at establishing Louis XIV's hegemony over the Holy Roman Empire by installing a French nominee on its throne; and at securing the acquiescence of the Austrians, the English, the Dutch, and every other European power in a Bourbon succession to the Spanish throne. The second army, led by John Churchill, then earl, later duke of Marlborough, with the assistance of Prince Eugene of Savoy, sought to preserve the existing balance of power, defend Hapsburg control of the imperial throne, and deprive Louis of his Spanish prize.

At stake, so nearly everyone supposed,[1] was the establishment of a universal monarchy in Europe and French dominion in the New World, and there was every reason to suppose that Louis would achieve this goal, which had been the object of his ambition during the entirety of his adult life. After all, on the field of the sword, France enjoyed a preeminence that no one dared deny. The French had occasionally been checked, but on no occasion in the preceding one hundred fifty years had an army of France suffered a genuinely decisive defeat.

---

[1] See Franz Bosbach, *Monarchia Universalis: Ein politischer Leitbegriff der frühen Neuzeit* (Göttingen : Vandenhoeck & Ruprecht, 1988), 107–21, and "Eine französische Universalmonarchie? Deutsche Reaktionen auf die europäische Politik Ludwigs XIV," in *Vermittlungen: Aspekte der deutsche französischen Beziehungen vom 17. Jahrhundert bis zur Gegenwart*, ed. Jochen Schlobach (Berne: Peter Lang, 1992), 53–68, as well as Steven C. A. Pincus, "The English Debate over Universal Monarchy," in *A Union for Empire: Political Thought and the Union of 1707*, ed. John Robertson (Cambridge, UK: Cambridge University Press, 1995), 37–62.

It thus came as a shock when all of Europe learned that the army commanded by Marlborough and Prince Eugene had annihilated the French force and captured Marshal Tallard.[2]

Had the Battle of Blenheim been a fluke, a genuine anomaly, Louis's defeat on this particular occasion would not have much mattered. At most, it would have marked a temporary if severe setback for French arms. In the event, however, this great struggle was but the first of a series of French defeats meted out by armies captained by Marlborough, and it foreshadowed the series of setbacks that would bedevil the French as the century wore on. If we are today ill informed concerning the events that took place at Ramillies, Oudenarde, Lille, and Malplaquet in the brief span of years stretching from 1706 to 1709, it is because we have become accustomed resolutely to avert our gaze from the fundamental realities of political life. In the United States, despite the leading role in the world that country long ago assumed, very few universities devote substantial resources to the study of armed conflict. Not one history department in twenty even offers a course focusing on the conduct and consequences of war. And yet Winston Churchill was surely right when he observed that "battles are the principal milestones in secular history," when he rejected "modern opinion," which "resents this uninspiring truth," and when he criticized "historians" who so "often treat the decisions in the field as incidents in the dramas of politics and diplomacy." "Great battles," he insisted, whether "won or lost, change the entire course of events, create new standards of values, new moods, new atmospheres, in armies and in nations, to which all must conform."[3]

So it was in France and in Europe more generally after 1713 when the Treaty of Utrecht brought an end to the War of the Spanish Succession. By dint of diplomatic skill and a canny exploitation of the partisan strife that erupted in England, Louis XIV managed to preserve his kingdom intact and even to secure the Spanish throne for his younger son.[4] But this did not alter the fact that his great project had proved unattainable. Nor did this turn of events disguise the fact that overreaching on his part had bankrupted France and very nearly brought down the polity. A sense of foreboding gripped his countrymen as they slowly digested what there was to be learned from their repeated defeats on the field of the sword. It is no accident that, as a thinker, Bishop Bossuet had in France no real heirs. Nor should it seem odd that the Regency came to be synonymous with decay. It was no longer possible to thrill to the vision of grandeur that had informed Louis's great effort, and no one at the time had an alternative vision to proffer. By 1715, it was perfectly clear to anyone with a discerning eye that, in France and elsewhere, the old order was bankrupt in more than one way.

---

[2] For the details, see Winston S. Churchill, *Marlborough: His Life and Times* (London: George G. Harrap, 1947), 1:711–868.

[3] See ibid., 2:95–627 (esp. 381).

[4] See ibid., 2:628–1005.

Europeans, then, began to look elsewhere for models. Prior to the first decade of the eighteenth century, no one on the continent had demonstrated much of an interest in England. The execution of Charles I had been noticed, of course, but it evoked only horror; and apart from the years in which Oliver Cromwell was in the ascendancy, England played no very prominent role in the affairs of Europe or the New World. From the perspective of Louis XIV, it was a mere pawn – a relatively inconsequential state virtually begging for manipulation. He is said once to have asked the English ambassador whether his country had any writers of note, and when Pierre Corneille was sent an English translation of *Le Cid*, he purportedly shelved it in his cabinet between the work's Slavonic and Turkish translations.[5] In seventeenth-century Europe, no one thought England, the English, their language, their literature, their institutions, their mode of conduct, and their way of seeing the world a proper object for contemplation.

After the Glorious Revolution, however – especially after Marlborough's magnificent victories in its defense – attitudes changed, and young Europeans of penetrating intelligence thought it necessary to read about and even visit the country that had put together, funded, and led the coalition that had inflicted on the Sun King of France so signal a defeat. Scots, such as David Hume, journeyed South. Frenchmen, such as François-Marie Arouet, whom we know best by his pen-name Voltaire, and Charles-Louis de Secondat, baron de la Brède et de Montesquieu, crossed the English channel and labored to master what their forebears had regarded as a barbarous language. Ambitious colonials, such as Benjamin Franklin of Pennsylvania, thought it essential to pay the old country a visit. London had become the center of the world. The English and their way of life, their practices, the form of government they had developed, and their turn of mind – these were all of interest, as was the manner in which Niccolò Machiavelli's *Discourses on Livy* informed the thinking of James Harrington, John Locke, Algernon Sidney, John Trenchard, Thomas Gordon, and the other writers embraced by the radical Whigs.

Marlborough's victories were made possible by credit. The United Provinces had learned from the city-states of Renaissance Italy a secret at the heart of modern statecraft – the manner in which a national debt can be a national blessing for a commercial republic intent on the projection of power and able to borrow from its own citizens – and their English allies in the age of William III had capitalized on the discovery made by the compatriots of their Dutch king.[6]

Political economy was a subject on which one might expect Machiavelli to have been well-versed. He was, after all, a Florentine. He had been reared, he

---

[5] See C. P. Courtney, "Montesquieu and English Liberty," in *Montesquieu's Science of Politics: Essays on* The Spirit of Laws, ed. David W. Carrithers, Michael A. Mosher, and Paul A. Rahe (Lanham, MD: Rowman and Littlefield, 2001), 273–90 (at 273).

[6] See John Brewer, *The Sinews of Power: War, Money, and the English State, 1688–1783* (New York: Knopf, 1989).

spent most of his life in a city dominated by merchants and bankers. He was a high-level civil servant in a government quite familiar with instruments of debt, and he had dealings with Venice, Genoa, and other commercial republics accustomed to taking advantage of public credit.[7]

Finance was not, however, Machiavelli's long suit. "If I were able to speak to you," he writes on 9 April 1513 to his friend Francesco Vettori (*O* 1131), "I would be unable to refrain from filling your head with castles in the air *(castelluci)* because Fortune has brought it about that, since I do not know how to reason about either the silk or the wool trade, either gains or losses, it is necessary that I reason concerning matters of state *(stato)*." Though he was born in a commune of tradesmen, Machiavelli dedicated his attention primarily to ancient polities governed by warriors and farmers. He was sensitive to the fact that his beloved Romans had financed their wars by enslaving the conquered and confiscating their land, and he recognized that changes in the *ius gentium* ruled out the implementation of such a policy in Christian Europe.[8] But he nowhere explained how to pay for modern wars. Repeatedly he denied that money is "the sinews of war" (*D* 2.10, *AW* 7.178–9).

In a famous letter written to Vettori on 10 December 1513, at a time when he had been deprived of employment and forced to live in his villa outside the city in a condition akin to house arrest, Machiavelli describes how he spends his days – trapping birds, passing time with the woodcutters in his employ, disputing over what is owed him, reading Dante and the lesser poets, daydreaming about his amours, gossiping at an inn, gambling with the innkeeper, a butcher, a miller, and two bakers, and quarreling with his companions over the pennies at stake. "Thus involved with these lice," he writes, "I scrape the mold off my brain and I satisfy the malignity of this my fate, being satisfied to be run over on this path so as to see whether fate will be ashamed of it." Only at the end of his account does Machiavelli abandon the pervasive tone of bitter

---

[7] Consider Roberto Ridolfi, *The Life of Niccolò Machiavelli*, tr. Cecil Grayson (Chicago: University of Chicago, 1963), 15–132, and Robert Black, "Machiavelli, Servant of the Florentine Republic," in *Machiavelli and Republicanism*, ed. Gisela Bock, Quentin Skinner, and Maurizio Viroli (Cambridge, UK: Cambridge University Press, 1990), 71–99, in light of Mark Jurdjevic, "Virtue, Commerce, and the Enduring Florentine Republican Moment: Reintegrating Italy into the Atlantic Republican Debate," *Journal of the History of Ideas* 62:4 (October 2001): 721–43; then, see Anthony Molho, "L'amministrazione del debito pubblico a Firenze nel quindicesimo secolo," in *I ceti dirigenti nella Toscana del Quattrocento* (Monte Oriolo: Papafava, 1987), 191–207, and "Lo Stato e la finanza pubblica. Un'ipotesi basata sulla storia tardomedioevale di Firenze," in *Origini dello Stato: Processi di formazione statale in Italia fra medioevo ed età moderna*, ed. Giorgio Chittolini, Anthony Molho, and Pierangelo Schiera (Bologna: Il Mulino, 1994), 225–80. The subject does come up in Machiavelli's personal correspondence: See Letters to Giovanni Vernacci on 20 April 1514 and on 15 February and 8 May 1521, in *O* 1173–4, 1201–2.

[8] Cf. *AW* 2.302–9 with 5.93–104; note *D* 2.6, and then consider the contrast that Machiavelli draws between the liberality of Cyrus, Caesar, and Alexander and the parsimony practiced in his own day by Pope Julius II, Louis XII of France, and Ferdinand of Spain (*P* 16).

self-mockery and reveal what he is really up to. "When evening comes," he reports,

I return to my house and enter my study. At the entrance I take off my daily attire, replete with mud and mire, and I put on my garments regal and courtly; and properly reclothed, I enter the ancient courts of ancient men, where, received by them in a loving fashion, I feed on the food which is mine alone, that for which I was born. There, I am not ashamed to converse with these men and to ask them the reason for their actions, and they in their humanity answer me. For four hours at a stretch I feel no boredom, I forget every pain, I do not dread poverty, death frightens me not. Entirely I give myself over to them.

It is in this connection, he remarks, that he has jotted down what he has gained from these imaginary conversations in a little work entitled *De Principatibus*, which should be "acceptable to a prince, especially a new prince" (O 1159–60). Classical antiquity was the starting point for his political ruminations.

By 1710, however, when it had become clear to all concerned that Louis XIV's martial France – modeled, as it was, on imperial Rome – could not withstand the modern Carthage on the other side of the English Channel, the cause of classical antiquity had worn rather thin. To discerning men, such as Hume, Montesquieu, and Franklin, the obsession with Roman greatness that had preoccupied Machiavelli seemed more and more an anachronism, and astute observers came to believe that one cannot reason concerning matters of state without studying the silk and wool trades, profit, and loss.[9]

That Machiavelli did not prove to be an anachronism himself is due to the fact that he did not take the ancients at their word – that he read them, as Markus Fischer has shown in the prologue to this book, "judiciously." In the process, as Marchamont Nedham and James Harrington, John Locke, Algernon Sidney, and the authors of *Cato's Letters* realized,[10] he had pioneered a new politics of interest, distinct from the ancient politics of principle – a politics of interest that could easily be adapted to a world more prosaic than the one that preoccupied the Florentine's dreams.[11] In the new world of the eighteenth century, in which commercial interests frequently took precedence over political interests, Machiavelli's influence may have been less obvious, but it was, in fact, greater than before.[12]

[9] In this connection, see Paul A. Rahe, "The Book That Never Was: Montesquieu's *Considerations on the Romans* in Historical Context," *HPT* 26:1 (Spring 2005): 43–89.
[10] See Chapters 1 through 3.
[11] See Sheldon S. Wolin, *Politics and Vision: Continuity and Innovation in Western Political Thought* (Boston: Little Brown, 1960), 232–3.
[12] See Albert O. Hirshman, *The Passions and the Interests: Political Arguments for Capitalism before Its Triumph* (Princeton, NJ: Princeton University Press, 1977). See also Istvan Hont, "Free Trade and the Economic Limits to National Politics: Neo-Machiavellian Political Economy Reconsidered," in *The Economic Limits to Modern Politics*, ed. John Dunn (Cambridge, UK: Cambridge University Press, 1990), 41–120.

Nedham, Harrington, Locke, and Sidney wrote in an age in which political liberty was under siege. It was by no means clear prior to 1704 that England would not end up as an absolute monarchy on the model of Hapsburg Spain and Bourbon France. It was only with the victories of Marlborough and with the Hanoverian succession that it gradually became evident that the Revolution Settlement was secure. As late as 1720, when John Trenchard and Thomas Gordon began to publish *Cato's Letters* in the public prints, there was still reason for fear.

By the 1730s and the 1740s, however, the fears that had originally driven republican and Whig speculation had subsided to a considerable degree, and to the discerning eye it was the old order on the continent of Europe that seemed in peril, its fragility repeatedly exposed on the field of the sword.[13] It was in this context that Hume and Montesquieu took note of Machiavelli's tacit acknowledgment that monarchy is compatible with a "civil way of life *(vivere civile)*" and even a "political way of life *(vivere politico)*."[14] It was in this context that they attended to his contention that the institutions of monarchical France were conducive to moderation and the rule of law (*P* 19; *D* 1.16.5, 19.2, 58.2, 3.1.5).[15] It was in this context that they came to the defense of the civilized monarchies established on the continent of Europe. It was in these circumstances that they set out to rethink political science from the ground up with an eye to the commercial revolution already well under way, asking what could be learned from the ancients, what from Machiavelli, and what from the Florentine's admirers among the English republicans and Whigs. Their task, as they saw it, was to restore the cause of prudence in the face of a new species of politics that at times seemed no less doctrinaire in its propensities than the political theology that had inspired the sectarian struggles of the sixteenth and early seventeenth centuries. Moderation they made their watchword, and Benjamin Franklin was their heir. If they struggled self-consciously to find a cure for one species of Machiavellianism, they were, nonetheless, intent on doing justice to the force of the argument that Machiavelli had pioneered, as we shall soon see.

Of the three, Franklin was the very model of a modern moralist, and Montesquieu was to do the most for political science – while David Hume (*EMPL* 42–3) explored moderation's philosophical supports, showing how

---

[13] See John Robertson, "Universal Monarchy and the Liberties of Europe: David Hume's Critique of an English Whig Doctrine," in *Political Discourse in Early Modern Britain*, ed. Nicholas Phillipson and Quentin Skinner (Cambridge, UK: Cambridge University Press, 1993), 349–73.

[14] Note the monarchical context within which Machiavelli speaks of the establishment of a *vivere civile* at Rome (*D* 1.9.1, 19.1). Note the manner in which, in a republic or monarchy, one can ordain a *vivere politico* and one can turn to a *vita civile* (*D* 1.25–6). A *vivere civile* is necessary to but not sufficient for the achievement of "a free way of life *(vivere libero)*": see *D* 1.2.7, 9.2, 25.

[15] See Elena Fasano Guarini, "Machiavelli and the Crisis of the Italian Republics," in *Machiavelli and Republicanism*, 17–40 (esp. 24–28, 34).

"a maxim" can "be true in *politics*, which is false in *fact*," demonstrating that Machiavelli (*D* 1.3.1) can be right in thinking it "a just *political* maxim, *that every man must be supposed a knave*," though it is far from true and folly to suppose that, in ordinary social intercourse, every man really will prove himself such. To come to grips with this paradox, Hume had to reconsider the philosophical foundations of Machiavelli's argument and to turn the skepticism of the Florentine against the dogmatism to which it had given rise. It is to his ruminations on this theme that we must now turn.

4

Getting Our Bearings

Machiavelli and Hume

John W. Danford

More than fifty years ago, political commentator Max Lerner called Machiavelli "the first modern analyst of power," and identified *The Prince* as "one of the half dozen books that have done most to shape Western thought."[1] Machiavelli deserves credit, according to this line of thought (and according to Machiavelli himself) for establishing the first *scientific* political science, based on steely-eyed scrutiny of actual human behavior and the passions that move human beings in all ages.[2] "Whoever considers present and ancient things easily knows that in all cities and in all peoples there are the same desires and the same humors, and there always have been," Machiavelli writes. "So it is an easy thing for whoever examines past things diligently to foresee future things in every republic" (*D* 1.39). It follows that history, or the register of "past things," is the laboratory in which the political scientist works. There is a remarkably similar passage in David Hume's writings:

Mankind are so much the same, in all times and places, that history informs us of nothing new or strange in this particular. Its chief use is only to discover the constant and universal principles of human nature, by showing men in all varieties of circumstances and situations, and furnishing us with materials from which we may form our observations and become acquainted with the regular springs of human actions and behavior.

(*EHU* 83)

It is thus not a coincidence that Machiavelli and Hume were both great historians, arguably two of the greatest historians of the last five hundred years. And there are other similarities. Both wrote unsentimentally. Both were philosophers of the greatest penetration. Both were notorious for religious heterodoxy, and

---

[1] In the editor's introduction to the Modern Library College Edition of *The Prince and the Discourses* by Niccolo Machiavelli (New York: Random House, 1950), xxvi.
[2] See C. Bradley Thompson, "John Adams's Machiavellian Moment," *RP* 57:3 (Summer 1995): 399–406, and Chapter 8 of this book.

I would like to thank Liberty Fund, where, as a senior research fellow in 1996–7, I drafted this chapter.

94

were accused of hostility to Christian teachings. Both were distinguished for breadth of classical learning. Moreover, readers of Hume can easily tell that he studied the writings of Machiavelli with care.[3]

But these similarities obscure a deeper difference between Hume and Machiavelli, having to do with their relative modernity. As Markus Fischer observes in the prologue to this book, Machiavelli, properly understood, teaches a "repudiation of the classical tradition." Far more often, however, over the past half-century, Machiavelli has been looked on as a republican or civic humanist, with distinctly ancient sympathies. In the words of one influential commentator, "Machiavelli not only presents a wholehearted defence of traditional republican values; he also presents that defence in a wholeheartedly traditional way."[4] His works praised the practices and political wisdom – in short, the virtue – of the ancient Romans, while mocking and denigrating the political sophistication of his contemporaries. By contrast, Hume wrote favorably of large modern commercial societies, including the eighteenth-century French monarchy, and argued that the ancient republics were uncritically appreciated by their admirers.[5] Thus we may be tempted to see Machiavelli as a transitional figure, at most a bridge to modern forms of political society, and Hume as their champion, and thus the more modern of the two. This would be too hasty, however. Each of these thinkers is notoriously difficult to classify.[6] Reading Machiavelli as a civic humanist requires that one ignore some of his most shocking recommendations, to say nothing of his centuries-old reputation as a teacher of evil.[7] As Fischer

---

[3] See, for example, the discussion of Machiavelli in Hume's essay, "That Politics May Be Reduced to a Science," in *EMPL* 22–3.

[4] Quentin Skinner, "Machiavelli's *Discorsi* and the Pre-Humanist Origins of Republican Ideas," in *Machiavelli and Republicanism*, ed. Gisela Bock, Quentin Skinner, and Maurizio Viroli (Cambridge, UK: Cambridge University Press, 1990), 141. See also J. G. A. Pocock, *The Machiavellian Moment: Florentine Political Thought and the Atlantic Republican Tradition* (Princeton, NJ: Princeton University Press, 1975); Hans Baron, "Machiavelli the Republican Citizen and Author of *The Prince*," in Baron, *In Search of Florentine Civic Humanism: Essays on the Transition from Medieval to Modern Thought* (Princeton, NJ: Princeton University Press, 1988), 2:101–51. The best brief summary of this line of scholarship is to be found in William J. Connell, "The Republican Tradition, in and out of Florence," in *Girolamo Savonarola: Piety, Prophecy and Politics in Renaissance Florence*, ed. Donald Weinstein and Valerie R. Hotchkiss (Dallas: Bridwell Library, 1994), 95–105. For a critique, see Vickie B. Sullivan, "Machiavelli's Momentary 'Machiavellian Moment': A Reconsideration of Pocock's Treatment of the *Discourses*," *Political Theory* 20:2 (May 1992): 309–18. See also Paul A. Rahe, "Situating Machiavelli," in *Renaissance Civic Humanism: Reappraisals and Reflections*, ed. James Hankins (Cambridge, UK: Cambridge University Press, 2000), 270–308.

[5] The most notable example of this is found in Hume's "Of Commerce," in *EMPL* 253–67, the first of his 1752 political economy essays. But see the companion essays, especially "Of Refinement in the Arts," in *EMPL* 268–80, which was originally titled "Of Luxury" – and thus addressed even in its title one of the bugbears of eighteenth-century republicans.

[6] Thus in the words of Hans Baron, "Machiavelli the Republican Citizen and Author of *The Prince*," 101, "few subjects humble and caution the student of history so much as the history of the interpretation of Machiavelli's works."

[7] See, for example, Sheldon Wolin, *Politics and Vision: Continuity and Innovation in Western Political Thought* (Boston: Little, Brown, 1960), 195–238; Isaiah Berlin, "The Originality of

puts it, according to Machiavelli, "necessary evil belongs to the effectual truth of...the civil way of life." As for Hume, there is similar controversy, though most commentators stop short of accusing him of being in league with the devil. Hume is variously seen, for example, as a conservative defender of the British political establishment, a liberal proponent of "the politics of progress,"[8] or even, as one commentator has argued, something of a civic humanist himself.[9]

I will try to show that the teachings of Hume and Machiavelli differ more profoundly than is commonly believed, but that the ground of their difference is not at all what the preceding characterization suggests. I will argue that in the most important respects Machiavelli is wholeheartedly and unequivocally modern, while it is Hume who has deeper sympathies with the perspective of his classical or ancient predecessors. In so arguing, I hope to shed light on what modernity itself means, in its most fundamental or radical formulation.

It will be clear to the reader that I read Machiavelli in much the same way as does Markus Fischer in the prologue to this book. But where Fischer traces the *political* implications of Machiavelli's views, I am concerned with the *philosophical* implications of Machiavelli's challenge to his ancient and medieval predecessors, because that is the plane on which Hume's views come into conflict with part of what Machiavelli taught. In a nutshell, this is because the consequences drawn by Machiavelli's modern philosophical successors (Francis Bacon, René Descartes, Thomas Hobbes, John Locke, and others) gave rise to a new understanding of the grounds of political life – and legitimacy – that posed, in the eighteenth century, a new problem. One could say that Hume was concerned with precisely the radical character of one of Machiavelli's core principles, namely, the principle that we should take our bearings from extreme or worst cases. For example, Hume saw the doctrine of the social compact, advanced by Locke and the radical Whigs, as a dangerous political teaching, a

---

Machiavelli," in *Against the Current: Essays in the History of Ideas*, ed. Henry Hardy (New York: Viking Press, 1980), 25–79; Leo Strauss, *Thoughts on Machiavelli* (Seattle, WA: University of Washington Press, 1969); *Natural Right and History* (Chicago: University of Chicago Press, 1953), 177–82; Harvey C. Mansfield, *Machiavelli's New Modes and Orders: A Study of the Discourses on Livy* (Ithaca, NY: Cornell University Press, 1979).

[8] The expression comes from Hiram Caton's excellent study, *The Politics of Progress: The Origins and Development of the Commercial Republic, 1600–1835* (Gainesville, FL: University of Florida Press, 1988). Caton discusses Hume's defense of the progress of the arts and sciences in 324–30. See also Paul A. Rahe, *Republics Ancient and Modern: Classical Republicanism and the American Revolution* (Chapel Hill, NC: University of North Carolina Press, 1992), 519–20, 587–9, 642.

[9] See John Robertson, "The Scottish Enlightenment at the limits of the civic tradition," in *Wealth and Virtue: The Shaping of Political Economy in the Scottish Enlightenment*, ed. Istvan Hont and Michael Ignatieff (Cambridge, UK: Cambridge University Press, 1983), 137–78. The section on Hume attempts to make the case that Hume saw economic progress as making possible the realization of the goal of civic humanists: "...with the general improvements and diffusion of martial and political virtues resulting from the industrious pursuit of luxury, it should become possible for everyone to cultivate the basic moral attributes of citizenship.... Quite simply, it was Hume's contention that as every individual is motivated by interest, so, by achieving the material sufficiency and independence for which interest strives, every individual may also be capable of the virtue required of a citizen" (159).

case of "false philosophy" or philosophy wrongly deployed as a tool to change the world, and one likely to have the most deleterious political consequences.

According to Hume, a political order develops gradually and incrementally: In today's terms, we would say it is an evolutionary order or a case of spontaneous order. He allows that "consent" in some form is necessary in a political community, but insists that

> even this consent was long very imperfect, and could not be the basis of a regular administration.... No compact or agreement, it is evident, was expressly formed for general submission; an idea far beyond the comprehension of savages: Each exertion of authority in the chieftain must have been particular, and called forth by the present exigencies of the case: The sensible utility, resulting from his interposition, made these exertions become daily more frequent; and their frequency gradually produced an habitual, and, if you please to call it so, a voluntary, and therefore precarious, acquiescence in the people.
> (*EMPL* 468–9)

So much Hume is willing to grant to the proponents of what he calls "Original Contract" theory:

> But philosophers, who have embraced a party (if that be not a contradiction in terms) are not contented with these concessions. They assert, not only that government in its earliest infancy arose from consent or rather the voluntary acquiescence of the people; but also, that, even at present, when it has attained full maturity, it rests on no other foundation. They affirm, that all men are still born equal, and owe allegiance to no prince or government, unless bound by the obligation and sanction of a *promise*. And as no man, without some equivalent, would forego the advantages of his native liberty, and subject himself to the will of another; this promise is always understood to be conditional, and imposes on him no obligation, unless he meet with justice and protection from his sovereign.
> (*EMPL* 469)

Such is the foundation of authority in every government, "according to these philosophers," Hume notes. This is what we are led to if we insist on reducing everyday affairs, or the surface of things, to first principles. "But would these reasoners look abroad into the world, they would meet with nothing that, in the least, corresponds to their ideas, or can warrant so refined and philosophical a system" (*EMPL* 469–70). In the conclusion of the essay ("Of the Original Contract"), Hume states his view in the most forceful terms: "Nothing is a clearer proof, that a theory of this kind is erroneous, than to find, that it leads to paradoxes, repugnant to the common sentiments of mankind, and to the practice and opinion of all nations and all ages. The doctrine, which founds all lawful government on an *original contract*, or consent of the people, is plainly of this kind" (*EMPL* 486).

Machiavelli and the Tradition

Let us begin with the claim that Machiavelli should be understood as restoring the perspective of classical republicanism. The cardinal principle of classical republicanism was surely what J. G. A. Pocock calls "the ancient belief that the fulfillment of man's life was to be found in political association."[10] As Aristotle had expressed it, "man is by nature a *polis* animal"*(Pol.* 1253a3). Since the nature of a thing can be seen only in its completion or perfection (its *telos*, or end), this amounts to the belief that anyone who is not fortunate enough to live in a *polis* cannot be said to live as a full human being or to realize his nature. Whatever we may think of Aristotle's claim (as repeated, of course, by centuries of classical writers, including Cicero and St. Thomas Aquinas), it is difficult to find such a teaching in Machiavelli's writings.[11] Indeed Machiavelli, who insists he is merely describing men as they are, maintains that "in every republic are two diverse humors, that of the people and that of the great," and "if one considers the end of the nobles and of the ignobles, one will see great desire to dominate in the former, and in the latter only desire not to be dominated" (*D* 1.4, 1.5). Machiavelli recognizes very clearly what we might call the "political impulse" that leads men to seek to rule, for the sake of honor and glory.[12] But he teaches us that this is found only in the few, not the many. And he never suggests that the many, who desire only to be left alone or not to be dominated, are "slavish" or less than human. On the contrary, we are told that "the common utility that is drawn from a free way of life" consists in "being able to enjoy one's things freely, without any suspicion, not fearing for the honor of wives and that of children, not to be afraid for oneself" (*D* 1.16).[13]

In fact, Machiavelli does not suggest that anything can or should be understood in terms of its end, or "fulfillment." According to Markus Fischer, notwithstanding the semantic continuity, Machiavelli "reject[s] the teleological account of man so fundamental to classical theorizing about politics." He famously eschews reflection on "how one should live," preferring "to write something useful," something oriented by what he calls the "effectual truth of the thing" (*P* 15). What matters, we learn repeatedly in his writings, is not the end or goal *(telos)* of a thing, but the cause or origin of the thing.

---

[10] See J. G. A. Pocock, "Between Machiavelli and Hume: Gibbon as Civic Humanist and Philosophical Historian," in *Edward Gibbon and the Decline and Fall of the Roman Empire*, ed. G. W. Bowersock and John Clive (Cambridge, MA: Harvard University Press, 1977), 104.

[11] According to Sebastian de Grazia, *Machiavelli in Hell* (Princeton, NJ: Princeton University Press, 1989), 268–9, "this ancient political idea" that man is a political animal "travels with the baggage of Aristotle and the Stoics from Greece to Rome, where it is rewrapped, taken up by Thomas Aquinas, and distributed among Christians everywhere." Some paragraphs later (269), he expresses Machiavelli's reaction: "There is, however, a disadvantage to the theory: it is untrue. A conduit running straight from man's inborn nature to his final worldly end? No. Unable to see it, Niccolo cannot claim it."

[12] See *P* 25, where Machiavelli, speaking of the ways in which men seek their various ends or goals, identifies two candidates for the role of "the end that each has before him." The two he names are "glories" and "riches." This seems to fit quite well with Machiavelli's distinction between the many, who care only about their own private concerns and do not wish to be oppressed, and the few (the lovers of honor or glory?) who love to rule.

[13] Cf. Montesquieu, *EL* 2.11.6: "Political liberty in a citizen is that tranquillity of spirit which comes from the opinion each one has of his security, and in order for him to have this liberty the government must be such that one citizen cannot fear another citizen." See the discussion in Rahe, *Republics Ancient and Modern*, 440–4.

Machiavelli classifies the different types of states not according to the end or ends that rulers aim at, as Aristotle had taught, but according to how power is acquired: "All states, all dominions that have held and do hold empire over men have been and are either republics or principalities. The principalities are either hereditary, ... or they are new. The new ones are either altogether new, ... or they are like members added to the hereditary state" (*P* 1; cf. *D* 1.2). It is difficult to find even a trace of classical teleology in Machiavelli; concern with causes and conditions, or the "effectual truth," seems wholly to supplant reflection on the proper or highest ends. And we are not left in the dark about why: For human beings there is no leisure to reflect on ends, because the constant motion of human desires makes survival or security (and acquisition of the power necessary thereto – "men cannot secure themselves except with power" [*D* 1.1]) the only concern we can afford.

Leisure, in the classical or Aristotelian account, is the proper end of action; wars are fought in order to have peace and leisure. Aristotle criticized the Spartans for reversing this ranking (*Pol.* 1334a5–10). According to Machiavelli's account, however, Aristotle was wrong and the Spartans correct. The art of war "is the only art which is of concern to one who commands"; Machiavelli observes that other writers praise Philopoemen, prince of the Achaeans, who was wise because "in times of peace he never thought of anything but modes of war" (*P* 14). The Romans, according to Machiavelli, "knew that war may not be avoided but is deferred to the advantage of others" (*P* 3), and knowing this, they were always on the lookout for future trouble.

The causes of things are not taken seriously enough primarily because they are obscure. The surface of things, Machiavelli suggests, is deceptive, and "the generality of men feed on what appears as much as on what is; indeed many times they are moved more by things that appear than by things that are" (*D* 1.25). This explains why men are so confused about how to guide their lives: "if one considers everything well, one will find something appears to be virtue, which if pursued would be one's ruin, and something else appears to be vice, which if pursued results in one's security and well-being" (*P* 15). Since "the vulgar are taken in by the appearance and the outcome of a thing, and in the world there is no one but the vulgar" (*P* 18), we should not be surprised that the causes of success are so poorly understood. Aristotle, of course, was quite critical of the capacities of the many or the vulgar. According to Aristotle, it is difficult to understand the natures of things since the nature of anything is revealed only when it can develop in nearly perfect conditions; thus the nature of a thing can only be glimpsed in circumstances that are rare and fragile. According to Machiavelli, things are hard to understand because the causes are hidden by deceitful appearances.

Take, for example, a civilized social order, a *polis*, the natural locus for the development of our full humanity according to the classical view. How does a civilized social order come into being? We learn less than we might like on this question from ancient writers. But they teach very clearly the difference between life *in a polis*, where freedom from necessity makes possible the serious consideration of issues of justice and honor, and life *outside* a *polis*, where necessity rules. When human beings are governed by necessity, or the requirements of survival, there is no place for the nicer questions of justice. Thucydides formulated this understanding in unforgettable terms in the Melian dialogue. Thus a civilized social order makes possible the emergence of the distinctively human considerations, or makes it possible for us to live as full human beings, as Aristotle said.

Machiavelli, who does speak at least indirectly about how civilized orders come into being, offers a radical challenge to this understanding. He does so by denying that we can ever transcend or escape from the requirements of the realm of necessity. We may believe that we can transcend necessity, and this is all the easier to believe because human beings are taken in by the surface of things, and things sometimes appear to be peaceful and quiet. In peaceful and quiet times, men are inclined to turn their thoughts to leisure and forget necessity. Those who are shrewder do not do so. In the chapter entitled "What Have Been Universally the Beginnings of Any City Whatever, and What Was That of Rome," Machiavelli shows how wise founders correct this inclination. "Men work either by necessity or by choice," he tells us, and "there is greater virtue to be seen where choice has less authority." Is it better, Machiavelli asks, to found a city in a fertile place (with the promise of leisure) or where "men are constrained to be industrious and less seized by idleness" as a consequence of "the poverty of the site"? The latter choice "would without doubt be wiser and more useful if men were content to live off their own and did not wish to seek to command others." But men are not content; they wish to dominate; and "since men cannot secure themselves except with power, it is necessary to avoid this sterility in a country and to settle in the most fertile places...as to the idleness that the site might bring, *the laws should be ordered to constrain it by imposing such necessities as the site does not provide*" (D 1.1; emphasis added).

A wise founder will find a way to compel men always to take account of the dictates of necessity. The fundamental human condition is one of competition and war, because ambition "is so powerful in human breasts that it never abandons them at whatever rank they rise to," and so "whenever engaging in combat through necessity is taken from men they engage in combat through ambition." As Machiavelli likes to observe, this is only natural. "The cause is that nature has created men so that they are able to desire everything and are unable to attain everything. So, since the desire is always greater than the power of acquiring, the result is discontent with what one possesses and a lack of satisfaction with it" (D 1.37). The same lessons are found in many places in Machiavelli's writings, literary as well as political. "Men willingly change their masters in the belief that they will fare better," for example, and "truly it is a very natural and ordinary thing to desire to acquire, and always, when men do it who can, they will be praised or not blamed" (P 3). "Human appetites are insatiable, for since from nature they have the ability and the wish to desire all things and from fortune the ability to achieve few of them there continually results from this a discontent in human minds and a disgust with the things they possess" (*D* 2.pref.).

The implication is clear: Human life is a constant struggle or competition. The ancient philosophers were blind to this because they allowed themselves to be taken in by the surface of things. In this conclusion, we glimpse Machiavelli's presentation of what we can call the fundamental orientation of modernity itself, which is a posture of skepticism.[14] If the surface of things deceives us always or even sometimes, we must resolve – if we hope for success in operating in such a world – to penetrate beneath the surface of things to find the truth. Machiavelli presents this in the form of political doctrine, advising us to orient ourselves by what happens in times of adversity or in extreme cases. "So whoever holds a state, whether republic or prince, should consider beforehand what times can come up against him, and which men he can have need of in adverse times; and then live with them in the mode that he judges to be necessary to live, should any case whatever come up" (*D* 1.32). It is, as he points out, "a common defect of men, not to take account of the storm during the calm"; this is why princes who have ruled states successfully ought not "accuse fortune when they have lost them afterwards, but their own indolence; for never having thought that quiet times could change. . . . when later the times became adverse, they thought of fleeing and not of defending themselves" (*P* 24).

The Romans, of course, always took their bearings from the worst that could happen. Machiavelli approves this as the posture of those who understand how the world works. It is better for a prince to base his rule on fear than on love, for example, because fear is the more reliable passion: "for love is held by a chain of obligation, which, because men are wicked, is broken at every opportunity for their own utility, but fear is held by a dread of punishment that never forsakes you" (*P* 17). By the same token it is unwise to rely on magistrates, as a prince is inclined to do in "quiet times," since lines of authority will not be clear when, in an emergency, the prince must direct things himself. It is better to take one's bearings from emergencies, because sooner or later they will arise. When things are quiet, "everyone promises, and each wants to die for him when death is at a distance; but in adverse times, when the state has need of citizens, then few of them are to be found" (*P* 9).

Though presented as a political doctrine, the implications of this posture toward the world go far beyond – and were understood by Machiavelli's successors to go far beyond – political science in the narrow sense. The cardinal tenet of Machiavelli's outlook can be described as the principle of reduction: The hard core of things lies beneath layers of appearance; we must penetrate beneath the confusing or misleading surface to find the reality beneath; we should orient ourselves according to the most basic, the lowest, or most fundamental layer. Here is one formulation of Machiavelli's teaching: "contrary to the opinion of many" who think Rome was lucky not to have been destroyed

---

[14] As Hume noted (*THN* 1.4.4), the "fundamental principle" of the "modern philosophy" is skepticism about the senses.

by *tumulti*, which would have happened "if good fortune and military virtue had not made up for its defects," Machiavelli confides that he "cannot deny that fortune and the military were causes of the Roman Empire; but it quite appears to me they are not aware that where the military is good, there must be good order; and too, it rarely occurs that good fortune will not be there" (*D* 1.4). He states this more plainly in *The Prince*: "The principal foundations that all states have, new ones as well as old or mixed, are good laws and good arms. And because there cannot be good laws where there are not good arms, and where there are good arms there must be good laws, I shall leave out the reasoning on laws and shall speak of arms" (*P* 12). Machiavelli prefers to get down to basics, and what is basic is force. We may not see the armed force on which all else, and certainly lawful behavior, depends. It is commonly hidden beneath the deceptive surface of things. But the wise prince or statesman knows what he should attend to, and reduces things to the layer where we find the things that really matter.[15]

Let us try to see what this means in slightly different terms by considering Machiavelli's comments on those who seek a "middle way." The idea that we can be moderate or balanced, in both our actions and in our understanding, was of course characteristic of Machiavelli's ancient or classical predecessors, most famously Aristotle. Aristotle knew that there is war as well as peace, and he knew that in time of war men are guided by necessity: We do what we have to do to survive. But Aristotle also taught that peace or leisure gives us freedom to act according to justice or honor, and to ask questions about ends – for example, how should we live? We no longer need to take our bearings from the lowest concern, survival; we can orient ourselves by what is highest. We can ask, for example, whether the life of a poet is higher than that of statesman. This is why Aristotle criticizes the Lacedaemonians for organizing their *polis* around the inevitability of war. That war is "for the sake of being at leisure and of peace," he writes, "is testified to by events as well as arguments." Cities such as Sparta "preserve themselves when at war, but once having acquired [imperial] rule they come to ruin...the reason is that the legislator has not educated them to be capable of being at leisure" (*Pol.* 1334a5–10).[16]

Machiavelli believed that peace is an illusion; the reality of human life is struggle and competition, even when these are hidden. Nonetheless we – and especially those who philosophize about politics – are tempted to look for a way to limit or avoid struggle and competition. Following Aristotle, we look for a middle ground, a way to order political life with an eye to war, for the sake of security, but yet aiming at peace and leisure. According to Machiavelli, "if someone wished...to order a republic anew, he would have to examine

---

[15] This could also be brought out by attending to Machiavelli's teaching about necessity (discussed previously); see, e.g., *D* 3.12.

[16] See also, for example, August. *De civ. D.* 19.12: "It is therefore with the desire for peace that wars are waged, even by those who take pleasure in exercising their warlike nature in command and battle. And hence it is obvious that peace is the end sought for by war."

whether he wished it to expand like Rome in dominion and in power or truly to remain within narrow limits" (*D* 1.6). To design a healthy but nonexpansionist republic might be possible, Machiavelli at first admits with some hesitation. "If it stays within its limits, and it is seen by experience that there is no ambition in it, it will never occur that one will make war for fear of it" (*D* 1.6). But we have reason to suspect that there cannot be any human institution with "no ambition in it," for reasons examined previously.

Machiavelli allows that "if the thing could be held balanced in this mode, it would be the true political way of life and the true quiet of a city." The subjunctive hints at his real conviction, however:

But since all things of men are in motion and cannot stay steady, they must either rise or fall; and to many things that reason does not bring you, necessity brings you. So when a republic that has been ordered so as to be capable of maintaining itself does not expand, and necessity leads it to expand, this would come about to take away its foundations and make it come to ruin sooner.

That is, a republic that has not oriented itself for contingencies or emergencies, or what "necessity" may compel it to deal with, will fail when an emergency arises. "On the other hand," Machiavelli continues (again in the subjunctive), "if heaven were so kind that it did not have to make war, from that would arise the idleness to make it either effeminate or divided; these two things together, or each by itself, would be the cause of its ruin" (*D* 1.6). Peace, leisure, and prosperity, in other words, are dangerous. If no outside threat compels a republic to unite or "get serious," then internal divisions, softness, or idleness will corrupt its vitality. To remain healthy, a political community requires an enemy.[17] Enemies are of course inevitable only if the aim is expansion.

There are thus only two genuine possibilities: division and decline if the republic is oriented toward peace and leisure, or healthy competition (sometimes called war) if the aim is cohesion and expansion. As Machiavelli concedes at the end of his analysis, there really is no middle way: "I do not believe one can find a mode between the one and the other" (*D* 1.6). The denial of the existence of a middle way is a lesson or principle repeated many times in different contexts. It is the basis of Machiavelli's famous recommendation that one's enemies should either be "caressed or eliminated" (*P* 3). It appears in slightly different form when Machiavelli discusses loyalty to princes. "Some say that with princes you should not wish to stand so close that their ruin includes you, nor so far that you would not be in time to rise above their ruin when they are being ruined. *Such a middle way would be the truest if it could be observed, but because I believe that it is impossible*, one must be reduced to the two modes written above – that is, either to distance oneself from or to bind oneself to them" (*D* 3.2; emphasis added). As he puts it in yet another context, "one cannot hold exactly to the middle way, for our nature does not consent to it" (*D* 3.21).

---

[17] Consider NM, *P* 19, in light of 9.

Machiavelli and His Successors

We turn now to the question of what Machiavelli's rejection of the classical and Christian tradition, as exemplified in the sort of principles we have identified, meant to – or in the hands of – his successors. I take for granted that Machiavelli was (and was understood by them to be) a philosopher, not merely a political tactician or advisor to princes.[18] Machiavelli declared forthrightly that he had decided "to take a path as yet untrodden by anyone" (*D* 1.pref.). To "write something useful," he had to "depart from the orders of others" (*P* 15).

He also knew that such a project was a dangerous undertaking (*D* 1.pref.; cf. *P* 6). Those determined to proceed along his new path also were cautious, at least about acknowledging any debt to the Florentine, and it is not surprising that Machiavelli's ideas show up, variously disguised but still unmistakable, without his name being mentioned. A century after his death, Machiavelli's principles emerged as cardinal tenets in the writings of those who launched the great intellectual revolution of the seventeenth century, the revolution associated with the development of modern natural science, or as Hume was later to call it, "the modern philosophy." In Markus Fischer's words, "Machiavelli's turn toward the 'effectual truth' gave an important impulse to the modern scientific project." In order to see clearly the relation between Machiavelli and Hume, one must attend to the connection between Machiavelli and the scientific revolution.

Perhaps the most fundamental of the continuities we are seeking is the understanding of philosophy itself. The ancient thinkers taught that philosophy is the highest or most fully human way of life, but they did not think of it as a practical enterprise. Philosophy meant the pursuit of wisdom for its own sake, and the fate of Socrates taught that such a pursuit is not without its dangers. Machiavelli gently mocks those who "have imagined republics and principalities that have never been seen or known to exist in truth"; he proposes instead, as we have seen, to "write something useful," and he suggests that it is "more fitting to go directly to the effectual truth of the thing than to the imagination of it" (*P* 15). A century later, in *The Great Instauration*, Francis Bacon complained that "the entire fabric of human reason which we employ in the inquisition of nature is badly put together and built up, and like some magnificent structure without any foundation." More particularly, according to Bacon, the philosophy of the ancients is useless: "for its value and utility it must be plainly avowed that that wisdom which we have derived principally from the Greeks is but like the boyhood of knowledge, and has the characteristic property of boys: it can talk, but it cannot generate, for it is fruitful of controversies but barren of works." The modern philosophy that Bacon proposes to establish will replace controversy, or "perpetual agitation," with effectual knowledge, which allows us to

---

[18] See Harvey C. Mansfield and Nathan Tarcov, "Introduction," in *D* xxxvi–xli: the section is entitled "Machiavelli the Philosopher?" See also Roger D. Masters, *Machiavelli, Leonardo, and the Science of Power* (Notre Dame, IN: University of Notre Dame Press, 1996), 29–47.

"command nature in action" (*WoFB* 4:7–8, 14, 24). Philosophy, in short, is to be understood as a tool, a "new organon," an instrument. "Human knowledge and human power meet in one," he wrote in his *Novum Organum* (1.3), "for where the cause is not known the effect cannot be produced" (*WoFB* 4:47). The philosophy of the ancients was useless and must be entirely replaced. One can trace in Descartes and Hobbes precisely the same attitude and the same hopes.[19]

In the new philosophy, the teleology of the ancients is to be rejected in favor of understanding things by looking at causes. To know something, according to Hobbes, is to be able to break it down or resolve it into its constituent parts, and then compose it or construct it. The second rule of Descartes' "method of rightly conducting the reason and seeking truth in the field of the sciences" is to divide any problem (anything one wishes to understand) into "as many parts as possible," after which one should "think in an orderly fashion, beginning with the things which were simplest and easiest to understand, and gradually and by degrees reaching toward more complex knowledge" (*DM* II). Things or wholes are unintelligible to us unless we approach them by means of this method; the idea that we can understand a thing in terms of its completion or perfection, its *telos*, is a foolish dream. Instrumental knowledge or what Machiavelli called the "effectual truth" can be described by the slogan "what is true is what works." And the key to scientific procedure as Hobbes understood it – he called it the resolutive-compositive method – is the procedure of reduction: We resolve or reduce wholes to parts or simples, and then compose or construct the whole out of these elements or variables. Today we call this "modeling"; the method is as pervasive in the social sciences as in physics or chemistry.

That it is indispensable to *have* a procedure or method is perhaps of more fundamental significance. We have already seen in Machiavelli the principle that the surface of things deceives us. The surface is unreliable as a guide to action, since the apparent calm of peaceful times is only hiding an underlying and ever-present competition, which results from insatiable human desires and ambition. The real implication of this principle may be obscured by the purely political form in which Machiavelli clothed it. For if appearances deceive us, at least sometimes, then if we wish to be secure we must be suspicious of appearances at all times. And this means we must be skeptical about what our senses, including common sense, tell us about the world around us. As Hume later noted, doubt about the evidence of the senses is the "fundamental principle" of the modern philosophy. It is ludicrously easy to find expressions of this notion in the writings of Bacon, Descartes, and Hobbes. "The sense," Bacon observes in *The Great Instauration*, "fails in two ways. Sometimes it

---

[19] Descartes, *DM* I; Hobbes, *Leviathan* IV.xlvi; *De Corpore*, Ep. Ded., in *EW* 1:vii–xii. It is worth quoting Hobbes's words from Chapter 46 of *Leviathan*. Referring to the philosophy of the Greeks, Hobbes asks, "But what has been the Utility of those Schools? What science is there at this day from their readings and disputings? . . . The natural philosophy of those Schools, was rather a Dream than Science."

gives no information, sometimes it gives false information. For first, there are very many things which escape the sense, even when best disposed and no way obstructed.... And again when the sense does apprehend a thing its apprehension is not much to be relied upon" (*WoFB* 4:26).[20] In the opening chapter of *Leviathan* (I.i), Hobbes briefly reviews basic scientific doctrines, pointing out that although the cause of sense is the "Externall Body, or Object, which presseth the organ proper to each sense," we are compelled to admit that sensible qualities are really only "fancies." Why? All of the "qualities called Sensible, are[,] in the object that causeth them, but so many several motions of the matter, by which it presseth our organs diversly."

The skeptical posture about the evidence of our senses is symptomatic of a profound skepticism about our place in the natural order. The ancients seem to have believed that human beings are equipped by nature for the place they occupy in the natural order. Our senses – and above all sight, the most human of the senses – are naturally suited to inform and guide us as to the nature of the beings around us. In Aristotle's account of the hierarchy of the senses, sight is highest (in Greek the words for seeing and knowing are cognates).[21] Touch – the sense shared even with earthworms and oysters – is lowest. But the moderns reverse this, as they learned to do from Machiavelli. "Everyone sees how you appear; few touch what you are" (*P* 18; cf. *Mandragola* 5.2, in *O* 888–9), he counseled, convinced that sight is most easily fooled by the surface of things while touch can be counted on. In Hobbes's account of the senses (*Leviathan* I.i), sight is presented as a "mediated" sense and therefore less reliable than the direct or "unmediated" sense of touch.

What is at stake here is whether we are by nature fitted or suited to know the world around us. If not, then our experience is unreliable insofar as it is not corrected by scientific method, by what we might call "rational reconstruction" of the world. Descartes laments that before our reason has a chance to develop (or we have a chance to apply it), we are spoiled or confused by nonrational influences. "We were all children before being men, at which time we were necessarily under the control of our appetites and our teachers, and...neither of these influences is wholly consistent.... It is therefore impossible that our judgments should be as pure and firm as they would have been had we the use of our whole reason from the time of our birth" (*DM* II). What we require, Hobbes and Descartes both teach, is to replace the defective conclusions we draw from experience, or common sense, with accounts of the world derived rationally, using scientific method. That this should be necessary indicates that earlier thinkers, the ancients above all, were far too complacent in their evaluation of the human situation. They thought the most important things to know could be known or learned directly from the world around us, but they were living in a fool's paradise. The human senses, as Bacon points out, are

---

[20] See also *The Great Instauration* and *The New Organon* 1.50, in *WoFB* 4:26, 58.
[21] *Eîdos* and *idéa*, the Greek terms we translate as idea or intelligible form, derive from *ideîn*, the verb "to see."

suited not to nature but to man, and we fail to see whole worlds of life and activity (microscopic animals and plants, for example, or light outside the visible part of the electromagnetic spectrum) that surround and affect us. Simple human experience, then, is a poor basis for the accumulation of genuine knowledge.

The demotion of experience as the source of knowledge, or rather the attempt to construct a science that does not rely on common sense or prudential knowledge, was justified by Descartes and Hobbes as the only way to achieve knowledge that is useful. To be useful, it must be certain. How do we achieve certainty? We must build on a reliable foundation, which requires that we take nothing for granted. Thus we must take our bearings from what will be true "no matter what," that is, what we see in "adverse times." In explaining human behavior, for example, we can admit that human beings sometimes act magnanimously or from disinterested motives. But when the chips are down, in an emergency, human beings can be counted on to act out of self-interest. "For nothing is more easily broken than a mans word," as Hobbes puts it (*Leviathan* I.xiv). The fact that we desire far more than we can attain to means that the human condition or the natural condition is one of discontent: In Hobbes's words, "I put for a generall inclination of all mankind, a perpetual and restlesse desire of Power after power, that ceaseth only in Death." Lest there be any doubt, he goes on: "Nor can a man any more live, whose desires are at an end, than he, whose Senses and Imagination are at a stand. Felicity is a continuall progresse of the desire, from one object to another; the attaining of the former, being still but the way to the later [sic]." As a corollary, Hobbes recognized that the human condition is fundamentally a condition of anxiety, and "anxiety for future time" is the seed not only of science but of religion (*Leviathan* I.xi).

The anxiety that is inescapable in the human condition justifies our attempt to orient ourselves by what is most reliable, and therefore justifies the procedure of reduction. If we aim to have reliable knowledge, there is no room for attempts at balance (for example, to consider both activity and leisure, or both peace and war, as possible alternatives). There is no middle way. We are better off (more secure in our understanding) if we regard peace as a temporary and even illusory interlude between episodes of war, which are the reality. "For Warre, consisteth not in Battell onely, or the act of fighting; but in a tract of time wherein the Will to contend by Battell is sufficiently known" (*Leviathan* I.xiii). And thus the natural condition of mankind is a condition of war – just as Machiavelli had taught.

These considerations justify a new conception of politics, the central concern of which is henceforth to be understood as the task of achieving peace, or such security as human beings can hope for. The ancient or traditional understanding held that the aim of civil or political life is the perfection of human faculties and cultivation of the virtues – in short, "human fulfillment." But on the new understanding, there is no room for (or no time for) such considerations; survival matters most in a condition of fundamental scarcity and insecurity. The aims of civic life are thus peace and "commodious living." Whatever else individuals may want or seek, survival and security are indisputably necessary; we can envision complete agreement on these goals. But this means, in turn, that the human faculties formerly regarded as highest, and even as partaking of divinity, such as reason, are now to be understood as tools or instruments for the satisfaction of the most important and more *basic* human needs. Our philosophy or science should serve the "low" ends (Aristotle would have said low; the new teaching says "basic" or "universal").

All this can be traced, as I have tried to show, to the principles of Machiavelli. Implicit in these principles is much of the broad program of modernity, in both its epistemological or scientific and its political aspects. These are sweeping generalizations, however, and we must be careful not to claim too much. There are significant differences between the understandings or the teachings of Machiavelli and Hobbes, as indeed there are between those of Bacon and Hobbes, or Descartes and Hobbes. Hobbes's *Leviathan* surely indicates, for example, that Machiavelli overestimated human inequality. Hobbes agreed with Machiavelli's teaching that there are basically two kinds of human beings – those who are "glad to be at ease within modest bounds," but also "some" who take "pleasure in contemplating their own power in the acts of conquest, which they pursue farther than their security requires." But on Hobbes's view, despite this division into two kinds, men should be seen to be equal politically because of a decisive point of equality: Every human being, even the strongest and smartest, is susceptible to being killed by others. Even "the weakest has strength enough to kill the strongest, either by secret machination, or by confederacy with others, that are in the same danger with himselfe" (*Leviathan* I.xi). Thus Hobbes corrects Machiavelli on the question of how civil societies come into being. The credit should be given not to the great glory-seeking armed prophets, but to the timid multitude who acquiesce in a covenant to escape from the terrible state of nature.

Notwithstanding such differences, it is proper to see Machiavelli as quite radically modern. He explicitly rejects the teaching of "many" who "have written about" virtue and vice, or "those things for which men and especially princes are praised or blamed." Not only does he offer a substitute for the teaching of the tradition, he tells us why the tradition must be supplanted: It is not useful. Not only does he reject it as useless, he teaches us how to orient ourselves so as to arrive at a more useful, because more reliable or certain, teaching. And in all these respects and others, Machiavelli's principles were apparently understood, and accepted, by successors as diverse as Bacon, Descartes, and Hobbes. Machiavelli is properly regarded as the founder of not just a new political science, but of a new science altogether, which became what we call modern natural science. And this is where Hume comes in.

Hume and Machiavelli

We may begin from the most important point of agreement between Hume and Machiavelli. Hume accepted Machiavelli's suggestion that the aims of political life as the classical thinkers conceived it were much too high. The chief concerns of government should be the security and prosperity of citizens or subjects rather than their virtue or salvation. Hume in fact devoted one of his best political essays to precisely this question, asking whether modern sovereigns should try to imitate the ancient republics in elevating the principle of public-spiritedness, which requires the sacrifice of private to the public good. He argues persuasively that they should not, and in the process explains that the ancient republics are not worthy of imitation: "ancient policy was violent, and contrary to the more natural and usual course of things" (*EMPL* 259). The ancient republics compelled their citizens to submit to "grievous burdens"; their policies were successful only because they existed in very special – and undesirable – circumstances. The modern policy of encouraging rather than disdaining "trade and manufactures" much more successfully promotes human happiness. Hume is justifiably regarded as the champion of large commercial societies, mainly because of the prosperity and individual liberty they not only permit, but promote.[22]

Machiavelli was full of praise for republican Rome, it is true, but the grounds of his praise are commonly misunderstood. Machiavelli praises the Romans because they grasped the fundamental truth about the human condition, which is that it consists of competitiveness, unsatisfied desire, and instability, and they based their policies on that truth. He was under no illusions about the priorities of ordinary human beings. "For one can say this generally of men: that they are ungrateful, fickle, pretenders and dissemblers, evaders of danger, eager for gain"; a ruler should take care "to abstain from the property of others, because men forget the death of a father more quickly than the loss of a patrimony" (*P* 17).

In a remarkable passage concerning the Roman Empire, Machiavelli asks the reader to think about "the times from Nerva to Marcus, and compare them with those that came before and that came later." If a prince were to make such a comparison:

let him choose in which he would wish to be born or over which he would wish to be placed.... For in those governed by the good he will see a secure prince in the midst of his secure citizens, and the world full of peace and justice; he will see the Senate with its authority, the magistrates with their honors, the rich citizens enjoying their riches, nobility and virtue exalted; he will see all quiet and all good, and, on the other side, all rancor, all license, corruption and ambition eliminated. *He will see golden times when each can hold and defend the opinion he wishes. He will see, in sum, the world in triumph, the prince full of reverence and glory, the peoples full of love and security.*

(*D* 1.10; emphasis added)

---

[22] For a nuanced discussion of Hume on the issue of liberty and commercial society, see Richard B. Sher, "From Troglodytes to Americans: Montesquieu and the Scottish Enlightenment on Liberty, Virtue, and Commerce," in *Republicanism, Liberty, and Commercial Society, 1649–1776*, ed. David Wootton (Stanford, CA: Stanford University Press, 1994), 368–402. The book contains a number of other good pieces related to this issue.

These are obviously not the words of a classical republican, since the "golden times" were achieved centuries after the republic had disappeared.[23] Machiavelli makes no mention of men being fulfilled or made fully human by political participation. And in any event, such participation was not widespread under the emperors.[24] Indeed, his description of the golden times includes freedom of opinion or conscience – a concern notably absent from the ancient *polis*, but characteristic of modern liberal societies.

Security and riches seem particularly important in the account Machiavelli offers. And this is consistent with the advice Machiavelli offers elsewhere, when he counsels a prince to "inspire his citizens to follow their pursuits quietly, in trade and in agriculture and in every other pursuit of men, so that one person does not fear to adorn his possessions lest they be taken away from him, and another to open up a trade for fear of taxes" (*P* 21). This is a far cry from the classical view that trade and commerce are unworthy of the attention of a gentleman, and that human fulfillment is to be found in participation in the life of the *polis*. The refocusing of political life on the concerns of prosperity, commerce, and trade is distinctly modern, as least as far as theory is concerned. As Hume notes in one of his earliest essays, "trade was never esteemed an affair of state until the last century; and there scarcely is any ancient writer on politics, who has made mention of it" (*EMPL* 88).

According to Machiavelli, it is wise to aim low because security and prosperity are the things people want anyway, and the attempt to elevate the goals of political life makes political stability that much harder to achieve. Political men, those who seek honor and glory, are never found in large numbers. The prince, Machiavelli, suggests, "should examine what causes are those that make [peoples] desire to be free. He will find that a small part of them desires to be free so as to command, but all the others, who are infinite, desire freedom so as to live secure" (*D* 1.16). In fact, Machiavelli supplies us with numbers: "For in all republics, ordered in whatever mode, never do even forty or fifty citizens reach the ranks of command." These can be dealt with, he suggests, "either

---

[23] It is worth comparing this passage to the similar account in Edward Gibbon, *History of the Decline and Fall of the Roman Empire*, ed. David Womersley (London: Penguin, 1994), 103: "If a man were called to fix the period in the history of the world during which the condition of the human race was most happy and prosperous, he would, without hesitation, name that which elapsed from the death of Domitian to the accession of Commodus."

[24] According to Hans Baron, *The Crisis of the Early Italian Renaissance: Civic Humanism and Republican Liberty in an Age of Classicism and Tyranny* (Princeton, NJ: Princeton University Press, 1955), 1:38–43, one of the challenges facing the early Florentine civic humanists, and in particular Leonardo Bruni – the author of what Baron calls "the birth certificate of a new period" (1:38) – was the fact that their beloved Dante had placed the murderers of Caesar in the lowest pit of hell, in the maws of Lucifer; see Dante Alighieri, *Inferno*, canto 34, line 65, in *The Divine Comedy*, tr. Allen Mandelbaum (New York: Knopf, 1995), 211. This seemed to suggest that Dante thought well of Caesar and perhaps of the period of his rule, and this in turn would surely disqualify Dante as far as civic humanist political judgment is concerned. Perhaps Machiavelli also spoke well of the "golden times" under the Roman emperors because he shared more with Dante than with Bruni.

by getting rid of them or by having them share in so many honors ... that they have to be in good part content." As for "the others, to whom it is enough to live secure," they can be satisfied if the prince or sovereign makes "orders and laws in which universal security is included" (*D* 1.16). Thus, he proposes a neat solution to satisfy both types of human beings: the few who care about glory or reputation, and the many who want only security and tranquillity – that is, to be left alone.

Despite substantial agreement between Machiavelli and Hume on the question of what the aims of political life should be, their views rest on somewhat different foundations. Machiavelli arrives at his policy recommendations by taking his bearings from the worst that can happen, or from "adverse times," as we have seen. In the issue now under consideration, we could say that Machiavelli assumes all men to be selfish or self-interested, some seeking honor while others care only about peace and security. Aiming low is more likely to satisfy both types, and thus to result in stability. Machiavelli's liberal successors adopted this principle, and denied the relevance of public-spirited political behavior altogether. One might describe this as an inversion of the classical approach. Where the ancients hoped to suppress the desire for private gain in order to promote the public good, Machiavelli suggests that the public good consists in satisfying the private appetites or "humors" of different types of men. Aristotle teaches us to understand the low in terms of (or for the sake of) the high; Machiavelli introduces quotation marks, and teaches us to recognize that the "high" is for the sake of the "low." In the view of Machiavelli and his successors, political society or the *polis* is an artifice, a human construction or instrument for the achievement of private, prepolitical goods or ends.

Hume's account breaks the symmetry we see when we compare the classical view with the view of Machiavelli. Aristotle teaches us to understand the private (the household) as existing for the sake of the public (the *polis*); Machiavelli and his successors teach us to understand political life as existing to satisfy private ends. Hume's account refuses both the classical suppression of the low for the sake of the high and Machiavelli's reversal. Hume accepts Machiavelli's account of what the goals of political life should be, but he is unwilling to accept the ground that Machiavelli offered for his recommendation, namely that the high things are illusory. One might say that for Hume it is not that the high things – for example, leisure and philosophy – are illusions or delusions, but that they are properly left in the private realm. Political communities should concern themselves with peace and security not because these are all that matter, but because political communities with the elevated goals of the ancient *polis* do violence to human nature and destroy liberty.

The disagreement we have uncovered is related to a deeper difference between Hume and Machiavelli, which we may describe as a difference in epistemology. We have tried to show that Machiavelli's policy recommendations flow from the principle of radical reduction, to which we are driven, as he sees it, by the impossibility of any "middle way." Because the surface of things sometimes deceives us, we must find a more reliable foundation for knowledge. In the thought of Machiavelli's successors (or as Hume would put it, in their "systems"), the need for certainty leads to an emphasis on method, which requires that we construct a rational account of the world to replace the commonsense world of experience or more precisely prescientific experience. Thus we construct a model to explain human behavior, for example, by assuming self-interested human beings, since self-interested behavior is most common or universal. Generous or disinterested conduct is, to use Hobbes's words, "too rarely found to be presumed on" (*Leviathan* I.xiv).

Hume's great philosophical contribution was epistemological: He supplied a critique of modern rationalism, undermining the vain hope that we can construct a science that escapes the limitations of knowledge from experience. On Hume's understanding, we cannot achieve clear and certain knowledge of the sort sought by Descartes or Hobbes anywhere outside the purely abstract or mathematical sciences, because all knowledge of the world or of "matters of fact" ultimately rests on the experiences and perceptions from what Hume liked to call "common life." This is as true of the natural as of the moral sciences. In both, we must be able to trace our reasoning back to common life, although Hume's account allows that there will be a slight difference. In moral reasoning or reasoning about the passions, Hume believes, it is unlikely that any satisfactory account can be given that seeks to "reduce all the various emotions of the human mind to a perfect simplicity." But in the natural sciences, as opposed to the moral sciences, we find more room for reduction. "The case is not the same in this species of philosophy [moral philosophy] as in physics. Many an hypothesis in nature, contrary to first appearances, has been found, on more accurate scrutiny, solid and satisfactory" (*EPM* 299).

Hume's reasoning about what he calls the "selfish system of morals" – attributed to Hobbes and Locke – will illustrate this clearly. According to Hobbes's reasoning, we can construct a reliable theory or model of human behavior (one that will serve to predict accurately, "if this be, that shall be . . . ," and so on), if we begin by taking nothing for granted. We will not assume that human beings are benevolent or disinterested, but assume the worst, namely that they are selfish and passion-driven, in constant motion trying to satisfy the endless succession of appetites and aversions in which human life consists. These individuals or atoms will be permanently in competition with each other for scarce goods. The result is not difficult to deduce: chaos and scarcity, danger and fear, and the life of man "solitary, poor, nasty, brutish, and short." The natural condition of mankind must therefore be admitted to be a state of war; in order to escape this terrible condition, the necessary means is the establishment of a civil order. The reason for the existence of civil society is thus exposed with stark clarity: Men live in society not for "human fulfillment" but out of "foresight of their own preservation, and of a more contented life" (*Leviathan* II.xvii). Hobbes's conclusions are not matters for argument. They can be demonstrated, according to him, with convincing reasoning, starting from simple truths with which no one can disagree, and assuming the worst wherever appropriate, so that nothing is taken for granted. At the very least, the world is as Hobbes describes it; it may be better, but that does not shake the basic truth. Therefore all men must accept Hobbes's new political science or "civil philosophy."

Hume appears to have believed that the political science of his predecessor was the product of an overdeveloped longing for simplicity or systematic philosophy. Reductive explanations – while they may be true in a *de minimis* sense – produce a different kind of problem, by distorting the phenomena they purport to explain. Moreover, they can have dangerous consequences. Hume addresses the reductive approach of the "selfish system of morals" both in the second *Enquiry* and in the *Essays*, using similar approaches. The reductive account of "an Epicurean or a Hobbist," as Hume explains, may "attempt, by a philosophical chymistry, to resolve the elements of this passion [friendship]...into those of another, and explain every affection to be self-love, twisted and moulded, by a particular turn of imagination, into a variety of appearances" (*EPM* 296–7). The attempt to find solid ground beneath disparate appearances cannot be successful, however, if the reduction manages to explain away the phenomenon we know as friendship in common life or ordinary speech. Some individuals are concerned about others; some are not. Hume says that he esteems the former, "as I hate or despise him who has no regard to anything beyond his own gratifications and enjoyments." These are characters we know from common life:

In vain would you suggest that these characters, though seemingly opposite, are at bottom the same, and that a very inconsiderable turn of thought forms the whole difference between them....And I find not in this more than in other subjects, that the natural sentiments arising from the general appearances of things are easily destroyed by subtle reflections concerning the minute origin of these appearances.   (*EPM* 297)

Hume recommends taking our bearings from "common feeling and our most unprejudiced notions." The philosophical reductionists ignore or deny the "obvious appearance of things." According to Hume, even "to the most careless observer there appear to be such dispositions as benevolence and generosity; such affections as love, friendship, compassion, gratitude. These sentiments have their causes, effects, objects, and operations, marked by common language and observation, and plainly distinguished from those of the selfish passions." What moves theorists such as Hobbes to deny the surface of things, complex as it is, and offer a reductive explanation? "All attempts of this kind have hitherto proved fruitless, and seem to have proceeded entirely from that love of simplicity which has been the source of much false reasoning in philosophy" (*EPM* 298).[25]

Hume's insight is that in this case we gain nothing by performing the reduction insisted on by philosophical systematizers. Suppose we allow that all

---

[25] See Donald Livingston, *Hume's Philosophy of Common Life* (Chicago: University of Chicago Press, 1984), 20–33, 91–111, who calls attention to Hume's use of the term "false philosophy."

human behavior is selfish, he suggests, imagining a dialogue with someone holding to the "selfish system of morals":

What say you of natural affection? . . . Is that also a species of self-love? Yes: All is self-love. Your children are loved only because they are yours: Your friend for a like reason: And your country engages you only so far as it has a connexion with yourself : Were the idea of self removed, nothing would affect you. . . . I am willing, reply I, to receive your interpretation of human actions, provided you admit the facts. That species of self-love, which displays itself in kindness to others, you must allow to have great influence over human actions, and even greater, on many occasions, than that which remains in its original shape and form.

He concludes the paragraph with an elegant piece of teasing: "Be you also one of these selfish men," Hume tells his antagonist, "and you are sure of everyone's good opinion and good will; or not to shock your ears with these expressions, the self-love of every one, and mine among the rest, will then incline us to serve you, and speak well of you" (*EMPL* 85).

It remains to say why reductive explanations can be dangerous. Hume was alert to the consequences of what we may call political rationalism – of which scientific reduction is the chief hallmark – in a way that his predecessors were not. He foresaw the rise of ideological politics long before the phenomenon itself was named or indeed even discerned. Philosophical systematizers are prone to lose their bearings in common life precisely because they mistrust common life or experience; in their search for an indisputable foundation for political reasoning (by reduction), they propound theories of the sort that can be used to delegitimize actual, and decent, political orders. "Parties from *principle*, especially abstract speculative principle, are known only to modern times, and are, perhaps, the most extraordinary and unaccountable *phœnomenon*, that has yet appeared in human affairs," according to Hume (*EMPL* 60).

Of particular concern to Hume was a party connected to the theoretical construct that Hume criticized under the term "original contract" theory. Original contract theory is one example of a speculative theory that "leads to paradoxes, repugnant to the common sentiments of mankind, and to the practice and opinion of all nations and all ages" (*EMPL* 486). As his footnotes indicate, Hume has in mind the theory of John Locke in the *Second Treatise*. Locke's adherents have not

scrupled to affirm, *that absolute monarchy is inconsistent with civil society, and so can be no form of civil government at all; and that the supreme power in a state cannot take away from any man, by taxes and impositions, any part of his property, without his own consent or that of his representatives.* What authority any moral reasoning can have, which leads into opinions so wide of the general practice of mankind, in every place but this single kingdom, it is easy to determine.   (*EMPL* 487)

The danger such a doctrine poses was nicely illustrated by the French Revolution, more than a decade after Hume's death. And "abstract, speculative" political doctrines have caused considerable damage in the two succeeding centuries.[26]

In Hume's view, "though an appeal to general opinion may justly, in the speculative sciences of metaphysics, natural philosophy, or astronomy, be deemed unfair and inconclusive, yet in all questions with regard to morals, as well as criticism, there is really no other standard, by which any controversy can ever be decided" (*EMPL* 486). Hume reaches this conclusion after a careful and lengthy analysis of the origins of civil society. "Reason, history, and experience shew us, that all political societies have had an origin much less accurate and regular" than the doctrine of original contract allows. In fact, "were one to choose a period of time, when the people's consent was the least regarded in public transactions, it would be precisely on the establishment of a new government" (*EMPL* 474).

The problem with abstract speculative theories in politics is that "there is no virtue or moral duty, but what may, with facility, be refined away, if we indulge a false philosophy, in sifting and scrutinizing it, by every captious rule of logic, in every light or position, in which it may be placed" (*EMPL* 482). The only remedy against such theories is solid grounding in history and experience – in what we earlier called the surface of things, which modern scientific reductionism eschews as the basis of solid knowledge. "Would these reasoners look abroad into the world, they would meet with nothing that, in the least, corresponds to their ideas, or can warrant so refined and philosophical a system" (*EMPL* 469–70).

We have tried to show that Machiavelli's distrust of the surface of things led, in the hands of his successors, to a certain approach to political issues that Hume regarded as detached from common life. Now of course Machiavelli was himself hardly a speculative or abstract philosopher. Whatever else he may have been, he was a historian, and it may seem churlish to charge him with responsibility for the speculative theories of which Hume is so critical. Hume himself admits that it is a "just *political* maxim, *that every man must be supposed a knave*," when we are "contriving any system of government, and fixing the several checks and controuls of the constitution" (*EMPL* 42). The principle here seems purely Machiavellian (see *D* 1.3), and it is surely one of the most important principles enshrined in the U.S. Constitution.[27] Hume is aware that the principle poses a problem for his own insistence on taking one's bearings from common life: "It appears somewhat strange, that a maxim should be true in *politics*, which is false in *fact*" (*EMPL* 42–3).

---

[26] An excellent discussion of "false philosophy" and its relation to politics and historical understanding is to be found in Donald W. Livingston, "Hume's Historical Conception of Liberty," in *Liberty in Hume's History of England*, ed. Nicholas Capaldi and Donald W. Livingston (Dordrecht: Kluwer, 1990), 105–53 (esp. 137–51).

[27] See Paul A. Rahe, "Jefferson's Machiavellian Political Science," *RP* 57:3 (Summer 1995): 449–81 (at 453–5), where the same passage from Hume is discussed, and Chapter 9 in this book.

His reasoning is instructive. "To satisfy us on this head, we may consider, that men are generally more honest in their private than in their public capacity, and will go to greater lengths to serve a party, than when their own private interest is alone concerned." That is, Hume makes a distinction between two areas of common life, and suggests that human behavior in groups (parties), though it operates on the same principles as it does when considered universally, leads to different results. "Honour is a great check upon mankind: But where a considerable body of men act together, this check is, in a great measure removed; since a man is sure to be approved of by his own party, for what promotes the common interest [of the party]; and he soon learns to despise the clamours of adversaries." Thus we are not taking leave of common life when we arrive at the political maxim, we are simply taking our bearings from a particular sort of human behavior or a special part of common life. "When there offers, therefore, to our censure and examination, any plan of government, real or imaginary, where the power is distributed among several courts, and several orders of men, we should always consider the separate interest of each court, and each order." And this is not the result of a speculative theory: "In this opinion I am justified by experience, as well as by the authority of all philosophers and politicians, both antient and modern" (*EMPL* 43).

Conclusion

Machiavelli presented himself as a pathbreaker. The famous lines of the Proemium to book one of the *Discourses* leave no doubt about this: "I have decided to take a path as yet untrodden by anyone, and if it brings me trouble and difficulty, it could also bring me reward through those who consider humanely the end of these labors of mine." Human nature being what it is, of course, he knew it is "no less dangerous to find new modes and orders than to seek unknown waters and lands" (*D* 1.pref.). These self-conscious pronouncements prompt us to ask where the new path was to lead, and they surely render dubious the claim that Machiavelli thought of himself as *recovering* the public-spirited politics of republican Rome.

We have seen that the Florentine's vision was more radically modern than many acknowledge, and that the new modes and orders include or project many of the features of the kind of liberal commercial society we live in. Such a social order would have been unthinkable to the ancients, not least because of the wealth generated by the two sides of Machiavelli's project: on the one hand, the liberation of human energies in commerce and trade, and on the other, the scientific conquest of fortune or nature in order to increase human powers. There is much to be grateful for in the vision of progress that Machiavelli launched. Those who should be most grateful are perhaps the beneficiaries who live in the most modern, and hence most Machiavellian, modern commercial society, the United States. No doubt Americans' much-decried indifference to politics is traceable in part to Machiavelli's suggestion that for most people happiness has little to do with political activity or the public realm.

We can allow that much of what is good in large modern commercial societies is traceable to Machiavelli without, however, denying that some of the most destructive excesses of modern social thought are also traceable to the pattern of thought he established. Specifically, Machiavelli's distrust of the surface and his denial that a middle way is possible have encouraged implausible, sometimes hilarious, and occasionally dangerous reductionism in attempts to understand the human world. Jonathan Swift satirized these tendencies to great effect in the third book of *Gulliver's Travels* some time before even Hume began to express his misgivings. And Hume's misgivings were not widely appreciated, at least not widely enough to forestall the overwhelming reductionism of, for example, Karl Marx, with all the baneful effects that are perhaps inevitable when you combine a determination to change the world with overconfidence in your understanding of it. The conviction that human history is driven by economics is only one of many forms of reductionism whose fundamental outline can be glimpsed in Machiavelli's teaching about the relation between force and law.

Hume adopted or at least shared Machiavelli's conviction that politics was overrated by the ancient thinkers when they claimed that a man who does not engage in political activity cannot be fully human. He shares the view that a prosperous and free society, with a flourishing commerce, where the arts and sciences can develop to enhance and adorn human life, where civil liberty as well as peace are enjoyed by the general population, should be the goal of every statesman as well as of political reflection. Hume's term for this human *telos*, easily discerned in the volumes of his *History of England*, is civilization or a civilized society. But Hume is considerably less sanguine than is Machiavelli about the possibility of achieving a civilized order by intentional human activity. He describes England as "a civilized nation," and suggests that the English "have happily established the most perfect and most accurate system of liberty, that was ever found compatible with government." But he advises that men recognize the fragility of the decent order they inhabit; a careful study of history should teach them "the great mixture of accident which commonly concurs with a small ingredient of wisdom and foresight, in erecting the complicated fabric of the most perfect government" (*HE* 2:525).

Though Hume was skeptical about the ability of human beings to design or arrange the complicated fabric of a perfect government, he was, as we have tried to show, less skeptical than was Machiavelli about taking our bearings from common life or the surface of things. That is, Hume was less pessimistic about the human place in the world, about the suitability of the world as a human abode. He tried to show that the "fundamental principle" of the modern philosophy, skepticism about the senses, induces us to try to construct rational systems of thought that eventually lead us into absurdities (*EHU* 149–60). All reasoning, whether in physics or morals, is about facts or experience, and can never escape the limitations of the imperfect human capacities. We should be, Hume teaches, *mitigated skeptics*, which is to say we should take a middle way between "the greater part of mankind" who are "naturally apt to be affirmative and dogmatical in their opinions," and those philosophical skeptics whose doubts lead them into insurmountable absurdities (*EHU* 161).

Hume was, in short, a proponent of the middle way, the very possibility of which Machiavelli denied. A nice illustration of this can be seen in one of Hume's earliest essays – an essay sometimes cited as showing the influence of Machiavelli on Hume – "That Politics May Be Reduced to a Science." Hume begins the essay by considering "whether there be any essential difference between one form of government and another? and, whether every form may not become good or bad, according as it is well or ill administered?" (*EMPL* 14). As the reader discovers only later, he takes up this issue because he has something to say about a "hot-button" political issue of the day (1741). The issue exercising his contemporaries is a debate about whether certain political ills are to be blamed on particular ministers in the current government, or on the British constitution itself (which makes it possible for such ministers to rise to power). The first part of what is for Hume a rather long essay traces the importance of constitutional order and fundamental laws, at least in a republican and free government (as opposed to an absolute government, in which matters depend much more on the character of those holding power). According to Hume, "a republican and free government would be an obvious absurdity, if the particular checks and controuls, provided by the constitution, had really no influence, and made it not the interest, even of bad men, to act for the public good" (*EMPL* 15–16). In a passage that shares something with Harrington,[28] Hume continues: "So great is the force of laws, and of particular forms of government, and so little dependence have they on the humours and tempers of men, that consequences almost as general and certain may sometimes be deduced from them, as any which the mathematical sciences afford us" (*EMPL* 16). What follows in the next ten pages is the apparently Machiavellian portion of the essay, intended to draw some "general and certain consequences" about the effect of certain specific political arrangements (for example, that the best form of aristocracy requires "a nobility without vassals"). "Here, then, is a sufficient inducement to maintain, with the utmost ZEAL, in every free state, those forms and institutions, by which liberty is secured, the public good consulted, and the avarice or ambition of particular men restrained and punished" (*EMPL* 26). But now Hume turns to what one might call his "ulterior motive" in composing the essay: After praising those who pursue the public good with "utmost ZEAL," he pulls back. "But this is a subject which needs not be longer insisted on at present. There are enow of zealots on both sides who kindle up the passions of their partizans, and under pretence of public good, pursue the interests and ends of their particular faction" (*EMPL* 27).

We now learn Hume's real aim in composing this essay. "For my part," he continues, "I shall always be more fond of promoting moderation than zeal; though perhaps the surest way of producing moderation in every party is to increase our zeal for the public. *Let us therefore try, if it be possible, from the*

---

[28] See Chapter 1 in this book.

foregoing doctrine, to draw a lesson of moderation with regard to the parties, into which our country is at present divided." He goes on to seek a middle way. "Those who either attack or defend a minister in such a government as ours, . . . always carry matters to an extreme, and exaggerate his merit or demerit with regard to the public. His enemies are sure to charge him with the greatest enormities, both in domestic and foreign management; and there is no meanness or crime, of which, in their account, he is not capable." But on the other hand, "the partizans of the minister make his panegyric run as high as the accusation against him, and celebrate his wise, steady, and moderate conduct in every part of his administration" (*EMPL* 27–8; emphasis added).

Hume's concern is now set forth unequivocally: "When this accusation and panegyric are received by the partizans of each party, no wonder they beget an extraordinary ferment on both sides, and fill the nation with violent animosities. But I would fain persuade these party-zealots, that there is a flat contradiction both in the accusation and panegyric, and that it were impossible for either of them to run so high, were it not for this contradiction" (*EMPL* 28). He spells it out at greater length than would be appropriate to quote here. To those who think the minister awful but the constitution excellent, Hume points out that an excellent constitution should have prevented the long tenure of an awful minister. To those who take the opposite side and defend the minister with too much zeal, Hume offers similar reasoning:

Is our constitution so excellent? Then a change of ministry can be no such dreadful event; since it is essential to such a constitution, in every ministry, both to preserve itself from violation, and to prevent all enormities in the administration. *Is our constitution very bad?* Then so extraordinary a jealousy and apprehension, on account of changes, is ill placed; and a man should no more be anxious in this case, than a husband who had married a woman from the stews, should be watchful to prevent her infidelity. Public affairs, in such a government, must necessarily go to confusion, by whatever hands they are conducted; and the zeal of *patriots* is in that case much less requisite than the patience and submission of *philosophers*.   (*EMPL* 30)

Hume's teaching in the essay is, in a word, moderation: "Would men be moderate and consistent, their claims might be admitted; at least might be examined. . . . I would only persuade men not to contend, as if they were fighting *pro aris & focis*" (*EMPL* 30–1). And it is in respect of this moderation that Hume is closer to the moderate views of, say, Aristotle.[29] Always attentive to common life, or common speech, Hume shares with Aristotle the conviction that reasoning about political matters always begins from what men say or believe in ordinary times. There is peace and there is war; both must be attended to and understood without attempting to resolve the one into the other. Some men behave selfishly and some have a regard to others – indeed, most of us are capable of both – and we only distort the moral and political

---

[29] See Stephen G. Salkever, *Finding the Mean: Theory and Practice in Aristotelian Political Philosophy* (Princeton, NJ: Princeton University Press, 1990), 139–42.

world if we claim one disposition is more basic or that one can be reduced to the other.

Hume's modern principles are genuine and undeniable, but they are mitigated by more than a touch of classical moderation. In this respect, he is easier to recognize as the intellectual kinsman of the hardheaded yet commonsensical spokesmen of the American founding generation. While we cannot deny that Machiavelli is, in important respects, the intellectual ancestor of both, we must conclude that the American statesmen owe more to their Scottish cousin than to their Florentine great-grandfather.

5

The Machiavellian Spirit of Montesquieu's Liberal Republic

Paul Carrese

It is now less controversial than it once was to claim that Machiavelli is a significant presence in Montesquieu's political philosophy. This change stems, Montesquieu might say, from two causes. The more elementary is the "influence scholarship" of the past century, which, after studying Montesquieu's library, the style and themes in his published works, and his comments in letters and notes, concludes that he was substantially indebted to Machiavelli.[1] For example, by 1726 – some eight years before publication of his *Considerations on the Causes of the Greatness of the Romans and Their Decline* and some twenty-two years before publishing his masterwork, *On the Spirit of Laws* – Montesquieu owned *The Prince* and the *Discourses on Livy* in Latin and French; eventually he came to possess the works of Machiavelli in Italian as well. However, the narrow methods of such scholarship tend to obscure the extraordinary character of each philosopher's thought and the dialogue a philosopher might have with a predecessor. Montesquieu himself boasts of having examined a sheep's tongue under a microscope (*EL* 2.14.2), but it is another matter to apply these methods to philosophic works such as Machiavelli's *Discourses on Livy* and Montesquieu's *Considerations on the Romans*.

The methods and spirit of influence scholarship point to the more interesting cause for lessened controversy over linking these philosophers: that being associated with Machiavelli is no longer scandalous. Montesquieu's most recent

---

[1] See Ettore Levi-Malvano, *Montesquieu e Machiavelli* (Paris: Champion, 1912), which is now available in English (*Montesquieu and Machiavelli*, tr. Anthony J. Pansini [Kopperl, TX: Greenvale Press, 1992]), and Robert Shackleton, "Montesquieu and Machiavelli: A Reappraisal," *Comparative Literature Studies* 1 (1964): 1–13. For other citations, see Neal Wood, "The Value of Asocial Sociability: Contributions of Machiavelli, Sidney and Montesquieu," in *Machiavelli and the Nature of Political Thought*, ed. Marvin Fleisher (New York: Atheneum, 1972), 282–307 (at 298, n. 52); Diana Schaub, *Erotic Liberalism: Women and Revolution in Montesquieu's Persian Letters* (Lanham, MD: Rowman and Littlefield, 1995), 161–2, n. 42. More generally, see Louis Desgraves, *Répertoire des ouvrages et des articles sur Montesquieu* (Geneva: Droz, 1988), nos. 1452, 2299–2322.

biographer reports that in the eighteenth century, "the reputation of Machiavelli in France, even with the relatively advanced thinkers, was unsavory," though he quickly adds that some thinkers (including Cardinal Richelieu and his secretary, Machon) rose above moral concerns to appreciate the Florentine's work and that "opinions abroad were different," especially in England.[2] Such respectable figures as Sir Francis Bacon, John Locke, James Harrington, and Algernon Sidney either cited or clearly echoed Machiavelli; Montesquieu's sojourn of over a year in England must have exposed him to these influences and to the Viscount Bolingbroke's more polemical usage of Machiavelli. Such observations support respectable conclusions about Machiavelli's important, if limited, influence upon Montesquieu, which is most evident in particular historical emphases and in a utilitarian attitude toward religion, climate, and terrain that appears in the years surrounding the publication of the latter's *Considerations on the Romans*. The Florentine's influence upon *The Spirit of Laws* is said to be even more limited. Nonetheless, Montesquieu's recourse to Machiavelli for "inspiration" on at least some themes gave "a modern and mature orientation to the French Enlightenment."[3]

Such judgments are true, but incomplete, for they misrepresent Machiavelli, Montesquieu, and the relation between them. We have taken for granted the main reason that linking these philosophers is now less controversial than it was in Montesquieu's day. We now think it "mature" to envisage Machiavelli not as a revolutionary philosopher or a teacher of evil but as a pillar of the classical republican tradition, indeed as its main restorer in modern times.[4] This reading, which informs the predominant view of the relationship between Machiavelli and Montesquieu, casts the Florentine as a great teacher of republican liberty. For some, he is even the originator of liberal pluralism and thus of modern civilization itself.[5]

This classical republican view of Machiavelli is attractive for defending civic humanism and helpful for its attention to the historical context of authors and ideas, but it misperceives both Machiavelli and his legacy. A representative

---

[2] See Shackleton, "Montesquieu and Machiavelli," 7 (with 5–9). See also Shackleton, *Montesquieu: A Critical Biography* (Oxford, UK: Oxford University Press, 1961), 22, 127, 142–3, 152, 165, 265–9, 292.

[3] See Shackleton, "Montesquieu and Machiavelli," 11–12.

[4] See the prologue of this book.

[5] See J. G. A. Pocock, *The Machiavellian Moment: Florentine Political Thought and the Atlantic Republican Tradition* (Princeton, NJ: Princeton University Press, 1975), 21, 427, 463, 465, 475, 484–5, 488, 491–2, 501, 516, 521, 526, 548. Fuller studies include Judith Shklar, "Montesquieu and the New Republicanism," in *Machiavelli and Republicanism*, ed. Gisela Bock, Quentin Skinner, and Maurizio Viroli (Cambridge, UK: Cambridge University Press, 1990), 265–79 (esp. 265–6); Wood, "The Value of Asocial Sociability," 289, 304–6. Wood quotes Sergio Cotta to the effect that Montesquieu's *Considerations on the Romans* provides "a new conception of political life," and he credits Cotta with linking its treatment of faction with that in *The Spirit of Laws*; see Cotta, "L'idée de parti dans la philosophie politique de Montesquieu," in *Actes du Congrès Montesquieu*, ed. Louis Desgraves (Bordeaux: Impriméries Delmas, 1956), 260. Wood correctly traces this new conception to Machiavelli.

problem is its inattention to an aspect of Machiavellism that Montesquieu himself criticized. It is not accidental to Machiavelli's philosophy but essential to and a mark of the ruler's *virtù* in all regimes that individuals be killed for the greater good when "necessity" arises. This is true whether they be innocent or not, whether (or however) found guilty, and thus whether justly punished or not – though Machiavelli does recommend a legal mode of execution if possible: "For if a citizen is crushed in a way ordered by law, even though he has been done a wrong, there follows little or no disorder in the republic (*D* 1.7)."[6] Machiavelli does praise a republican virtue of self-sacrifice for the common good. He also teaches that the common good can require the sensational sacrifice of some one or few who, being imprisoned, exiled, or dead, enjoy neither any common good nor the warm feeling of exercising civic virtue.[7]

While some readers of Machiavelli think it easy to extract from his work a hard-nosed republicanism while leaving behind the ferocity, Montesquieu, who attempted such a distillation, thought it a more difficult and delicate task.[8] His relationship to Machiavelli is both complex and problematic. Machiavelli's political science deeply shaped his own, though he labored to hide this and to prove that one could modify Machiavelli's principles in such a manner as to avoid their harsher consequences. This complicated influence would be most evident from a thorough comparison of their masterful works on Rome, Machiavelli's *Discourses on Livy* and Montesquieu's *Considerations on the Romans*. Examining the relationship more comprehensively would be even more daunting, since both spoke of the "infinite" scope of their inquiries and wrote political philosophy in several genres, from history and comedy to treatise and letter. The themes requiring comparison range from their views on morals, religion, and the family to their distinctive attention to climate and history.[9] Here it is enough to show that the doctrine for which Montesquieu is most famous, the separation of powers, accepts but moderates Machiavelli's

---

[6] As to *The Prince*, note the simultaneous ascriptions of virtue and criminality to Agathocles (*P* 8), Hannibal (*P* 17), and Severus (*P* 19). See Victoria Kahn, "*Virtù* and the Example of Agathocles in Machiavelli's *Prince*," in *Machiavelli and the Discourse of Literature*, ed. Albert R. Ascoli and Victoria Kahn (Ithaca, NY: Cornell University Press, 1993), 195–217.

[7] See Harvey C. Mansfield, "Machiavelli's Virtue" and "Machiavelli's Politics," in Mansfield, *Machiavelli's Virtue* (Chicago: University of Chicago Press, 1996), 6–52, 233. See also Vickie B. Sullivan, *Machiavelli's Three Romes: Religion, Human Liberty, and Politics Reformed* (DeKalb, IL: Northern Illinois University Press, 1996); Patrick Coby, *Machiavelli's Romans: Liberty and Greatness in the Discourses on Livy* (Lanham, MD: Lexington Books, 1999).

[8] Cf. the efforts by Shackleton, "Montesquieu and Machiavelli," 11; Wood, "The Value of Asocial Sociability," 307; Shklar, "Montesquieu and the New Republicanism," 266.

[9] For work in this vein on Montesquieu's major works, see Schaub, *Erotic Liberalism*, 11–12, 20, 24, 42, 98, 101–2, 111, 147, 168, n. 2, 170–1, n. 9; David Lowenthal, "Introduction," in *Considerations on the Causes of the Greatness of the Romans and their Decline*, ed. and tr. David Lowenthal (Indianapolis: Hackett, 1999), 1, 6–12, 19; Thomas L. Pangle, *Montesquieu's Philosophy of Liberalism: A Commentary on* The Spirit of the Laws (Chicago: University of Chicago Press, 1973), 5, 86–7, 136–7, 162–4, 322–3, n. 8. Cf. Mark Hulliung, *Montesquieu and the Old Regime* (Berkeley, CA: University of California Press, 1976), 11–13, 17–24, 140–72, 185–9, 204–5, 224–5.

revolutionary advocacy of factional politics in his *Discourses on Livy*. This understanding in turn reveals that the importance of the rule of law and the judiciary in modern liberal democracies finds its germ, however modified by Montesquieu and his legacy, in Machiavelli's political science.

Necessity and Republican Faction

As Markus Fischer demonstrates in the prologue to this book, the early chapters of Machiavelli's *Discourses on Livy* thematically argue that faction is necessary for republican imperialism, and that such imperialism is itself a necessity. The political psychology informing this dynamic republicanism states that "men never work any good unless through necessity; but where choice abounds, and one can make use of license, at once everything is full of confusion and disorder" (*D* 1.3). Machiavelli only slowly reveals the profound implications of these principles, unfolding them over several chapters.[10] As Fischer also observes, Machiavelli knew that classical political philosophy condemned faction, especially in republics, both for its own injustice and disorder – its violation of the higher ends that nature ordains for man and politics – and for its tendency to produce a tyrant who would claim to restore order. Machiavelli grants the balance or stability of the Spartan republican model, and of the mixed regime of ancient political philosophy. Nonetheless, he argues that such a republic is blind to or incapable of coping with necessity, which forces a republic to seek "greatness":

> ...since all things of men are in motion, and cannot stay steady, they must either rise or fall, and to many things that reason does not lead you, necessity leads you....In ordering a republic there is need to think of the more honorable part, and to order it so that if indeed necessity leads it to expand, it can conserve what it has seized....I believe that it is necessary...to tolerate the enmities that arise between the people and the Senate, taking them as an inconvenience necessary to arrive at Roman greatness.
>
> (*D* 1.6)[11]

Though he rejects the Epicurean retirement from politics, Machiavelli revives the Epicurean materialism that rivaled the metaphysics and physics of qualities, forms, and ends propounded by Plato and Aristotle.[12] Machiavelli asserts the

---

[10] On the manner and substance of Machiavelli's writing, see Leo Strauss, *Thoughts on Machiavelli* (Chicago: University of Chicago Press, 1958); Harvey C. Mansfield, *Machiavelli's New Modes and Orders: A Study of the Discourses on Livy* (Ithaca, NY: Cornell University Press, 1979). See also Victoria Kahn, *Machiavellian Rhetoric: From the Counter-Reformation to Milton* (Princeton, NJ: Princeton University Press, 1994), 26, 32, and Chapter 3 of this book.

[11] On demotion of the good and orientation by necessity, see Pierre Manent, "Machiavelli and the Fecundity of Evil," in Manent, *An Intellectual History of Liberalism*, tr. Rebecca Balinski (Princeton, NJ: Princeton University Press, 1995), 10–19; Markus Fischer, *Well-Ordered License: On the Unity of Machiavelli's Thought* (Lanham, MD: Lexington Books, 2000).

[12] A manuscript of Lucretius's *De rerum natura* survives with notations in Machiavelli's hand; see Sergio Bertelli and Franco Gaeta, "Noterelle Machiavelliane; un codice di Lucrezio e di Terenzio," *Rivista Storico Italiana* 73 (1961): 544–57. For another view on premodern science

primacy of the political and human over the natural, of the human passions over any natural order that might guide or restrain them. We must, he claims, judge man by what we can know and have observed, by the effectual truth of political life and the human things, not by "imagined republics and principalities" (*P* 15) – whether Plato's republic, Epicurus' garden, or Augustine's City of God. In this fashion, he repudiates the authority central to scholastic philosophy, Aristotle, whose political science draws upon a natural teleology that provides each species with an ordained end as well as the means for its achievement. "If nature," Aristotle contends, "makes nothing either incomplete or in vain, then she has necessarily made all these things for the sake of human beings" (*Pol.* 1256b). Machiavelli replaces this progression toward a set end with a chaotic natural world that permits only the fittest, most adaptable beings to survive. His discourse on the eternity of the world and the history of mankind thus compares the fact that "nature" often "moves by itself and produces a purge that is the health" of "simple bodies" with the plagues, famines, and floods that purge and renew the "mixed body of the human race . . . so that men, having become few and beaten, may live more advantageously and become better" (*D* 2.5).

Such a science compels a redefinition of virtue, "the honorable part," to account for necessity and provide for man's way in the world. The Spartan, Platonic, and Aristotelian conceptions of a republic attempted to impose stability and order in accord with man's natural inclinations, thereby providing for leisure and a higher life, whether moral, political, or philosophic. For Machiavelli, such attempts fail to achieve stability because they overlook the necessity of either rising or falling. A static government fails to protect itself against external enemies, but also lays itself open to internal threats, for even if "heaven were so benign that it did not have to make war, from that would arise the idleness to make it either effeminate or divided" (*D* 1.6).

This is neither advocacy of faction for its own sake nor blithe approval of the tumults of politics. Throughout the *Discourses on Livy*, Machiavelli indicates his acceptance of faction as dangerous yet necessary – necessary to rising, itself a necessity.[13] On this basis, he coins a maxim at the root of the politics of mistrust later institutionalized as the separation of powers, that "it is necessary to whoever disposes a republic and orders laws in it to presuppose that all men are bad, and that they always have to use the malignity of their spirit" whenever possible (*D* 1.3).[14] As for institutions to secure these aims, that of "the tribunes of the plebs" in Rome "made the republic more perfect," a perfection shown to derive from institutionalizing the factious dispute between the Senate and the plebs. Hatred between claimants to rule – kings, nobles,

---

in Machiavelli's philosophy, see Anthony J. Parel, *The Machiavellian Cosmos* (New Haven, CT: Yale University Press, 1992).

[13] Machiavelli asserts that faction was "the first cause of keeping Rome free" (*D* 1.4.1), then admits that at "the time of the Gracchi," it was "the cause of the ruin of a free way of life" (1.6). See *D* 1.12–13, 37, 47, 52, 54, 2.25, 3.30, for "disunion" or "tumults" bringing ruin if not managed.

[14] On the "politics of mistrust," see Chapter 9 of this book.

the people – should be harnessed, not eradicated, by structuring institutions to check each claim or passion by another. He commends the tribuneship as an office "with so much eminence and reputation" that those holding it could counter "the insolence of the nobles" (*D* 1.3).[15] One must tolerate factions as an inconvenience necessary for greatness, since a machine that works by the conflict or opposition of forces moves more powerfully and quickly than a system that permits no internal opposition (*D* 1.6). Indeed, "in every republic are two diverse humors, that of the people and that of the great," and so "every city ought to have its modes with which the people can vent its ambition, and especially those cities that wish to avail themselves of the people in important things" – such as the expansion necessary for rising (*D* 1.4).[16] The centerpiece of this institutionalization of factious energy is the public accusation of crimes against the republic. Through accusations made by the people's tribunes to the people themselves, such as that against the nobleman Coriolanus, "an outlet is given by which to vent, in some mode against some citizen, those humors that grow up in cities." Institutionalizing this vengeance avoids the "extraordinary modes" that destroy republics, for "there is nothing that makes a republic so stable and firm, as to order it in a mode so that those alternating humors that agitate it can be vented in a way ordered by the laws." It does not matter who is accused or for what; as long as a citizen is "crushed in an ordered way," there will be little if any harm or disorder for the republic, "even though he has been done a wrong" (*D* 1.7.1).[17]

Montesquieu accepted many elements of Machiavelli's turn away from the ancient condemnation of faction, as had Marchamont Nedham, Locke, and Sidney before him.[18] The French philosophe's decisive contribution was to make such conflict safer for each individual and less ferocious in general. His debt to Machiavelli is most obvious regarding faction in ancient Rome, since the *Discourses on Livy* deeply informs the analysis in his *Considerations on the Romans*. But Machiavelli's linkage of expansion and faction also reappears in *The Spirit of Laws*. A moderated Machiavellism is at the heart of Montesquieu's political science and conception of a modern republic in his doctrine of the separation of powers.

Indeed, Montesquieu's interest in Machiavelli and in political faction long predates his travels to England or his writing of the *Considerations on the Romans*, let alone his drafting of *The Spirit of Laws*. This is most obvious in the earliest of his surviving works, the "Dissertation on the Policy of the Romans in Religion" of 1716, though it mentions neither the *Discourses on Livy* nor its

---

[15] Further endorsements of the balance or equilibrium achieved by the contest of internal forces occur in *D* 1.40, 42.

[16] See John P. McCormick, "Machiavellian Democracy: Controlling Elites with Ferocious Populism," *APSR* 95:2 (June 2001): 297–313.

[17] On the consequences of accusation by the tribunes, compare Machiavelli's praise for the Coriolanus affair (*D* 1.7.1) with Livy's view (2.36–42); but Machiavelli nearly admits the near-disaster this brought to Rome in *D* 1.29.

[18] See Chapters 1 through 3 of this book.

author.[19] Faction is a topic evident in his first major work of political philosophy, *Lettres Persanes* (1721), although the influence of Machiavelli is not as obvious here.[20] *Persian Letters* regularly praises a constitutional equilibrium of action and reaction among separated powers, first in a striking consideration of "what kind of government most conforms to reason" (*LP* 80). The protagonist and chief letter-writer, Usbek, concludes that "the most perfect is that which attains its goal with the least friction," namely that which "leads men in a manner which is most suited to their interests and their inclinations" (*LP* 80). The greater rationality of mild government appears in its justice and tranquillity, while the "injustice and vexations" of despotism testify to its irrationality. Subsequent letters regularly connect moderate government and its reduction of any "friction" frustrating desires to another mechanical metaphor, an equilibrium or balance between powers that produces security and tranquillity for individuals.[21] *Persian Letters* then amplifies this liberalism in two thematic discussions, on government in Europe and England and on "the history and origin of republics" (*LP* 102–4, 131). These discussions of liberty and faction, revolution and the balancing of powers – in Greece, Rome, the Germanic tribes, and England – foreshadow the analyses in both the *Considerations on the Romans* and *The Spirit of Laws*. To the extent that these are Machiavellian themes, his first major work quietly reveals Montesquieu's early study of *The Prince* and the *Discourses on Livy*. His debt is noticeably greater in his *Considerations on the Romans*, even though here, too, he neither mentions nor cites either the *Discourses on Livy* or Machiavelli. Such silence, however, is an aspect of Montesquieu's intention to write with care and subtlety. He explicitly states this regarding *Persian Letters*, which he later said contained a "secret and, in some respects, hitherto unknown chain" of meaning, and it is discernible in his other works.[22]

The crux of his *Considerations on the Romans* is its diagnosis of the two causes of Rome's ruin, its imperial expansion, "the greatness of the empire," and its granting of citizenship to all conquered peoples, which produces "the greatness of the city" (*Rom.* 9). Montesquieu digresses from the second cause – that Rome fractured under such a wide granting of citizenship – to rebut the view of "the authors" that Rome never was united but always was riven by

---

[19] See *Dissertation sur la politique des Romains dans la religion*, in *WoM* 1:81–92. For Montesquieu's reliance upon the *Discourses on Livy* here, see Levi-Malvano, *Montesquieu e Machiavelli*, passim; Shackleton, "Montesquieu and Machiavelli," 1–13.

[20] Schaub, *Erotic Liberalism*, points out several Machiavellian moments in *LP*; see footnote 9, above.

[21] *LP* 92 laments the decline of *parlements* (judicial bodies) as a check on the French monarchy; see also *LP* 138, 140.

[22] See "Quelques Réflexions sur les *Lettres Persanes*" (1754) in *WoM* 1:129. On the manner of Montesquieu's writing, see David Lowenthal, "Book I of Montesquieu's *The Spirit of the Laws*," *APSR* 53:2 (June 1959): 485–98; Pangle, *Montesquieu's Philosophy of Liberalism*, 11–19. In the preface to his *Spirit of Laws* (*EL* pref.), Montesquieu asks that "one approve or condemn the whole book, and not some few phrases," and warns that "many of the truths will not make themselves felt until after one sees the chain which links them to the others."

faction. This digression resumes his analysis of the conflict between the patrician Senate and the plebeians as "a secret war" within Rome. In addition to praising the Senate and criticizing the aggrandizement of the plebeians, this earlier analysis argues that "the most fortunate" republic is one where authority is not hereditary, implying that Rome's class warfare between people and Senate is unfortunate (*Rom.* 8). Yet his subsequent defense of Rome argues that, despite its internal commotion, it was "a city whose people had but a single spirit, a single love of liberty, a single hatred of tyranny, a city where the jealousy of the Senate's power and the prerogatives of the great, always mixed with respect, was only a love of equality" (*Rom.* 9). Indeed, he deems faction an essential requirement for any free republic. Montesquieu here employs an obviously Machiavellian – and Newtonian – conception of politics and distills many points from his *Persian Letters*:

> It was very necessary there be dissensions in Rome.... To ask, in a free state, for men who are bold in war and timid in peace is to wish the impossible: and, as a general rule, whenever we see everyone tranquil in a state that calls itself a republic, we can be sure that liberty does not exist there.
>
> What is called union in a body politic is a very equivocal thing: the true kind is a union of harmony, whereby all the parts, however opposed they may appear, cooperate for the general good of society, as dissonances in music cooperate in producing overall concord. There can be union in a state where we seem to see nothing but disorder, that is to say, a harmony resulting in happiness, which alone is true peace. It is as with the parts of the universe, eternally linked together by the action of some, and the reaction of others.
>
> But, in the concord of Asiatic despotism, that is to say, of all government which is not moderate, there is always real dissension.... [For] some oppress the others without resistance: and, if we see any union there, it is not citizens who are united but dead bodies buried one next to the other.   (*Rom.* 9)

Proper government is moderate, a commotion of cooperation or a harmony of dissonances that provides happiness and true peace for both parts and whole. The rationale for such balance and tranquillity is Machiavellian necessity: Rome simply had to aggrandize other states if it was to be great, and to think otherwise would be to wish the impossible. Tranquillity in a republic is therefore antithetical to liberty, namely, the freedom to satisfy wants and thus to aggrandize power in both domestic and foreign affairs. In both *Persian Letters* and his *Considerations on the Romans* Montesquieu argues that it is better to let the passions go, with motion reinforcing motion so that the total energy of the political system increases and projects outward. This embrace of harmony over absolute unity recalls Aristotle's criticism of the extreme unity of Socrates' ideal city in *The Republic*, that "as a city advances and becomes more of a unity, it will cease to exist" (*Pol.* 1261a).[23] However, while

---

[23] See Arist. *Pol.* 1261a10–1261b15, and 1263b27ff, where Aristotle warns against reducing "a many-voiced harmony to unison or rhythm to a single beat."

Montesquieu seeks to distinguish his philosophy from extreme or simplistic analyses, his target is not so much Plato as the rationalism of earlier liberal philosophers.[24] That said, Montesquieu's particular criticism of unity presupposes his rejection of not only the Platonic but also the Aristotelian concern for virtue and justice as the fulfillment of man's political and rational nature. Excessive unity is despotic because it denies nature as necessity – the necessity of leaving people free to pursue their passions or "happiness" and to pursue the expansion necessary for the survival and happiness of any political community.

This is a Machiavellian view, an influence already evident from the fact that Montesquieu's *Considerations on the Romans* examines politics through the lens of greatness or power and not through that of the best regime as discussed in Plato, Aristotle, and the medieval philosophers.[25] This is so despite the initial impression given by Montesquieu's arguments about the two causes of Rome's ruin, which seem antithetical to expansion. His claims that "the greatness of the empire ruined the republic," that "the greatness of the city ruined it no less," and that it was "solely the greatness of the republic" that "changed popular tumults into civil wars" seem to prefer, against Machiavelli, the Spartan model over the Roman. Soon thereafter, however, Montesquieu states that "good laws" are those "which have made a small republic grow large," that "their natural effect was to create a great people," and that "there is a considerable difference between good laws and convenient laws, between those that enable a people to make itself master of others, and those that maintain its power once it is acquired" (*Rom.* 9).

Montesquieu's political science follows Machiavelli and modern science in understanding both nature and human nature in terms of matter, motion, and power. His debt is nowhere more evident than in these remarks on the political necessity of expansion, despite the fact that neither Machiavelli nor the *Discourses on Livy* ever appear. The subscription to Machiavelli's tumultuous republicanism also shows through in his earlier analysis of faction in Rome. He initially criticizes the "malady internal to man" that made Rome's plebeians attack patrician privilege: "a secret war was going on within its walls,"

---

[24] The famous chapter in *EL* on the constitution of England (2.11.6) closes by criticizing utopianism, arguing that Harrington sought liberty "only after misunderstanding it," and thus "built Chalcedon with the coast of Byzantium before his eyes"; the previous chapter (*EL* 2.11.5) closes in similar fashion, arguing that to "discover political liberty in [the English] constitution, not much trouble need be taken. If it can be seen where it is, if it has been found, why seek it?" On Montesquieu's critique of rationalism, see Harvey C. Mansfield, *Taming the Prince: The Ambivalence of Modern Executive Power* (New York: Free Press, 1989), 213–24, 232–3; Paul Carrese, "Montesquieu's Complex Natural Right and Moderate Liberalism: The Roots of American Moderation," *Polity* 36:2 (January 2004): 227–50.

[25] I am much indebted here to Lowenthal, "Introduction," 6–12. See also Paul A. Rahe, "The Book That Never Was: Montesquieu's *Considerations on the Romans* in Historical Context," *History of Political Thought* 26:1 (Spring 2005): 43–89.

and its "fires were like those of volcanoes which burst forth whenever some matter comes along to increase their activity." This classical condemnation of faction fades, however, when he states that the only real problem was the plebeians' degree of success in aggrandizing the patricians. With the Senate effectively conquered, the internal contest could not continue; the Senate had been correct in fearing that "the populace would elevate some tribune to tyranny" (*Rom.* 8).[26] A significant difference between the two philosophers does arise, however, because Montesquieu does not endorse Machiavelli's animus toward Rome's nobles. Machiavelli depicts a balanced contest between the two, but Montesquieu praises the Senate's wisdom and notes the plebeians' malicious determination to strip the nobles of all privileges. Similarly, Montesquieu praises the patrician institution of censors for achieving stability through reforming "everything that could introduce dangerous novelties, change the heart or mind *(esprit)* of the citizen, and deprive the state – if I dare use the term – of perpetuity." Nonetheless, Machiavelli's general influence remains, since the real reason for praising this "very wise institution" is that it "continually examined" and corrected the constitution, ever changing the political order to achieve a stable motion or equilibrium amid factious agitations (*Rom.* 8).[27] Indeed, Montesquieu defines free government as being "always subject to agitation" and thereby doomed if it is not "capable of correction" or constantly reformed "by its own laws." This foreshadows the striking conclusion to not only the discussion of the causes of Rome's ruin but to Montesquieu's treatment of Roman faction. The problem in Rome was not motion and change but the ultimate cessation of motion or the timing thereof: "It lost its liberty because it completed the work it wrought too soon" (*Rom.* 8–9).

The meaning of this cryptic judgment becomes clearer in light of Montesquieu's mature treatment of political motion and an equilibrium of forces in *The Spirit of Laws*, which also moderates the Machiavellian teaching upon which it, too, draws. Perhaps the Romans should not have completed their quest for empire but instead should have stayed in perpetual motion; perhaps they completed that quest too quickly to consolidate their gains and reconstitute themselves in new circumstances, failing to maintain a dynamic imperial dominion instead of a static one. Either way, the moral of the story recommends a moderation of Machiavellian aims, not their rejection.

---

[26] Montesquieu later notes, "The emperors were vested with the power of tribunes," and "it is on this basis that so many men were put to death" (*Rom.* 14). Ronald Syme, *The Roman Revolution* (Oxford, UK: Clarendon Press, 1939), 336–7, dates the "revolution" that founded the empire to that moment when Augustus had the *tribunicia potestas* given him for life.

[27] Cf. NM, *D* 3.49 (the final discourse) with Montesquieu, *Rom.* 9, on the redistribution of the people among the tribes by the censor Quintus Fabius (each citing Livy 9.46). While Machiavelli qualifies his support for the plebeians (e.g., *D* 1.37, 54), other passages maintain his initial stance (for example, *D* 1.50). His *Florentine Histories* is more sympathetic to nobles. Montesquieu's more consistent neutrality, or even favor for patricians, in the name of moderation may be an amplification of Machiavelli's own sense of the need for limits to factious conflict.

The Moderation of Machiavellism in *The Spirit of Laws*

Montesquieu's softening of Machiavelli's political philosophy appears most fully in *De l'Esprit des Lois* (1748),[28] where there are four references to the Florentine. Three of these obviously criticize Machiavelli and his teachings. First, and perhaps most crucially, Montesquieu cites the *Discourses on Livy* to criticize Machiavelli's insistence upon a popular jury for cases of high treason in a republic (*EL* 1.6.5). The second reference praises the fact that commercial Europe "has begun to be cured of *machiavélisme*," defined as the "barbarism" of "great acts of authority" and violent abuses of rule termed "coups d'État," with the cure being "more moderation in councils" (*EL* 4.21.20).[29] In the fourth reference (*EL* 6.29.19), Machiavelli joins Plato, Aristotle, More, and Harrington in the list of "legislators" who failed to overcome their "passions and prejudices" in proposing laws: "Machiavelli was full of his idol, Duke Valentino" (Cesare Borgia).

These passages distinguish Montesquieu's political science from Machiavelli's but do more as well. As with the complicated references to Lucretius and Epicureanism in *The Spirit of Laws*, Montesquieu signals some affinity or agreement while indicating important points of contrast. Thus, praise and respect for Machiavelli shine through amid the criticism. Unlike the earlier works, *The Spirit of Laws* cites the *Discourses on Livy*, even though – as the word *machiavélisme* indicates – its author's name was synonymous with ruthless politics and the teaching of evil. It is even more noteworthy that in his first mention of Machiavelli, early in the work, Montesquieu calls him "this great man," though the occasion is a disagreement about trials and judging (*EL* 1.6.5). *The Spirit of Laws* makes no further reference to the *Discourses on Livy*, but it is the work of a great man, and no other criticisms arise. In the fourth reference, amid criticism of prejudiced "legislators," Machiavelli stands alongside important ancient and modern political philosophers – indeed, in the central position among the five. Moreover, while Montesquieu laments that all of them let their passions distort their philosophy, only Machiavelli is called a "great man" elsewhere in the work, even if there are many more references to Plato and Aristotle.

Amid these moderately critical remarks, Montesquieu's third reference points the reader to "what Machiavelli says of the destruction of the old Florentine nobility" (*EL* 6.28.6). Although no work is cited, he presumably has in mind the *Florentine Histories*. If so, *The Spirit of Laws* quietly treats, as

---

[28] In the view of Lowenthal, "Introduction," 19, there is an "inner kinship" between the republicanism of Machiavelli's *Discourses of Livy* and that of Montesquieu's *Considerations on the Romans*, while "the republicanism of *The Spirit of the Laws* is meant to be, and is, much more prudent."

[29] Throughout I revise Montesquieu, *The Spirit of the Laws*, tr. Anne Cohler, Basia Miller, and Harold Stone (Cambridge, UK: Cambridge University Press, 1989). I have also consulted the 1750 translation praised by Montesquieu and his circle: Montesquieu, *The Spirit of the Laws*, tr. Thomas Nugent (New York: Hafner, 1949).

authoritative, Machiavelli's analysis and qualified endorsement of faction, which Montesquieu had more openly adopted in his *Considerations on the Romans*. In the Proem to the *Florentine Histories*, Machiavelli distinguishes his study from earlier efforts for its attention to Florence's "civil discords and internal enmities, and the effects arising from them." Its extraordinary factiousness, being more complex and bloody than Rome's, both revealed and increased its greatness:

> And truly, in my judgment, no other example appears to me to demonstrate so well the power of our city, as the one derived from these divisions, which would have had the force to annihilate any great and very powerful city. Nonetheless ours, it appeared, always became greater from them: so great was the virtue of those citizens and the power of their genius and their spirit to make themselves and their fatherland great, that as many as remained free from so many evils were more able by their virtue to exalt their city, than could the malignity of those accidents that had diminished the city overwhelm it.
>
> (*FH* Proem)[30]

Three of Montesquieu's four references to Machiavelli in *The Spirit of Laws*, then, are somewhat favorable and perhaps substantially so. Still, the second one seems damning. A declaration that Europe has been "cured of *machiavélisme*" endorses the respectable opinion that the Florentine is such an exponent of ruthlessness that one can contrast "coups d'État" with "moderation in councils" simply by reference to his name (*EL* 4.21.20). However, this condemnation lies within a general analysis of commerce that is a moderated version of Machiavellian political hedonism, with its rejection of Platonic and Aristotelian philosophy. In this second of three books on commerce, Montesquieu reiterates his contention that the spread of commerce will soften and moderate politics because rulers and ruled will be more concerned with their own interest, profit, and success than with their pride, mastery, or greatness. He does not argue that Europe has turned toward the Aristotelian moral virtue of moderation, only that increased commerce, through its capacity to increase the appetite for comfort and security, has moderated a customary ruthlessness. The lionlike barbarism of political brutality has given way to market-driven demands for a more foxlike, cunning politics, since "men are in a situation such that, though their passions inspire in them the thought of being wicked, they nevertheless have an interest in not being so" (*EL* 4.21.20).[31] The great risk in this argument, which owes much to Bernard Mandeville's claim that private vices can become

---

[30] In *EL* 6.28.6, Montesquieu seems to point to Books II and III of the *Florentine Histories*; Machiavelli compares the "reasonable" faction in Rome with the "injurious and unjust" kind in Florence (*FH* 3.12) and comments that the people's victory in an earlier battle inflicted "ruin" upon the nobles to a shameful degree (*FH* 2.41–2). Montesquieu may have learned from Machiavelli that only moderate faction is productive and beneficial.

[31] For the fundamental importance of commerce for his political philosophy, see Pangle, *Montesquieu's Philosophy of Liberalism*, 200–48; Catherine Larrère, "Montesquieu on Economics and Commerce," in *Montesquieu's Science of Politics: Essays on the Spirit of Laws*, ed. David W. Carrithers, Michael A. Mosher, and Paul A. Rahe (Lanham, MD: Rowman and Littlefield, 2000), 335–73.

public virtues, is its moral dubiousness. Montesquieu thus emphasizes the benefits of reducing conflict, war, and insecurity, and does so by forcefully distinguishing commerce from *machiavélisme*.[32] He quietly teaches a lesson of lowered expectations for politics and man learned from Machiavelli, while defusing any moral qualms by invoking the typical reader's condemnation of Machiavellism.

This spirit of moderated Machiavellism also informs the conception of tempered political commotion and party faction in *The Spirit of Laws*, just as it underlies that work's explicit criticism of the *Discourses on Livy* regarding popular juries for treason trials. Both temperings of Machiavelli's doctrines helpfully reveal the blending of prudence and science evident in Montesquieu's mature work, balancing a prudential attention to everyman's fears or wants with a scientific observation of the equilibrium achieved by interacting bodies. *The Spirit of Laws* emphasizes a complex constitutionalism and, more quietly, the judicial power as indispensable means to the relative equilibrium appropriate to each historical situation and people. A liberal constitutionalism, especially one suffused with judicial power, would provide for the "degrees of liberty each one of them can enjoy," and attain as moderate a government as possible given the necessities of each (*EL* 2.11.20).[33]

Separation of Powers and the Constitutional Politics of Moderation

The basic premise of Montesquieu's constitutional principle of the separation of powers is that politics is best understood and practiced according to a blend of Newtonian dynamics and Machiavellian faction. But *The Spirit of Laws* uses modern physics and Machiavelli's revolutionary political science to elaborate a possibility not explored by Machiavelli, a liberal constitutionalism. Montesquieu's version also owes much to Hobbes and Locke, though it is less doctrinaire and rigorously deductive. The equilibrium that Montesquieu discerns and advocates in politics is also characteristic, then, of his own philosophy, which tempers the extremes of preceding philosophers by blending their teachings or balancing one with another.[34]

The Spirit of Laws builds slowly toward the moderate constitutionalism embodied by its widely read chapters on the English constitution, and an early preparation for that peak occurs when it examines "the principle of monarchy." Honor or ambition may be "pernicious in a republic," but they are nonetheless advantageous in a monarchy, for if honor checks honor, an equilibrium of selfishness "gives life to the government," even as it prevents the worst effects of

---

[32] Montesquieu twice (*EL* 1.7.1, 3.19.8) cites Mandeville's *Fable of the Bees* (1714) as authoritative, although he never provides its subtitle: *Or, Private Vices, Public Benefits*.

[33] In the opening book of his *Spirit of Laws* (*EL* 1.1.3), Montesquieu declares, "It is better to say that the government most in conformity with nature is the one whose particular disposition best relates to the disposition of the people for whom it is established."

[34] See Carrese, "Montesquieu's Complex Natural Right and Moderate Liberalism," 227–50.

what, "philosophically speaking," is "a false honor" (*EL* 1.3.7). Montesquieu makes the Mandevillean notion of private vices as public virtues more scientific and also more relative to the particular necessities and forces shaping each people or government.

The principal consequence of these Newtonian political mechanics is Montesquieu's emphasis upon moderation, understood both as a lowering of moral standards and a softening of political action. Indeed, his great interest in moderation leads, as his book unfolds, to a successively greater emphasis on the distinction between moderate and immoderate governments, which comes to overshadow his early classification of political regimes as republics, monarchies, and despotisms. The title of one early book refers to these "Three Governments" (*EL* 1.3.title), but an important chapter therein distinguishes "moderate" from despotic governments (*EL* 1.3.10). This eclipse of the initial typology of governments culminates in the constitutionalism that arises from his first thematic study of England. This influential sketch of a liberal constitution ignores or transcends the initial classification into three governmental structures and the principle moving each, for it emphasizes that "liberty is found only in moderate governments"; that "in most kingdoms in Europe the government is moderate" because the judicial power is independent of the king, who unites the other two powers; and that the "extreme political liberty" of England should not "humble" governments having "only a moderate one," since "the excess even of reason is not always desirable," and "men almost always accommodate themselves better to middles than to extremities" (*EL* 2.11.4, 6). Montesquieu ultimately recommends that we "seek out in all the moderate governments we know the distribution of the three powers and calculate thereupon the degrees of liberty each one can enjoy," and he leaves the reader to consider the links between political moderation, a constitution of separated powers, and liberty (*EL* 2.11.20).

In fact, Montesquieu prepared for this first study of the constitution of England by stating that political liberty is found only in moderate governments. Even in those "moderate states" where moderation results not from the structure of government but from other causes – perhaps the character of the ruler, or general mores – the citizen cannot have liberty (*EL* 2.11.4).[35] Since he then defines liberty as that "tranquillity of spirit which comes from the opinion each one has of his security" (*EL* 2.11.6), there is no tranquillity even when political moderation prevails if there is no governing structure to ensure moderation and thus secure liberty; without this, there is no security of knowing that power will not be abused. Montesquieu then offers his influential prescription

---

[35] Another passage early in *The Spirit of Laws* that emphasizes moderate government and foreshadows Montesquieu's discussion of the separation of powers occurs after an extensive discussion of despotism: "In order to form a moderate government, one must combine powers, regulate them, temper them, make them act; one must give one power a ballast, so to speak, to put it in a position to resist another; this is a masterwork of legislation that chance rarely produces and prudence is rarely allowed to produce" (*EL* 1.5.14).

for moderate government and liberty, which reads almost as a précis of the early chapters of Machiavelli's *Discourses on Livy*:

[Political liberty] is present only when power is not abused; but it has eternally been observed that any man who has power is led to abuse it; he continues until he finds limits. Who would say it! even virtue has need of limits.

So that one cannot abuse power, power must check power by the disposition of things. A constitution can be such that no one will be constrained to do the things the law does not oblige him to do, or be kept from doing the things the law permits him to do. (*EL* 2.11.4)[36]

Montesquieu dares to say it: Even virtue has need of limits. This develops Machiavelli's treatment of faction, albeit toward the softened, liberal aim of constitutionalism. Montesquieu is more concerned with the tranquillity and security of all than with the glory of one alone. He offers a more humane and pedestrian account of providing for oneself in a world of harsh necessity, in part because he is more concerned to watch over all mankind than is Machiavelli.[37]

Montesquieu thus adopts Machiavelli's marriage of the ideal and the actual in a lowered ideal. However, Montesquieu's perception of the human manifestations of Newton's laws about the equilibrium and conservation of momentum produces a political philosophy more egalitarian and liberal than Machiavelli's, since it argues that an equilibrium of forces, or a moderating of any extreme force, is the effectual truth about nature and human nature. A striking instance of this occurs in Montesquieu's long analysis of commerce, where he explicitly rejects Aristotle's condemnation of usury. He criticizes both classical political philosophy and Christianity for an unrealistic concern with virtue precisely in the chapter where he rejects *"machiavélisme"* in favor of "moderation in councils." Usury and commerce have reduced the harshness of politics so much that Europe's persecuted but persistent merchants, the Jews, have raised the prospects for themselves and for all. By linking lowered moral expectations with a criticism of political brutality, Montesquieu adapts Machiavelli's orientation by interest to a moderation of both the ends and means of Machiavellian man (*EL* 4.21.20).[38]

This political science of moderation is most famous for its endorsement, especially with respect to England, of factional republicanism as a corollary of the separation of powers. Indeed, Montesquieu's doctrine of the separation of powers differs from that of Locke by blending the classical "balanced constitution" or mixed regime model, which accords representation to distinct classes, with a model delineating the powers of government. This blending first appears in the dual use of the term "three powers" in the first thematic chapter

---

[36] Note the Machiavellian tenor in Locke's view of the separation of powers in *TTG* 2.7.93, 12.143.
[37] Consider Montesquieu's praise for the Stoics (*EL* 5.24.10) in light of *EL* pref.
[38] Shortly after this, Montesquieu (*EL* 4.22.21–2) draws several lessons: first, "extreme laws for good give rise to extreme evil"; then, "affairs must go forward, and a state is lost if everything falls into inaction"; and, finally, "I shall continue to repeat, it is moderation which governs men, not excesses."

on England, where the phrase is initially used to refer to legislative, executive, and judging powers and then more often deployed to identify lower and upper legislative houses and a separate executive, which represent, respectively, popular, aristocratic, and monarchical orders (*EL* 2.11.6). Intrinsic to this blending is the constitutionalizing of party faction, a device employed in part to animate a constitutional machine that is so separated and internally opposed. Thus, while *The Spirit of Laws* maintains the endorsement of faction more obviously evident in Montesquieu's *Considerations on the Romans*, it moderates faction by applying Newtonian dynamics and its law of equilibrium. Montesquieu's final statement on the conflict between patricians and plebeians, principally in the chapters on Rome that follow the first crucial chapter on England in his *Spirit of Laws*, removes the air of empire, power, and ruthlessness that in part characterizes his *Considerations on the Romans*. The candid brutality of Machiavelli's *Discourses on Livy*, with its claim that the "tumults" never sent "more than eight or ten citizens into exile" and "killed very few of them," producing "not any exile or violence unfavorable to the common good but laws and orders in benefit of public freedom," stemmed from the necessity to secure oneself and even to rule as one alone (*D* 1.4). Montesquieu adopts only the aim of individual security, and this in its humane and pedestrian version: security for all. The constitutionalized, Newtonian conception of faction in Montesquieu's book is so soft that he resorts to a floral metaphor to describe the conflict in ancient Rome:

> States are often more blossoming *(fleurissent)* during the imperceptible shift from one constitution to another than they are under either constitution. At that time all the springs of the government are strained; all the citizens have claims; one is attacked or flattered; and there is a noble rivalry between those who defend the declining constitution and those who put forward the one that prevails.   (*EL* 2.11.13)[39]

This constitutionalizing of faction, moderating its passions through the bloodless mechanism of Newtonian equilibrium, is even more evident in Montesquieu's second extended discussion of the English constitution in *The Spirit of Laws*. He returns to the English to study "the effects that had to follow" from "the principles of their constitution," especially "the character that was formed from it, and the manners that result from it" (*EL* 3.19.27). There is liberty for all the passions in such a constitution, especially those productive of vice. Montesquieu even praises this licentiousness for its beneficial fostering of conflict between partisans of the "two visible powers, legislative power and executive power." A conflict between Tories and Whigs, supporters of Crown and Parliament, arises over the "great expectations" generated by the executive among seekers of patronage, since it "has all the posts at its disposal."

---

[39] In addition to emphasizing judicial procedures and mild criminal laws throughout *The Spirit of Laws*, Montesquieu (*EL* 1.7.17) praises mildness in government more generally, including a discussion of "Administration by Women": "their very weakness gives them more gentleness and moderation, which, rather than the harsh and ferocious virtues, can make for good government." Cf. Machiavelli's recommendation of brutal methods for dominating the woman *fortuna* (*P* 25).

Its supporters are those who stand to gain, while it is "attacked by all those who could expect nothing from it." Rome's partisans struggled over matters of life and death, liberty and oppression, but the Newtonian mechanics of a liberal constitution lower the stakes. In the modern constitution of liberty, such controlled agitation is a necessary source of momentum and energy within an equilibrium of forces, a balance that always will maintain itself so as to protect liberty. It even can tame the distinctively Machiavellian passion for distinction:

As all the passions are free there, hatred, envy, jealousy, and the ardor for enriching and distinguishing oneself would appear to their full extent; and if this were otherwise, the state would be like a man who, laid low by disease, has no more passions because he has no more force.

The hatred between the two parties would endure because it would always be powerless.

As these parties are made up of free men, if one party gained too much, the effect of liberty would be to lower it, while the citizens, like hands which relieve the body, would come and raise the other party.   (EL 3.19.27)

Since neither the nurturing of character nor the activity of contemplation is the aim of such a constitutionalism, stability in authority and law is not a prerequisite. Indeed, this Newtonian science of dynamics elevates the factional agitation condemned by the ancients to the level of constitutional principle. Montesquieu's political science endorses passion, faction, and injustice because they maintain the free motion and activity of the separated parts, thus the liberty of the parts and also that of the whole: "they would even have the good effect of straining all the springs of the government, and rendering all the citizens attentive" (EL 3.19.27). The costs of this republican faction are thought to be only the "terrors" or "empty clamors and insults" needed to maintain liberty. This is a significant moderation of the supposedly "few" murders, exiles, confiscations, and fines that Machiavelli thought an acceptable price for the achievement of a liberty that was itself a means to republican imperialism.

The Moderating Spirit of Judging and the Rule of Law

The indispensable institution for maintaining the moderate Machiavellism of separated powers is, curiously, the power Montesquieu refers to in his first study of England as "invisible and null," the one he later implicitly charges with moderating the dispute between "the two visible powers" – namely, the judging power (EL 2.11.6, 3.19.27). An early indication of the important role assigned to judging is Montesquieu's first reference to Machiavelli in *The Spirit of Laws*, where he seeks to moderate Machiavelli's ferocious republicanism precisely regarding the use of popular juries for treason trials (EL 1.6.5). However, this crucial instance of Montesquieu's concern for judicial power and the rule of law may well be indebted to Machiavelli's praise of France's ordered monarchy and of its *parlements* in particular.⁴⁰ The *parlements* were assemblies of nobles dating from the Middle Ages, established first in Paris then in all the regions, which had shared legislative and political functions with the monarch but by the early modern period were confined to judicial activity. In *The Prince*, Machiavelli declares that "among the well-ordered and governed kingdoms in our times is that of France. And in it are infinite good institutions, on which the liberty and security of the king depend, [and] the first of these is the *parlement* and its authority" (P 19). His *Discourses on Livy* echoes this praise: France "lives under laws and under orders more than any other kingdom. These laws and orders are maintained by *parlements*, and especially that of Paris" (D 3.1).⁴¹ In the case of faction, Montesquieu tempers the Machiavellian ruthlessness of a "few" murders and exiles toward greater protection of the life, liberty, and property of individuals. Regarding public prosecutions and judging, however, he pointedly rejects the *Discourses on Livy*, seemingly having learned from Machiavelli himself of the importance of judging and the rule of law.

Montesquieu challenges Machiavelli's commentary on the expulsion of the Florentine secretary's own employer, Piero Soderini, from Florence in 1512 by a Spanish army, which led to the restoration of the Medici. Machiavelli claims that if Soderini had been charged, judged, and executed, or exiled by the people, the republic would have remained: "For to accuse one powerful individual before eight judges in a republic is not enough; the judges need to be very many, because the few always behave in the mode of the few" (D 1.7). Montesquieu comments that Machiavelli attributes "the loss of liberty in Florence to the fact that the people as a body did not judge the crimes of high treason committed against them, as was done in Rome," because, "states Machiavelli, few are corrupted by few." Montesquieu's critique reveals his greater concern with individual security and tranquillity and the priority he gives to civil or private matters over political ones. Further, the essential means to these ends are the judicial power and due process, the general topics of this particular book of *The Spirit of Laws*:

I would gladly adopt this great man's maxim; but as in these cases political interest forces, so to speak, civil interest (for it is always a drawback if the people judge their offenses themselves), it is necessary, in order to remedy this, that the laws provide, as much as they can, for the security of individuals.   (EL 1.6.5)

---

⁴⁰ See Elena Guarini, "Machiavelli and the Crisis of the Italian Republics," in *Machiavelli and Republicanism*, 26–8, 32, on Machiavelli's report (after a diplomatic mission) on France, the *Ritratto di cose di Francia*, and the remarks on France in his *Discourses on Livy* and *The Prince*. Guarini overlooks the importance for Montesquieu of Machiavelli's praise of French laws and orders, especially its judicial order.

⁴¹ See also NM, D 1.16 (France and its king are "secure and content" due to the "infinite laws in which the security of all its people is included"), 19 (France is maintained by its "ancient orders"), and 58 (France is "moderated more by laws than any other kingdom of which knowledge is had in our times"); see also D 1.55. Paul A. Rahe notes the link between Machiavelli, Montesquieu, and judging in *Republics Ancient and Modern: Classical Republicanism and the American Revolution* (Chapel Hill, NC: University of North Carolina Press, 1992), 1002, n. 173.

Montesquieu then cites two protections afforded to the "civil interest" in ancient Rome that, he implies, Machiavelli overlooks: Accused men could exile themselves before judgment was passed, and the people could not confiscate the goods of an accused man.[42] Further, he links this analysis of judicial formalities or due process with his subsequent study of the constitution of political liberty, remarking that "other limitations placed on the people's power to judge will be seen in Book 11" (*EL* 1.6.5). This apparently refers to the limits on popular juries, emphasized early in the chapter on England's constitution, and to the "supreme authority" later attributed to the upper house of the legislature to moderate any and all laws. It may also refer to the treatment of Rome that follows, in which the chapter on Roman judging is the longest. Interestingly, Montesquieu's views on Roman judging are at odds with Machiavelli's endorsement of the tribunes' handling of the Coriolanus affair and with the praise he bestows on the general transformation of judging from a patrician to a popular function (*EL* 2.11.6, 18).

This explicit and pointed criticism of Machiavelli's disregard for the security of individuals occurs within Book 6 (the first extended treatment of judging in *The Spirit of Laws*), where Montesquieu catalogues various abuses and reforms of the judging function in terms of such security. One of the distinguishing, if little noted, marks of Montesquieu's political science is this humane emphasis upon judging and the administration of justice for individuals, and it explains his strong disagreement on this issue with a "great man" to whom he is so indebted.[43] Montesquieu was for many years a senior judge *(président à mortier)* in the *parlement* of Bordeaux and thus drew upon his experience as well as his theoretical acumen to support his constitutional emphasis on the judging power. Indeed, just prior to his critique of Machiavelli, he declares that "justice," understood in judicial terms as "the formalities of justice" or due process, is "the thing in the world that it is most important for men to know" (*EL* 1.6.2). Nonetheless, throughout the work he discusses the role of judging in facilitating the security and tranquillity of individuals within the larger context of moderate government and the separation of powers. His central innovation in liberal constitutionalism, as compared to Hobbes and Locke, is an independent judicial power that tempers the constitutional conflict between classes and among the separated powers, thus moderating the making and execution of laws affecting individual security and tranquillity. These liberal, life-protecting purposes for judicial power explain the other striking statements about it scattered throughout *The Spirit of Laws* – that "among a free people"

---

[42] For Montesquieu's references to Socrates and Plato in discussing self-exile, see the notes to *EL* 1.6.5. In discussing the Roman constitution, Polybius (6.14.7) specifically praises the practice of voluntary self-exile.

[43] I discuss this at length in Paul Carrese, *The Cloaking of Power: Montesquieu, Blackstone, and the Rise of Judicial Activism* (Chicago: University of Chicago Press, 2003), as well as recent English and French scholarship on this theme. A more historical interpretation of judging in Montesquieu's political philosophy is Rebecca Kingston, *Montesquieu and the Parlement of Bordeaux* (Geneva: Droz, 1996).

the "masterwork of legislation is to know how to place well the power of judging," that individual security (already identified as the essence of liberty) "is never more attacked than in public or private prosecutions," that a knowledge of "the surest rules one can observe in criminal judgments concerns mankind more than anything else in the world," and that "it is only on the practice of this knowledge that liberty can be founded" (2.11.11, 12.2). Since Montesquieu may have seen Machiavelli's praise of *parlements* and the rule of law in France as, paradoxically, a key to turning the drive for glory toward liberal preservation and tranquillity for all, Montesquieuan judging reveals itself as distinctly, if softly, Machiavellian.

Machiavellian Moderation and the Perpetuation of Liberal Constitutionalism

Montesquieu, and Machiavelli's influence upon him, should not be remote concerns in liberal democracies. Montesquieu's prominent place in the thought of the American founders, especially at the time of the framing and establishment of the 1787 Constitution, is evident to any reader of *The Federalist*.[44] Through America's influence on the world's liberal democracies, whether parliamentary regimes or governments based on a separation of powers, Montesquieu's distinctive imprint shines through in the prominence of pluralism, faction, judicial power, federalism, and globalization – the worldwide reach of commerce and the moderate government that it requires. Yet for all the achievements of the modern liberalism he promoted – from personal and political liberty, to general prosperity, to military prowess – he would be among those friends of liberal democracy who acknowledge its defects. He would recognize the problems diagnosed by Rousseau and Nietzsche in terms of "alienation" or "individualism," although he surely would prefer Tocqueville's more moderate formulations. These concerns arise across the contemporary academic and political spectrum in America, voiced by liberal theorists, communitarians, and conservatives, as the lack of a "politics of meaning," "habits of the heart," or "civility," as the need for "personal responsibility," "family values," or "character," or with reference to such symptoms as "defining deviancy down," "bowling alone," or "democracy's discontent."

The second most famous chapter in *The Spirit of Laws* reveals Montesquieu's prescient awareness of the potential for such problems in modern liberalism. When he observes how English laws shape the mores, manner, and character

---

[44] Donald Lutz, "The Relative Influence of European Writers on Late Eighteenth-Century American Political Thought," *APSR* 78:1 (March 1984): 189–97, argues that Montesquieu was the most widely cited author in America in the 1780s and 1790s, more so than Locke. I discuss this in Paul Carrese, "The Complexity, and Principles, of the American Founding: A Reply to Alan Gibson," *HPT* 21:4 (Winter 2000): 711–17, and in "Montesquieu's Complex Natural Right and Moderate Liberalism," 227–50. Note also Fareed Zakaria's reliance on Montesquieu's conception of liberal constitutionalism in Zakaria, *The Future of Freedom: Illiberal Democracy at Home and Abroad* (New York: W. W. Norton, 2003).

of the nation, he describes English politics as a dynamic equilibrium that moderates the passions by promoting private enterprise and commercial opportunity for individuals (*EL* 3.19.27). His mixed portrait of this liberal people anticipates Tocqueville's concerns regarding liberal democracy, suggesting that for all the benefits that the English constitution produces in the character of its people, the "extreme liberty" that Montesquieu had earlier noted in fact produces an extreme individualism, an antireligious ire, and polarized or sectarian thinking among intellectuals.[45] That said, Montesquieu was less concerned with, or attuned to, these issues than his fellow Frenchman subsequently would be, and a paradox associated with recovering an understanding of Montesquieu's philosophy today is that we must consider how much its own resources can be used to moderate its own tendencies toward extremes. There are discernibly Montesquieuan roots to the past century's judicialism and the individualism it enforces – an unintended consequence of his emphasis on individual tranquillity and an independent judiciary empowered to protect and enhance it. A range of contemporary political theorists has challenged the judicialized conception of liberalism that arose in the twentieth century, warning that such a politics reduces any higher civic and moral aims to litigious disputes about individual claims and entitlements, even regarding elections to the highest political offices.[46]

Indeed, a quite public pairing of Montesquieu with Machiavelli in the nineteenth century in a dialogue on liberalism – and especially the ultimate fate of that pairing – reinforces our recognition of the paradox that aspects of Montesquieu's moderate liberalism have subsequently damaged the philosophe's own aims. French author Maurice Joly sought to champion the enlightened liberalism of Montesquieu by ranging it against the illiberalism of Machiavelli,[47] but this well-laid plan suffered a shocking fate. Something within modern liberal Europe was capable of transforming this defense of humane liberty into the protofascist and anti-Semitic Protocols of the Learned Elders of Zion, and of using it to achieve the most illiberal of aims.[48] Montesquieu's

---

[45] See Schaub, *Erotic Liberalism*, 142–4. Recent studies that find Montesquieu moderating modern liberalism with ancient elements include Paul A. Rahe, "Forms of Government: Structure, Principle, Object, and Aim," and Sharon Krause, "Despotism in *The Spirit of Laws*," both in *Montesquieu's Science of Politics*, 69–108, 231–71, as well as Carrese, "Montesquieu's Complex Natural Right and Moderate Liberalism," 227–50.

[46] Compare the defense of a juridical liberalism by John Rawls, *Political Liberalism* (New York: Columbia University Press, 1993), 231–40, 212–13, with the criticisms aimed at it by Michael Sandel *Democracy's Discontent: America in Search of a Public Philosophy* (Cambridge, MA: Harvard University Press, 1996), 28, 39–47, 92–101, 279–80, 286–8. I discuss these issues in Carrese, *The Cloaking of Power*, 231–64.

[47] See [Maurice Joly], *Dialogue aux enfers entre Machiavel et Montesquieu: ou, La politique de Machiavel au XIXe siècle* (Brussels: A. Mertens, 1864), which is now available in an English translation: See Joly, *The Dialogue in Hell between Machiavelli and Montesquieu*, ed. and tr. John S. Waggoner (Lanham, MD: Lexington Books, 2002).

[48] See Shackleton, "Montesquieu and Machiavelli," 1–13; Schaub, *Erotic Liberalism*, 176–7, n. 20.

liberal apology was discarded, the Jews were given Machiavelli's lines, and the moral of the story was the need to combat such characters with a similarly Machiavellian ruthlessness. Montesquieu had thought that Jews, and the rest of us, would find security within a factional liberalism of commerce and mutual self-interest. The most enlightened and educated of peoples proved in the twentieth century, however, that the turn away from virtue and the good is not always easily kept moderate or civilized. Such concerns about tendencies in modern liberalism to uproot or undermine its own principles do not suggest that American constitutionalism is thoroughly, even if moderately, Machiavellian, or that our founders intended it to be so. Nor do they suggest that moderation and the separation of powers are all bad. Rather, the issue is a restoration of aspects of our complex constitutional tradition that were intended by its founders to balance others. Moderate expectations for civic virtue, public-spiritedness, and political civility were once thought conditions necessary for protecting individual rights, and our complex constitutional republic originally was constituted to promote such qualities. Similarly, a classic common law jurisprudence once tempered the atomistic, rationalist tendencies of the Lockean legal theory with which it was blended.[49] Montesquieuan moderation may well be more humane than the more severe and doctrinaire versions of liberal modernity. Even a moderately Machiavellian liberalism, however, cannot by itself provide what it promises to deliver – individual security and tranquillity. The distinctly modern versions of moral and political moderation may need moderating through recourse to other principles and traditions.

---

[49] See Harvey C. Mansfield, "Separation of Powers in the American Constitution," in Mansfield, *America's Constitutional Soul* (Baltimore, MD: Johns Hopkins University Press, 1991), 115–27; James R. Stoner, *Common Law and Liberal Theory: Coke, Hobbes, and the Origins of American Constitutionalism* (Lawrence, KS: University Press of Kansas, 1993), 1–9, 223–5, and *Common Law Liberty* (Lawrence, KS: University Press of Kansas, 2003); Carrese, *The Cloaking of Power*, passim.

6

Benjamin Franklin's "Machiavellian" Civic Virtue

Steven Forde

At first glance, it might seem that Benjamin Franklin is the least Machiavellian of the American founders. He abhorred war, though he thought the American Revolutionary War necessary. He despised the classical ideal of heroism insofar as it was wedded to the glories of war. The ideal that he self-consciously proposed to replace it, through his *Autobiography* and other writings, is unabashedly at peace with commerce, wealth, and creature comforts. His ideal also has strong elements of public service and civic virtue, but this virtue is not understood as heroic or even self-sacrificing. Franklin's virtue seems far indeed from the martial republican virtue that Machiavelli hoped to revive in modernity. Indeed, despite the central role he played in the politics and diplomacy of American independence, Franklin might have been less concerned with politics per se than any of the founders. He devoted his energies as a writer and thinker much more to what we would call social or private affairs.

But by Franklin's day, the influence of Machiavelli was felt in the world of social and private affairs as much as anywhere. That influence, modified by Montaigne, Bacon, Locke, and others, had created a distinctive modern outlook and a distinctly modern world – the grandchild, not the child, of Machiavelli. In statecraft, the moralized Machiavellianism of *raison d'état* was a reigning doctrine.[1] Machiavelli's bloody and expansive lust for glory had been replaced

---

[1] See Friedrich Meinecke, *Machiavellism: The Doctrine of Raison d'État and Its Place in Modern History*, tr. Douglas Scott (Boulder, CO: Westview Press, 1984). *Raison d'état* is Machiavellian in giving over the world of politics, especially international politics, to amoral calculations of power and interest. But it justifies this by appealing to the national interest as an overriding moral interest. See Leo Strauss, *Thoughts on Machiavelli* (Seattle, WA: University of Washington Press, 1969), 61–3, 79–80; Harvey C. Mansfield, "Machiavelli's *Stato* and the Impersonal Modern State," in Mansfield, *Machiavelli's Virtue* (Chicago: University of Chicago Press, 1996), 281–94; Paul A. Rahe, *Republics Ancient and Modern: Classical Republicanism and the American Revolution* (Chapel Hill, NC: University of North Carolina Press, 1992), 263. See also Thomas L. Pangle, *The Spirit of Modern Republicanism: The Moral Vision of the American Founders and the Philosophy of Locke* (Chicago: University of Chicago Press, 1988), 63–4.

by more sedate means of serving bodily security and following the promptings of nature. It was in the wholehearted embrace of these goals that Machiavelli's influence was seen, rather than in sanguinary political recommendations. That is, his influence was deep rather than apparent. On the surface a repudiation of Machiavelli, the new philosophy in fact rested on and carried forward his overthrow of preexisting notions of man's proper goals.[2] The increasing weight that the philosophy of liberalism gave to private and social affairs, specifically their divorce from politics, was paradoxically a part of this project. Franklin's participation in this movement is seen in nothing more clearly than the twin poles of his moral compass, *humanity* and *civility*. Classical catalogues of virtues could be scoured without finding these qualities. Indeed, the classical philosophers would not grant the title "virtue" to either of them, since humanity and civility, as understood by the post-Machiavellians, are divorced from what the older philosophy regarded as the essential and higher aspirations of mankind. They are instead the names of qualities that had risen to the status of virtues in the egalitarian world that followed from Machiavelli's attack on the old, perfectionist ideals. They presuppose Machiavelli's repudiation of the moral and metaphysical arguments on which that perfectionism was based, and on his decision to seek the good of mankind in a humbler, material sense.

No denizen of the eighteenth century was more attuned to the new outlook, or more comfortable in the world it had created, than Benjamin Franklin. Franklin, the oldest of the American founders, was more broadly familiar with the contemporary European intellectual currents than most of his colleagues. As a colonial postmaster, printer, bookseller, and scientific investigator, he was more intimately exposed to those currents than almost anyone in the colonies. As a long-time inhabitant of London and Paris, he imbibed the new spirit with unrivaled gusto. Franklin was a man at home in his age as few men ever have been. He also contributed to its development more than most, though not always in conspicuous ways.

Franklin's *Realpolitik*

References to Machiavelli in Franklin's writing are virtually nonexistent, though the few that exist make approving use of Machiavellian texts to bolster diplomatic arguments.[3] In his long career as a diplomat – first representing several of the colonies in London, then representing the United States in France during the War of Independence – Franklin displayed considerable appreciation for

---

[2] For a much more thorough account of this development, see Rahe, *Republics Ancient and Modern*, Book Two; Leo Strauss, *Natural Right and History* (Chicago: University of Chicago Press, 1953), 165–251. Some elements of the development will be elaborated in this chapter.

[3] In the thirty-six published volumes of Franklin's papers, only two references by Franklin to Machiavelli are indexed. One is in a 1760 London pamphlet on the advisability of British expansion in Canada in the wake of the defeat of the French there. In 1766, also in London, Franklin included an excerpt from the *Discourses* in an essay about the Stamp Act controversy (*PBF* 9:92, 13:28).

the realities of power politics. His awareness of these realities, and especially of the need for armed force as a guarantee for security, predates these experiences. During the 1740s and 1750s, at the beginning of Franklin's involvement in public affairs, Pennsylvania confronted threats from French and Spanish privateers by sea, and combined French and Indian forces by land on the frontier. Franklin took the lead first as a private citizen, then as a member of the Pennsylvania House of Burgesses, to organize citizen militias and provide defensible ramparts, armed with cannon, for the Philadelphia waterfront. This took some doing, given the predominance of the pacifist Quakers in the colony and its Assembly. Franklin was by and large successful in maneuvering around the Quakers' pacifism, but he makes it clear in his *Autobiography* that he thought religious pacifism a rather silly indulgence, given the realities of the world. Indeed, he notes, when confronted with actual danger, even sectarians were generally willing to allow their principles to lapse. "Common Sense aided by present Danger," he quips, "will sometimes be too strong for whimsicall Opinions" (*ABF* 232).[4]

Lest we miss this crucial point, Franklin discusses in some detail the Quakers' various embarrassments in dealing with the issue of defense. This series of episodes draws our attention because it represents the most pointed and sustained critique of religious doctrine in the *Autobiography*, where Franklin otherwise professes the greatest respect for the beliefs of all sects (*ABF* 182–91).[5] Being a British colony with a frontier, Pennsylvania experienced threats stemming from the geopolitical struggles of the European powers in the New World, and from the unsettled frontier (though the frontier threats usually were stirred up by geopolitics). Franklin makes it clear that these realities essentially constituted a refutation of pacifist principles, and that the sectarians themselves were obliged to bow to this reality. They allowed military defense to proceed only by subterfuge, so that they would not have to disavow their principles overtly. The gulf between their religious principles and political reality became increasingly uncomfortable, though, and the Quakers eventually took to refusing public service in order to avoid it, "Chusing rather to quit their Power than their Principle" (*ABF* 191). In Franklin's view, they could not have both.

In 1757, Franklin was appointed colonial agent to London, and at age fifty-one embarked on his diplomatic career proper. Throughout that career, he displayed a keen awareness of the importance of the geopolitical balance of power. His principal interest, naturally enough, was the place of the New World in the global balance. Before the revolutionary struggle, he took the view that the heart of British power was its American colonies, and that these would only increase in importance with time (*WrBF* 760–1). He saw the brightest future for the Anglo-American empire, if strategic obstacles to its expansion

---

[4] Cf. *ABF* 182–91. This remark is made in connection with the pacifism of the Moravians, not the Quakers. All my quotations from Franklin will be as found in the editions cited, with orthography and emphases unchanged.

[5] Cf. *ABF* 146, 157, 162.

could be removed. He was in London during the late 1750s and early 1760s as the Seven Years' War with France raged, and this experience made him an advocate of unrestricted imperial expansion. While the outcome of the war was still in doubt, a policy debate developed in London over whether Britain should maintain possession of all of Canada in the event of success or cede some of it back to the French. Franklin entered the pamphlet war unequivocally on the side of expelling the French entirely. His "Canada pamphlet" of 1760 is a monument to *raison d'état*.[6] Another pamphleteer had argued that Canada should be returned, on the grounds that Britain had alleged no claim to the territory before the war, and had not included such a conquest in its war aims. Franklin vehemently disagreed: The progress of British arms might justify larger claims after the war than beforehand. Britain might not have had any rightful claim to Canada before, but "Advantages gain'd in the course of this war may increase the extent of our rights" (*PBF* 9:61). It is important to Franklin's argument that the war as a whole is a just one on the part of Britain, but he clearly also believes that power can confer a measure of right. The case is sealed, in his view, by the consideration that the possession of Canada would allow England's American colonies to expand without stint. He both expects and approves such expansion; another war with France is inevitable, he asserts, if France retains any presence in Canada (*WrBF* 532, 761).

One argument used by Franklin's opponent in this exchange of pamphlets was that a French presence in Canada was to Britain's advantage, as a means of preventing the British American colonies from becoming too great and ultimately overbearing to the mother country. This argument, prescient as it might seem in retrospect, is rebuffed indignantly by Franklin. His vision of the British Empire was a single English-speaking nation straddling the Atlantic Ocean, whose center of gravity was inexorably shifting to the New World. In the controversies leading up to independence, his view of the importance of the American colonies to British power emboldened him in his assertion of the rights of the colonies. Once the breach came, the inherent strength of the American strategic position as he saw it shaped his diplomacy at the French court. He had ample reason to know how precarious the American cause was at times, but he maintained throughout that triumph was inevitable in the fullness of time. For all his courting of the French, and all his gratitude for the assistance they provided, Franklin refused to promise or concede them too much because of his assessment of the underlying relations of power and the future prospects of an independent United States. "Poor as we are," he wrote to John Jay in 1780, "I know we shall be rich" (*WrBF* 1029). With Franklin's encouragement, the Continental Congress initially proposed a treaty of alliance with France that bound the French not to invade any British holdings in America – despite the

---

[6] "The Interest of Great Britain Considered with Regard to Her Colonies and the Acquisitions of Canada and Guadaloupe, to Which are Added Observations Concerning the Increase of Mankind, Peopling of Countries, & c," in *PBF* 9:59–100. See also the satirical piece on the same subject, *WrBF* 532–5.

fact that the British had only recently taken many of these from France – on the grounds that they were the future destiny of the United States.[7]

His understanding of the dynamics of force accounts for Franklin's behavior during the eventual peace negotiations with the British. His sense of underlying American strength led him to negotiate rather firmly, rebuffing all attempts to locate the frontier of the new nation anywhere east of the Mississippi, and insisting on full use of the Mississippi for navigation (*WrBF* 1029, 1055).[8] To the surprise of many, the British actually agreed to these conditions. They balked, however, at Franklin's suggestion that they cede all of Canada to the new United States. His rationale for this bold, if not presumptuous, proposal was the same he had given earlier for British retention of this territory upon its conquest from France. Now, though, it was the power and security of an independent United States that was at stake.

Franklin's hard-nosed *Realpolitik*, his "Machiavellianism" in foreign affairs, did not come from close study of his Florentine predecessor in the diplomatic corps. It came from Franklin's exposure to the international realities of his day, through which he had to navigate first as a colonial statesman, then as the emissary of an infant power to the great courts of Europe. The policies of those courts, and thus the environment to which he had to adapt, had been decisively if indirectly shaped by post-Machiavellian *raison d'état*. Franklin himself was far from unconcerned with justice – he believed the American revolutionary cause to be supremely just – and he professed to believe at least one nation, France, to be moved more by honor than by interest (*WrBF* 1043). Nevertheless, he did not base his hopes for American success on the justice of the cause, nor did he truly expect France or any other nation to assist the United States except on the basis of shared interests. Franklin's diplomacy on behalf of the United States consistently accepted the principle that the weaker could gain favors from the stronger only by serving their interests. By the same token, he had no inhibitions against treating still weaker powers as pawns. His attitude toward Canada, both as an imperialist in London during the Seven Years' War and as American peace negotiator in Paris, would be difficult to imagine outside this Machiavellian context. Within that context, it was taken for granted that such territories could be treated as mere bargaining chips in the contests of greater powers. The wishes of their inhabitants, whatever they may be, scarcely entered into his, or anyone else's, calculations of power and interest.

Franklin and Modern Science

Political practice was just one arena in which the influence of Machiavelli was visible by the end of the eighteenth century. Philosophy had been even more

---

[7] See Esmond Wright, *Franklin of Philadelphia* (Cambridge, MA: Harvard/Belknap, 1986), 276.

[8] Opposition was felt from the Spanish as well as the British on these points – and even, to some degree, the French. Gerald Strouzh, *Benjamin Franklin and American Foreign Policy* (Chicago: University of Chicago Press, 1954), 130.

profoundly affected. By Franklin's time, the split between natural philosophy – that is, science – and speculative philosophy was virtually consummated. Both branches of this endeavor were heavily if indirectly indebted to Machiavelli, and Franklin participated in each of them in different ways. In the new field of natural science, Franklin was without peer among Americans.

The key link between Machiavelli and modern natural science is their shared use of human reason as an instrument for analyzing the empirical world, with the explicit purpose of controlling or subduing it to the advantage of man. Machiavelli's image of conquering the woman Fortune in the penultimate chapter of *The Prince* is the most famous epitome of this in his work (*P* 25). Machiavelli rejects the old, purely contemplative ideal of reason in the name of a new empiricism and activism. He makes reason an instrument rather than an end in itself or the vehicle of some higher human perfection, and the cause in which it is enlisted is advancing the preservation and the physical comfort of mankind. The ancients never attempted such an approach because of their different, and more exalted, understanding of the life of reason and of man's place in the cosmos. Bacon, Descartes, and other knowing or unknowing disciples of Machiavelli applied the new understanding to the natural world and created a science devoted to controlling nature for the sake of easing man's estate. In the process, they furthered Machiavelli's wholesale assault on the older moral philosophy.[9]

It was as a scientist in this mold that Franklin first made an international reputation for himself. Scientific investigation pleased him more than almost any other activity. In 1748, when he had accumulated what he regarded as a "sufficient tho' moderate Fortune," he more or less retired from business with the intention, he says, to devote himself exclusively to "Philosophical Studies" in the form of experiments with electricity (*ABF* 196). His design was thwarted by the many demands for public service that were pressed upon him, and which he accepted. He continued to insist, though, that scientific investigation was his true love (e.g., *WrBF* 454). Despite the political "distractions," Franklin's correspondence, and the rest of his *oeuvre*, is filled with remarkably penetrating observations on a remarkably wide range of scientific subjects. There is no doubt that Franklin had a scientific genius, untutored though it was, and his contributions, especially in the field of electricity, were truly deserving of international renown.

Franklin's mind was continually on the useful applications of science. In this sense, despite his complaints about giving up one for the other, science

---

[9] The link to Machiavelli is seen most explicitly in Bacon; see, for example, his explicit homage to the Florentine in the essay "Of Goodness, and Goodness of Nature," in *WoFB* 6:403–5. In *The Great Instauration*, an overview of his intellectual project, Bacon speaks of his science as an attempt to subdue nature and proclaims its goal to be a humanitarian one (*WoFB* 4:7–8, 13–33). Descartes knew how revolutionary, and hence subversive, his new natural philosophy was, especially vis-à-vis the ancient alternative; see, for example, René Descartes, *DM* passim (esp. I, VI). Descartes discusses the humanitarianism of his project in the same work (*DM* VI). John Locke also saw science as an exercise in "charity" (*ECHU* 4.12.11–12).

and public service were not divergent for him. The lightning rod is the clearest expression of their convergence in the field of electricity, and Franklin worked to increase the use of this initially controversial device like a proselyte. Bifocal glasses are another example. When in Paris, Franklin was fascinated by the useful applications that might be made of the lighter-than-air balloons that were then first appearing. He wondered about the possibility of a floating harness that, among other applications, might assist him in getting about despite his gout.[10] His writings are full of such ideas – means of increasing the navigability of canals, using knowledge about the Gulf Stream (whose nature he first explored) to expedite shipping, as well as his notorious satirical proposal for a scientific competition to find a way to give intestinal gas a pleasant odor.[11] In that proposal, Franklin (*WrBF* 954) asks, "Are there twenty Men in Europe at this Day, the happier, or even the easier, for any Knowledge they have pick'd out of Aristotle?" The benefit to mankind in liberating flatulence from public disgrace, he continues, would be a more signal service than Descartes' theory of vortices or the calculations of Newton. This proposal, and the arguments advanced on its behalf, are only partially ironic. Even his purest scientific researches were closer to useful applications than was the theory of gravitation. In the *Autobiography*, Franklin makes special mention of one of his more humble inventions, the famous "Franklin stove." This stove was based on Franklin's thorough investigations of drafts, convections, and the problem of "smokey chimneys" in the houses of his day. The stove was designed to avoid these problems, and to heat more efficiently with less wood. In the *Autobiography*, Franklin mentions that he was offered a patent on its design, but he declined, preferring to make it available to one and all (*ABF* 191–2). His principle, he informs us, was that, just as we benefit from the inventions of others, we should be willing likewise to benefit others when occasion offers. This is one version of a more general precept that Franklin recommended throughout his life: that favors should be passed on, as a way of expressing gratitude for favors one has received in the past (*WrBF* 475, 1040). It is entirely typical that Franklin should apply this general principle of social good works to scientific endeavor. For him, "pure" science was never far from its applications, and those applications were dedicated to increased human comfort and security.

One of the themes implicit in the modern scientific project is progress. Franklin could be considered almost the incarnation of this idea. His conviction, which breathes in every page of his scientific writing, was that science is an engine for virtually limitless progress in the mastery of natural principles for the comfort of man. More than once, Franklin half-seriously expressed the wish that he had been born a century or more later, so as to behold the wondrous improvements that must be made in science (*WrBF* 1017, 1074, 1167).

---

[10] Franklin discusses balloons in *WrBF* 1074–8; see also Claude-Anne Lopez, *Mon Cher Papa: Franklin and the Ladies of Paris* (New Haven, CT: Yale University Press, 1990), 215–21.

[11] Franklin discusses canals in *WrBF* 832–4; the proposal on intestinal gas may be found in *WrBF* 952–5.

This optimism was not unjustified – immense technological advancements have indeed been made in the last two centuries, advancements that would gratify and amaze him. There is one outgrowth of the belief in scientific progress, however, that Franklin distinctly did not share. Many in the Enlightenment (and many more in the nineteenth century) were persuaded that scientific progress augured indefinite progress in society and human affairs generally. Franklin, for all his enthusiasm about progress in natural science, was much more pessimistic about progress in "moral Science" (*WrBF* 1017). In fact, when contemplating human shortcomings, Franklin's normally sunny disposition could turn surprisingly black. He decried human selfishness, which overpowers reason and leads to unnecessary and fruitless conflict in politics, trade, and war (e.g., *WrBF* 806–7, 822–3, 1017). He once chided a doctor for practicing his art: "Half the Lives you save are not worth saving, as being useless; and almost the other Half ought not to be sav'd, as being mischievous" (*WrBF* 803). In a 1782 letter to Joseph Priestly, Franklin laments once again his lack of leisure for scientific pursuits, and contrasts the joys of scientific investigation with his travails in his dealings with men:

I should rejoice much, if I could once more recover the Leisure to search with you into the Works of Nature; I mean the *inanimate*, not the *animate* or moral part of them, the more I discover'd of the former, the more I admir'd them; the more I know of the latter, the more I am disgusted with them. Men I find to be a Sort of Beings very badly constructed, as they are generally more easily provok'd than reconcil'd, more disposed to do Mischief to each other than to make Reparation, much more easily deceiv'd than undeceiv'd, and having more Pride and even Pleasure in killing than in begetting one another.   (*WrBF* 1047–8)

Then, in what must be the low point of this type of reflection in Franklin, he suggests that it might be better to use boys and girls in scientific experiments, rather than to "murder" so many "honest, harmless mice."

Before we label Franklin a "Machiavellian" on the grounds of these bleak statements concerning human nature, we have to recognize that they do not represent Franklin's final or considered view. After all, he devoted his life to public service in the hope that he could do some good and prevent some evil, and he undertook numerous projects of public education that betray a hope that improvement – modest, perhaps, but significant – was possible. Franklin is Machiavellian in finding that the darker side of human nature cannot be done away with, and that it places strict limits on the progress of society. He is equally Machiavellian in the philosophical basis on which he places his moral philosophy.

Franklin and Modern Philosophy

To some it may seem perverse to place Franklin within the modern philosophical tradition, or any philosophical tradition. One of the clearest themes of his *Autobiography* is the futility of philosophical speculation, an endeavor Franklin says he was enamored of in his youth but later abandoned. At age forty he wrote to a friend of his attitude toward metaphysical reasoning: "The great Uncertainty I have found in that Science; the wide Contradictions and endless Disputes it affords . . . have given me a Disgust to what I was once extreamly fond of" (*WrBF* 435).[12] In marked contrast to some of his fellow founders, Franklin was reluctant to speak of such philosophical abstractions as the "rights of man," the "state of nature," and so on.[13] At bottom, he found such doctrines too uncertain to be the basis of a creed – or, no doubt, of a revolution. At the Federal Convention of 1787, while some of his fellow founders debated grand theoretical points, Franklin was concerned only with practical outcomes. In his final speech at that convention, Franklin simply stated that, human reason being as fallible as it is, the objections he conceives to the proposed Constitution may well be wrong, and moreover, that "there is no *Form* of Government but what may be a Blessing to the People if well administered" (*WrBF* 1140).[14]

Franklin was clearly more skeptical than his colleagues about the ability of reason to produce grand theories, such as the natural-rights theory of John Locke that guided the framing of the Declaration of Independence and the Constitution. Was Franklin then a misologist who had grown cynical of the capability of reason to guide our actions? And were his own admittedly strong convictions simply arbitrary? In order to make sense of Franklin's position, we have to see that he developed it not in repudiation of modern philosophy, or even of Locke. Rather, he hewed self-consciously to a prominent, antimetaphysical strain of the post-Machiavellian tradition.

A key part of Machiavelli's assault on his predecessors was his rejection of their grand speculative systems, especially in ethics, as vain "imaginings" (see NM, *P* 15). Machiavelli attempted to show that experience of the real world revealed these systems to be groundless. He replaced them with a new political philosophy rooted in the insights he claimed to have gleaned from a clear-eyed view of practical reality. As a result, Machiavelli bequeathed to his successors not only political realism and modern natural science, but a metaphysical skepticism that made experience rather than abstract speculation the touchstone for philosophical truth. Thus Descartes began his intellectual project by rejecting all previous philosophy out of hand. He took radical doubt as the beginning point of his thought, and it is a matter of debate how far he ever got

---

[12] Cf. *WrBF* 1016, *ABF* 113–15.

[13] Franklin was willing to make occasional use of the doctrine of the rights of man for rhetorical purposes, though even here he was much more reticent than his fellows. This was not only because he was skeptical of such doctrines, but because they could be politically counterproductive. During the years in which he was trying to find a reconciliation between the Americans and the British, Franklin thought the absolutist rhetoric of rights too hostile to compromise. See Wright, *Franklin of Philadelphia*, 173, 197, 232; Edmund S. Morgan, *Benjamin Franklin* (New Haven, CT: Yale University Press, 2002), 93–4, 142–3, 149, 155. One of the hard lessons the young Franklin learns in the *Autobiography* is that speculative reasoning in general is more conducive to dispute and social ill-will than to truth (*ABF* 60, 64–5, 114).

[14] Franklin here echoes one of his favorite authors, Alexander Pope (cf. *Essay on Man*, 3.303–4).

beyond it. Subsequent philosophy, at least to the end of the eighteenth century, was fundamentally oriented around the problem of the *limits* of human reason, specifically its inability to ground the grand metaphysical structures of the past. Hume's empiricism questioned our knowledge of the external world and denied the rationality of inferences such as causality. Immanuel Kant, inspired by Hume's skeptical empiricism, built a philosophical system grand enough in itself, but founded on the notion that the underpinnings of reality are opaque to us, and that reason cannot definitively answer many of the traditional questions of philosophy.[15] Both these philosophers were deeply influenced by John Locke. For Locke, who is best known today as the apostle of universal natural rights, was at least as well known in the century after his death as an empiricist and a skeptic.

Franklin had the greatest admiration for Locke, an admiration he expressed even after his disillusionment with speculative philosophy was complete. He made efforts to augment Locke's reputation among his fellow Americans. In his *Poor Richard's Almanack* for 1748, Franklin inserted a commemoration of Locke's death (which had occurred in 1704), calling him "the *Newton* of the *Microcosm*," that is, of the human mind (*WrBF* 1249). The only work of Locke that this commemoration mentions is his *Essay Concerning Human Understanding*. In fact, only two works of Locke have a great explicit presence in Franklin's writing: the *Essay* and *Some Thoughts Concerning Education*. In his *Autobiography*, Franklin identifies the *Essay* as one of the books he read when very young (*ABF* 64). The approach of that work could serve as a pattern for Franklin's own moral thought.

Locke explains at the outset of the *Essay* that the work had its origin in a philosophic conversation that he and some friends were unable to bring to a satisfactory conclusion. This put Locke in mind of the limits of human reason; he concluded that the subject of their conversation was beyond the capacity of the human mind, and that the first task of philosophy had to be to find the limits of that capacity (*ECHU* Epistle to the Reader). Locke does not enlighten us further about that occasion, but one of those present later recalled that the subject had been morality and revealed religion.[16] In the *Essay*, Locke proclaims his primary goal to be to show what reason can know, and what it cannot, in order to prevent us from wasting our intellectual efforts on the one hand, and to preserve us from complete skepticism or intellectual despair on the other (*ECHU* 1.1.7).[17] For, Locke assures us, though we might not be able

---

[15] See Hume, *THN* 3–4; Immanuel Kant, "Preface to First Edition," in Kant, *Critique of Pure Reason*, tr. Norman Kemp Smith (New York: St. Martin's Press, 1965), 328–421.

[16] The recollection is James Tyrrell's (cited in Rahe, *Republics Ancient and Modern Ancient and Modern*, 307).

[17] Thus I hope it is clear that when I speak of the "skepticism" of the post-Machiavellian tradition, I mean only its skepticism regarding the grander claims for human knowledge made by previous philosophy. These philosophers regarded their humbler project as an inoculation against the complete skepticism that could arise from the collapse of the older metaphysics. See Descartes, *DM* III, VI.

to resolve the most exalted metaphysical questions, our intellect is adequate to the purposes of human life, and in particular to the derivation of rules, moral and otherwise, for the conduct of life (*ECHU* 1.1.5).[18] Of course, this implies that the "purposes" of human life are humbler than was thought by the classical philosophers, for whom the more exalted wisdom was the truest human perfection. Locke does say that the purposes that men propose for themselves are tied up with their various visions of happiness, and that these visions are in turn the origin of every moral system. For men call moral that which accords with their happiness – and they are right to do so (*ECHU* 1.3.6, 2.28.5).[19]

This collection of precepts is virtually a program for the development of Franklin's own thought. In his youth, Franklin became rather enamored of high-flown metaphysical and theological speculation, owing in part to the books of "polemic Divinity" he found in his father's library. This was a most unfortunate circumstance, Franklin says in the *Autobiography*, since it helped give him a contentious and disputatious turn. He quickly discovered that this was a vice (*ABF* 58, 60, 64–5, 71, 212–13). In due course, he also concluded that the theological and metaphysical subjects he liked to debate were beyond the grasp of the human mind. The young Franklin wrote two pamphlets, on separate occasions, arguing opposite conclusions about necessity, free will, and morality. This experience, the older Franklin tells one of his correspondents, left him with a conviction that such matters could not be resolved by human reason.[20] This is when he became "disgusted" with the whole enterprise of such speculation – not only, he says, on account of its uncertainty, but of the evil consequences that errors in this type of reasoning can have in life (*WrBF* 435). When Franklin forcefully takes the same position in his *Autobiography*, the repudiation of metaphysics becomes a part of his official public teaching, as it were.

The account he gives of this in the *Autobiography* is a remarkable one, and easily misunderstood. Franklin retraces his intellectual journey. Among the books in his father's library, he begins, were some directed against deism. But his own reading of these tracts led him to become "a thorough Deist": "For the Arguments of the Deists which were quoted to be refuted, appeared to me much stronger than the Refutations" (*ABF* 114).[21] Young Franklin's astuteness

---

[18] Evidently, the moral subjects discussed in Locke's colloquy with Tyrrell and others dealt with moral speculation more metaphysical than that which Locke's philosophy supports.

[19] Cf. Pangle, *The Spirit of Modern Republicanism*, 193.

[20] Letter to Benjamin Vaughan on 9 November 1779, in *WrBF* 1015–17. The two pamphlets were *A Dissertation on Liberty and Necessity, Pleasure and Pain* (*WrBF* 57–71), written in London in 1725 when Franklin was 19, and *On the Providence of God in the Government of the World* (*WrBF* 163–8), written five years later in Philadelphia.

[21] Rahe, *Republics Ancient and Modern*, 950–1, n. 87, archly speculates that one of these books may have been Locke's *Reasonableness of Christianity*. By Rahe's analysis, Franklin's reading of this work would not have been particularly objectionable to Locke (302–13). Pangle, *The Spirit of Modern Republicanism*, 196, 203, 211, would make the same point even more strongly.

as a reader only got him in trouble, however, when he converted some of his friends to his new creed. These friends later wronged him without compunction, and Franklin became convinced that deism was responsible for it. He came to regard this as an effectual refutation of the doctrine itself. Specifically, he concluded "that this Doctrine tho' it might be true, was not very useful" – a strikingly misologist formulation, it seems. He does allow that some error must have crept into his thinking and infected the whole ("as is common in metaphysical Reasonings"), but it is clearly his experience rather than any renewed speculation that has convinced him of this. Franklin abandoned his deism for a creed based on a new-found conviction that "*Truth, Sincerity and Integrity* in Dealings between Man and Man, were of the utmost Importance to the Felicity of Life" (*ABF* 114). This, too, came from experience rather than speculation.

If this movement of thought is misologist, it is the misology of post-Machiavellian metaphysical skepticism. Franklin's argument rests on the notion that the truth of a doctrine like deism is, strictly speaking, beyond human ken; but we are entitled on the basis of other, empirical, signs to reject it. These signs include its effects on the conduct of life and especially on our happiness, which henceforward become the touchstone for our beliefs. Thus metaphysical agnosticism allows us to reject deism on the grounds that it is not useful, laying aside the (irresolvable) question of its truth. As Locke said, though our minds are too limited to settle many of the classical problems of philosophy, they are adequate to the guidance of life. Locke's own procedure in seeking such guidance is to explore the conditions of human preservation and happiness, taking human beings as we find them, not as philosophy might imagine them. He also suggests that probabilistic rather than mathematical reasoning may be appropriate to these questions (*ECHU* 1.1.5, 2.21.70, 4.17.16). Descartes had spoken of a "provisional" moral code that was to guide his conduct while he called all into doubt. The heart of this code was obedience to law and adoption of moderate or measured maxims of conduct (*DM* III). But Descartes was typical of the movement of early modern thought when he placed in the center of his moral system, apparently during all phases of his thinking, the general principle of benevolence to mankind. He insisted repeatedly that this is a "law" or general "duty" for all, and he used it partially to explain his intellectual project as a whole (*DM* VI).

The combination of metaphysical skepticism and generalized humanitarianism is characteristic of the entire post-Machiavellian movement. Franklin is more averse to philosophical speculation than many in this movement, though no more so than Montaigne, one of Machiavelli's earliest progeny, who was a true humanitarian and a stranger to metaphysical speculation.[22] We have already seen the key role played by benevolence in the scientific project launched

---

[22] For a discussion of Montaigne's outlook and its place in the modern development see Rahe, *Republics Ancient and Modern*, 267–73. For his humanitarianism, see especially his essays "Des Cannibales" and "De la Cruauté," in Michel de Montaigne, *Oeuvres Complètes* (Paris: Bibliothèque de la Pléiade, 1962), 200–13, 400–15.

by thinkers such as Bacon and Descartes. In fact, benevolence, or humanity, could be said to anchor the entire moral understanding of this movement. These thinkers, following Machiavelli, rejected the older moral metaphysics (and theology) and replaced it with a generalized good will to mankind. This impulse is Machiavellian inasmuch as Machiavelli's project was motivated by the desire to liberate mankind from the tyranny of Christianity and the suppression of human nature characteristic of all the old, perfectionistic ethics. Given the groundlessness of the old ethics, it is much more humane simply to allow human nature – actual, empirical human nature – to express itself. Machiavelli's bleak assessment of the necessities of politics prevented him from advocating humanity at the level of ordinary politics.[23] But his successors saw, or thought they could create, a much tamer human world, which freed them to spread the gentle balm of humanity far and wide. By Franklin's time, this was most clearly seen in the philosophies of moral sentiment, which put a general moral inclination to benefit mankind at the center of their theories. Francis Hutcheson, Adam Smith, and even Jean-Jacques Rousseau can be put in this category.[24] We may also include David Hume, a philosopher with whom Franklin had a small correspondence. In a letter, Franklin congratulates Hume on advocating "the *Interest of Humanity*, or common Good of Mankind," something "too little thought of by selfish Man" (*WrBF* 776).[25]

Franklin did not subscribe to the specific theories propounded by this school – perhaps his assessment of the selfish side of human nature prevented it[26] – but these philosophers' humanitarianism, like the humanitarianism of the other post-Machiavellians, was extremely congenial to him. Within the philosophical context they created, his notion that we simply learn the moral principles of "*Truth, Sincerity and Integrity* in Dealings between Man and Man" from experience is unobjectionable. For to say that we learn those principles from experience means that we learn from experience that they are most conducive to our happiness. Franklin denies that these principles have any intrinsic moral weight in and of themselves (nor, he explicitly adds, do they gain such weight from the authority of revelation); actions are not good or bad *because of* their conformity to moral injunctions. Rather, he says, the injunctions gain their authority from the fact that certain actions are harmful or beneficial to

---

[23] Machiavelli's classic statement of his humane motivation is in *D* 1.pref.; for his rejection of retail humanitarianism in politics, see especially *D* 3.19–23, 1.28–32, as well as *P* 18. See Strauss, *Thoughts on Machiavelli*, 290.

[24] See Francis Hutcheson, *A Short Introduction to Moral Philosophy*, in *Collected Works of Francis Hutcheson* (Hildesheim, Germany: Georg Olms, 1969), 4:14–20, 49–53; Adam Smith, *The Theory of Moral Sentiments*, ed. D. D. Raphael and A. L. Macfie (London: Oxford University Press, 1976), esp. 1.1.1, 2.2.1–3; Jean-Jacques Rousseau, *Discours sur l'origine et les fondements de l'inégalité parmi les hommes*, in Rousseau, *Oeuvres Complètes* (Paris: Editions du Seuil, 1971) 2:204–67, esp. 210, 223–5.

[25] Franklin is commenting on one of Hume's essays on free trade, a subject that interested Franklin a great deal. For Hume's analysis of the "moral sense," see *THN* 3.1.2.

[26] He (*WrBF* 201) once wrote, "Men are *naturally* benevolent as well as selfish."

us, "in their own Natures, all the Circumstances of things considered" (*ABF* 115; cf. 158). In other words, benefit or harm to ourselves is the true standard of morality. Morality is grounded in human nature (and social reality), by way of those things that lead to our true happiness. Here we are on solid Lockean ground. Franklin's well-known view that "nothing [is] useful that [is] not honest" reflects neither the morality of a shopkeeper, as some have charged, nor is it particularly novel; rather, it is grounded in Franklin's well-considered notion of what brings happiness and the reverse to men (*ABF* 54).[27] This is where experience plays a determinative role, for only experience can show us what is to our true benefit, though reason might play an important role in sifting that experience, in distinguishing true from false happiness.

If experience rather than a priori reasoning is the true source of moral insight, then a document like Franklin's *Autobiography*, a well-tailored account of one man's experience, might be the best, the most pertinent, account of virtue and of life properly lived. A treatise, an abstract or speculative work, could not serve as well. The most distinctive problem created by the post-Machiavellian political dispensation was the problem of reconciling the individual and the public good. Under this dispensation, individuals were allowed, indeed encouraged, to pursue their own interests primarily, and it was understood that the interests of the individual are not naturally or intrinsically connected to the common good. Different approaches to this problem were taken. Theories of moral sentiment alleged that men get natural gratification from certain types of service to others. Theories of social contract were based on the interest that individuals have in the maintenance of social order. Both are attempts to make the "honest" and the "useful" coincide. The difficulty they share, though, is that they hold only generally, or most of the time. There are key moments in public life when interest and inclination will instead lead individuals to take advantage of others with impunity, and philosophical theories may not be *persuasive* enough to prevent them. Here is where a work like Franklin's *Autobiography* may be uniquely serviceable. It is the portrait of a life of virtue and of public service, which at the same time brought its author wealth, esteem, and a kind of happiness that every reader will find enviable. The portrait is narrated in such a way as to show how the congruence of public interest and private happiness was not fortuitous but intrinsic, once the proper virtues were found and cultivated. And it shows how anyone might cultivate these virtues, to find the same kind of happiness. Precisely by eschewing "metaphysical reasoning," and showing in practice how the new morality and happiness coincide, the *Autobiography* presents a more full-blooded account of virtue, and a more compelling argument

---

[27] For Locke's similar statements, see *ECHU* 1.3.6, 2.28.5. For the accusation that Franklin's is just a "shopkeeper's" morality, see D. H. Lawrence, "Benjamin Franklin," in Lawrence, *Studies in Classic American Literature* (New York: Viking Press, 1964), 9–21; Charles Angoff, "Benjamin Franklin," in *Benjamin Franklin and the American Character*, ed. Charles L. Sanford (Boston: DC Heath, 1955), 53–7; Max Weber, *The Protestant Ethic and the Spirit of Capitalism* (New York: Charles Scribner's Sons, 1958), 48–56, 151.

for its choiceworthiness, than do the treatises of Franklin's fellows in the modern philosophic movement.[28] For a long time, in America and elsewhere, its influence was immense in helping to make good citizens for the new societies of the post-Machiavellian world.

Humanity and Religion

Once the philosophical and theological foundations of earlier moral philosophy were cleared away, the rationale for the austere or difficult virtues predicated on them dissolved. The old outlook was stringently perfectionist, since it saw man as a being with a higher calling. The post-Machiavellians saw man more simply as a natural creature, possessed of appetites and instincts, and perhaps some simple spiritual needs. The new outlook found no justification for the arduous self-mortification characteristic of the old virtue. Indeed, it typically found such "virtue" to be barbaric, *inhuman* – not truly virtue at all, but the product of false pride.[29] What took its place was a much more easygoing outlook, seeking a happiness closely allied to comfort and based upon accommodating our nature as much as possible. Its cardinal virtues were humanity and civility.

Franklin's sympathy with this movement is complete. It is no accident that when he proposed the formation of a party of men devoted to the cultivation of virtue, its name was to be "the Society of the *Free and Easy*" (*ABF* 161–3). As to the "heroic" virtues, while some of his fellow founders emulated classical models, Franklin had no use for them. In *Poor Richard's Almanack* for 1748, he included the following verses:

> Alas! That Heroes ever were made!
> The *Plague*, and the *Hero*, are both of a Trade!
> Yet the Plague spares our Goods which the Heroe does not;
> So a Plague take such Heroes and let their Fames rot.
> (*WrBF* 1248)

In the same almanac, Franklin noted the birthday of Louis XV, then king of France: "He bids fair to be as great a mischief-maker as his grandfather; or in the language of poets and orators, a Hero" (*PBF* 3:249). Regarding the antique moral code that supported heroic virtue, Poor Richard had earlier intoned, "The ancients tell us what is best; but we must learn of the moderns what is fittest" (*WrBF* 1208).[30] His praise of the ancients for finding what is "best" is equivocal. At the most, it is an admiration of the magnificent thoughts and deeds inspired by the ancient outlook. In truth, for Franklin as for the other post-Machiavellians, what is best is the "fitting" – fitting to our nature as creatures of

---

[28] See Lorraine Smith Pangle and Thomas L. Pangle, *The Learning of Liberty: The Educational Ideas of the American Founders* (Lawrence, KS: University of Kansas Press, 1993), 278.

[29] See Descartes, *DM* I; Locke, *ECHU* 2.28.10.

[30] This is from the year 1738. Cf. Descartes, *DM* I.

this world rather than inhabitants of a metaphysically or theologically inspired utopia.

Franklin's best-known statement of his moral code is the section of his *Autobiography* in which he discusses his "Art of Virtue," and lists the thirteen virtues to which that art is directed (*ABF* 148–60). The humble character of these virtues is the first thing that strikes the reader. Traits like "silence," "cleanliness," "frugality," and "industry" would not be found in any classical catalogue of virtues. These are virtues accessible to all – Franklin, typically, provides us with a *method* by which all may attain them – and fitting to a society of comfortable individualists. Franklin was positive that self-sacrifice was not the essence of virtue (*WrBF* 242–4); virtue is rather the proper means to happiness within society. For that reason, one clear emphasis of his list of virtues is sociability: speaking kindly of others, doing good for society, curbing one's own feelings of resentment when injured. In a sense, the *Autobiography* as a whole is a gloss on this list, and one of its clearest lessons is the advantage, as well as the delight, of cultivating harmonious social relations. All Franklin's efforts are bent to showing how marvellously habitable is the common ground between the individual and social good. But we can inhabit it only on condition that we agree with Franklin to make the rules of this common ground the center of our moral code. The old, heroic morality is one potential obstacle to this, though not one of great practical importance by Franklin's day. More ominous was the possible opposition of religious zeal, a problem Franklin recognized in common with all the post-Machiavellians.

In general, post-Machiavellian moral philosophy was harsher on classical thought than on Christianity. This was partly, but only partly, for tactical reasons. The classical notions of human perfection and of the *summum bonum* were rejected outright, while only a softening or humanizing of Christianity was sought. The goal was to make Christianity more tolerant of human nature, including socially benign human selfishness ("the pursuit of happiness"), and to make Christians more tolerant of one another.[31] The means by which the softening took place was a winnowing of Christian doctrine, submitting it to the test of the new humanitarianism. The claim that this only recovered "true Christianity" from its merely human accretions proved rhetorically quite successful.[32] In the American context, Locke's "reasonable Christianity" achieved a very wide circulation and influence during the colonial period.[33] But Franklin

---

[31] See Rahe, *Republics Ancient and Modern*, 313–15. On Locke's approach to this problem, see Pangle, *The Spirit of Modern Republicanism*, 196, 198–209; Steven Forde, "Natural Law, Theology, and Morality in Locke," *American Journal of Political Science* 45:2 (April 2001): 396–409, esp. 405–8.

[32] Compare Descartes' pointed praise of that religion whose precepts are given by "God alone" (*DM* II). The disingenuousness of this is seen particularly in the fate of a virtue like charity in the new, moderate Christianity; see Pangle, *The Spirit of Modern Republicanism*, 144.

[33] Pangle, *The Spirit of Modern Republicanism*, 21–4, provides a concise discussion of this theological movement in colonial America.

goes further than Locke in the latitude of toleration for which he publicly pleads. Indeed, the breadth of his proposals can take the reader by surprise even now.

Franklin may have repudiated deism owing to its deleterious effect on morals, but the creed that he adopted in its place itself must be called a species of deism. In the *Autobiography*, Franklin lists its tenets:

> That there is one God who made all things.
> That he governs the World by his Providence.
> That he ought to be worshipped by Adoration, Prayer and Thanksgiving.
> But that the most acceptable Service of God is doing Good to Man.
> That the Soul is immortal.
> And that God will certainly reward Virtue and punish Vice either here or
>   hereafter.   (*ABF* 162)

Franklin has simply taken basic deist doctrine and added general and particular providence to it, including divine attention to prayer and good works, with the application of rewards and punishments. In laying out these doctrines, he claims that he has captured "the Essentials of every known Religion," and that his creed will shock none. We might wonder whether any of Franklin's fellow Americans would balk at his implicit claim that such doctrines as the divinity of Jesus and the divine origin of Scripture are inessential to religion. Nevertheless, Franklin's intention in promulgating this creed is twofold: to put good works as much as possible at the center of religion, and to advance the cause of religious toleration. Both reveal Franklin's project of judging religion by the standards of social good.

Though he is not shy about broadcasting this creed, Franklin does not insist that others adopt it. He tells us that he has supported all religious causes that came to him for help, regardless of denomination. He consistently set himself against attempts to undermine peoples' faith in their own sect, for religious belief is a key support to virtue in most people (*WrBF* 336, 426–7, 1180).[34] Even as he did so, however, he ranked some sects and some believers above others, for their proximity in practice to his "Essential creed." Of the American denominations, he says, "I respected them all, tho' with different degrees of Respect as I found them more or less mix'd with other Articles which without any Tendency to inspire, promote or confirm Morality, serv'd principally to divide us and make us unfriendly to one another" (*ABF* 146). He never tired of criticizing those who thought religious ritual to be more important than good works, who believed the delivering or hearing of sermons to be more important than assisting one's fellow man. Above all, he had little patience for those who desired to advance the cause of their sect before advancing the cause of mankind. He tells us that he stopped attending the sermons of his local Presbyterian minister when it became clear that he was concerned in his

---

[34] Of particular note is Franklin's harsh reaction to an essay an unknown correspondent sent to him, arguing against particular providence. Refusing to debate the substance of the matter, Franklin merely notes the harmful tendency of such an argument (*WrBF* 748).

sermons "rather to make us Presbyterians than good citizens" (*ABF* 147; cf. 145, *WrBF* 476).

In Franklin's view, the focus of all denominations should be the same essential – and essentially this-worldly – moral teaching. He regards all religious doctrines beyond these as purely speculative. These doctrines may support morality as Franklin has defined it, but sometimes they undermine it, and they always hold the possibility of divisiveness. The one sect that Franklin praises most highly in the *Autobiography* is the Dunkers, who never committed a creed to writing, since they were not sure that they were in possession of the full or final truth. "This Modesty in a Sect," Franklin marvels, "is perhaps a singular Instance in the History of Mankind, every other Sect supposing itself in Possession of all Truth" (*ABF* 191; cf. *WrBF* 673). He contrasts them with the Quakers in particular, whose rigidly pacifist views constituted an obstacle to the public defense. Franklin wishes that all such "extraneous" doctrines might be abandoned, or at least downplayed, in the name of social utility and toleration.

There is no denying that Franklin's toleration, based on his own "essential creed," is rooted in a rather serious critique of much of Christian theology – or perhaps of all of it, since by his reckoning the divinity of Christ is one of the "nonessential" doctrines of faith. In a well-known letter to Ezra Stiles near the end of his life, Franklin avers that the "System of Morals" devised by Jesus of Nazareth is the best the world has seen, but that Jesus's divinity is doubtful, "tho' it is a question I do not dogmatize upon." He adds that he is not about to enter into speculations on the question now, "when I expect soon an Opportunity of knowing the Truth with less Trouble" (*WrBF* 1179). It was well known in Franklin's day, of course, that many denied the divinity of Jesus, but for Franklin to plead with a wide audience, especially an American one, to regard the whole matter as "nonessential" to religion was bold, to say the least. Clearly, the most Franklin actually hoped for was toleration for those on both sides of the issue, but even that requires giving the issue much less weight than believers had traditionally done. This is the only point on which Franklin allows such a wide gulf to become evident between himself and the bulk of his readers, where he is willing to risk serious controversy. But religion is an area where all of Franklin's moral concerns converge, with urgency. The "essential creed" he espouses is the only one that does not fall prey to speculative excess, and that accordingly serves the human good without distractions. Franklin minimizes the shock of his proposal by emphasizing its wholesomely moral thrust and its congeniality to society, and by making clear that others are perfectly free to continue in their own confessions. His hope is that, even if his creed is not adopted by many, its favorable reception will insensibly cause sectarians to regard those parts of their confession not related to moral virtue as less important. Toleration for moral deists will soften religion overall, and direct it toward the good of mankind. The goal of humanity will then be doubly served, by the increased focus on social morality and the increased civility among religions.

Civility

Civility, the near relation of humanity, is a key part of Franklin's moral outlook, as it is of the post-Machiavellian movement in general. Franklin's treatment of religion highlights as well as anything could the meaning of this virtue. As with humanity, civility is a trait that would not be found in classical catalogues of the virtues. Virtuous men of old would of course have treated each other civilly, but this would fundamentally be a consequence of their shared devotion to other virtues such as magnanimity. These other virtues, *higher* virtues, were in turn grounded in the metaphysical or theological analyses rejected by Machiavelli and his successors. The distinctly modern virtue of civility, while suffused with the warmth of humanity, is at the same time cooler and more distant than Christian charity, or the friendship and emulation of Aristotelian gentlemen.[35]

The rejection of the old moral ideals simply leaves human beings with less in common. Instead of the shared quest for a single moral perfection, individuals now share only the desire to pursue their own happiness, defined as idiosyncratically as may be. Civility is the key social virtue demanded of such individuals. Its paradigmatic form can be seen in Hobbes, for whom all the laws of nature reduce to the simple principle that everyone should be nice to everyone else, wherever possible (*Leviathan* I.xiv–xv).[36] The goal of Hobbes's natural law is social peace, not moral elevation, and individuals obey it only because social peace serves their own good. Civility is a means of constructing society based not on a common definition of the *summum bonum*, but on the simple social need for individuals to accommodate each other. Franklin's religious minimalism follows this paradigm. He would have Christians lay aside the disputes about the precise nature of the theological good – disputes that had set them at each others' throats for centuries – in the name of the more humble common good of peace and humanity. Franklin's position is openly agnostic on the more suble theological issues, which he would prefer to jettison from religion entirely. Failing this, different positions must at least be tolerated. This is the underlying principle of modern civility: Citizens may indulge whatever fantasies they like about the ultimate goals or higher goods of human existence, and they are free to pursue such goals if they wish; but when it comes to relations with their fellow citizens, they must agree to disagree.

Civility is thus in a sense less a virtue than a replacement for virtue. Or rather, it becomes a virtue as a result of the post-Machiavellian rejection of virtue in the old, perfectionist sense. Precisely for this reason, however, it is the central social virtue of the new order. Franklin would have learned as much from reading Locke's thoughts on education, where the distinctive virtues of the new dispensation are a prominent theme. Locke argues that all the other

---

[35] See, e.g., Nathan Tarcov, *Locke's Education for Liberty* (Chicago: University of Chicago Press, 1984), 194.

[36] See also Pangle, *The Spirit of Modern Republicanism*, 228.

virtues become as naught unless given the sociable grace of civility. For "the happiness that all men so steadily pursue consisting in pleasure, it is easy to see why the civil are more acceptable than the useful," that is, than those who are useful but lack the socially accommodating polish of civility (*STCE* 143).[37] Since the goal of virtue itself is our own happiness, civility might thus be said to have priority over all the rest of virtue.[38] Among other vices that Locke said civility must be summoned to cure is the inclination to disputatiousness and curtness of speech (*STCE* 143). This was a cure Franklin was forced to take, as he so prominently narrates in the *Autobiography*. In the end, civility of speech is the primary meaning that Franklin assigns to the quality of "humility" in his catalogue of virtues (*ABF* 159).[39] It is the one virtue, he intimates, that he devoted the greatest effort to developing, and that contributed most perhaps to his success and happiness (*ABF* 159).

Civility was important enough to Franklin that he allowed it to intrude on the privileges of his own chosen profession, printing. Given Franklin's prominent and lifelong membership in the Fourth Estate, his lukewarmness as a defender of absolute freedom of the press is striking. This has drawn him some criticism, but Franklin's position only reveals the priority of civility in his thinking. When publishing his *Philadelphia Gazette*, Franklin periodically inserted apologies for any offense that might have been given by one or another item in the paper. He explained, as his colleagues in the press always have done, that some offense is a necessary consequence of free public debate. He protested, however, that he had on occasion taken it upon himself to refuse items that might have given too great offense (see *WrBF* 171–7, 283–5, 954, 1148–50).[40] He regarded some degree of self-censorship, in the name of civility and social grace, as the responsibility of printers, and he did not regard their freedom as absolute. In one biting piece near the end of his life, Franklin went so far as to propose that if printers insisted on abusing the liberty of the press, perhaps victims of their slander should be extended a countervailing "*liberty of the Cudgel*" (*WrBF* 1153).[41] Or if that be thought too extreme, Franklin says, perhaps the legislature should define the

---

[37] Franklin cites extensively from this work in his own "Proposals Relating to the Education of Youth in Pennsylvania" (*WrBF* 323–44). A man possessing virtue but lacking civility might resemble Jean-Baptiste Molière's *Misanthrope*. It is revealing that Rousseau sides with the misanthrope; his attack on the *politesse* of modern society is an attack on its foundation in civility. See Jean-Jacques Rousseau, *Lettre à d'Alembert* (Paris: Garnier-Flammarion, 1967), esp. 96–110; *Discours sur les sciences et les arts*, in *Oeuvres Complètes*, 2:52–68.

[38] See Tarcov, *Locke's Education for Liberty*, 195.

[39] This is doubly peculiar, given Franklin's initial gloss on humility, "Imitate Jesus and Socrates." Civility is also central to Franklin's understanding of "Moderation": "Avoid Extreams. Forbear resenting Injuries so much as you think they deserve" (*ABF* 150). On Franklin's painful cure from contentiousness, see *ABF* 60, 65, 71.

[40] Wright, *Franklin of Philadelphia*, 51, criticizes Franklin nonetheless for being too weak a defender of freedom of the press.

[41] Franklin makes a sharp distinction between offense given by discussion of political issues and by personal attacks. Only the latter are abuses of the press, but Franklin claims they are far too common.

proper limits of press freedom; for no institution should be allowed to threaten the harmony and the pleasure that civility is capable of furnishing us.

Freedom of the press is only one example of the difficulty of balancing civility with individualism and individual liberty in modern society. Franklin did not see the general problem as starkly as did Hobbes, for whom human nature was violently antisocial. It is impossible to miss the great joy Franklin gets from social relations, or the spontaneity with which he practices his benevolent virtues. Still, he was never willing to say that man is simply sociable by nature, and he acknowledged that Hobbes probably has more truth in him than his idealistic opponents.[42] However much Franklin delighted in his sociable life of virtue, and wanted us to share that delight, he never lets us forget that virtue is fundamentally rooted in what is useful to us and to society. Franklin's own delight is partly a product of his intellectual appreciation of the fact that the harmony between his own happiness and that of society is to some extent of his own making, that it is in some measure the product of art. In the *Autobiography*, we see the young Franklin struggling with his own uncivil tendencies, principally his strong inclination for contentiousness and eristic. Only with time and hard experience did he come to appreciate the futility of this. He resolved thereafter to practice civility in speech, a "Mode," he says, "which I at first put on, with some violence to natural Inclination." For it required him to foresake the "Pleasure" of abruptly contradicting others (*ABF* 159).[43] This is the most significant instance in the *Autobiography* of Franklin curbing his nature for the sake of virtue, that is, suppressing a natural inclination for the sake of greater overall happiness. Franklin emphasizes the importance of this particular lesson and this particular virtue again and again.

At the same time, paradoxically, Franklin confesses that he never really acquired the "*Reality*" of this virtue, only its "*Appearance*" (*ABF* 159).[44] He is not particularly remorseful for this, for civility is more an external than an internal virtue. Given the nature and purpose of civility, the appearance is enough, for the purpose of this virtue is not to perfect the soul so much as to smooth social relations. If Franklin secretly harbors his pride, and even gets pleasure from it, no one will, or should, object. The *public face* of humility or civility, meanwhile, as Franklin tells us in this very passage, was instrumental in bringing him influence, and making social relations much more pleasant for himself

---

[42] Reviewing one essayist, Franklin wrote, "It seems to me that the Author is a little too severe upon Hobbes, whose Notion, I imagine, is somewhat nearer the Truth than that which makes the State of Nature a State of Love." He suggests the truth lies somewhere in the middle (*WrBF* 425).

[43] Ralph Lerner provides an insightful discussion of Franklin's many uses of concealment and subterfuge in the *Autobiography*: See Lerner, "Franklin, Spectator," in Lerner, *The Thinking Revolutionary: Principle and Practice in the New Republic* (Ithaca, NY: Cornell University Press, 1987), 50–1. See also Steven Forde, "Benjamin Franklin's *Autobiography* and the Education of America," *APSR* 86:2 (June 1992): 357–67, esp. 365–6.

[44] Poor Richard noted that pride "is said to be the *last* vice the good man gets clear of" (*WrBF* 1254).

(*ABF* 160).[45] The element of contrivance in modern civility in fact helps to account for the peculiar remoteness that some have detected behind Franklin's trademark *bonhomie*. However much warmth he gives, and receives, from his fellow men, Franklin always seems to be holding something in reserve, something that is not engaged by his supremely sociable exterior.[46] His very deepest thoughts and sentiments remain somehow elusive. Many of the lessons he gives us in the *Autobiography* are lessons of concealment, lessons tied to the requirements of getting along more smoothly in society. When proposing a significant project, for example, Franklin counsels that it is best to present it not as one's own idea but that of "a Number of Friends," so that no one thinks the project aimed only at increasing one's own reputation (*ABF* 143).[47] Civility consists in not affronting others' pride. Franklin liked to tell a story about a youthful encounter he had with Cotton Mather, whose *Essays to Do Good* were an early influence on his thinking. When leaving Mather's house, he once hit his head upon a low beam, which inspired Mather to advise him, "Let this be a Caution to you not always to hold your Head so high; Stoop, young Man, stoop – as you go through the World – and you'll miss many hard Thumps" (*WrBF* 881; cf. 1092). For the sake of society, Franklin learned, and for the sake of one's own effectiveness, one is well advised to conceal one's very superiority.

"Stoop, young Man, stoop": This is surely as vivid an expression of the death of heroic virtue and its replacement by civility as anything could be. Yet Franklin relished this advice, and did not consider that it reflected any defect in the social order. It is merely a price to be paid for enjoying the pleasures of society, for benefiting and being benefited by it. For his readers, Franklin paints such a pleasing portrait of life in the new social order that it is easy to forget that there once were fundamentally different visions of the good life and the good society. The older visions rested on the most exalted ambitions for human perfection, and from their perspective, Franklin and all his post-Machiavellian colleagues have forsaken man's true nobility for mere comfort and social peace. In Franklin we see as eloquent a case as may be made for the new order of things. It is true that heroism has no place here, but Franklin's outlook begins with a critique of the theology and metaphysics that grounded this heroism. Absent that foundation, man looks indeed like a simple animal, a merely natural creature with merely natural needs and desires. The modern project in politics was to find the political order that best suits this creature, while in morals it discovered humanity and civility as his most natural and convenient virtues. A

---

[45] On Franklin's indulgence of pride, in himself and others, see *ABF* 44.

[46] See Lerner, "Franklin, Spectator," 53, 58; Carl L. Becker, "Benjamin Franklin," in *Dictionary of American Biography*, ed. Allen Johnson and Dumas Malone (New York: Charles Scribner's Sons, 1931) 6:585–98, esp. 597; Ormond Seavey, *Becoming Benjamin Franklin* (University Park, PA: Pennsylvania State University Press, 1988), 32. It is surprising how readily Franklin allowed his correspondence with his French friends, among whom he had lived for nine years, to languish upon his return to the United States; see Lopez, *Mon Cher Papa*, 303, 307.

[47] Franklin is careful to add that, in the end, the original proponent will get full credit for the project.

whisper of the older objection, though, has always echoed through this project. In the end, does it provide for a form of happiness and a way of life that can be called rich and fulfilling in a truly *human* way? Franklin's *Autobiography*, and the whole record of his life, provide perhaps the most compelling answer to this question that is possible. Antique heroism is indeed lacking in it, as is the true selflessness of pure religious virtue. But Franklin, living on the new terrain, has perfected his natural faculties, including his intellectual faculties. He has lived a life suffused with comfort, but not a despicable comfort. His life of public service and private happiness cannot be called bestial, or even simply selfish. It deserves to be called a richly rewarding, and a richly human life, if any distinctively modern life could.

PART III

THE AMERICAN FOUNDING

I n at least one particular, the American Revolution bears comparison with the execution of Charles I and with Marlborough's great victory at the Battle of Blenheim. Like these two prior events, it occasioned a sea change in political thought by altering decisively the political world within which a particular group of exceptionally able men found themselves situated. As a consequence, it, too, marked an epoch in the reception of Machiavelli's republican ruminations.

Had it not been for the revolution, George Washington, Thomas Jefferson, and James Madison would not have had occasion to encounter John Adams and Alexander Hamilton. They would have eked out their lives in Virginia, playing the prominent role in local politics accorded the gentry of that colony, no doubt, but doing little if anything else of note. Adams and Hamilton would have suffered a similar fate. None of them would have been called upon to tackle the great questions that they confronted in the wake of 4 July 1776. Of this fact, they were acutely aware.

John Adams spoke for all of the individuals discussed in the chapters that follow when he celebrated the fact that his generation had "been sent into life at a time when the greatest lawgivers of antiquity would have wished to live" (*WoJA* 4:200). As the historian David Ramsay had occasion to observe firsthand while a member of the Continental Congress, the American Revolution made a difference in the lives of these men. It

called forth many virtues, and gave occasion for the display of abilities which, but for that event, would have been lost to the world. When the war began, the Americans were a mass of husbandmen, merchants, mechanics, and fishermen; but the necessities of the country gave a spring to the active powers of the inhabitants, and set them on thinking, speaking, and acting, in a line far beyond that to which they had been accustomed. . . . In the years 1775 and 1776, the country, being suddenly thrown into a situation that needed the ability of all its sons, these generally took their places, each according to the bent of his inclination. As they generally pursued their objects with ardour, a vast expansion of the human mind speedily followed. . . . It seemed as if the war not only required, but created talents. Men whose minds were warmed with the love of liberty, and whose abilities were improved by daily exercise, and sharpened with a laudable ambition to serve their distressed country, spoke, wrote, and acted, with an energy far surpassing all expectations which could be reasonably founded on their previous acquirements.[1]

When the poet Philip Freneau predicted in 1771 that his compatriots would soon be able to boast of their own "Scipio's, Solon's, Cato's, sages, chiefs," he was not overstating his case.[2] In light of the ancient Greek practice of worshiping the founders of cities as heroes after they had died, it was entirely appropriate that Thomas Jefferson, in a letter to John Adams, should speak of the Federal Convention as "an assembly of demigods" (*AJL* 1:196), for that it was.

The Founding Fathers were profoundly sensitive to their own potential stature. Alexander Hamilton disclosed something of their spirit in 1778 when he remarked,

The station of a member of C——ss, is the most illustrious and important of any I am able to conceive. He is to be regarded not only as a legislator, but as the founder of an empire. A man of virtue and ability, dignified with so precious a trust, would rejoice that fortune had given him birth at a time, and placed him in circumstances so favourable for promoting human happiness. He would esteem it not more the duty, than the privilege and ornament of his office, to do good to mankind; from this commanding eminence, he would look down with contempt upon every mean or interested pursuit.

(*PAH* 1:580–1)

Five years later, an anonymous "North American" caught James Madison's attention with an exhortation to his compatriots to reform the defective constitutions hastily adopted in the various states in the wake of the Declaration of Independence. "Let them," he wrote,

by a government adequate to the ends of society, secure those blessings to which the virtues, sacrifices and sufferings of America have an undeniable claim. – Let them do this – and then, when corroding time, shall separate pure and immortal virtues from attendant frailties, which at first obscure their lustre – when envy and jealousy shall be no more – a just and grateful fame will rank them amidst those idolized patriots of Greece and Rome, whose names antiquity has already consecrated at her venerable shrine."[3]

There can be little doubt that a great many members of the revolutionary generation were swept away by the longing to accomplish something brilliant, something noble and worthy of remembrance.

---

[1] See David Ramsay, *The History of the American Revolution* (London: John Stockdale, 1793), 2:315–16.

[2] See Philip Freneau, "The Rising Glory of America" (1771), in *Poems of Freneau*, ed. Harry Hayden Clark (New York: Harcourt, Brace, and Co., 1929), 13.

[3] See The North American no. 1, *Pennsylvania Journal*, 17 September 1783, in "Two Neglected Madison Letters," ed. Irving Brant, *WMQ* 3:4 (October 1946): 569–87 (at 572).

The author of *The Prince* and of the *Discourses on Livy* was far less fortunate. He was ambitious – there can be no doubt – but a founder he was not. Nor, strictly speaking, was he even a citizen, much less a statesman. He was rendered ineligible for public office in the republic he served by the meanness of his birth, and by the time that he began his career as a writer, he was no longer the servant of Florence or of any republic: He was an unemployed bureaucrat, down on his luck, suspect to the authorities. He was very much in need of a job and willing to put himself at the disposal of virtually anyone – prince, even merchant – who could pay his keep.

In the two great books that he penned, Machiavelli had much to say regarding glory, but on the subject of justice he was notoriously reticent. As a civil servant, he had concerned himself for over fourteen years with foreign affairs, with the struggle for power in Italy, and with the creation of a militia for Florence. If he had an occasion to display an interest in domestic affairs, it was always almost solely with an eye to the projection of power abroad. His had always been, in certain crucial regards, a limited perspective, and so it remained. In *The Prince* and in his *Discourses on Livy*, he deliberately eliminated from consideration the concerns that defined the horizon of the statesman. There was at the heart of these political works something profoundly unpolitical.

The American founders could hardly ignore Machiavelli. The nation that they hoped to establish would have to make its way in an international arena that the doctrine of *raison d'état* had done much to shape. This they knew. They were also acutely aware of the threat to domestic tranquillity posed by the sectarian divisions that had emerged within Christendom in the sixteenth and seventeenth centuries, and, if they had any doubts in the beginning, they soon came to recognize that to blunt such a threat, one might very well be forced to make use of one or more of the devices of Machiavellian statecraft. But when and where they opted for political indirection, the projection of power abroad was rarely, if ever, their chief concern. After all, the American Revolution had been fought in the name of justice, and with its achievement in this particular the men discussed in the last five chapters of this book were deeply concerned. They were not adventurers intent on acquisition; they were founders. That they would and that they should be held responsible for their accomplishments and their failures in this regard they were agreed.

Appropriately, no American was as sensitive to the dictates of responsibility as was their chief of men. That George Washington was the one figure among his contemporaries who commanded near universal respect is by no means an accident. It is only by reflecting on his character that we can come fully to understand the character of the American enterprise and begin to grasp thereby the manner in which the writings of Niccolò Machiavelli shaped and failed to shape the republic established on the North American continent in the last quarter of the eighteenth century.

7

The American Prince?

George Washington's Anti-Machiavellian Moment

Matthew Spalding

Over the course of the American founding, there was hardly a moment when George Washington was not in a position of authority and influence. The de facto leader of the colonial struggle, the personification of the American Revolution as military commander, constitution-maker, and president, he was early on considered "the father of his country." By the time of his death, many spoke of the era as nothing less than "the age of Washington."

In a private letter written soon after becoming the first president, Washington recorded his thoughts on the beginning of the new nation: "It was to be, in the first instance, in a considerable degree a government of accommodation as well as a government of Laws. Much was to be done by *prudence*, much by *conviction*, much by *firmness*." He fully understood the unique part he played in the American founding; more often than not it was *his* prudence, *his* conviction, and *his* firmness that carried the day. He also knew that circumstances demanded the prudence, convictions, and firmness of one man. "In our progress towards political happiness my station is new; and, if I may use the expression, I walk on untrodden ground," he wrote. "Few who are not philosophic spectators can realize the difficult and delicate part which a man in my situation had to act" (*WrGW* 30:495–6; emphasis added).

Much of Niccolò Machiavelli's writing, as Markus Fischer observes in the prologue to this book, centers on the beginnings of new states and the reforming of corrupt ones, on founding and refounding. The notorious Florentine rightly understood that such moments are periods of turmoil and danger in politics, and that these situations require the unique skills, wit, and daring of a great man to seize the day. "This should be taken as a general rule," he concluded in the *Discourses*, "that it never or rarely happens that any republic or kingdom is ordered well from the beginning or reformed altogether anew outside its old orders unless it is ordered by one individual. Indeed, it is necessary that one alone give the mode and that any such ordering depend on his mind." Machiavelli recommends matter-of-factly that the one who seeks to be the founder of a republic "should contrive to have authority alone" (*D* 1.9.29).

Might George Washington's philosophical spectator be Machiavelli ? Washington understood many of Machiavelli's most important lessons, after all. He knew firsthand the value of one's own arms, and consistently sought to free his nation from a dependence on mercenaries and foreign military power. When it became necessary to turn to France during the Revolution for military aid, he warned Congress of a fatal reliance on foreign alliances and alien soldiers; he wanted a permanent, standing army trained and disciplined for the rigors and depravations of war.[1] In his Farewell Address, he famously warned of a slavish dependence on foreign countries and the dangers of permanent alliances and foreign entanglements, urging America to seek the strength and consistency necessary to give the nation "the command of its own fortunes" (*WrGW* 35:214–38).

Washington was not incapable of seemingly Machiavellian deeds. In 1776 and again in 1777, when Congress was forced to abandon Philadelphia in the face of advancing British troops, General Washington was granted virtually unlimited powers to maintain the war effort and preserve civil society, powers not unlike those assumed in an earlier era by Roman dictators – and recommended by Machiavelli.[2] At one point, Washington ordered farmers to harvest, thresh, and deliver their grain to him according to specific timetables or have it seized by the army. At another, he proclaimed that all persons not taking an oath of loyalty within thirty days would be considered "enemies of the American states" and treated accordingly. In reorganizing the continental army in 1776, Washington instructed his officers that their primary duty was to attend to his orders, obey them rigidly, communicate and explain their meaning to the troops, and punish every case of neglect and misbehavior.[3] To enforce discipline and inspire raw recruits in battle, he recommended that cowards be punished by death and encouraged the swift execution of mutinous soldiers.[4] In early July 1780 when a line of the Pennsylvania militia did mutiny, Washington called for

---

[1] "I am sincere in declaring a full persuasion, that the succour will be fatal to us if our measures are not adequate to the emergency." GW to President Joseph Reed, 28 May 1780, in *WrGW* 18:438. Washington warned that "no prudent statesman" could ignore the maxim that no nation – enemy or friend – was to be trusted "farther than it is bound by its interest." In establishing a nation, without the "sufficient vigor and maturity" to recover from any false steps, Americans ought to be "particularly cautious" of foreign alliances: GW to Henry Laurens, 14 November 1778, in *WrGW* 13:256.

[2] Washington was given the "full power to order and direct all things relative to the department, and to the operations of war." Resolution of Congress, 12 December 1776, in *WrGW* 6:354n. See also, Garry Wills, *Cincinnatus: George Washington and the Enlightenment* (New York: Doubleday, 1984), 17–23.

[3] See Proclamation, 20 December 1777, in *WrGW* 10:175; Proclamation, 25 January 1777, in *WrGW* 7:61–3; Washington, General Orders, 1 January 1776, in *WrGW* 4:203.

[4] "A Coward, when taught to believe, that if he breaks Ranks, and abandons his Colours, will be punished with Death by his own party, will take his chance with the Enemy; but the Man who thinks little of the one, and is fearful of the other, Acts from present feelings regardless of consequences." GW to the President of Congress, 9 February 1776, in *WrGW*, 4:316; GW to Robert Howe, 22 January 1781, in *WrGW*, 21:128–9.

a declaration of martial law throughout the state and the use of force against the militia "with a boldness and vigor suited to the emergency" (*GWC* 151).

It is hard to imagine a more daring question: Was George Washington the American prince? The answer will tell us much not only about the man but also about the American founding, for if the founder was Machiavellian, it is hard to imagine that the regime rests on more noble principles.

But let us hesitate before proceeding down this path of inquiry. We must keep in mind a clear distinction between the advice and observations of Machiavelli, which are often neither new nor controversial, and the broader teachings of Machiavellian political science, which are. There has always been and always will be a place for harsh, even shocking, actions in politics; the existence of such actions does not necessarily make the American founding, or any other political event, a Machiavellian moment. Most if not all of Machiavelli's observations on political practice can be found in the political thought and seen in the political action that preceded him. He was simply the first to openly and proudly make these observations the centerpiece of his theory of politics.[5]

Another reason for hesitation is Machiavelli's attractiveness. His political theory seems to account for every contradiction and complication of political life, yet viewing political life through Machiavellian glasses can be misleading. Assuming that Machiavelli is the key to understanding Washington – or the American founding, for that matter – might cause the observer to misperceive the political phenomenon at hand. Just as Gilbert Stuart's famous stone-faced portraits of Washington obscure the man, so drawing a Machiavellian face on Washington may mask the statesman underneath. And since its essence is the concealment of one's motives, Machiavellianism is ultimately nonfalsifiable; that everything Washington did contributed to his glory is proof enough that this must have been his motivation. Like a grand conspiracy theory of politics, it is impossible to disprove.

Politics is about the principles and purposes of human action, and political science should begin by understanding political actors – "the stepping stones of historical narrative," as Winston Churchill put it.[6] Any theoretical explanation that is foreign to political action cannot provide an adequate account of political phenomena. Let us begin, then, not by studying Machiavelli, or how Machiavelli might have perceived Washington, but by trying to understand Washington as he understood himself. Instead of using a Machiavellian lens to view Washington's project, let us look first to Washington for an account of his thoughts and actions, assessing Washington's principles and purposes within his own terms, his own life, and his own circumstances. Only then can one be a "philosophic spectator" of Washington's prudence, conviction, and firmness.

When one considers Washington in a book about Machiavelli's influence on America, a few themes come to mind. Perhaps the most important theme in both Machiavelli's (and Washington's) worldview is virtue and its relation to politics. A similarity or difference on this point would be telling. Another

---

[5] See Leo Strauss, *Thoughts on Machiavelli* (Chicago: University of Chicago Press, 1958), 10.
[6] See Winston Churchill, *Great Contemporaries* (Chicago: University of Chicago Press, 1973), 9.

is Washington's understanding of the meaning of the American founding and his self-perceived role in the overall enterprise. What did he understand to be the end for which the Revolution was fought? Lastly, we must assess Washington's view of the executive and how he understood and shaped the American presidency. Only after considering these ideas (at the very least) can one possibly suggest some broader conclusions about Washington, Machiavelli, and the relationship between the two.

Washington's Virtue

Washington is best known to us not for his long resume but for his good character. The Continental Congress appointed him to be commander in chief of all continental forces in 1775 because he had military experience and was from Virginia, to be sure, but most of all because he displayed the qualities of character – courage, integrity, loyalty, dedication – that they believed were needed to build and lead a republican army. "On the whole," Thomas Jefferson wrote of Washington in 1814, long after the passions and conflicts of the early Republic had subsided, "his character was, in its mass, perfect, in nothing bad, in few points indifferent; and it may truly be said, that never did nature and fortune combine more perfectly to make a man great, and to place him in the same constellation with whatever worthies have merited from man an everlasting remembrance" (*WrTJ* [ed. Peterson] 1318–19).

That Washington is known for his character is no accident. It is evident in one of his earliest writings, an adolescent copybook record of one hundred and ten "Rules of Civility and Decent Behavior in Company and Conversation."[7] Because Washington believed that an early and proper education in both manners and morals formed the leading traits of one's life, he urged on correspondents the development of good habits and the unremitting practice of moral virtue, warning of "the necessity of paying due attention to the moral virtues" and avoiding the "scenes of vice and dissipation" often presented to youth (*WrGW* 30:248.). "To point out the importance of circumspection in your conduct, it may be proper to observe that a good moral character is the first essential of man, and that the habits contracted at your age are generally indelible, and your conduct here may stamp your character through life," he advised George Steptoe Washington. "It is therefore highly important that you should endeavor not only to be learned but virtuous" (*WrGW* 30:163).

The first object of education, according to Washington, was to acquire as much knowledge as one could, thereby establishing the habits of earnestness, industry, and seriousness. And while the beginnings of education depended upon it, the end product of education was never unattached in Washington's

---

[7] Drawn from an early etiquette book, these social maxims concern everything from how to treat one's superiors ("In speaking to men of Quality do not lean nor look them full in the face") to how to moderate one's own behavior ("Let your recreations be manful not sinful") to more significant expressions of civility ("keep alive in your breast that little spark of celestial fire called conscience"). *GWC* 8–13.

mind from moral character. The "advantages of a finished education," he told George Washington Parke Custis, were both a "highly cultivated mind, and a proper sense of your duties to God and man" (*WrGW* 35:341). While recognizing its higher, speculative qualities, Washington considered education's most important public purpose to be the teaching of citizens to know and defend their rights, to distinguish between oppression and lawful authority, and "to discriminate the spirit of liberty from that of licentiousness – cherishing the first, avoiding the last."[8] The "best means of forming a manly, virtuous and happy people, will be found in the right education of youth," he noted in a letter written to George Chapman in 1784. "Without this foundation, every other means, in my opinion, must fail." Education and knowledge were to be encouraged for "qualifying the rising generation for patrons of good government, virtue, and happiness" (*WrGW* 28:13–14).

Washington's own life was a constant striving to control the passions and habituate the qualities of good character. As a young man, he displayed high ambitions and a desire for military glory; accepting one early military command, he noted in writing to Warner Lewis that he would have to give up "what at present constitutes the chief part of my happiness; i. e., the esteem and notice the country has been pleased to honour me with" (*WrGW* 1:162). But for Washington what ultimately mattered was that his reputation was deserved: Self-respect preceded public respect, and self-respect required virtuous intentions and behavior. The best way to establish a good reputation, Washington believed, was to be, in fact, a good man. "I hope I shall always possess firmness and virtue enough to maintain (what I consider the most enviable of all titles) the character of an honest man," he told Alexander Hamilton, "as well as prove (what I desire to be considered in reality) that I am" (*WrGW* 30:67).

Individuals with self-respect were motivated by honor in the highest and best sense.[9] Washington's favorite play, Joseph Addison's *Cato: A Tragedy*, makes this point.[10] When Henry Lee urged him in 1788 to accept the presidency out of a regard not only for the happiness of the American people but also for his own fame and reputation, Washington responded that he would not act for the sake of the latter: "Though I prize, as I ought, the good opinion of my fellow citizens; yet, if I know myself, I would not seek or retain popularity at the expense of

---

[8] Washington believed that mathematical investigations trained the mind and were "peculiarly worthy of rational beings." Such investigations also encouraged higher theoretical knowledge: "From the high ground of mathematical and philosophical demonstration, we are insensibly led to far nobler speculations and sublimer meditations." See GW to Nicholas Pike, 20 June 1788, in *WrGW* 30:2–3. See also GW, First Annual Message to Congress, 8 January 1790, in *WrGW* 30:493.

[9] On Washington and honor, see Lorraine Smith Pangle and Thomas L. Pangle, *The Learning of Liberty* (Lawrence, KS: University of Kansas Press, 1993), 231–49.

[10] "Honour's a sacred tie, the law of kings, /The noble mind's distinguishing perfection, /That aids and strengthens virtue where it meets her, /And imitates her actions, where she is not." See "Cato: A Tragedy," in *The Works of the Right Honorable Joseph Addison*, ed. Richard Hurd (London: George Bell and Sons, 1883), 189, 198. Washington had "Cato" performed for his troops at Valley Forge.

one social duty or moral virtue.... And certain I am, whensoever I shall be convinced the good of my country requires my reputation to be put in risque, regard for my own fame will not come in competition with an object of so much magnitude" (*WrGW* 30:97). Jefferson, for one, thought that Washington was risking his fame by becoming president: "I am sensitive of the immensity of the sacrifice on your part," he remarked to his fellow Virginian. "Your measure of fame was full to the brim: and therefore you have nothing to gain. But there are cases wherein it is a duty to risk all against nothing, and I believe this was exactly the case" (*WrTJ* [ed. Ford] 5:94–5).

Washington's understanding of character extended to his countrymen, and his concept of character as a political principle cannot be overlooked when it comes to exploring his view of the American founding. He believed that the formation of character – whether of a man or a nation – was the first and most important step toward independence, prosperity, and greatness. "[T]he first transactions of a nation, like those of an individual upon his first entrance into life," Washington wrote to John Armstrong at the time of the ratification of the Constitution, "make the deepest impression, and are to form the leading traits in its character" (*WrGW* 29:465). The success of the American experiment would require good laws and good citizens, and Washington set out to establish a nation of both. The way to do so, he concluded, was to establish rightly from the beginning a sense of character as a nation. "To form a new Government, requires infinite care, and unbounded attention," Washington wrote to John Augustine Washington in 1776, "for if the foundation is badly laid the superstructure must be bad, too much time therefore, cannot be bestowed in weighing and digesting matters well" (*WrGW* 5:92).

The Washingtonian Moment

In the *Discourses on Livy*, Machiavelli argues that republics must renew themselves every so often by returning to their "first principles" (*D* 3.1). George Washington shared the sentiment, and used similar language in his letters after the Revolution, warning George Mason at one point that "unless the bodies politick will exert themselves to bring things back to first principles, correct abuses, and punish our internal foes, inevitable ruin must follow" (*WrGW* 15:300). By "first principles," as Markus Fischer observes in the prologue, Machiavelli meant reimposing the punishment and reviving the fear that made the citizens good at the beginning; if constitutional government was possible, it was only because of a constant recurrence to its violent, unconstitutional origins. When Washington used the phrase, however, he meant something entirely different. His call was for a return not to the circumstances of the Revolution but to the political principles of the founding.[11]

---

[11] The Fairfax Resolves (written by George Mason and introduced by Washington) speak of "the fundamental Principle" of representative government based on popular consent. See Fairfax County Resolves, 18 July 1774, in *The Papers of George Mason, 1725–1792*, ed. Robert A. Rutland (Chapel Hill, NC: University of North Carolina Press, 1970), 201–2. Likewise, the

Early in the Revolution, Washington reported that "abler heads" – probably Mason and Jefferson – had convinced him that the British laws being enforced in America were "subversive of the laws and constitution of Great Britain itself." But it was "an innate spirit of freedom" that led him to conclude "that the measures, which [the British] administration hath for some time been, and are now most violently pursuing, are repugnant to every principle of natural justice."[12] Writing to John Armstrong, he later praised *The Federalist Papers* because they "have thrown new light upon the science of Government," and "have given the rights of man a full and fair discussion, and explained them in so clear and forcible a manner, as cannot fail to make a lasting impression" (*WrGW* 29:466). Washington used arguments drawn from the common law principles of the British constitution, but always as a reflection of the more fundamental laws of nature. He understood the rights of human nature to be the moral ground of the American Revolution; it was the establishment of civil and religious liberty that induced him to take to the field.[13]

Designing and establishing a government that would secure and protect these rights was the difficulty. The Articles of Confederation created little more than a league of friendship and quickly proved both insufficient to the task of supporting the war effort and an obstacle to the establishment of the stronger union that he and other nationalists supported. Mired in their own local concerns and prejudices, the states had become hotbeds of political corruption and poor management. As a result, the common interests of America were moldering and sinking into irretrievable ruin. The breakdown of political and economic order, Washington explained to James Warren, "afford[s] too many melancholy proofs of the decay of public virtue" (*WrGW* 14:312).

Yet at the very height of his power, and at the moment when the war was turning in the Americans' favor, Washington rejected the opportunity to become a true American prince. He did not seize Colonel Lewis Nicola's infamous offer of monarchy in the spring of 1782 but instead repudiated it as inappropriate in republican America and dishonorable for himself.[14] Likewise, Washington rejected the option of using military force (with or without his participation) to strengthen the national government and take control of the government. In

---

Virginia Bill of Rights states that "no free government, or the blessings of liberty, can be preserved to any people, but by a firm adherence to justice, moderation, temperance, frugality, and virtue, and by a frequent recurrence to fundamental principles."

[12] Washington believed that the acts of Parliament were "no longer governed by the principles of justice," and that the crisis had finally arrived when Americans must assert their rights "or submit to every imposition, that can be heaped upon us, till custom and use shall make us as tame and abject slaves, as the blacks we rule over with such arbitrary sway." See GW to Bryan Fairfax, 24 August 1774, in *WrGW* 3:232–4.

[13] See GW to the Ministers, Elders, Deacons, and Members of the German Reformed Congregation of New York, 27 November 1783, in *GWC* 271.

[14] See GW to Colonel Lewis Nicola, 22 May 1782, in *WrGW* 24:272–3. This was the only time during the whole war that Washington obtained written statements from his aides that the letter had been properly sealed and sent. James Flexner, *George Washington in the American Revolution (1775–1783)* (Boston: Little Brown, 1968), 491–2.

1783, Alexander Hamilton recognized that the frustrated army might use force to "procure justice to itself," and urged Washington to "take the direction of them" in order to "do justice to the creditors of the United States . . . and supply the future wants of government" (*PAH* 3:253–5).[15] Washington cautioned young Hamilton that an army "is a dangerous instrument to play with," and was perplexed that he did not realize "the fatal tendency of such a measure" for the republican project.[16] In speaking on this occasion, Washington condemned what became known as the Newburgh Conspiracy, pointedly alluding to "the Ides of March," and urging his officers to express their "utmost horror and detestation" of the one who wished to "overturn the liberties of our Country, and who wickedly attempts to open the flood Gates of Civil discord, and deluge our rising Empire in Blood." To oppose such an effort, he averred, would be "one more distinguished proof of unexampled patriotism and patient virtue" (*WrGW* 26:222–7). "The moderation and virtue of a single character," Jefferson later observed in a letter to Washington, "probably prevented this Revolution from being closed, as most others have been, by a subversion of that liberty it was intended to establish" (*PTJ* 7:106).

Instead, Washington recommended fundamental political reform. America needed a transformation of its conduct, and this required much more than radical changes in the financial or legal structure. The narrow, local prejudices that dominated the Confederation had to be replaced by a sense of interest in and patriotism for a common, national good. Washington was convinced that "the honor, power, and true Interest of this Country must be measured by a Continental scale," and feared that local prejudices and state politics would distract the people and prevent them from realizing their potential as a nation. Americans, he explained to the Marquis de Lafayette, must be convinced of the "more liberal and extensive plan of government which wisdom and foresight, freed from the mist of prejudice, would dictate" (*WrGW* 26:298). Washington saw this path as the only alternative to the twin evils of anarchy or despotism.

Washington held that having increased power and authority in a national government – an idea many thought repugnant to the principles of republicanism – was necessary for establishing a workable republican government. And republican government at a national level required a national character to encourage the habits of self-government and to build a nation out of the loose and disorganized confederation that then existed. "We now stand an Independent People, and have yet to learn political tactics," Washington wrote to Lafayette in the spring of 1783. "We are placed among the Nations of the Earth, and have a character to establish" (*WrGW* 26:298). The successful outcome of the Revolutionary War, and the recognition of America's independence as a nation, afforded the opportunity for such a venture.

Washington first laid out his case for an American national character as the centerpiece of political and moral reform in his final Circular to the States,

[15] See also AH to GW, 17 March 1783, in *PAH* 3:290–3.
[16] See GW to AH, 4 March and 4 April 1783, in *WrGW* 26:186, 293.

announcing his intention to retire his military commission on 8 June 1783. The peace had been won, political independence established, and a vast territory was now in America's sole possession. Finding themselves in the most enviable of conditions, it was now in the power of the American people to decide their own future and determine whether the Revolution was "a blessing or a curse" for themselves and the rest of the world. "This is the time of their political probation," he proclaimed, for "this is the moment when the eyes of the World are turned upon them; this is the moment to establish or ruin their national Character forever; this is the favorable moment to give such a tone to our Federal Government, as will enable it to answer the ends of its institution...."

Nothing better illustrated the significance of this moment than the "happy conjuncture of times and circumstances" under which America had declared its independence, referring less to the physical conditions than to the intellectual and moral preconditions of America coming into existence as a nation. "The foundation of our empire was not laid in the gloomy age of Ignorance and Superstition," he wrote in one of his most striking statements,

but at an Epocha when the rights of mankind were better understood and more clearly defined, than at any former period; the researches of the human mind, after social happiness, have been carried to a great extent; the Treasures of knowledge, acquired through a long succession of years, by the labours of Philosophers, Sages and Legislatures, are laid open for our use, and their collected wisdom may be happily applied in the Establishment of our forms of Government; the free cultivation of Letters, the unbounded extension of Commerce, the progressive refinement of Manners, the growing liberality of sentiment, and above all, the pure and benign light of Revelation, have had a meliorating influence on mankind and increased the blessings of Society.

In describing the times and circumstances in this broad way, Washington saw America's founding in line with the deeper philosophical and theological roots of the Revolution. The rights of mankind were better understood and more clearly defined than ever before. Yet at the same time, the enlightened citizen respected the principles of reason *and* revelation – the collected wisdom of the ages as well as the pure and benign light of divine revelation. Far from being contradictory, the great truths of reason and revelation cooperated and collaborated in the American moment. The occasion afforded "infinite delight to every benevolent and liberal mind," regardless of whether it is viewed "in a natural, a political, or moral point of light." At its best, the character of the American people would reflect these truths.

While these unique circumstances were favorable, they did not guarantee success. In order to "seize the occasion and make it [their] own," Washington recommended the policies he regarded as essential to the well-being of America's independence and character as a nation. First, he advocated a permanent union of the states, for without union the "fruits of the Revolution would have been made in vain." Second, Washington recommended a strong commitment to public justice in law, contracts, and debts, to be built upon "the same good faith" that was found in "private engagements." This would strengthen the government and allow individuals to reap the benefits of their labor. Third, he recommended the adoption of a proper peace establishment for the defense of the republic; it was essential that the militia be built upon a single system of organization, and that its formation, discipline, arms, and supplies be uniform throughout the nation. Finally, Washington observed that republican government required "a pacific and friendly Disposition among the People of the United States, which will induce them to forget their local prejudices and policies, to make those mutual concessions which are requisite to the general prosperity, and in some instances, to sacrifice their individual advantages to the interest of the Community." These four ideas made up the "Pillars on which the glorious Fabrick of our Independency and National Character must be supported" (*WrGW* 26:483–96)

Washington always understood the American founding to be an auspicious moment that would prove the viability of republican government. It demanded institutional arrangements strong enough to build a great nation without violating republican principles. But the decisive act in the formation of the new nation was the establishment of the principles of good government and the habits of citizenship that would stamp the nation with an indelible character and make its people capable of ruling themselves.

New Modes and Orders?

As he retired from public life in 1783, Washington had no doubt that the many problems faced by the new nation would in due time be corrected. America would "work its own cure," he wrote to George William Fairfax, "as there is virtue at the bottom" (*WrGW* 27:58). Nevertheless, he was increasingly pessimistic about the actual road to political reform. Although he believed that "all things will come right at last," he expressed his fear to Virginia Governor Benjamin Harrison in January 1784 that "like a young heir, come a little prematurely to a large inheritance, we shall wanton and run riot until we have brought our reputation to the brink of ruin," only then "to do what prudence and common policy pointed out as plain as any problem in Euclid, in the first place" (*WrGW* 27:305–6).

By late 1785, he had concluded that the Confederation was "a shadow without the substance," and that Congress was "a nugatory body." So far had things declined that, "from the high ground on which we stood, we are descending into the vale of confusion and darkness" (*WrGW* 28:290). All of the jealousies, vices, and narrow opinions that Washington lamented continued to engulf greater portions of the public mind, especially the political leadership. Mortified by what he saw, Washington observed in May 1786 that "virtue, I fear has, in a great degree, taken its departure from us; and the want of a disposition to do justice is the source of the national embarassments" (*WrGW* 28:431–2). Three months later, Washington remarked to John Jay that "we have probably had too good an opinion of human nature in forming our confederation." Only

a vigorous, national, republican government could demonstrate that governments "founded on the basis of equal liberty" were not "ideal and fallacious"
(*WrGW* 28:502–3).

Although Washington long hesitated to participate in the Constitutional
Convention, ultimately he agreed, explaining in a letter to James Madison that
the gathering "is a measure of equal necessity and magnitude; and may be the
spring of reanimation" that was needed to save the country (*WrGW* 29:71).
Once he decided to participate, he recommended to James Madison that the
convention adopt "no temporizing expedient," but instead "probe the defects
of the Constitution to the bottom, and provide radical cures." A complete revision of the system was the "only constitutional mode" to remedy the defects of
the Confederation. He agreed with Madison that any new constitutional structure must give adequate powers and energy to the federal government, allow for
the secrecy and dispatch characteristic of good administration (of which more
later), and have the confidence and ability to exercise national powers and
pursue national policies. "[A] conduct like this, will stamp wisdom and dignity on the proceedings," he noted (*WrGW*, 29:191–2).[17] Washington presided
over the convention as its president, and both publicly and privately urged
bold action. Although he did not publicly participate in the ratification debate,
Washington staunchly supported the Constitution in his correspondence.[18] His
prestige and backing were essential to its eventual approval: "Be assured,"
James Monroe wrote to Jefferson, "his influence carried this government"
(*PTJ* 13:352).

Washington had good reasons to support the resulting document: It established a national government, created a strong executive, and formed the legal
framework necessary for a commercial republic. In a letter to Lafayette in
February 1788, Washington – fully aware that his words would "become known
to all the world" – gave his primary reasons for supporting the Constitution.
First, the new government was invested with no more power than was absolutely necessary for good government; it was to be a limited government with
powers restricted by a written constitution. Second, these powers were distributed into three branches of government – legislative, executive, and judicial –
so as to prevent the degeneration of the government into a despotic or oppressive form. The Constitution provided for energetic government, yet at the same
time the separation of powers preserved its republican form, and frequent elections kept it close to the people. But Washington did not believe that these
new institutional arrangements – which owed much, as the contributors to this
book have attempted to make clear, to the speculations of Montesquieu and

---

[17] Madison responded by sending to Washington his outline of a new system based on the creation
of a supreme national government and a change in the principle of representation.

[18] Washington was unequivocal and decided on the issue of ratification; he increased his correspondence with key political leaders, especially in Virginia, and invited others to circulate and
communicate his strong support for the new Constitution. Washington also monitored the political debates and voting in each state and closely followed the pamphlet debate for and against
the proposed Constitution – encouraging the dissemination of the Federalist Papers.

his predecessors among Machiavelli's seventeenth-century admirers – were sufficient by themselves to solve the republican dilemma. In his judgment, the new Constitution could prevent degeneration into despotism only "... so long as there shall remain any virtue in the body of the people." The new government took advantage of the progress of the science of politics by proposing more checks and barriers against tyranny than any government "hitherto instituted among mortals." But a good constitution, no matter how well constructed, did not remove the need for moral citizens. Washington continued:

> I would not be understood my dear Marquis to speak of consequences which may be produced, in the revolution of ages, by corruption of morals, profligacy of manners, and listlessness of the preservation of the natural and unalienable rights of mankind; nor of the successful usurpations that may be established at such a juncture, upon the ruins of liberty, however providently guarded and secured, as these are contingencies against which no human prudence can effectually provide. (*WrGW* 29:409–10)[19]

Washington saw the new Constitution as the framework for the restoring of the American character. The debate and ratification of the Constitution (and the first elections thereafter) were the first steps in this restoration. Rejoicing at every step that was taken to preserve the union and establish good government, Washington knew, as he explained to Benjamin Lincoln, that it still remained to be seen whether "there is good sense and virtue enough left to recover the right path" (*WrGW* 30:11).

Washington's most mature statement about the institutional arrangements of the founding and the moral character of the people is the Farewell Address of 1796. There he urges Americans to assess the immense value of the Union to their collective and individual happiness so that they might come to "cherish a cordial, habitual and immoveable attachment to it," and warned of those who might seek to "enfeeble the sacred ties which now link together the various parts." The cornerstone of this sacred compact was the uniting of the states and the people under a new constitution of "as much vigour as is consistent with the perfect security of Liberty," yet strong enough "to maintain all in the secure and tranquil enjoyment of the rights of person and property." A formal Union, unlike the confederation government, offered greater strength, resources, and security, as well as the economic advantages of a commercial republic, and made for "an indissoluble community of Interest as one Nation." What made the Constitution sacred, however, was not interest or security as much as its basis in just principles of government. The new Constitution's grounding in the consent of the governed, according to Washington, made it "sacredly obligatory upon all" until it was formally changed "by an explicit and authentic act of the whole People." The rule of the majority is a sacred substitute for original unanimity because of the necessity of the acquiescence of the minority to the rule of the majority, but also because the majority itself (and thus the government) is ruled and restricted by rights equally possessed by all (*WrGW* 35:214–38). "All,

---

[19] See Chapters 1 through 3 and 5.

too, will bear in mind this sacred principle," Jefferson would later write in his First Inaugural, "that though the will of the majority is in all cases to prevail, that will to be rightful must be reasonable; that the minority possess their equal rights, which equal law must protect, and to violate would be oppression" (*WrTJ* [ed. Peterson] 492–3).

Washington's declaration of the natural-rights grounding of constitutional government, which would seem to allow an unlimited pursuit of private interest, is followed in the Farewell Address by a discussion of the virtues needed for self-government. The new Constitution, Washington argues, will encourage moderation and good habits of government. First, the separation of powers and the system of checks and balances thwarted governmental despotism and encouraged responsibility in public representatives. A responsible government, in turn, bolstered responsible people. Second, the legitimate constitutional amendment process allowed democratic reform at the same time that it elevated the document above the popular passions of the moment, thereby encouraging deliberation and patience in the people. Good opinions in the people, and good government, would have a complementary effect on politics.

But republican government was possible only if the public and private virtues needed for civil society and self-government remained strong and effective. The consent that was necessary for just government must be informed by knowledge of the rights of man: "Promote, then, as an object of primary importance, institutions for the general diffusion of knowledge. In proportion as the structure of a government gives force to public opinion, it is essential that public opinion should be enlightened." The civic responsibility and moderation of public passion also required the moderation of private passion through the encouragement of private morality. According to Washington, the "great Pillars of human happiness" and the "firmest props of the duties of Men and citizens" inhered in religion and morality: "Of all the disposition and habits which lead to political prosperity, Religion and morality are indispensable supports." Religion and morality are the props of duty, the indispensable supports of the dispositions and habits that lead to political prosperity, and the great pillars of human happiness. They aid good government by teaching men their moral obligations and creating the conditions for decent politics. Neither the religious nor the political man can ignore this fact: "The mere Politician, equally with the pious man ought to respect and to cherish them" (*WrGW* 35:214–38).[20]

Thoughts on Machiavelli and Washington

Let us turn our thoughts back to Machiavelli for a moment, and consider the executive in the American constitutional structure. The modern doctrine of

[20] See Matthew Spalding and Patrick J. Garrity, *A Sacred Union of Citizens: George Washington's Farewell Address and the American Character* (Lanham, MD: Rowman and Littlefield, 1996).

executive power, after all, begins with Machiavelli, the first political thinker to present the executive as the centerpiece of his political theory. In order not to be weak and vulnerable, states require an executive or prince who is liberated to practice not only the art of war but also the new virtue. To the extent that there remains a "common good," as Markus Fischer has made clear, it is no longer defined in terms of moral or even philosophical virtue – as in imagined republics and principalities – but is instead based on the common objectives desired by all societies: independence, stability, prosperity, empire. For this reason, the Florentine hardly ever mentions justice. Anything and everything that is concretely beneficial to the new ends of political society thus narrowly conceived is to be wholeheartedly embraced. *Virtù*, as understood by Machiavelli, is no longer what it was for Aristotle and his Christian admirers: the mean between two vices. It is, instead, a calculated mix of virtue and vice designed as a tool for the pursuit of political society's new ends.

The new executive is not subject to the ends of nature but only to necessity, for its purpose is to overcome necessity and thereby conquer fortune. He must be able to practice the skills of both the fox and the lion – and to use both virtue and vice according to the requirements of the circumstances. The executive must "learn to be able not to be good, and to use this and not use it according to necessity" (*P* 15). He must excel in decisive and secret actions, the dispensing of swift punishment, public executions, and a willingness to exercise emergency dictatorial powers. And the new ends justify and determine the proper means: "So let a prince win and maintain a state: the means will always be judged honorable, and will be praised by everyone" (*P* 18). Thus Machiavelli's executive, and an unlimited power to execute his own decisions without appeal, exemplify the new emphasis on survival as the ground of politics.[21]

In the modern world, models of republics were few and far between; even in the ancient world they were notoriously unstable and weak. To correct this problem, the Americans incorporated into their constitutional order inventions of political science that were unknown to the ancients, including a new source of vigor: the office of the presidency, vested with the executive power. But the executive had undergone much change before it reached America, by which time the harsh edges had been worn off and the office domesticated and legitimated. As Margaret Michelle Barnes Smith and Paul Carrese have pointed out in Chapters 2 and 5 of this book, John Locke tempered the executive by placing it under the structure of a constitution and making it serve the ends of constitutional government, and Montesquieu further moderated the executive through the addition of an independent judiciary and the doctrine of the separation of powers.[22] The dilemma for the Americans was that while

---

[21] See Harvey C. Mansfield, "Machiavelli and the Modern Executive," in Mansfield, *Machiavelli's Virtue* (Chicago: University of Chicago Press, 1996), 295–314.

[22] For a discussion of the development of the modern executive, see Harvey C. Mansfield, *Taming the Prince: The Ambivalence of Modern Executive Power* (New York: Free Press, 1989).

it was understood that executive power was needed for good government, it was presumed that "a vigorous executive is inconsistent with the genius of republican government" (*Fed.* 70). They solved this problem by republican-izing the executive through regular elections and a written constitution that brought executive powers under the rule of law and the consent of the gov-erned. The Americans mixed the strength of monarchical governments with the requirements of republicanism, thereby allowing for the energy that republics need to survive without sacrificing the liberties that make self-government possible.

In Federalist 70, Publius observes that "energy in the executive is a leading character in the definition of good government." The ingredients of energy remind us of the recommendations of Machiavelli. Unity, the first ingredient, is the most familiar. It is required because of the need for unanimity during critical emergencies, when decisions are most necessary; emergencies require the decisiveness, secrecy, and dispatch of one man acting alone. The unique ingredient of energy, however, is duration in office. Duration allows not only for stability in execution but also for the participation of the "noblest minds," whose ruling passion is the love of fame (*Fed.* 70–2). This invitation to great men has the added advantage of providing an opening for the participation of men of great virtue. Indeed, Publius argues that the Constitution affords a "moral certainty" that the president will have more than "talents for low intrigue and the little arts of popularity," and predicts a "constant probability" that the office will be filled by "characters preeminent for ability and virtue" (*Fed.* 68). The republican principle demands that elected representatives be governed by the "deliberate sense of the community," not every sudden breeze or transient impulse; it is the "duty" of statesmen to withstand such delusions to allow "time and opportunity for cool and sedate reflection." This demands men of courage and magnanimity to rule wisely despite popular displeasure (*Fed.* 71).[23]

In the end, Publius recognizes necessity – and the need for an executive who can address the requirements of necessity – but does not accept the conclusion of Machiavellian political science that necessity determines the course of politics. This recognition must be seen in light of the executive's higher purpose, which is to preserve the constitution for the sake of constitutional government and the rule of law. Thus, as Harvey Mansfield notes in his study of the modern executive, executive power in the American context does not become "an excuse for doing ill, but an incentive for doing better than what is merely necessary," for "constitutional powers broad enough to meet necessities may also be strong

---

[23] John Marshall wrote in his monumental biography of Washington that Washington always respected "the real and deliberate sentiments of the people, [as] their gusts of passion passed over, without ruffling the smooth surface of his mind," yet at the same time "had the magnanimity to pursue [the nation's] real interests, in opposition to its temporary prejudices." See Marshall, *The Life of George Washington* (Fredricksburg, VA: Citizens' Guild of Washington's Boyhood Home, 1926), 5:377.

enough to satisfy virtue."[24] By anticipating necessity, the American founders placed it in the service of a greater good.

In the end, the executive in the American regime, while informed by varied and numerous sources, cannot be understood apart from the nation's first president. Washington was always an advocate of strong leadership and pushed for more energy and responsibility in government. During the war, he acted for all intents and purposes (both with and without the permission of Congress) as the chief executive of the nation. When it came to the new federal Constitution, while he supported checks on the president's power, he advocated a strong and independent executive over the anarchy, gridlock, and weakness associated with the Articles of Confederation.[25] An examination of Washington's voting record at the Constitutional Convention shows his consistent support for a strong executive and strong national powers.[26] "No man is a warmer advocate for proper restraints and wholesome checks in every department than I am," Washington wrote to Bushrod Washington in 1787, "but I have never yet been able to discover the propriety of placing it absolutely out of the power of men to render essential Services, because a possibility remains of their doing ill" (*WrGW* 29:312). Washington was energetic as president and defended his prerogatives when needed and his position when challenged.

But Washington was also aware of the unique characteristics of the American executive: He symbolized the new government as well as the whole American project. The other founders thought as much of Washington, for they were willing to create such an executive only because of his personification of their ideal. The vast powers of the presidency, as Pierce Butler noted some months after the Constitutional Convention of 1787, would not have been made as great "had not many of the members cast their eyes towards General Washington as president; and shaped their ideas of the powers to be given to a president, by their opinions of his virtue" (*RFC* 3:302). Washington understood the presidency's great potential for raising the moral tone of the government and the citizenry – a task for which he was preeminently and uniquely qualified. To John Armstrong in 1788, he expressed his hope that "those persons who are chosen to administer [the new government] will have wisdom enough to discern the influence which their example as rulers and legislators may have on the body of the people, and will have virtue enough to pursue that line of conduct which will most conduce to the happiness of their Country" (*WrGW* 30:465).

---

[24] "As a formal possibility, Aristotle's kingship of virtue remains in the Constitution.... The Constitution adopts that which precludes kingship in order to create a republican executive rather than a king; nevertheless, constitutional powers broad enough to meet necessities may also be strong enough to satisfy virtue. The Machiavellian principle of anticipating necessity by the use of *virtù* may be interpreted in the interest of virtue." Mansfield, *Taming the Prince*, 252, 275.

[25] See Glenn Phelps, *George Washington and American Constitutionalism* (Lawrence, KS: University of Kansas Press, 1993), 104–6.

[26] See William B. Allen, "Washington and Franklin: Symbols or Lawmakers? Their Significance in the Constitutional Convention of 1787," *Political Science Reviewer* 17 (Fall 1987): 109–38; Phelps, *George Washington and American Constitutionalism*, 99–109.

Washington's understanding of virtue and its role in America's new constitutional structure is reflected in his First Inaugural. Rather than recommend measures to Congress for consideration – he did no more than point toward the objects defined in "the great constitutional charter" – Washington chose to speak of "the talents, the rectitude, and the patriotism, which adorn the characters selected to devise and adopt" the laws. It was here primarily and not in the institutional arrangements that he saw the "surest pledges" of wise policy, ensuring that neither local prejudices nor party animosities would misdirect the efforts of the representatives and guaranteeing that "the foundation of our national policy will be laid in the pure and immutable principles of private morality." This would prove that free government might be "exemplified" by attributes worthy of the affections of its citizens. Washington was moved to "dwell on this prospect" for profound reasons:

[T]here is no truth more thoroughly established than that there exists in the economy and course of nature, an indissoluble union between virtue and happiness; between duty and advantage, between the genuine maxims of an honest and magnanimous policy, and the solid rewards of public prosperity and felicity: since we ought to be no less persuaded that the propitious smiles of Heaven can never be expected on a nation that disregards the external rules of order and right, which Heaven itself has ordained: and since the preservation of the sacred fire of liberty, and the destiny of the republican model of government, are justly considered as deeply, perhaps as finally, staked on the experiment entrusted to the hands of the American people.

The connection between private morality and public policy is not made here for merely utilitarian purposes. For Washington, there is "no truth" more thoroughly established in the economy and course of nature than the "indissoluble union" between virtue and happiness. This formulation implies that some degree of virtue according to the external rules of order and right – as in the pure and immutable principles of private morality – is necessary for the preservation of liberty and the destiny of republican government, a destiny placed in the hands of the American people. Indeed, the great theme of Washington's statesmanship was the formation of an American character, both private and public (*WrGW* 30:291–6).

Conclusion

What is controversial about Machiavelli is his claim to have discovered a new political teaching based on a new moral worldview. The Florentine argues that the ancient view of man aimed too high and thus overshot man's nature, making the classical conception of politics unrealistic and improbable; his new approach to politics ceases to take its bearings from virtue and instead lowers the standard to focus on life as it is actually pursued. Men are understood to be directed not toward the virtues of reason or revelation but instead are under the necessity to use virtue, in the new sense of prudent selfishness, to satisfy the needs of their passions. The greatest passion of the greatest men is glory – especially the glory of being a new prince in a new state, a founder of new modes and orders.[27]

George Washington recognized the interested and passionate character of individuals and politics. During the Revolution, he warned against relying on virtue to the point of ignoring man's natural self-interest. And he believed as firmly in individual freedom, in the pursuit of economic well-being, in the material fruits of modern science, as any of the most "modern" founders. To the extent that these commitments presupposed a general acceptance of Machiavelli's understanding of the new conditions of politics, Washington could be said to be Machiavelli's heir. But Washington rejected the Florentine's narrow conception of the ends of politics. He believed that America could and must be something more than a collection of individuals and interests, and he defined a regime that maintained the possibility of decent and elevated political life. "And you will," Washington told his officers at Newburgh in mid-March, 1783, "by the dignity of your Conduct, afford occasion for Posterity to say, when speaking of the glorious example you have exhibited to Mankind, 'had this day been wanting, the World had never seen the last stage of perfection to which human nature is capable of attaining'" (*WrGW* 26:227).

In the draft of his First Inaugural, Washington referred to "the eternal line that separates right from wrong" that holds true in both private and public life (*GWC* 458). As he noted in his final text, there is "no truth more thoroughly established than that there exists in the economy and course of nature, an indissoluble union between virtue and happiness." He was "no less persuaded that the propitious smiles of Heaven can never be expected on a nation that disregards the external rules of order and right, which Heaven itself has ordained" (*WrGW* 30:294). Washington's connection between private morality and national character, between virtue and happiness, hardly seems Machiavellian. The idea of liberty as the emancipation of the passions had no place in Washington's conception of things; the phrase "external rules of order and right" suggests that morality and policy are informed by principles that are permanent and teleological. And while we cannot prove (and do not claim) that Washington was uninterested in glory, there is no reason to doubt that his efforts were undertaken not simply for the sake of glory but for nobler purposes. "All see, and most admire, the glare which hovers round the external trappings of elevated office," Washington wrote to Catherine Macaulary Graham in January 1790. "To me there is nothing in it, beyond the lustre which may be reflected from its connection with a power of promoting human happiness" (*WrGW* 30:495–6). Indeed, the idea of the American regime as Washington understood it – which is not to say that he understood it differently from the other founders – in certain crucial

---

[27] See Leo Strauss, "Niccolo Machiavelli," in *History of Political Philosophy*, 2nd edition, ed. Leo Strauss and Joseph Cropsey (Chicago: University of Chicago Press, 1972), 271–92; Leo Strauss, *What Is Political Philosophy?* (Chicago: University of Chicago Press, 1988), 40–9; Mansfield, *Machiavelli's Virtue*, passim; the prologue of this book.

regards markedly points *away from* rather than *toward* the political science of
Machiavelli.[28]

The Athenian stranger of Plato's *Laws* (708d, 712a) notes that "lawgiving
and the founding of cities is the most perfect test of manly virtue," and that
"the natural genesis of the best regime, and laws to match," occur only when
great power coincides with a man of great prudence and moderation. By per-
sonifying and elaborating the traits of good character, Washington sought to
moderate the passions of citizens and ennoble the deeds of statesmen. To the
extent that his words and his model placed an emphasis on these two qualities – moderation and nobility – Washington should be judged not according to
Machiavelli's political science but rather the classical principles of statesmanship and political life. Perhaps it is here that we should look for a philosophic
spectator to understand the phenomenon of Washington.

---

[28] See Strauss, *Thoughts on Machiavelli*, 13.

8

John Adams's Machiavellian Moment

C. Bradley Thompson

Scholars have debated for many years the role that Machiavelli's ideas may or may not have played in the founding of the United States. Some argue that Machiavelli resurrected a lost tradition of classical republican theory and practice, which was then transmitted to America via the so-called Commonwealthmen of seventeenth- and eighteenth-century English politics.[1] Others credit Machiavelli with having initiated a revolution in political thought that paved the way for the modern natural-rights teaching of Hobbes, Locke, and the American Revolution.[2] And, of course, some deny that Machiavelli had any influence whatsoever in America.

Those who argue for an explicit Machiavellian connection are confronted by one massive problem: There is simply no tangible evidence to suggest that Machiavelli positively influenced any of the American founders. One searches in vain for a direct and recognizable link to Machiavelli in the writings of Jefferson, Madison, or Hamilton. Thus, much of the work on this question has attempted to show how certain Machiavellian ideas were distilled and culturally transmitted to America. In other words, we are led to believe that eighteenth-century Americans were Machiavellians without knowing it.

John Adams was an exception to the rule. He was unique among the founders in that he actually read and took seriously Machiavelli's ideas. Adams quoted extensively from Machiavelli, and he openly acknowledged an intellectual debt to the Florentine statesman. Adams even claimed to have been a

---

[1] See J. G. A. Pocock, *The Machiavellian Moment: Florentine Political Thought and the Atlantic Republican Tradition* (Princeton, NJ: Princeton University Press, 1975); Lance Banning, *The Jeffersonian Persuasion* (Ithaca, NY: Cornell University Press, 1978), 21–91.

[2] See Thomas L. Pangle, *The Spirit of Modern Republicanism: The Moral Vision of the American Founders and the Philosophy of Locke* (Chicago: University of Chicago Press, 1988), 41–128; Paul A. Rahe, *Republics Ancient and Modern: Classical Republicanism and the American Revolution* (Chapel Hill, NC: University of North Carolina Press, 1992), 231–782.

This essay is adapted from C. Bradley Thompson, "John Adams's Machiavellian Moment," *RP* 57:3 (Summer 1995): 399–406, and reprinted with permission.

"student of Machiavelli."[3] Adams's political writings are replete with references to Machiavelli and his writings. In the first volume of his great opus *A Defence of the Constitutions of Government of the United States of America*, he classified Machiavelli, along with Sidney and Montesquieu, as a philosophic defender of mixed government. To that end, he transcribes in its entirety Machiavelli's chapter on "The Different Kinds of Republics, and of What Kind the Roman Republic Was," from the *Discourses on Livy*. In the second volume of the *Defence*, he copied over one hundred pages from the *Florentine Histories*, and he reprinted Machiavelli's *Discourse upon the Proper Ways and Means of Reforming the Government of Florence*, which he retitled "Machiavel's Plan for a Perfect Commonwealth." Scattered throughout the *Defence* are several shorter quotations from Machiavelli that Adams cites approvingly and disapprovingly (*WoJA* 4:408, 410, 559; 5:95; 6:4, 394, 396).

Adams freely admitted that he was often uncertain as to when Machiavelli spoke the truth and when he dissimulated, "whether he was in jest or in earnest." He also seems to have known that there were two Machiavellis: Machiavelli the restorer of ancient republican institutions, and Machiavelli the teacher of evil. Years later he would say of the Florentine that his "writings contain a good deal of wisdom, though it is unfortunately mixed with too much wickedness."[4] Adams took from Machiavelli what he needed, and he rejected much.

It is no exaggeration to suggest, then, that Machiavelli cast a long shadow over one of America's most serious students of the political sciences. But even the most thoughtful reader of the *Defence* is hardly prepared when Adams advances on behalf of the Florentine a series of stunning claims. At one point, Adams refers to Machiavelli in the manner of James Harrington as "the great restorer of true politics." Elsewhere in the *Defence*, he insisted that the "world" was much indebted to Machiavelli for "the revival of reason in matters of government." He also praised Machiavelli for having been "the first" to have "revived the ancient politics."[5]

What could Adams have meant by these extraordinary statements? What were the "true politics" that Adams thought Machiavelli had restored and how had this Florentine statesman resurrected "reason" in the affairs of political life? And what specific tradition of the "ancient politics" did Adams think Machiavelli had revived? By examining these interesting questions, this chapter hopes to open new avenues of scholarship on the question of Machiavelli and the American founding.

John Adams's intellectual debt to Machiavelli was unique and rather different from the intellectual tradition that the Florentine is alleged to have deposited in America. In what follows, we examine the direct intellectual confrontation between Adams and Machiavelli. Our task is therefore a limited one: to examine how Adams understood and then used and rejected many of Machiavelli's ideas

---

[3] JA to Francis Adrian Vanderkemp, 9 August 1813, *PJAM* Reel 95.
[4] JA to Francis Vanderkemp, 19 March 1813 and 9 August 1813, *PJAM* Reel 95.
[5] Consider *WoJA* 4:559, 5:95, 6:4, in light of Chapter 1 of this book.

and methods, forms and formalities, modes and orders. Readers must determine for themselves whether Adams understood the true Machiavelli.

"Reason in Matters of Government"

In 1784, Dr. Richard Price, the English dissenting minister, published as an appendix to his *Observations on the Importance of the American Revolution* a letter he had received from the famous French philosophe, the Baron Anne-Robert Turgot. The letter criticizes America's revolutionary constitutions for slavishly imitating the checks and balances of England's mixed constitution. Adams understood Turgot's letter to be a celebration of Pennsylvania's unicameral constitution and a condemnation of his own Massachusetts constitution, as well as all other state constitutions with bicameral legislatures. Adams wrote his *Defence of the Constitutions of Government of the United States of America, against the Attack of M. Turgot*, to repel the advance of a French virus onto American shores.

The first and most influential volume of the *Defence* is divided into three large sections. The first section studies twenty-five democratic, aristocratic, and monarchical republics of the modern world. The second section examines the opinions and philosophies of Swift, Franklin, Price, Machiavelli, Montesquieu, Harrington, Polybius, Dionysius of Halicarnassus, and Plato. The last third studies seventeen democratic, aristocratic, and monarchical republics of the ancient world. The second volume and part of the third "contain three long Courses of Experiments in Political Philosophy," as Adams explained to Thomas Jefferson, a trilogy of case studies that examine the Italian republics of the Middle Ages (*AJL* 1:192). The last half of the third volume is an analysis and critique of Marchamont Nedham's essay on *The Excellency of a Free State, or the Right Constitution of a Commonwealth*, published in 1656.

The *Discourses on Davila*, which one can appropriately describe as the fourth volume of the *Defence*,[6] consists of thirty-two essays, eighteen of which are straight translations from the Italian historian Enrico Caterino Davila's *Historia delle guerre civili di Francia* (1630). The *Discourses* recount the battles, intrigues, factions and assassinations during forty years of French civil war in the late sixteenth century. Davila's historical narrative is interrupted after the first discourse, however, by fourteen essays of "useful reflections" that discuss the "constitution of human nature," drawn in part from Adam Smith's *Theory of Moral Sentiments*.

Historians have been puzzled over the years as to why Adams would write such a "strange" and difficult text.[7] Any serious study of the *Defence* must,

---

[6] Adams often referred to the *Defence* and his *Discourses on Davila* (1790–1) as his four volumes on government, and it was his intention that they be read as a single, unified work; see *WoJA* 6:482; 10:96, and *AJL* 2:356–7. For the purpose of the present study, I will, therefore, treat Adams's *Discourses* as the "fourth volume" of the *Defence*.

[7] Adams himself referred to the *Defence* as a "strange" book. See JA to Richard Cranch, 15 January 1787, in *WoJA* 1:432.

sooner or later, confront the almost universal scholarly opinion that the work lacks order, coherence and a unifying plan.[8] As it stands, the *Defence* is cumbersome and uninviting; indeed, it is seemingly without method. Why did John Adams feel compelled to respond to Turgot's letter criticizing the American constitutions with a three-volume treatise? More to the point, who did he think would read such a tome and what did he think his audience would do with the information once read?

Buried among his unpublished papers is a set of rough notes from which Adams pieced together much of the *Defence*. Included in this material is an extraordinary fragment that permits the historian to access a new way of viewing this "strange" book.[9] Never published as part of the *Defence*, this note provides a key to decoding the mystery of a book that seems at first sight to be merely a "disordered conglomeration" of uncontrollable material. The fragment reveals in dramatic fashion the scientific tradition from which Adams developed his theory of political architecture, and it helps the reader to unlock a new entrance into the organization, purpose, and meaning of this obscure treatise.[10]

The stated purpose of this fragment is first to illuminate "the true method of pursuing the Study of the Arts and Sciences," and second to enumerate "the great Men to whom We are indebted for the ancient discovery and modern revival of it." Adams's negative purpose is to counter "some celebrated Academicians" who had lately advanced the thesis that "experience and examples" have nothing to do with one of the most important of the sciences, "that of Government." In all likelihood, Adams is here referring to Turgot, Condorcet, and others among the French philosophes and encyclopedists. Adams clearly identified two opposed traditions of scientific reasoning in the fragment: one advocating an empirical – a posteriori – inductive mode of reasoning, and another advancing a rationalist – a priori – deductive method. By challenging what he considered bad science and by developing a "right method of philosophizing," Adams hoped to lay the methodological groundwork for a science of politics that could distinguish between "attainable and unattainable knowledge" (*PJAM* Reel 188). In other words, he is challenging the deductive method of hypothesis and system building with the inductive method of fact and experience.

Interestingly, Adams argued that the revolution in modern science usually associated with Francis Bacon and Isaac Newton had actually originated in the ancient world. "It is not true," he claims, "to say that the right use of Reason and the right conduct of the Understanding in the Investigation of Truth, and

---

8 Gordon S. Wood, *Creation of the American Republic, 1776–1787* (New York: W. W. Norton, 1969), 568, for instance, has described the *Defence* as a "bulky, disordered, conglomeration of political glosses on a single theme."

9 See "Literary Drafts and Notes," *PJAM* Reel 188.

10 For a fuller discussion of the relationship between this fragment and the organization of the *Defence*, see C. Bradley Thompson, *John Adams and the Spirit of Liberty* (Lawrence, KS: University Press of Kansas, 1998).

the Acquisition of knowledge is a late discovery." He identifies Hippocrates, Democritus, and "some of the Writings of Aristotle" as having first comprehended "that Observation and Experience were the only means of acquiring a knowledge of Nature." Adams preferred the "experimental Philosophy" of Aristotle's *History of Animals* to the "Conjecture," the "fictions of Imagination, and the Spirit of System" found in his *Physics*. And when a new generation of men in the modern era had "little by little, introduced a new science," and seemingly smashed all that had gone before it, Adams found they had really "only revived a Method which had been practised in Antiquity" (*PJAM* Reel 188).

Adams credits "Chancellor Bacon" with initiating a revolution in modern science, a revolution grounded on resurrected modes of reasoning that had laid dormant for over a millennium. Adams thought Bacon the "first among the moderns" to have "abandoned a vague and obscure Philosophy." It was Bacon who had left "words for things" and who "sought in the observation of Nature, a real knowledge, founded in fact." It was Bacon who first "opened a wider field" and who perceived the "general Principles which ought to be fundamental in the study of Nature." And it was Bacon who "dared to form the design of rebuilding Science from the foundations which he had laid on the rock of Nature." Adams considered this last achievement to have been Bacon's greatest. Though his Lord Verulam "hinted at a great number of discoveries which have since been made," it was his reconstruction of science on the basis of a new method that marked his true greatness (*PJAM* Reel 188).

Descartes followed Bacon and was credited by Adams for opening "some courses in experimental Philosophy." But Adams was suspicious of Descartes for having admitted of "certain inward Sentiments of Evidence which it is not easy to comprehend and which may misguide Us in the conduct of the Understanding." He saw in Descartes the beginning of the hypothetico-deductive method. Adams did credit Descartes, though, with discovering certain principles in "Geometry and Algebra," if only because they "pointed out the path to Newton."

For Adams, as for almost every educated person of the eighteenth century, the development of modern science reached its zenith in the work of Sir Isaac Newton. Adams, however, was much less impressed with Newton's actual scientific discoveries than he was with Newton's formulation of a new conception of science, of its methods and modes of analysis. The Newtonian revolution was based, according to Adams, on "the Art of introducing Geometry and Algebra into natural Philosophy and by combining Experiment with Calculation." Adams maintained that Bacon rediscovered the method of induction but that Newton had subsequently applied the theory in brilliant fashion to astronomy and optics, thereby validating and extending its methodological premises. What Bacon had only suggested in the way of an experimental method, Adams saw as having been brought to fruition by Newton.

The last philosopher considered by Adams to have contributed to the development of this empirical science of nature was "Mr. Locke, whose Writings

demonstrated that all materials, the elements and Principles of human knowledge, are derived only from Experience and Analogy." Those who attempt to
read this "enlightened Phylosopher," Adams notes,

are Conducted through a Course of experimental Phylosophy, and are Shown that every
Sensation and every Reflection is an Experiment. There is a continual appeal to his own
Apprehensions, Judgements, Reasonings and Arrangements, and to his own Reflections
on his own Intellectual operations. He is perpetually [. . . .] to analyze his own Ideas and
Notions, to compare them with the nature of Things, to be accurate in his definitions
and steady and sincere in the use of words.   (*PJAM* Reel 188)

But how could the methods and the modes of reasoning peculiar to the natural sciences be applied to things political? What sort of political epistemology
should law-givers use and employ when designing constitutions? These were
the central questions for Adams.

In the very same way that Adams saw two methods of reasoning in the natural sciences, he also identified two modes of reasoning in the political sciences.
On the one hand, there was a tradition of political epistemology – a tradition he
often identified with Plato, Rousseau, Paine, and Condorcet – that built political systems on the basis of "Imagination, Hypothesis [and] Conjecture" (*PJAM*
Reel 188).[11] The tradition of political science that Adams felt the greatest kinship with, however, is best seen in an April 1814 letter to John Taylor, where he
explicitly states that he had fortified himself in the *Defence* behind the writings
of "Aristotle, Livy, Sidney, Harrington, Dr. Price, Machiavel, Montesquieu,
Swift, &c." (*WoJA* 6:492). To that list he might well have added Cicero,
Polybius, and David Hume, all of whom he mentioned on separate occasions
as having influenced his theory of political architecture.[12]

The pivotal figure here is Machiavelli. In the same way that Adams credits
Bacon with having recovered a methodological tradition in the natural sciences
reaching back to classical antiquity, he also claimed that the "world" was "much
indebted" to Machiavelli "for the revival of *reason* in matters of government."
Machiavelli was for Adams a kind of missing link, an important bridge between
the political science of the ancient world and the empirical political tradition
of the modern age (*WoJA* 5:95, emphasis added). Adams thought Machiavelli
the central figure in the resurrection of an empirico-inductive tradition of
political science. It is no small coincidence and should be kept in mind that
Bacon – the man Adams described as having "introduced a new science" based
on a "revived Method which had been practised in Antiquity" – thought the best
method for the political sciences was "that which Machiavel chose wisely and
aptly for government; namely, *discourse upon histories or examples*" (*WoFB*
3:453).

---

[11] See JA to TJ, 28 June 1812 and 16 July 1814, in *AJL* 2:308–11, 434–9. See also JA to Benjamin
Rush, 19 September 1806, in *The Spur of Fame: Dialogues of John Adams and Benjamin Rush,
1805–1813*, ed. John A. Schutz and Douglass Adair (San Marino, CA: Huntington Library,
1966), 65–6.

[12] See *WoJA* 4:294–6, 435–45, and JA to Samuel Adams, 18 October 1790, in *WoJA* 6:415.

But Machiavelli – certainly the Machiavelli of the *Prince* – would seem to be an odd candidate, at least from the perspective of a revolutionary republican, for the honor of being crowned the "restorer of true politics." What could Adams have meant by this? At the very least, he probably meant to say that Machiavelli had resurrected in his *Discourses on Livy* the constitutional tradition of mixed government associated with Sparta, Carthage, and Rome. That he would describe Machiavelli as having restored *"reason"* in the matters of government suggests that he meant something more. In all likelihood, it was the Florentine statesman's methodological approach to the political sciences that impressed Adams.

Machiavelli began the *Discourses* by identifying his audience and by describing his purpose in writing. His book was intended to guide a certain kind of man (that is, young men of merit worthy of governing) toward the knowledge necessary to found, perpetuate, or reform civic institutions. He planned to share with this audience his "long practice and a continual reading" into the course of human affairs. In particular, he would provide his readers with a "true knowledge of histories" (*D* Ep. Ded., 1.pref., 3.43).[13] A certain kind of reasoning about political things was a key element in Machiavelli's political philosophy and reform project.

The *Discourses* are written in the form of a commentary on Livy's history of ancient Rome. It empirically observes and analyzes the policies and actions of Rome's rulers and citizens between 753 and 293 B.C. Machiavelli recounts the events, persons, and processes by which Rome was formed and brought to greatness, and he charts the causes for its decline. To that end, he examines the evolution of Rome's constitution, its political institutions and military organization, its internal dissensions and external growth, and the virtues and vices of its greatest statesmen and soldiers. In this way, Machiavelli's modes of reasoning are very different, for instance, from those found in Plato's *Republic*, Hobbes's *Leviathan*, or Rousseau's *Social Contract*. The *Discourses*, the *Florentine Histories*, and even *The Prince* employ a method that seems much closer to that of Aristotle (*Pol.* 1260b27–1261a9) and the classical historians, Polybius (1.1.36) in particular. Adams credits Machiavelli's political science, like Bacon's natural science, with initiating a revolution by resurrecting a certain kind of classical political reasoning.

At the heart of Machiavelli's political science was a methodological approach that encouraged the political scientist to study man as he really *is* rather than as he *ought* to be, and history provides the best way to examine man as he is (*P* 15). This "scienza nuova" excised metaphysical and theological considerations from its approach. Armed with this rule of procedure, Machiavelli claimed to have introduced "new modes and orders" as dangerous to discover as "unknown waters and lands." He claimed to have opened "a path as yet untrodden by anyone" (*D* 1.pref.).

---

[13] See the prologue of this book.

But how does the explorer find his way in uncharted seas? In the very same way that developments in the navigational sciences permitted Columbus to explore unknown seas and continents and that advances in the optical sciences magnified Galileo's sight, so it was Machiavelli's development and application of a new political science, a new constitutional compass, that permitted the constitutional pilot to chart new seas and to discover lost and forgotten worlds. Machiavelli's political science examined the histories of states, ancient and modern. These political bodies or social organisms he called "mixed bodies," which, like "all worldly things have a limit to their life." Feigning a kind of decayed Aristotelianism, Machiavelli said of these "mixed bodies" that they have a natural course, a telos, "ordered for them by heaven." But the history of most regimes demonstrated that their lives had been unusually short. Very few republics had run their entire course and fulfilled their natural end. This was because most republics throughout history had allowed their constitutional forms and structures to become "disorder[ed]." Indeed, "in everything," Machiavelli said, "some evil is concealed that makes new accidents emerge" (D 3.1, 11).

Just as Newton established certain *"Regulae Philosophandi"* in the natural sciences, Machiavelli prescribed certain *"regola generale"* for rulers, legislators, and students of political science. After studying how men really do live, the fundamental axiom on which Machiavelli built his science of politics was the premise that human nature has always been and is everywhere the same. Man was the same in pagan Greece as he is in Christian Florence. In the thirty-ninth chapter of the first book of the *Discourses*, Machiavelli established the primary *"regola generale"* that guided his approach to politics:

Whoever considers present and ancient things easily knows that in all cities and in all peoples there are the same desires and the same humors, and there always have been. So it is an easy thing for whoever examines past things diligently to foresee future things in every republic and to take the remedies for them that were used by the ancients, or, if they do not find any that were used, to think up new ones through the similarity of accidents. But because these considerations are neglected or not understood by whoever reads, or, if they are understood, they are not known to whoever governs, it follows that there are always the same scandals in every time.

The historical observation of all states, Machiavelli argued, demonstrates that men and governments do not change "their motion, order, and power" (D 1.pref., 39). Thus the natural state of human affairs, according to Machiavelli, is to be in perpetual "motion," which always is in one of two directions: States are either healthy and ascending, or they are cancerous and declining. Countries may differ entirely from one another in their manners and mores, but they are all rising or falling according to the same laws of nature (D 2.pref.). What was most obvious to Machiavelli, even from a superficial examination of world history and the events of his own day, was that states seem to follow a regular pattern of relative health and growth, followed by internal decay and eventual decline.

Because of the uniformity and constancy of human nature, history can provide the political scientist with a kind of laboratory in which to observe and compare the nature, origin, and course of all governments. The world of ancient Rome provided Machiavelli with an experimental field for the verification of phenomena observed in his own time. If social and political phenomena could be reduced to a few basic elements and if their constituent parts do not substantially change over time, the student of politics should be able to discern certain patterns in the history of government that are fundamental and repeating. It would be possible, therefore, for the political scientist to establish from an observation of certain political phenomena rules intrinsic to the nature of political development.

By collecting and collating a wide variety of observable political phenomena and by analyzing the way consequences proceed from certain causes in political life and human nature, Machiavelli thought he had found the key to establishing a universally valid political science. History for Machiavelli – and for the entire empirical tradition – was not progressing toward some ideal state of perfection. Despite all of the changes and upheaval known in human history, the rise and fall of states follow a familiar and recurring order. Machiavelli thought the lessons of the past are therefore applicable to the present and the future. On this view of human nature and history, he was able to claim for political science the ability to draw valid generalizations or rules for governing and constitution-making and the power to predict the future of most governments. By taking human nature as always and everywhere the same and by studying history as the social phenomena of the political scientists' empirical observations, Machiavelli laid the basic groundwork for a style of historical writing and a mode of political science that would develop over the course of the next three centuries (*D* 3.43).[14]

Among the modern students of the Machiavellian political science was Bolingbroke. In his *Letters on the Study and Use of History* (1738), Bolingbroke developed and extended the insights of Machiavelli's empirical political science. Bolingbroke self-consciously attempted to develop a science or philosophy of history that would uncover the underlying rules and principles that exemplified "the invariable nature of things." Such principles are discoverable by induction from historical example. "He who studies history as he would philosophy," Bolingbroke wrote, "will soon distinguish and collect them, and by doing so will soon form to himself a general system of ethics and politics on the surest foundations, on the trial of these principles and rules in all ages, and on the confirmation of them by universal experience" (*WoLB* 2:193–4).

---

[14] On the development of the historical sciences as a part of the empirical study of politics, see Carl Becker, *The Heavenly City of the Eighteenth-Century Philosophers* (New Haven, CT: Yale University Press, 1932); Ernst Cassirer, *The Philosophy of the Enlightenment* (Boston: Beacon Press, 1951); Herbert Davis, "The Augustan Conception of History," in *Reason and Imagination: Studies in the History of Ideas, 1600–1800*, ed. J. A. Mazzeo (New York: Columbia University Press, 1962), 213–29.

Bolingbroke's science of history extended and deepened the empirical approach to politics. The statesman's study of the past, Bolingbroke argued, must encompass the experience of as wide a variety of actors and events as is possible: "History, therefore, of all kinds, of civilised and uncivilised, of ancient and modern nations, in short, all history that descends to a sufficient detail of human actions and characters, is useful to bring us acquainted with our species, nay, with ourselves." Historical study provides man with a "map of the country," by which "to guide ourselves." According to Bolingbroke, history provided men with an empirical basis for moral and political action. By history, though, Bolingbroke did not mean the antiquarian collection of facts, nor did he mean the recitation of events and heroic deeds for imitation. The ultimate goal of history was to dig beneath the surface for the "immediate and remote causes" of events. Here, at the level of cause and effect, history becomes "philosophy teaching by examples." The ultimate goal of history, then, was to "reduce all the abstract speculations of ethics, and all the general rules of human policy, to their first principles" (*WoLB* 2:191, 222–3, 229–30). This was a philosophy of history that John Adams could take hold of and apply to his science of politics.[15]

On the title page of his personal set of Enrico Caterino Davila's *Historia delle guerre civili di Francia*, Adams copied from Bolingbroke's fifth letter *On the Study and Use of History* a passage describing one of the principal purposes for which philosophers and statesmen could use history:

Man is the subject of every history; and to know him well, we must see him and consider him, as history alone can present him to us, in every age, in every country, in every state, in life and in death. History, therefore, of all kinds, of civilised and uncivilised, of ancient and modern nations, in short, all history that descends to a sufficient detail of human actions and characters, is useful to bring us acquainted with our species, nay, with ourselves.   (*WoLB* 2:229–30)

This entry provides an important clue as to the nature and purpose of Adams's own *Discourses on Davila*. At the end of the first discourse, Adams interrupted Davila's historical narrative to turn his readers' thoughts "for a few moments to the constitution of the human mind" (*WoJA* 6:232). He then follows with a lengthy discussion of human nature over the next eleven chapters.

Historians have often wondered why Adams chose the writings of an obscure Italian historian as the basis of a political treatise published for an American audience in the 1790s. What was his point in using Davila's *History*? Were Adams's *Discourses* on Davila's *Historia delle guerre civili di Francia* written in

---

[15] That Adams was greatly influenced by Bolingbroke can be little doubted. In his *Autobiography*, Adams mentions that when he went to Worcester in 1756 to begin teaching Latin at the local public school, he carried with him "Lord Bolingbroke's Study and Use of History, and His Patriot King"; see *Diary and Autobiography of John Adams*, ed. L. H. Butterfield (Cambridge, MA: Harvard University Press, 1962), 3:264. Adams' *Diary* is full of references to Bolingbroke; see *Diary and Autobiography*, 1:11–12, 35–6, 38, 40, 73, 176, 200, 2:386, 3:272. See also JA to TJ, 25 December 1813, in *AJL* 2:410.

self-conscious imitation of Machiavelli's *Discourses* on Livy's *History of Rome*? The answers to these questions are found in Bolingbroke.

Adams, like Bolingbroke, did not study history randomly; he did not think all histories or chronicles equally good, nor did he simply study the events of history for their imitative value. History for Adams and Bolingbroke meant something much more. We can only surmise what Adams learned from his reading of Bolingbroke, but it does seem likely that he was shaken from his historical slumbers when he read the famous fifth letter from *The Study and Use of History*. For it was here that Bolingbroke would have taught Adams that "Naked facts, without the causes that produced them, and the circumstances that accompanied them, are not sufficient to characterise actions and councils." It was important, therefore, for statesmen to examine and compare the works of different historians. Some obviously would be preferable to others in that they illuminated a deeper level of the human experience. The one historian recommended by Bolingbroke, the one who had achieved this higher purpose, was the "noble historian" Enrico Caterino Davila. Our plot thickens when we learn that Bolingbroke thought Davila's work "equal in many respects to Livy" (*WoLB* 2:228–9).

There can be little doubt that Bolingbroke's recommendation of the Italian historian influenced Adams. According to Bolingbroke, Davila had been suspected "of too much refinement and subtlety." He had been accused of penetrating "the secret motives of actions," and "in laying the causes of events too deep" (*WoLB* 2:228–9).[16] But it was precisely this quality that recommended Davila to Bolingbroke and Adams, and it was this quality that linked Davila with his near contemporary Machiavelli in the mind of John Adams. In his commentary on Machiavelli's *Florentine Histories* in the second volume of the *Defence*, Adams quotes Machiavelli to the effect that, "'The most useful erudition for republicans is that which exposes the causes of discord; by which they may learn wisdom and unanimity from the examples of others'" (*WoJA* 5:11). Adams was most interested in historians like Machiavelli and Davila – that is, those who sought to find the remote causes of events, causes that were "too deep" for most historians to see. Adams chose historical narratives such as Machiavelli's *Florentine Histories* and Davila's *Historia delle guerre civili di Francia* precisely because they sought to "'unravel the secret springs'" that govern the political life of all nations. In fact, all the historians and philosophers that Adams uses in the *Defence* – Polybius, Dionysius Halicarnassus, and even Plato[17] – could

---

[16] See John E. Paynter, "The Ethics of John Adams: Prolegomenon to a Science of Politics" (Ph.D. dissertation, University of Chicago, 1974), 97–101.

[17] Given this methodological standard – the heavy emphasis on experience and history as opposed to rationalism and philosophy – some may wonder why Adams would quote in the *Defence* so approvingly from Plato's *Republic*. The vast bulk of Adams's quotations from Plato is drawn from the eighth and ninth books. It is here that Plato describes the rise and fall of all pure forms of government into their corrupt forms. What impressed Adams was not Plato's unique, noncyclical theory of regime change, but rather his account of the reasons, the underlying causes of this change: "Plato has given us the most accurate detail of the natural vicissitudes of manners

be said to have fulfilled to a greater or lesser degree this necessary historical criterion. Indeed, their selection for inclusion in the *Defence* was intimately linked with their ability to get beneath the surface of social phenomena (*WoJA* 5:11, 6:365). In contrast to the theories of philosophes like Condorcet, Adams described the *Defence* as "an attempt to place Government upon the only Philosophy which can ever support it, the real constitution of human nature, not upon any wild Visions of its perfectibility." Thus, paraphrasing Bolingbroke, Adams could write that "History is philosophy and policy teaching by example – every history must be founded in philosophy and some policy."[18]

Reviving the "Ancient Politics"

Not only did Machiavelli revive and apply certain ancient modes of reasoning to political questions, but he was also the first, according to Adams, to have "revived the ancient politics" (*WoJA* 4:559). After centuries of the canon and feudal systems, Machiavelli initiated a revolution in the political sciences first to restore and then improve upon the republican political institutions of the ancient world. In particular, Machiavelli resurrected the theory of the mixed constitution, which subsequently enjoyed a renewed intellectual and political respectability in English political theory and practice.

There were, according to Adams, three periods in English history when "the principles of government" had been intensively studied. The first period, that of the Reformation, began with Machiavelli's restoration of what Adams called the "true politics" or the political theory of the mixed regime. The Florentine's prescriptions for mixed government were imported into England via John Poynet's "Short Treatise of Politicke Power," published in 1556. The second period, that of the Interregnum between 1640 and 1660, saw the publication of James Harrington's *Commonwealth of Oceana* (1656). The third period, that of the Glorious Revolution, produced Algernon Sidney, John Locke, Benjamin Hoadley, John Trenchard, Thomas Gordon, and Plato Redivivus (*WoJA* 6:3–4).

With the revolution in political philosophy that attended these three periods came a restored appreciation for "the essential principles of liberty" and the theory of mixed government. Adams had no doubt that it was Machiavelli who had "revived the ancient politics," thereby provoking the modern revolution in political thought. John Milton, Harrington, and Sidney, according to Adams, "were intimately acquainted with the ancients and with Machiavel." Adams identified Locke as a student of the Machiavellian tradition, and "Montesquieu," Adams charged, "borrowed the best part of his book from Machiavel, without acknowledging the quotation" (*WoJA* 4:559, 6:4).

---

and principles, the usual progress of the passions in society, and revolutions of governments into one another." See *WoJA* 4:448.

[18] See JA to Rev. De Walter, October, 1797, *PJAM* Reel 119; JA to Francis Adrian Vanderkemp, 20 April 1812, *PJAM* Reel 118.

Adams begins the second volume of the *Defence* with a running commentary on books two through seven of Machiavelli's *Florentine Histories*. The general purpose of this commentary is to demonstrate to Americans how governments resembling Turgot's democratic theory of "All Authority in one Centre" had actually worked in history. More to the point, Adams's Machiavellian commentary will teach future constitution-makers and statesmen how to study history in order to uncover the true causes of political conflict. Machiavelli's history, like Davila's history of the French civil wars, provided Adams with an experimental laboratory in which to see the cause and effect relationship between constitutional organization and human action. As we have already seen, Adams recommended Machiavelli's political science to potential constitution-makers because it exposed "'the causes of discord.'" The *Florentine Histories*, according to Adams, are "full of lessons of wisdom, extremely to our purpose." That purpose was to demonstrate "that the predominant passion of all men in power, whether kings, nobles, or plebeians, is the same; that tyranny will be the effect, whoever are the governors, whether the one, the few, or the many." Adams will also demonstrate, as a counter factual, how a constitutional order that institutionalized "equal laws, made by common consent, and supported, protected, and enforced by three different orders of men *in equilibrio*," could have ended the continual revolutions between "tyranny and anarchy" that characterized the government of Florence in the years between 1215 and 1492 (*WoJA* 5:5, 9–11). Thus begins Adams's subtle and important criticism or revision of Machiavelli.

The Florence chronicled by Machiavelli is in a state of constant civil disorder. The internecine battles between noble families, followed by the never-ending conflicts between the nobles and commons and then commons and plebeians, had left Florence in a state of constant political stasis. Machiavelli's history was useful for Adams's purposes because it clearly demonstrated to Americans that "it may be seen and considered that human nature is the same in a mob as upon a throne, and that unbridled passions are at least as brutal and diabolical, and unlimited power as tyrannical, in a mob, as in a monarch or senate." Indeed, Adams warns, "they are worse, for there is always a number among them who are under less restraints of shame and decency." Adams was in complete agreement with Machiavelli that the human passions most relevant to political life – aristocratic ambition and democratic envy – can be studied and "carefully traced" in order to observe their operation in political affairs (*WoJA* 5:11, 19). But Adams breaks with Machiavelli at this point.

According to Adams, Machiavelli had "an accurate idea of the evil" that bedeviled Florence, but he was thoroughly "confused" as to how to "remedy" the problem. Adams and Machiavelli seem to agree that human nature is "utterly incapable" of contentment and moderation, and both agreed that it "is action, not rest, that constitutes our pleasure." They both understood that faction was the cancer that ruined Florence. Equally important, Adams credits the Florentine with knowing something of the remedy to the problems of Florence, that is, Adams knew that Machiavelli was as "clear and full for a mixed government as any writer." And yet Adams thought there was a "mist" before Machiavelli's eyes – "eyes so piercing, so capable of looking far through the hearts and deeds of men" (*WoJA* 5:39–40, 44, 66).[19]

Machiavelli, according to Adams, did not fully understand or explain the causes that kept Florence in a state of perpetual revolution. Throughout the *Histories*, Machiavelli attempted to explain why certain uprisings occurred at a particular time. Every factional conflict seemed unrelated to the previous one because new characters were fighting for new prizes. Machiavelli therefore blames one conflict on the " 'the restless ambition ' " of the nobleman Corso Donati. In comparing how the factional feuding of Florence differed from that of ancient Rome, Machiavelli attributed his city's problems to its destiny or to *fortuna*. At another place, he blames the battles in Florence on the " 'iniquity of the times' " (*WoJA* 5:29–30, 42–5, 48). In other words, it was the ceaseless ambition or envy of certain individuals or factions in ever-changing social contexts that metabolized or unleashed a destructive solvent common to all regimes because it is inherent in human nature. Despite his great admiration for Machiavelli and the *Florentine Histories*, Adams criticized Machiavelli in the end for reducing the civil dissensions of Florence simply to the inconstancy and insatiability of the human passions operating in a world of *fortuna*.

Adams found Machiavelli's analysis of the destruction of Florence ultimately incomplete. Corso, or any other quarrelsome or ambitious individual, should not be blamed for the problems of Florence. "If Corso had not existed," Adams retorted, "the people would have found some other leader and confidant." There will always be men like Corso, and there will always be times when the people will "seek of Cassius, Mælius, Manlius, or Corso" aid and protection against the "oppressions of nobles." Likewise, the destiny or problems that Machiavelli claimed "peculiar" to Florence were, from Adams's vantage, "common to every city, nation, village, and club." The political scientist should not, according to Adams, blame *fortuna* or the inconstancy of human nature for the peculiar problems that bedeviled Florence. "Why should the people be deceived with insinuations that those evils arose from the destiny of a particular city," asked Adams, "when we know that destiny is common to all mankind" (*WoJA* 5:29, 45).

The critical moment in Machiavelli's history, according to Adams, occurred sometime around 1282, when, after the failure of two still-born constitutions (the so-called *Anziani* and *Buoni Homini* constitutions), the Florentines constructed a third that was the primary cause of the city's never-ending fluctuation between tyranny and anarchy. This new constitution, later to be called the *signori*, "huddled together" in one general body the one *(buoni Homini)*, the few *(credenza)* and the many (great council) with a balancing counterweight in the form of a second assembly confirming the laws of the first. The problem with this constitution was that "the aristocratical and democratical parts of the community were mixed in each" of the two bodies. The result, according to Adams, was that there could never be "harmony in either, both being

---

[19] See also NM, *D* 1.pref.

naturally split into two factions." But the greatest defect in the Florentine constitution was its provision of executive power (the power of disposing of public
honors and offices) to the mongrelized great council. It was an inevitable consequence, observed Adams, that the two councils would immediately divide into
factions for "loaves and fishes." In the end, however, it would be the nobility,
because of their superior electoral influence, that would dominate and control the entire government. But their control of the government could never be
hegemonic or uniform. Two mixed assemblies controlled by the nobility would
soon turn into a "mere football continually kicked from one side to another
by three or four principal families." From this moment forward, Adams told
his readers, "Unhappy Florence" would be destined "to never-ending factions,
seditions, and civil wars!" (*WoJA* 5:17–18, 26). And so it was. The remainder
of Machiavelli's history recorded by Adams walks the reader through more
than two hundred years of perpetual civil war.

The ultimate cause, then, of Florence's instability was intimately connected
to her flawed constitutional design. Mankind's ambitious and envious nature
is a given, according to Adams, but should not be blamed solely for a state of
recurring political and social conflict. Adams thought that Machiavelli should
have "laid the blame upon the constitution" rather than on the restless spirit of
the nobility or on the shoulders of a particular individual. Adams noted over and
over again throughout his commentary on the *Histories* that "It is the defect in
the government and the wants of the people, that excite and inspirit the ambition
of private men." And the temper of the people is the "natural and necessary
effect" of an improperly framed constitution. In his strongest statement on this
question, Adams corrected Machiavelli's "essential mistakes." Only properly
designed constitutions could restrain the ambition and envy common to all
people everywhere. Without such a restraint,

ambition cannot be prevented; nature has planted it in every heart. The factions of their
ancestors ought not to have been imputed to the iniquity of the times, for all times
and places are so iniquitous. Those factions grew out of the nature of men under such
forms of government; and the new form ought to have been so contrived as to produce
a remedy for the evil. This might have been done; for there is a way of making laws
more powerful than any particular persons or families. (*WoJA* 5:29–30, 48–9)[20]

At one place we find Adams heartily agreeing with Machiavelli that "'All
republics, especially such as are not well constituted, undergo frequent changes
in their laws and manner of government.'" But he considers inadequate
Machiavelli's explanation that the cause of these frequent constitutional
changes was due to "'downright oppression on one hand, or unbridled licentiousness on the other.'" On one level, Adams could agree with Machiavelli that
oppression and license are the known or obvious causes of political instability

---

[20] Adams's interpretation of the *Florentine Histories* should be read in the light of what Machiavelli says in the *Discourses on Livy* of the cause and effect relationship between the Roman
constitution and that city's good laws, good education, and good examples. See NM, D 1.4.

and constitutional degeneration. But for Adams there are deeper causes standing behind oppression and license. In fact, what are causes for Machiavelli turn out to be effects for Adams. The true cause of faction and party violence is a flawed or ill-designed constitution that serves as a host body for those passions destructive of civil society. Conversely, a well-designed constitution might serve as a filter through which the malignancies that destroy constitutions could be controlled and even directed toward the public good. Machiavelli would have come much closer to the truth had he "imputed all these evils to their true cause," namely, "an imperfect and unbalanced constitution of government" (*WoJA* 5:66, 82).

Machiavelli's mistake from Adams's perspective was that he did not have a clear enough idea of the institutional arrangements necessary to establish good government. The modern constitutional principles devised by the English and perfected by the Americans – representations, instead of collections of the people; a total separation of the executive from the legislative power, and of the judicial from both; and a balance in the legislature, by three independent, equal branches – were thought by Adams the necessary if not the sufficient conditions by which to arrest constitutional revolutions permanently (*WoJA* 4:284). Indeed, he thought it possible to channel the passions in such a way that they could be exploited to serve the public good:

When the three natural orders in society, the high, middle, and the low, are all represented in the government, and constitutionally placed to watch each other, and restrain each other mutually by the laws, it is then only, that an emulation takes place for the public good, and divisions turn to the advantage of the nation.   (*WoJA* 5:90)

Although Machiavelli was an advocate of mixed government and was the catalyst for its revival in modern times, he did not understand, according to Adams, what would later come to be the modern invention of a "separate executive, with power to defend itself" as the means of remedying the "fatal effects of dissensions between nobles and commons." Ironically, Adams criticizes Machiavelli for not understanding the nature and importance of a single executive with a legislative veto. Such an idea, Adams says, "seems never to have entered his thoughts" (*WoJA* 5:44–5).

At one point in the *Histories*, Adams thought Machiavelli was about to stumble on the solution of an independent executive, armed with the whole executive power and a legislative veto, as a sufficient means by which "to mediate, at all times, between the nobles and the commons." The Florentine had said what Adams thought to be "near the truth" – namely, that the separate interests of the few and the many must be harmonized by the "'spirit and fortune of one man alone.'" But this was insufficient to the hyperlegal mind of this New England constitutionalist. Machiavelli would have come closer to the truth of the matter had he said that "parties must be upheld together by the constitutional, legal authority of one man alone." In its legislative capacity, an independent executive intervening between the few and the many could help to foster or direct partisan or partial claims toward the common good and the pursuit of fully just laws. In its executive capacity, a well-armed single magistrate could "preserve the energy of the laws" that is absolutely necessary to retain the loyalty and attachment of the regime's best citizens. As long as the people's representatives retained control of the purse, the making of laws, and "the inquest of grievances, abuses, and state crimes," Adams thought the passions peculiar to those who sit in executive power could likewise be tamed and directed toward the public good (*WoJA* 5:67–8).

Adams applauded Machiavelli for having been a defender (albeit a flawed one) of the mixed form of government. The Florentine statesman's great failing, however, was that he had been an insufficient advocate of a "fixed" constitution. As Adams knew from his reading of the *Discourses on Livy*, Machiavelli preferred Romulus' incomplete or evolutionary founding of Rome to the perfect or complete Lycurgan founding of Sparta. Machiavelli believed that the great success of the Roman constitution was a consequence of its having institutionalized and tamed over time the conflict between the few and the many. As a mixed government, the Roman Republic was better able to withstand the forces that spark and perpetuate the cycle of revolution common to all regimes. The tension between nobles and plebeians fueled both the internal health and external growth of the republic. In the end, however, Machiavelli's Roman constitution relied on supraconstitutional (for example, the Dictator) or extraordinary political means (for example, the terror inspired by periodic refoundings) to prevent decay and degeneration. Because Machiavelli thought it "'impossible'" for any "'legislator or founder of a republic entirely to prevent feuds and animosities in it, it ought to be his chief care to provide against their growing into factions'" (*WoJA* 5:89). This Rome did by institutionalizing a variety of political devices or safety valves, such as public accusations. For Machiavelli, there was not and could not be a founding moment that permanently and unalterably fixed a nation's constitutional order. Civic health almost always meant a periodic return to the insecurity and original terror associated with first foundings. But only the form (the primeval state of necessity) and never the substance (the constitution) of the founding could be restored. One of the principal purposes of *The Prince*, therefore, was to instruct present and future rulers on how and when to induce, re-create, or respond to a state of crisis or fear. At the same time, of course, Machiavelli was rearming his reforming provocateurs with new modes and orders, training them in the proper use of violence and coercion (*D* 3.1, 22, 30).

Adams, on the other hand, thought it possible and best to establish a perpetual or nearly perfect constitution at one founding moment. He would have learned from Aristotle, Plutarch, Harrington, and even from Rousseau that building a new regime required a deliberate founding at a special point in time. Adams therefore called on the Americans to "begin right" their experiment in revolutionary constitution–making (*WoJA* 4:298, 587). This meant, of course, that he put a much higher premium on the ability of a single law-giver or a special constitutional convention to design a "fixed" or written constitution that would, at one moment in time, mix and balance *in equilibrio* the one, the few, and the many. Quoting Jonathan Swift's *Discourse of the Contests and Dissensions between the Nobles and Commons of Athens and Rome*, Adams could write in the *Defence* that "some physicians have thought, that if it were practicable to keep several humors of the body in an exact *balance* of each with its opposite, it might be immortal; and so perhaps would a political body, if the *balance of power* could be always held exactly even" (*WoJA* 4:384–5).

The difficult question for Adams and America's revolutionary founders was how to make this fundamental law higher law – that is, how to distinguish it from statutory law or the arbitrary rule of a Machiavellian prince. Their answer was to develop procedures and institutions – such as special constituting and ratifying conventions – that would separate and elevate constitutions above ordinary acts of legislation. On this crucial question of first foundings, Machiavelli's model law-giver was Romulus, whose founding act was shrouded under the veil of divine fraud and the immoral violence of fratricide, while for Adams, America's founding moment was impressive for its having rejected force and fraud in the name of reflection and choice (cf. NM, *D* 1.9 with *WoJA* 4:291–4).

Conclusion

John Adams's Machiavellian moment was a crucial event in the development of his political theory. Adams learned from and thought Machiavelli's teachings important and useful for American constitution-makers, but they were also valuable as a negative example of insufficient or flawed reasoning. Adams's commentary on Machiavelli was intended to revive but ultimately to surpass Machiavelli's new modes and orders.

The study of history provided for both a kind of laboratory in which certain laws of nature or human action could be discovered. Adams and Machiavelli agreed that history demonstrated human nature to be unchanging and everywhere the same, and that it is driven by powerful passions – aristocratic pride and democratic envy being the two most important. On that basis, they could also agree that the history of all societies is roughly the same, that all societies fall into repeating patterns of growth and decay. Latent in all societies because latent in human nature are forces of dissension that set in motion certain recurring processes of degeneration and decline.

Adams and Machiavelli parted company, however, over the important question of how to prevent or withstand the natural forces of social conflict. As John Adams read Machiavelli, the Florentine statesman's solution to this problem was inadequate. Machiavelli understood and appreciated the need for mixed government, but his teaching on that subject was incomplete. From Adams's perspective, the Florentine did not fully know what would come to be the modern teaching of the separation of powers and did not understand the need to mix and balance in the legislative branch the one, the few, and the many.

Machiavelli was much more pessimistic or fatalistic than Adams as to whether the cycle of revolution could be arrested (*D* 1.49, 3.39). And because

Machiavelli thought *fortuna* an omnipresent force in human affairs, his solution was *political*. Machiavelli therefore wrote for those who govern, those who conduct the affairs of state – princes, administrators, and diplomats. His are maxims, derived from experience and history, for rule. Machiavellian *virtù* would provide temporary embankments and dikes against the unpredictable and uncontrollable forces of human nature. His books would everywhere and forever be relevant and useful to those who govern.

John Adams, however, did think it possible to end the cycle. Permanent embankments and dikes could be established to withhold and diffuse nature's fury, even channeling it toward the public good. Adams's solution was therefore *constitutional*. That is why he put a much greater emphasis than did Machiavelli on the idea and importance of a "founding." To that end, Adams wrote for a much smaller audience: He wrote the *Defence* as a guidebook for law-givers or constitution-makers. The principal purpose of the *Defence* is the education of the law-giver. When viewed in this light, the *Defence* becomes something more than just the anomalous, antirepublican tract of a disordered mind described by modern historians; it may be seen now as a new and positive contribution to a trans-Atlantic debate over the science of politics in revolutionary societies.

9

Thomas Jefferson's Machiavellian Political Science

Paul A. Rahe

It would be easy to argue that Thomas Jefferson owed next to nothing to Niccolò Machiavelli. The Virginian was exceedingly erudite, and he was keenly interested in the education of the young. On more than one occasion, he took care in outlining a course of study for a protégé. But, in doing so, he never saw fit to include on his list of recommended books *The Prince*, the *Discourses on Livy*, the *Florentine Histories*, *The Art of War*, or any of Machiavelli's lesser works.[1] Indeed, in his only book, the *Notes on the State of Virginia*, in his public writings and speeches, and in his letters, he mentions the Florentine but once – and then only to denounce a wayward colleague in the Continental Congress. Regarding John Francis Mercer, in a letter written to James Madison in early May 1784, Jefferson had nothing good to say: "*He is very mischievous. He is under no moral restraint. If he avoids shame he avoids wrong according to his system.* His fondness for *Machiavel* is *genuine* and founded on a true *harmony* of *principle*" (*PTJ* 7:228). Jefferson's allusion to Machiavelli's reliance on appearances suggests that he had both read *The Prince* and assimilated the critique of virtue elaborated in chapters fifteen through eighteen.[2] That he had not adopted as his own the advice proffered therein by the connoisseur of cunning is evident as well.

---

[1] See, for example, TJ to Robert Skipwith, 3 August 1771; to Peter Carr, 19 August 1785 and 10 August 1787; to John Garland Jefferson, 11 June 1790, in *PTJ* 1:76–81, 8:405–8, 12:14–19, 16:480–2. See also TJ to John Minor, 30 August 1814 (with enclosure), in *WrTJ* (ed. Ford) 9:480–5.

[2] On the argument that Machiavelli presents in these chapters, see Clifford Orwin, "Machiavelli's Unchristian Charity," *APSR* 72:4 (December 1978): 1217–28; Richard H. Cox, "Aristotle and Machiavelli on Liberality," in *The Crisis of Liberal Democracy*, ed. Kenneth L. Deutsch and Walter Soffer (Albany, NY: State University of New York Press, 1987) 125–47.

This essay was reworked while I was a Fellow of the National Endowment for the Humanities and the Woodrow Wilson International Center for Scholars in Washington, DC, in 1993–4. I am indebted to these two institutions for support. It is adapted from Paul A. Rahe, "Thomas Jefferson's Machiavellian Political Science," *RP* 57:3 (Summer 1995): 449–81, and reprinted here with permission. All translations are my own.

There was, of course, another Machiavelli who was less easily dismissed – the republican author of the *Discourses on Livy*.[3] And Jefferson was by no means unaware of his existence. In late July 1791, at a tumultuous moment in the midst of the French Revolution, the Chevalier de Pio wrote to his old friend from Paris, remarking, "Actually, before my eyes, I have none but Locke, Sidney, Milton, J. J. Rousseau, and Th. Payne; that is my entire library; I have burned the rest, except for *Machiavel*, whom all diplomats possess, though they dare not confess it, and whom free men ought to place alongside the *Declaration of Rights*" (*PTJ* 20:662–3). Jefferson may never have acknowledged or even recognized what his own republicanism owed to the thinking of this Machiavelli, but that he was as deeply in debt to the Florentine as was the Chevalier de Pio we need not doubt. One does not have to cite an author or, for that matter, even peruse his works to absorb something of his doctrine and to come under his sway. Many an artist and many a thinker echoed Rousseau in the nineteenth century without having studied him in depth or even read him at all, and the same can be said for Martin Heidegger in more recent times. Debts acquired at secondhand remain debts whether we are witting or not; and despite his well-earned reputation as a teacher of evil,[4] Machiavelli exercised a species of intellectual hegemony over republican thought in the eighteenth century exceeded by none but John Locke.

The character of that hegemony demands attention. In recent years, it has become common among scholars to speak of Machiavelli and Locke as if they represented rival and opposed traditions in political thought: Machiavelli is often depicted as a "civic humanist" or classical republican, and Locke is treated in turn as the paradigmatic liberal.[5] That the two were at odds on some important questions, such as the status of natural right, is clear enough, and this deserves considerable emphasis. But, at a deeper level, as Margaret Michelle Barnes Smith has made clear in the second chapter in this book, in repudiating Aristotle's understanding of the character of politics and its foundations in human nature and in rejecting all his putatively evil works, especially those of his Christian henchmen, they were in complete accord. Their dispute concerning the natural foundations of justice was a family quarrel as to the implications of a set of presumptions concerning the relationship between reason and passion that they both accepted; and insofar as the Machiavellian strain of republicanism remained a genuine force within the English-speaking world after the

---

[3] In this connection, see *Machiavelli and Republicanism*, ed. Gisela Bock, Quentin Skinner, and Maurizio Viroli (Cambridge, UK: Cambridge University Press, 1990).

[4] See Victoria Kahn, *Machiavellian Rhetoric: From the Counter-Reformation to Milton* (Princeton, NJ: Princeton University Press, 1994).

[5] See J. G. A. Pocock, "Virtue and Commerce in the Eighteenth Century," *Journal of Interdisciplinary History* 3:1 (Summer 1972): 119–34; *The Machiavellian Moment: Florentine Political Thought and the Atlantic Republican Tradition* (Princeton, NJ: Princeton University Press, 1975); "The Myth of John Locke and the Obsession with Liberalism," in *John Locke: Papers Read at a Clark Library Seminar, 10 December 1977*, ed. J. G. A. Pocock and Richard Ashcraft (Los Angeles: William Andrews Clark Memorial Library, 1980), 3–24.

Restoration of Charles II, it did so chiefly as an element integrated within, rather than as one excluded from and opposed to, the liberal republican thinking of Marchamont Nedham, James Harrington, Algernon Sidney, John Locke, John Wildman, Walter Moyle, John Toland, John Trenchard, Thomas Gordon, Lord Bolingbroke, David Hume, the baron de Montesquieu, James Burgh, William Blackstone, and the like.[6]

The Politics of Distrust

Politically, Machiavelli can perhaps best be described as a disciple of Heraclitus. As Markus Fischer points out in the prologue to this book, the foundation of his teaching concerning politics is his claim that "all the things of men are in motion and cannot remain fixed." By this he meant to convey something closely akin to what Thomas Hobbes (*Leviathan* I.iii.3–5, viii.14–16) and David Hume (*THN* II.iii) had in mind when they asserted that reason is the slave of the passions. As Machiavelli put it by way of explanation, "the human appetites" are "insatiable"; "by nature," human beings "desire everything," while "by fortune they are allowed to secure little"; and since "nature has created men in such a fashion" that they are "able to desire everything" but not "to secure everything," their "desire is always greater than the power of acquisition *(la potenza dello acquistare)*." As a consequence of accepting this doctrine, the Florentine dismissed as utopian the moral and political teachings advanced by his classical and Christian predecessors; and under its guidance, he rejected the Aristotelian doctrine of the mean, arguing that the pursuit of moderation is a species of folly, and contending that in a world in constant flux, there simply is not and cannot be "a middle road *(via del mezzo)*" (*D* 1.6, 37, 2.pref.). Instead of succumbing to the snares of moral reason and the moral imagination, he asserted, one must take one's bearings from an appreciation of what he termed, in an elegant turn of phrase, "the effectual truth of the matter." His position, which he slyly attributed to "all who reason concerning civic life *(vivere civile)*," was that anyone intent on setting up a republic and ordaining its laws must "presuppose that all men are wicked *(rei)* and that they will make use of the malignity of their spirit whenever they are free and have occasion to do so" (cf. *D* 1.3 with *P* 15).

By Jefferson's day, this premise had become the common wisdom of the age. In the mid-seventeenth century, as I have pointed out in the first chapter of this book, James Harrington elaborated a revolutionary, new, and thoroughly modern scheme of republican political architecture on the presumption that

---

[6] For an extended analysis of the character of Anglo-American republican thought in the early modern period, see Paul A. Rahe, *Republics Ancient and Modern: Classical Republicanism and the American Revolution* (Chapel Hill, NC: University of North Carolina Press, 1992), 231–782. See also Vickie B. Sullivan, *Machiavelli, Hobbes, and the Formation of a Liberal Republicanism in England* (New York: Cambridge University Press, 2004); Lee Ward, *The Politics of Liberty in England and Revolutionary America* (New York: Cambridge University Press, 2004); and Chapters 1 through 6 of this book.

Machiavelli had been correct in presuming human desire insatiate and that Hobbes was similarly right in concluding that reason is enslaved to the passions. In consequence, he joined Machiavelli and Hobbes in concluding that self-interested rule is the effectual truth of the matter. And in making these claims, he set the tone for constitutional prudence from his day through the American Revolution.

David Hume is a case in point, as John Danford has noted in the fourth chapter in this book. It is indicative of the moderate and skeptical pose that he cultivated that he should soften and smooth the rough edges of the doctrine that Harrington had adapted from Machiavelli and Hobbes while reasserting its substance in relation to politics. "Political writers have established it as a maxim," he observed,

that, in contriving any system of government, and fixing the several checks and controuls of the constitution, every man ought to be supposed a *knave*, and to have no other end, in all his actions, than private interest. By this interest we must govern him, and by means of it, make him, notwithstanding his insatiable avarice and ambition, co-operate to public good. Without this, say they, we shall in vain boast of the advantages of any constitution, and shall find, in the end, that we have no security for our liberties or possessions, except the good-will of our rulers; that is, we shall have no security at all.

Hume acknowledged that it might appear "somewhat strange, that a maxim should be true in *politics*, which is false in *fact*," but he contended nonetheless that it is "a just *political* maxim, *that every man must be supposed a knave*." He explained this paradox by drawing attention to the fact "that men are generally more honest in their private than in their public capacity." In defense of partisan principles and in pursuit of what they represent to themselves and others as the common good, they are willing to commit misdeeds that they would never even consider if acting simply and solely on their own behalf. It was, strangely enough, man's generous, public-spirited propensity for partisanship that rendered institutional checks of the sort devised by Harrington so essential to good government (*EMPL* 42–6, esp. 42–3).

I quote Hume's carefully hedged restatement of the Machiavellian and Hobbesian position at length because, in that form, it was exceedingly popular in America. The young Alexander Hamilton cited the passage with approbation in a pamphlet that he published in 1775 on the eve of the American Revolution (*PAH* 1:94–5). John Adams did the same in a letter written to his cousin Samuel in October 1790, at a time when the former was vice-president of the United States (*WoJA* 6:415). Moreover, in his massive, three-volume *Defence of the Constitutions of Government of the United States of America*, Adams not only expressed his approval of the claim, advanced in Machiavelli's *Discourses on Livy*, that a legislator must presume all men knaves, he demonstrated in detail that the same view was espoused by Thomas Hobbes, James Harrington, Bernard Mandeville, the baron de Montesquieu, Lord Bolingbroke, and Jean Louis de Lolme as well as by Joseph Priestley and Richard Price (*WoJA* 4:408–15, 556–8). He need not have stopped there. Few if any English Whigs and few

American patriots were inclined to challenge Montesquieu's claim that "every man who possesses power is driven to abuse it"; few doubted that such a man would "go forward until he discovers the limits" (*EL* 2.11.4). This was their common creed.

James Madison summed up the convictions of the great majority of his English-speaking contemporaries on both sides of the Atlantic in *The Federalist* when he remarked, "If men were angels, no government would be necessary. If angels were to govern men, neither external nor internal controuls on government would be necessary. In framing a government which is to be administered by men over men, the great difficulty lies in this: You must first enable the government to controul the governed; and in the next place, oblige it to controul itself" (*Fed.* 51). This was a presumption common to Federalists and Anti-Federalists alike: Like the earlier successors of James Harrington, they disputed concerning the political architecture appropriate to a modern republic but not about the political problem that this architecture was meant to address. Under the guidance of Machiavelli, Harrington, and the Whig writers of the seventeenth and eighteenth centuries, America's Whigs had become practitioners of what we might call "the politics of distrust."

Wolves and Sheep

Among those who accepted something like Madison's reformulation of Machiavelli's argument, Thomas Jefferson was arguably the most eloquent. During his sojourn as an American diplomat in Paris, he was persuaded that he had observed the consequences of this fundamental truth firsthand. In a well-known letter, written in January 1787 to his friend and fellow Virginian Edward Carrington, he observed that, in Europe, "under pretence of governing they have divided their nations into two classes, wolves and sheep." He feared that the same could only too easily happen in the infant republics in America. "Cherish therefore the spirit of our people, and keep alive their attention," he urged his correspondent. "Do not be too severe upon their errors, but reclaim them by enlightening them. If once they become inattentive to the public affairs, you and I, and Congress, and Assemblies, judges and governors shall all become wolves. It seems to be the law of our general nature, in spite of individual exceptions; and experience declares that man is the only animal which devours his own kind" (*PTJ* 11:48–50).

This particular observation owes more to Machiavelli than one might at first suppose. From his premise that the founder of a republic must operate on the presumption that all men are wicked, the Florentine drew a series of conclusions that astonished his contemporaries and that would have surprised the ancients at least as much: that classical Rome was as a republic Lacedaemon's superior, that in a republic the people are safer and better guardians of liberty than the nobles, and that Roman liberty was rooted in a salutary political turbulence. In Machiavelli's judgment, those whom Jefferson feared might turn into wolves and sheep are to be found wherever there is liberty. Those, he wrote, who are inclined to denounce political turmoil and to argue for social and political harmony "have not considered how it is that in every republic there are two diverse humors – that of the people, and that of the great ones *(grandi)* – and that all the laws that are made in favor of liberty are born from this disunion." He insisted that "good examples arise from good education, good education from good laws, and good laws from the tumults *(tumulti)* which many so inconsiderately condemn." To those who thought this last claim preposterous, he replied that "every city ought to have modes by which the people can vent their ambition," arguing that "the demands of a free people are seldom pernicious and rarely endanger their liberty: they arise from oppression or from the suspicions that they entertain that they are about to be oppressed; and when these opinions are false, there is a remedy in the public assemblies where a good man can stand up and, in speaking, demonstrate to the people that they are in error." The crucial fact, he insisted, which one has to keep always in mind, is that the people "have less of an appetite for usurpation" than the *grandi*; if one ponders the ends that "the nobles" pursue and those pursued by "the ignoble," one will recognize that the former's purposes arise from "a grand desire for domination" and the latter's "solely from a desire not to be dominated" – that the former "desire to acquire," while the latter "fear to lose what they have acquired" (*D* 1.4–5).[7]

Institutions vs. Tumults

Not all of Machiavelli's admirers shared his taste for *tumulti*. As I have noted in the first chapter of this book, the most influential of these dissenters was Thomas Hobbes, and in this particular James Harrington was his devoted disciple. Although he rejected the case for enlightened despotism advanced by the Malmesbury philosopher, Harrington was equally critical of Machiavelli's taste for political disorder. Where the Florentine had proposed to rely on the spirit of the people and their capacity to assert themselves through tumults as a constraint on abuse by the *grandi*, he looked to institutions. In promoting social and political harmony between what he called "the natural aristocracy" and "the natural democracy," where Machiavelli had purportedly failed, Harrington asserted that one might easily succeed – by establishing a bicameral legislature and consigning the representatives of the former to a deliberative assembly and those of the latter to a voting assembly called together to approve or disapprove the proposals advanced by this "natural aristocracy."

Thomas Jefferson read Harrington and borrowed his language. He, too, spoke of "the natural aristocracy," and in using that phrase, he referred to those of his compatriots with a potential for accomplishment that would enable them in the wrong circumstances to present themselves as "wolves." But if he honored Harrington for his recognition of the political problem posed by the

---

[7] See, in this connection, Quentin Skinner, *The Foundations of Modern Political Thought I: The Renaissance* (Cambridge, UK: Cambridge University Press, 1978), 180–6; *Machiavelli* (New York: Hill and Wang, 1981), 48–77. For the ancient commitment to political and social harmony, see Rahe, *Republics Ancient and Modern*, 15–229.

natural division between those intent on domination and aggrandizement and those eager to escape domination and retain their possessions, he was in no way persuaded by the claim that with well-designed institutions the English republican or anyone else could eliminate the threat that this "natural aristocracy" posed to "the natural democracy." When Jefferson wrote from Paris to Edward Carrington to urge him to "cherish...the spirit of our people, and keep alive their attention," and then cautioned him against being "too severe upon their errors," he had in mind what he took to be an overreaction on the part of his compatriots to the uprising in western Massachusetts that came to be known as Shays's rebellion. In his letter, he described this event quite self-consciously in the language pioneered by Niccolò Machiavelli as "the tumults in America" (*PTJ* 11:48–9).

With regard to the question of political turbulence, the republican from Virginia was indistinguishable from his Florentine predecessor. He, too, believed what Machiavelli had said: that every political community "ought to have modes by which the people can vent their ambition"; he, too, was persuaded that "the demands of a free people are seldom pernicious and rarely endanger their liberty." Like Machiavelli, he was convinced that such demands "arise from oppression or from the suspicions that they entertain that they are about to be oppressed," and that, "when these opinions are false, there is a remedy in the public assemblies where a good man can stand up and, in speaking, demonstrate to the people that they are in error." Thus, after warning Carrington against being "too severe upon" popular error, Jefferson emphasized that he should, instead, seek to "reclaim" the people "by enlightening them." As he put it by way of explanation:

I am persuaded myself that the good sense of the people will always be found to be the best army. They may be led astray for a moment but will soon correct themselves. The People are the only censors of their governors: and even their errors will tend to keep these to the true principles of their institution. To punish these errors too severely would be to suppress the only safeguard of the public liberty.   (*PTJ* 11:49)

In letters dispatched soon thereafter to Abigail Adams and James Madison, Jefferson once again spoke in a Machiavellian vein, "The spirit of resistance to government is so valuable on certain occasions," he wrote to the former, "that I wish it to be always kept alive. It will often be exercised when wrong, but better so than not to be exercised at all. I like a little rebellion now and then. It is like a storm in the Atmosphere." To the latter, he remarked that political "turbulence" is an "evil...productive of good. It prevents the degeneracy of government, and nourishes a general attention to public affairs.... It is a medecine necessary for the sound health of government" (*PTJ* 11:92–7, 174–5).

Prerogative

In endorsing Machiavelli's conviction that popular ire is rooted in oppression, in a justified fear of oppression, or in unjustified suspicions that are quite easily dispelled, Thomas Jefferson was by no means peculiar. Few, if any, credited the more extreme claims that James Harrington had advanced on behalf of his scheme of political architecture. Indeed, apart, perhaps, from Harrington's close friend and colleague Henry Neville, the English republican was alone among those who contributed to the Whig canon in thinking that constitutional structures would in and of themselves be sufficient to obviate the need for popular vigilance. John Locke is an especially revealing example, for his position on this question was quite similar to Jefferson's, and it owed much more to Machiavelli than to Hobbes or Harrington.[8] From the outset, even before the Restoration, Locke was inclined to ground his politics on the supposition that "our passions ... dispose of our thoughts and actions." To a friend, he then wrote, "Tis Phansye that rules us all under the title of reason.... We are all Centaurs and tis the beast that carries us" (*CJL* 1:122–6). But from this premise he eventually drew conclusions opposed in one crucial regard to those of his monarchist predecessor and in another to those of that individual's most effective republican critic.

In his *Two Treatises of Government*, Locke presented himself as a proponent of "moderated" monarchy, but he did not hesitate to describe this regime as "the mighty *Leviathan*" (cf. *TTG* 2.14.159 with 8.98). His choice of language was by no means fortuitous, for, in contrast with Harrington, he made a point of entrusting the execution of the laws to a single individual. In fact, he insisted on lodging the conduct of war and foreign policy – which he called the federative power – in the same individual's hands. He was convinced that the maintenance of domestic tranquillity and a provision for the common defense are inseparable; and though committed in principle to governance "by establish'd *standing Laws*, promulgated and known to the People," he clearly shared Machiavelli's belief that "the things of men" are too much "in motion" to be consistently administered in so orderly and reasonable a way. Moreover, he clearly felt the force of the case that the Florentine had made on behalf of the Roman dictatorship, and he had apparently pondered the argument advanced by Hobbes on behalf of absolute monarchy. In consequence, Locke deemed it appropriate that his monarchical executive be conceded considerable discretion to contravene the precise letter of the law, to suspend it, to act where it is silent, to mitigate the severity of its penalties, and to pardon offenders. He was also quite happy to grant England's king the right to veto acts of Parliament; and while insisting that his ministers be held responsible for all that they did under his direction, he nonetheless asserted the sanctity of the king's person.[9] In the course of Locke's account of executive prerogative, the "wise and godlike" monarch who rules "by established laws of liberty" gradually gives way to something more akin to Machiavelli's Roman dictator who manages to sustain popular support while acting "without or contrary to the Letter of the

---

[8] See Chapter 2.
[9] Cf. Locke, *TTG* 2.12.145–8, 13.151, 154, 156, 14.168, 18.205–10, 19.222, with 7.87, 9.131, and consider NM, *D* 1.34, in light of 1.6 and *P* 18.

Law" (cf. *TTG* 2.5.42 with 14.165–6). In Locke's estimation, the public interest requires a remarkable concentration of power and authority in the hands of a single man.

On the face of it, Thomas Jefferson would appear to be opposed to Locke on this point. At the time of the Revolution, he was certainly no friend to the executive power. In 1776, when he designed a constitution for Virginia, he was prepared to embrace the notion of a unitary executive, but he saw fit in each of the three drafts that he penned to specify a long list of powers once accorded the king that, in his opinion, should be expressly denied the official he designated as "the administrator" (*PTJ* 1:329–65, esp. 341–2, 349–50, 359–60). In 1783, when he proposed a new constitution for his state, he specified that "by Executive powers we mean no reference to those powers exercised under our former government by the crown as of it's prerogative"; and once again he expressly listed and denied to Virginia's executive what he termed "the praerogative powers" (*PTJ* 6:294–308, esp. 298–9). Moreover, in his *Notes on the State of Virginia*, he denounced in round terms those in the general assembly of Virginia who had proposed, at a time of great distress in 1776 and again in 1781, conferring temporary emergency powers in the Roman manner on a dictator. As he put it,

One who entered into this contest from a pure love of liberty, and a sense of injured rights, who determined to make every sacrifice, and to meet every danger, for the re-establishment of those rights on a firm basis, who did not mean to expend his blood and substance for the wretched purpose of changing this master for that, but to place the powers of governing him in a plurality of hands of his own choice, so that the corrupt will of no one man might in future oppress him, must stand confounded and dismayed when he is told, that a considerable portion of that plurality had meditated the surrender of them into a single hand, and in lieu of a limited monarch, to deliver him over to a despotic one!

In making his argument, Jefferson took care to respond to the case advanced by the proponents of the dictatorship, intimating, to begin with, that he understood the linkage between Machiavelli's defense of the Roman institution and Locke's case for prerogative. There is, he insisted, no provision for such an office within the constitution of Virginia, which not only "provides a republican organization," but "proscribes under the name of *prerogative* the exercise of all powers undefined by the laws." To those who reiterated Machiavelli's appeal to "the necessity of the case," he responded that "necessities which dissolve a government, do not convey its authority to an oligarchy or a monarchy. They throw back, into the hands of the people, the powers they had delegated, and leave them as individuals to shift for themselves." In any event, he added, "the necessity" faced by his fellow Virginians was neither "palpable" nor "irresistible." In answering those who followed Machiavelli in asserting Roman precedent, he contended that "it had proved fatal." Rome was "a republic, rent by the most bitter factions and tumults, where the government was of a heavy-handed unfeeling aristocracy, over a people ferocious, and rendered desperate by poverty and wretchedness." In that polity, there were "tumults which could not be allayed under the most trying circumstances, but by the omnipotent hand of a single despot. Their constitution therefore allowed a temporary tyrant to be erected, under the name of a Dictator; and that temporary tyrant, after a few examples, became perpetual." In Jefferson's estimation, when his fellow Virginians contemplated electing a dictator, they came close to turning their backs on America's nascent experiment in republicanism. As he put it, "the very thought alone was treason against the people; was treason against mankind in general; as rivetting for ever the chains which bow down their necks, by giving to their oppressors a proof, which they would have trumpeted through the universe, of the imbecility of republican government, in times of pressing danger, to shield them from harm" (cf. *NSV* 13.126–9, with NM, *D* 1.34).

To this one might add that, throughout his life, Jefferson was an exceedingly strict constructionist in expounding the Constitution.[10] "I own," he told James Madison quite early on, "that I am not a friend to a very energetic Government. It is always oppressive" (*PTJ* 12:442). No one spoke with greater force in favor of what Locke called governance "by establish'd *standing Laws*, promulgated and known to the People." And yet Jefferson, as president, was prepared to sanction what, he had no doubt, was a breach of the Constitution, and he justified his act in negotiating the Louisiana Purchase and that of Congress in ratifying the treaty and in appropriating the requisite funds in a manner indicating his recognition that Machiavelli, Hobbes, Locke, Montesquieu, Bolingbroke, Blackstone, and Lolme were correct in supposing that necessity dictates, even within a republic, the presence of a prince capable of meeting the emergencies forever incident to human affairs. He, too, believed that the world is in constant motion.[11]

In pondering "whether circumstances do not sometimes occur, which make it a duty in officers of high trust, to assume authorities beyond the law," Jefferson argued that the question was "easy of solution in principle, but sometimes embarrassing in practice." As he put it in a letter written to J. B. Colvin in late September 1810:

> A strict observance of the written laws is doubtless *one* of the high duties of a good citizen, but it is not *the highest*. The laws of necessity, of self-preservation, of saving our country when in danger, are of higher obligation. To lose our country by a scrupulous adherence to written law, would be to lose the law itself, with life, liberty, property and all those who are enjoying them with us; thus absurdly sacrificing the end to the means.
>
> (*WrTJ* [ed. Ford] 9:279–82)

---

[10] See David N. Mayer, *The Constitutional Thought of Thomas Jefferson* (Charlottesville, VA: University Press of Virginia, 1994).

[11] For a thorough examination of the role played by the prince in modern republican speculation, see Harvey C. Mansfield, *The Taming of the Prince: The Ambivalence of Modern Executive Power* (New York: Free Press, 1989).

In *The Federalist*, Alexander Hamilton had hinted at something of the sort, alluding to the precedent set by Rome's dictatorship, arguing that the distinction between a workable republic and one incapable of providing for domestic tranquillity and the common defense turns largely on the provisions made to ensure the "decision, activity, secrecy, and dispatch" necessary to this end, and contending that the president's extended term of office would enable a public-spirited executive "to expose himself" when necessary, to save "the people from very fatal consequences of their own mistakes," and to procure for himself "lasting monuments of their gratitude" for having had "courage and magnanimity enough to serve them at the peril of their displeasure" (*Fed.* 70–1).

In making this argument, Hamilton was exceedingly cautious: If one were to ignore Hamilton's allusion to the Roman dictatorship, one could easily read the latter passage simply and solely as a defense of the executive veto. In his letter to Colvin, Jefferson was much more candid, specifying just what was involved. "It is incumbent," he wrote, "on those . . . who accept of great charges, to risk themselves on great occasions, when the safety of the nation, or some of its very high interests are at stake. An officer is bound to obey orders; yet he would be a bad one who should do it in cases for which they were not intended, and which involved the most important consequences." That "the line of discrimination between cases" might be "difficult," he was perfectly happy to acknowledge. His point was simply that "the good officer is bound to draw it at his own peril, and to throw himself on the justice of his country and the rectitude of his motives" (*WrTJ* [ed. Ford] 9:279–82).

Anticipation, Resistance, and Revolution

The willingness of Harrington's Whig successors to embrace the notion of a unitary executive posed a grave difficulty for the proponents of republican liberty: how to prevent an abuse of what Locke called "Prerogative" on the part of an executive graced with dictatorial discretion. It was in part with this problem in mind that Locke asserted the right of popular resistance and made the people's representatives in the legislature and the executive ultimately accountable to the people themselves for their conduct in office. Like Machiavelli, the English philosopher was persuaded that the people are the best, if not the only, safe guardians of their own liberty.[12] Some would, he conceded, attack him for laying "the Foundation of Government in the unsteady Opinion, and uncertain Humour of the People." But such men were in error – and to demonstrate that this was the case, Locke borrowed and adapted the arguments made by

---

[12] Note NM, *D* 1.4–8, 58; consider Julian H. Franklin, *John Locke and the Theory of Sovereignty: Mixed Monarchy and the Right of Resistance in the Political Thought of the English Revolution* (Cambridge, UK: Cambridge University Press, 1978); and see Nathan Tarcov, "Locke's *Second Treatise* and 'The Best Fence against Rebellion,'" *RP* 43:1 (Winter 1981): 198–217 (esp. 211–17); Thomas L. Pangle, "Executive Energy and Popular Spirit in Lockean Constitutionalism," *Presidential Studies Quarterly* 17:2 (Spring 1987): 253–65 (esp. 259–64).

Machiavelli against the very same objections. The many may be inclined to resist when "*generally ill treated*," he contended, but they are "not so easily got out of their old Forms, as some are apt to suggest." In fact, if anything, they are too steady in their opinions and too certain in their humors. For the people "are more disposed to suffer, than right themselves by Resistance," and they are "not apt to stir" until "the mischief be grown general, and the ill designs of the Rulers become visible, or their attempts sensible to the greater part." As a consequence, the many tend not to resist oppression until it is already too late for them to be effective; and even when they do, they nearly always fail to initiate the institutional reforms necessary to prevent a recurrence (*TTG* 2.19.223–4, 230).[13]

To counteract the "slowness" of the people, to lessen if not expunge their "aversion" to change, and to encourage them to anticipate oppression to come, Locke introduced a new rhetoric of popular resistance to be deployed by spirited and ambitious *grandi* of the sort that Machiavelli had deemed "worthy to be princes." To arouse the ardor of these natural aristocrats and to elicit from them the requisite jealousy, vigilance, and *virtù*, he mocked the traditional Christian doctrine of "*Passive Obedience*" and "quiet Submission" to authority, and he rejected the classical commitment to communal solidarity and trust; and in their place, he exalted the prudence and foresight, the independence of mind, and the wiliness that had enabled Odysseus to rescue himself from the Cyclops Polyphemus (*TTG* 2.19.223, 228).

Locke harbored no illusions concerning the few men endowed with what he called "a busie head, or turbulent spirit," and he said nothing in their defense. He remained persuaded that reason is dependent on the passions and that "the busie mind of Man" can "carry him to a Brutality below the level of Beasts." He had learned from long and painful experience that the human "imagination is always restless and suggests variety of thoughts, and [that] the will, reason being laid aside, is ready for every extravagant project." "In this State," Locke tells us, "he that goes farthest out of the way, is thought fittest to lead, and is sure of most followers." Consequently, the English philosopher readily acknowledges that "the Pride, Ambition, and Turbulency of private Men have sometimes caused great Disorders in Commonwealths," while "Factions have been fatal to States and Kingdoms." As for those who lay "the foundation for *overturning* the Constitution and Frame of *any Just Government*," he holds them responsible "for all those mischiefs of Blood, Rapine, and Desolation, which the breaking to pieces of Governments bring on a Countrey"; and in his judgment, this makes them "guilty of the greatest Crime" he can imagine "a Man...capable of" (*TTG* 1.6.58, 2.19.230).

But despite or perhaps even to some degree because of their shortcomings, Locke is eager to enlist these turbulent spirits under the banner of liberty, for he is confident that this natural aristocracy will understand how to make "the

[13] Note also Locke, *TTG* 2.14.168, and *Some Considerations of the Consequences of Lowering the Interest and Raising the Value of Money*, in WoJL 5:71.

ill designs of the Rulers... visible" and their "attempts sensible" to the people as a whole. From studying the example that he provides in his *Two Treatises of Government*, they can learn how to unmask the tyranny that lies hidden under "ancient Names, and specious Forms." It was in pursuit of this Machiavellian end that Locke redeployed the natural-rights theory devised for other purposes by that enemy of tumults, Thomas Hobbes. The rhetoric that Locke employed in his great political tract, in particular his appeal to natural rights as a standard by which to judge the conduct of administration, is an instrument fashioned in such a manner as to enable busy heads to make "visible to the People" the "design" that underlies and accounts for "a long train of Abuses, Prevarications, and Artifices, all tending the same way." When enlightened by the jealous and watchful few, the many "cannot but feel, what they lie under, and see, whither they are going"; and when they both feel and see, "'tis not to be wonder'd, that they should then rouze themselves, and endeavour to put the rule into such hands, which may secure to them the ends for which Government was at first erected" (*TTG* 2.19.225, 230).

That his "Doctrine" of anticipation, resistance, and revolution may be "destructive to the Peace of the World," Locke tacitly concedes. But, like Machiavelli, he demands that his readers consider whether the peace so often inculcated from the pulpit can be distinguished from "Violence and Rapine," and he concludes that this peace is "maintain'd only for the benefit of Robbers and Oppressors." Moreover, in posing a rhetorical question, he employs an analogy between man and beast that would soon be appropriated in America by Jefferson. "Who would not think it an admirable Peace betwixt the Mighty and the Mean," he asks, "when the Lamb, without resistance, yielded his Throat to be torn by the imperious Wolf?" (cf. *TTG* 2.19.228 with NM, *D* 2.2, 3.1).

The English philosopher resorts to sarcasm in this context because he clearly discerns an alternative to arbitrary rule. Civil disorder may, he confesses, be "an *Inconvenience*... that *attends all Governments* whatsoever," but that is only because "the Governours have brought it to this pass, to be generally suspected of their people." Such a condition is "the most dangerous state which [rulers] can possibly put themselves in." But "they are the less to be pitied, because it is so easie to be avoided," for it is "impossible for a Governor, if he really means the good of his People, and the preservation of them and their Laws together, not to make them see and feel it" (*TTG* 2.18.209).

In restating, elaborating, and adapting Machiavelli's argument that the people are the best guardians of their own liberty, Locke stopped just shy of fully endorsing the case that the Florentine had made in defense of tumults, and he failed at the same time to reiterate the Florentine's closely related contention that, in a free state, liberty depends upon a frequent recurrence to first principles (*D* 3.1, 3, 49). If some, such as Blackstone and Hume, thought Locke a mite reckless in elaborating a rhetoric of popular resistance, others, chiefly among the radical Whigs, were apparently persuaded that he had erred on the side of caution – and, as Vickie Sullivan points out in the third chapter of this book, they could cite the pronouncements of the Whig martyr Algernon Sidney in their defense.[14] Like Sidney and his admirers on both sides of the Atlantic, Thomas Jefferson repeatedly echoed Machiavelli's conviction that corruption and lethargy can easily deprive a people of the capacity to defend their own liberty.[15]

The Logic of Jefferson's Legislative Program

Some among Jefferson's contemporaries shared Alexander Hamilton's conviction "that there is always a body of firm patriots," and that they can easily "shake a corrupt administration" (*RFC* 1:381–2). Jefferson was not so confident. In November 1787, in writing to yet another correspondent on the subject of Shays's Rebellion, he observed, "God forbid we should ever be 20. years without such a rebellion." He was not especially disturbed by the ignorance of the people; he considered them fully capable of taking instruction. The real danger was that his compatriots would "remain quiet under" their "misconceptions." In this he perceived "a lethargy" that he described as "the forerunner of death to the public liberty." He asked, "What country can preserve it's liberties if their rulers are not warned from time to time that their people preserve the spirit of resistance?" And then he concluded, "Let them take arms. The remedy is to set them right as to facts, pardon and pacify them. What signify a few lives lost in a century or two? The tree of liberty must be refreshed from time to time with the blood of patriots and tyrants. It is it's natural manure" (*PTJ* 12:355–7). It was with the danger of public lethargy in mind that Jefferson fashioned his great program of legislative reform for Virginia.[16]

In 1776, when the general assembly asked him to revise the laws of the commonwealth in light of the decision to break with the mother country, Jefferson took his commission as an occasion for disassembling the artificial supports

---

[14] After reading Neal Wood, "The Value of Asocial Sociability: Contributions of Machiavelli, Sidney and Montesquieu," in *Machiavelli and the Nature of Political Thought*, ed. Martin Fleisher (New York: Atheneum, 1972), 282–307 (esp. 282–98), consider Blair Worden, "The Commonwealth Kidney of Algernon Sidney," *Journal of British Studies* 24:1 (January 1985): 1–40 (esp. 13–38); Jonathan Scott, *Algernon Sidney and the English Republic, 1623–1677* (Cambridge, UK: Cambridge University Press, 1988), and *Algernon Sidney and the Restoration Crisis, 1677–1683* (Cambridge, UK: Cambridge University Press, 1991); Alan Craig Houston, *Algernon Sidney and the Republican Heritage in England and in America* (Princeton, NJ: Princeton University Press, 1992); Sullivan, *Machiavelli, Hobbes, and the Formation of a Liberal Republicanism in England*, 199–226; and Chapter 3 of this book in light of Sidney, *DCG* 2.13–14, 24, 26. See also Walter Moyle, *An Essay on the Lacedaemonian Government* (1698), in *The Whole Works of Walter Moyle* (London: J. Knapton et al., 1727), 57–8.

[15] Consider Jefferson, *NSV* 13.120–1, 17.161, 19.164–5, in light of Alfredo Bonadeo, *Corruption, Conflict, and Power in the Works and Times of Niccolo Machiavelli* (Berkeley, CA: University of California Press, 1973); Riccardo Breschi, "Il concetto di 'Corruzione' nei 'Discorsi sopra la prima deca di Tito Livio,'" *Studi Storici* 29 (1989): 707–35.

[16] See Ralph Lerner, "Jefferson's Pulse of Republican Reformation," in Lerner, *The Thinking Revolutionary: Principle and Practice in the New Republic* (Ithaca, NY: Cornell University Press, 1987), 60–90.

sustaining what little there was in that state reminiscent of England's *ancien régime*. To lessen the probability that the clergy would exercise through priestly guile an hegemony over the minds of his fellow citizens, he proposed disestablishing the Episcopalian church. As drafted, Jefferson's bill attacked "the impious presumption of legislators and rulers, civil as well as ecclesiastical, who, being themselves but fallible and uninspired men, have assumed dominion over the faith of others" (*PTJ* 2:545–53). In this fashion, Jefferson disposed of the clergy's pretensions to tutelage. He then struck a blow at inherited wealth and position. To lessen the likelihood that riches would corrupt and birth dazzle his fellow Virginians, Jefferson "laid the axe to" what he described to John Adams in October 1813 as "the root of Pseudo-aristocracy" by convincing the assembly to outlaw entails and abolish primogeniture. Deprived of legal props, with their land and their other property being gradually divided by the succession of generations and ultimately dispersed, the great families of Virginia would wither and soon disappear (*AJL* 2:387–92).[17]

After eliminating the privileges reinforcing the power and influence of the clerical and secular *grandi* who stood as rivals to what he termed the "natural aristocracy," Jefferson concerned himself with promoting the advancement of young men of genius who might become genuinely worthy of high office. To encourage the emergence of a class of talented and well-informed individuals suited for public service, and to prepare ordinary Virginians for the task of selecting nature's noblemen from among the pretenders, he proposed what he later described in his autobiography as "a systematical plan of general education" (*WrTJ* [ed. Ford] 1:66). From 1779 on, he urged the Virginia General Assembly to pass his Bill for the More General Diffusion of Knowledge and thereby establish throughout the commonwealth a system of publicly supported elementary schools (*PTJ* 2:526–35).[18] In a curriculum lasting three years, these schools would instruct all of the state's young residents (male and female alike) not only in reading, writing, and arithmetic but also in the history of the spirited peoples who had pioneered free institutions – the Greeks, the Romans, the English, and their American successors. These schools were to be under the supervision of a visitor who would choose annually from among the children of parents who lacked the resources to provide for their son's further education "the boy, of best genius in the school," and send him on at state expense to study Greek, Latin, geography, and mathematics at one of the twenty grammar schools to be established within Virginia. After a year or two, "the best genius" was to be selected from among the scholarship students within each class at each of the grammar schools. The others would then be dismissed, and the one boy chosen would continue his studies until he had completed a six-year term. "By

---

[17] For the laws abolishing entails and primogeniture, see "Bill to Enable Tenants in Fee Tail to Convey Their Lands in Fee Simple," 14 October 1776, and "The Revisal of the Laws, 18 June 1779: 20. A Bill Directing the Course of Descents," in *PTJ* 1:560–2, 2:391–3.

[18] For a later version, see TJ to Joseph C. Cabell, 9 September 1817, with draft of "An Act for Establishing Elementary Schools," in *WrTJ* (ed. Lipscomb and Bergh) 17:417–41.

this means," Jefferson remarked, "twenty of the best geniusses will be raked from the rubbish annually, and be instructed, at the public expence, so far as the grammar schools go." Upon completion of this extended course of study, ten of the twenty would receive public support to go on to study "all the useful sciences" at the university level. "By that part of our plan which prescribes the selection of the youths of genius from among the classes of the poor," Jefferson observed, "we hope to avail the state of those talents which nature has sown as liberally among the poor as the rich, but which perish without use, if not sought for and cultivated" (*NSV* 14.146–9).

The proprietor of Monticello drafted this proposal decades before he first conceived the notion of establishing a university in the Piedmont region of central Virginia.[19] At the time, the only institution of higher education in the state was his own alma mater, the College of William and Mary. Persuaded that this institution, as constituted, failed to meet Virginia's needs in the new era of independence, in 1779 he urged a thoroughgoing reform of its bylaws and of the curriculum "to aid and improve that seminary, in which those who are to be the future guardians of the rights and liberties of their country may be endowed with science and virtue, to watch and preserve the sacred deposit." To this end, Jefferson set out to change what had been an Anglican establishment into an institution wholly secular, with a thoroughly modern course of study including mathematics as well as political and natural science. To achieve this, he argued for dropping the chairs in theology and oriental languages. After his reform, there would be eight professorships: one to give instruction in moral philosophy, the laws of nature and of nations, and the fine arts; and others to teach law and police, history, mathematics, anatomy and medicine, natural philosophy and natural history, ancient languages, and modern languages (*PTJ* 2:535–43).

Unfortunately, despite considerable and persistent effort on Jefferson's part, his "systematical plan of general education" never passed into law. The general assembly did make a feeble attempt to encourage the establishment of elementary schools on the local level; and, as Jefferson tells us in his autobiography, he was himself able to effect a partial reform of the College of William and Mary in 1779 when he served as a visitor to that ancient institution (*WrTJ* [ed. Ford] 1:66–70). But these meager accomplishments left him unsatisfied.[20] To John Adams, in 1813, he expressed his dismay that his "system" had never been enacted:

The law for religious freedom … having put down the aristocracy of the clergy, and restored to the citizen the freedom of the mind, and those of entails and descents nurturing an equality of condition among them, this on Education would have raised the mass

---

[19] For the history of Jefferson's efforts on behalf of education, see Merrill D. Peterson, *Thomas Jefferson and the New Nation: A Biography* (Oxford, UK: Oxford University Press, 1970), 145–52, 961–88.

[20] See TJ to Dr. Joseph Priestley, 27 January 1800, and "A Memorandum (Service to My Country)," in *WrTJ* (ed. Ford) 7:413–16, 475–7.

of the people to the high ground of moral respectability necessary to their own safety, and to orderly government; and would have compleated the great object of qualifying them to select the veritable aristoi, for the trusts of government, to the exclusion of the Pseudalists.   (*AJL* 2:387–92)

Despite its virtues, Jefferson's plan never recommended itself to the general public.

Ultimately, Jefferson had to settle for the establishment at Charlottesville of the University of Virginia on lines similar to those laid out in his plan to transform the College of William and Mary.[21] It is indicative of the Machiavellian roots of his program that he insisted that, had he been given the option, he would have preferred the general education of the many to the higher education of the few. To one close collaborator, he wrote, "Were it necessary to give up either the Primaries or the University, I would rather abandon the last, because it is safer to have a whole people respectably enlightened, than a few in a high state of science, and the many in ignorance. This last is the most dangerous state in which a nation can be. The nations and governments of Europe are so many proofs of it."[22] But Jefferson was denied the opportunity to choose. Though disappointed, he could nonetheless take consolation from the prospect that, at the university that he had instituted, the future leaders of Virginia would receive a proper political education and imbibe Machiavelli's politics of distrust as they read Algernon Sidney's *Discourses Concerning Government*, John Locke's *Second Treatise*, the Declaration of Independence, *The Federalist*, Washington's Farewell Address, and the Virginia Resolutions of 1799 while attending the

---

[21] For the overall plan as it developed, see "Report of the Commissioners for the University of Virginia (Rockfish Gap Report)," 4 August 1818, in *Early History of the University of Virginia as Contained in the Letters of Thomas Jefferson and Joseph C. Cabell*, ed. Nathaniel F. Cabell (Richmond, VA: J. W. Randolph, 1856), 432–47; "An Exact Transcript of the Minutes of the Board of Visitors of the University of Virginia during the Rectorship of Thomas Jefferson," 5 May 1817 to 7 April 1826, in *WrTJ* (ed. Lipscomb and Bergh) 19:361–499 (esp. 407–8, 413–16, 433–51, 454–61). In the mid-1790s, Jefferson toyed with the idea of shifting the Academy of Geneva to Virginia; in 1800, he began talking of establishing a new, thoroughly modern university in the Piedmont. See TJ to François d'Ivernois, 6 February 1795, and to Dr. Joseph Priestley, 18 and 27 January 1800, in *WrTJ* (ed. Ford) 7:2–6, 406–10, 413–16; TJ to Littleton Waller Tazewell, 5 January 1805, in *WrTJ* (ed. Peterson) 1149–53; TJ to Joseph C. Cabell, 9 September 1817, with draft of "An Act for Establishing Elementary Schools," in *WrTJ* (ed. Lipscomb and Bergh) 17:417–41. In this connection, see TJ to Messrs. Hugh L. White and Others, 6 May 1810, in *WrTJ* (ed. Washington) 5:520–2. To this project, he turned his attention a few years after he left the presidency. At first, he focused on the establishment of an academy in Albemarle County. See TJ to Peter Carr, 7 September 1814, in *WrTJ* (ed. Lipscomb and Bergh) 19:211–21. Perhaps the clearest testimony of the degree to which Jefferson was dedicated to this project is the fact that, though very nearly bankrupt, he nonetheless kept his promise and left his library to the university. See "Thomas Jefferson's Will," in *WrTJ* (ed. Lipscomb and Bergh) 17:465–70 (at 469), 19:x. See also Peterson, *Thomas Jefferson and the New Nation*, 961–88, 989–92, 1006–7.

[22] See TJ to Joseph C. Cabell, 13 January 1823, in *Early History of the University of Virginia*, 266–8.

lectures of an orthodox Whig.[23] As Jefferson put it, in Feburary 1826, in the very last letter he wrote to James Madison, "In the selection of our Law Professor, we must be rigorously attentive to his political principles." Before the Revolution, this would have been easy, he explained, for "our lawyers were then all Whigs." Even now, he added, "they suppose themselves, indeed, to be Whigs, because they no longer know what Whigism or republicanism means. It is in our seminary that that vestal flame is to be kept alive" (*WrTJ* [ed. Lipscomb and Bergh] 16:156–7).

Popular Education, Ward Republics, and Political Jealousy

The same set of concerns that animated first Machiavelli and then Locke account for Jefferson's frustration at the failure on the part of the framers of the Constitution to include a bill of rights within the document.[24] He harbored few illusions regarding the strength of parchment barriers as a bulwark against the tyrannical rule of a popular majority, but he did think them useful as a rallying point against oppression on the part of a corrupt and distant government. "Above all things," he wrote to James Madison in December 1787 with this question in mind, "I hope the education of the common people will be attended to; convinced that on their good sense we may rely with the most security for the preservation of a due degree of liberty" (*PTJ* 12:442). Citizens who were fully informed of their rights were much more likely to be able to defend those rights.

Jefferson's commitment to the freedom of the press is explicable in precisely the same terms. In his letter to Edward Carrington, he argued, with regard to tumults, that "the way to prevent these irregular interpositions of the people is to give them full information of their affairs thro' the channel of the public papers, and to contrive that those papers should penetrate the whole mass of the people." He was persuaded that "the basis of our governments" is "the opinion of the people," and that "the very first object should be to keep that right." "Were it left to me to decide whether we should have a government without newspapers, or newspapers without a government," he wrote, "I should not hesitate a moment to prefer the latter. But I should mean that every man should receive those papers and be capable of reading them" (*PTJ* 11:49).

Thirty years subsequent to his presentation of the Revisal of the Laws to the Virginia General Assembly, after observing the manner in which his political enemies in New England had employed the town meetings to rally the populace of that region against his embargo, Jefferson added an amendment to his

---

[23] See "An Exact Transcript of the Minutes of the Board of Visitors of the University of Virginia during the Rectorship of Thomas Jefferson," 4 March 1825, in *WrTJ* (ed. Lipscomb and Bergh) 19:460–1.

[24] See TJ to JM, 20 December 1787; to Alexander Donald, 7 February 1788; to GW, 4 November 1788; to Francis Hopkinson, 13 March 1789; and, again, to JM, 15 March 1789, in *PTJ* 12:438–43, 570–2, 14:328–32 (at 328), 649–51, 659–63.

original proposals. For the purpose of establishing local elementary schools, he had long supported dividing the counties into "hundreds" or "wards." Now he sought the institution of such small districts for another end as well: They were, he believed, ideally suited for the establishment of self-government within the localities, and as such they could do much to form the political character of the nation's citizens and to head off political lethargy and corruption. Here again he had in mind Machiavelli's defense of *tumulti*. The wards were designed to make the general public attentive to political affairs; they were to function as "a regularly organized power" enabling the people "to crush, regularly and peaceably, the usurpations of their unfaithful agents," free "from the dreadful necessity of doing it insurrectionally."[25] "By making every citizen an acting member of the government, and in the offices nearest and most interesting to him," Jefferson hoped, as he told Samuel Kercheval in July, 1816, to "attach him by his strongest feelings to the independence of his country, and its repub-lican constitution" (*WrTJ* [ed. Ford] 10:40–1). As he put it in a letter written to Joseph C. Cabell the previous February:

Where every man is a sharer in the direction of his ward-republic, or of some of the higher ones, and feels that he is a participator in the government of affairs, not merely at an election one day in the year, but every day; when there shall not be a man in the State who will not be a member of some one of its councils, great or small, he will let the heart be torn out of his body sooner than his power be wrested from him by a Caesar or a Bonaparte.... As Cato, then, concluded every speech with the words, "*Carthago delenda est* [Carthage must be destroyed]," so do I every opinion, with the injunction, "divide the counties into wards."   (*WrTJ* [ed. Washington] 6:540–4)

It is essential to recognize that Jefferson did not give primacy to political participation as an end in itself.[26] His desire to foster self-government in the localities had the same roots as his long-standing commitment to states' rights.

[25] See TJ to John Tyler, 26 May 1810; to Samuel Kercheval, 12 July and 5 September 1816; and to John Taylor, 21 July 1816, in *WrTJ* (ed. Ford) 9:276n–8n, 10:37–45, 45n–46n, 50–5; TJ to JA, 28 October 1813, in *AJL* 2:387–92; to Joseph C. Cabell, 2 February 1816, in *WrTJ* (ed. Washington) 6:540–4; to Major John Cartwright, 5 June 1824, in *The Memoirs, Correspondence, and Private Papers of Thomas Jefferson*, ed. Thomas Jefferson Randolph (London: H. Colburn and R. Bentley, 1829), 4:405. See also TJ to Joseph C. Cabell, 28 November 1820, in *Early History of the University of Virginia*, 184–8. As this missive and TJ's letter to Joseph C. Cabell, 2 February 1816, in *WrTJ* (ed. Washington) 6:540–4, make clear, the ward proposal was closely linked with Jefferson's campaign to establish primary schools. The passage quoted in the text is to be found in the second of the two letters to Samuel Kercheval.

[26] Cf. Hannah Arendt, *On Revolution* (New York: Viking Press, 1963), 111–285 (esp. 115–37, 234–85), and Garrett Ward Sheldon, *The Political Philosophy of Thomas Jefferson* (Baltimore, MD: Johns Hopkins University Press, 1991), 53–111, with Jean Yarbrough, "Republicanism Reconsidered: Some Thoughts on the Foundation and Preservation of the American Republic," *RP* 41:1 (Winter 1979): 61–95 (esp. 84–92). Yarbrough errs only in attributing the "North-American" letters to Madison: See Note on "The North-American," nos. 1 and 2, in *PJM* 7:319–46.

Like the Anti-Federalists, he wished to minimize the responsibilities of those elements of the government set at a great distance from the people and to maximize vigilance on the part of the people by fostering popular control of local affairs. His animating principle is visible in the passage that he inserted in his draft of the Kentucky Resolutions of 1798, arguing that "confidence is everywhere the parent of despotism," that "free government is founded in jealousy, and not in confidence," and that "it is jealousy and not confidence which prescribes limited constitutions, to bind down those whom we are obliged to trust with power" (*WrTJ* [ed. Ford] 7:304).

This Machiavellian predilection for distrust helps explain why Jefferson looked on the Supreme Court of the United States with such suspicion, railing against what he perceived as a propensity for judicial "despotism" and "oligarchy." It was Jefferson's conviction that to concede political supremacy to courts composed of men appointed to office for life would be to make the Constitution, as he put it to Spencer Roane in September 1819, "a mere thing of wax in the hands of the judiciary, which they may twist and shape into any form they please" (*WrTJ* [ed. Ford] 10:140–3). It was his conviction, he told William Charles Jarvis a year later, that "to consider the judges as the ultimate arbiters of all constitutional questions" was "a very dangerous doctrine indeed," for there was and could be "no safe depository of the ultimate powers of society but the people themselves." And he insisted that, "if we think them not enlightened enough to exercise their control with wholesome discretion, the remedy is not to take it from them, but to inform their discretion by education" (*WoTJ* 12:161–4).

Precisely the same concern with promoting popular vigilance dictated the desire, which Jefferson shared with the Anti-Federalists and with many a Federalist as well, that the individual citizens of the United States be armed and that they be organized locally under their own officers as a militia. Those who proposed the pertinent provisions in the various state bills of rights, those who enacted the relevant state laws, and those who requested, framed, and ratified what we now know as the Second Amendment to the federal constitution took as a given William Blackstone's exposition of the parallel passage in the English bill of rights. In the United States of America, as in England, the individual's right to bear arms was deemed an "auxiliary right" comparable to freedom of speech and freedom of the press. It was established as a legal or even constitutional right because it was thought essential as a safeguard for the more fundamental, natural rights to life, liberty, and property. To be precise, the right to keep and bear arms was "a public allowance, under due restrictions, of the natural right of resistance and self-preservation, when the sanctions of society and laws are found insufficient to restrain the violence of oppression."[27] Even those who greatly feared political turmoil recognized that measures aimed at suppressing tumults or rendering them

---

[27] See William Blackstone, *Commentaries on the Laws of England* (Oxford, UK: Clarendon Press, 1765–9), 1:119–41 (esp. 139).

impossible or exceedingly difficult might open the way for an elimination of public liberty.[28]

Jefferson never strayed from the position that he outlined in his missive to Edward Carrington. In his last communication, a letter that he drafted in late June 1826 in declining an invitation to attend festivities scheduled for the fiftieth anniversary of America's Declaration of Independence, he wrote of that event:

May it be to the world, what I believe it will be, (to some parts sooner, to others later, but finally to all,) the signal of arousing men to burst the chains under which monkish ignorance and superstition had persuaded them to bind themselves, and to assume the blessings and security of self-government. That form which we have substituted, restores the free right to the unbounded exercise of reason and freedom of opinion. All eyes are opened, or opening, to the rights of man. The general spread of the light of science has already laid open to every view the palpable truth, that the mass of mankind has not been born with saddles on their backs, nor a favored few booted and spurred, ready to ride them legitimately, by the grace of God.   (*WrTJ* [ed. Ford] 10:390–2)

From the outset, Jefferson's goal was to prevent America's *grandi* from becoming wolves who would treat their fellow citizens as if they were sheep. Because he was mindful of the Machiavellian dictum that a legislator must presume all men wicked, he was persuaded that the only way to accomplish this end was to see to it that the American people were never in any fashion sheeplike at all. Such was for Jefferson – as it had been for Machiavelli, Locke, and their admirers before him – the central core of his understanding of the spirit that one must foster if one is to sustain republican liberty.

---

[28] Cf. Robert E. Shalhope, "The Ideological Origins of the Second Amendment," *Journal of American History* 69:3 (December 1982): 599–614, with Lawrence Delbert Cress, "An Armed Community: The Origins and Meaning of the Right to Bear Arms," *Journal of American History* 71:1 (June 1984): 22–42, and see David T. Hardy, "The Second Amendment and the Historiography of the Bill of Rights," *Journal of Law and Politics* 4 (1987): 1–62; Joyce Lee Malcolm, *To Keep and Bear Arms: The Origins of an Anglo-American Right* (Cambridge, MA: Harvard University Press, 1994). If I am correct in asserting (*Republics Ancient and Modern*, 254–9, 321–34, 347–56, 409–747) that Whigs of all stripes, in America as well as in Britain, were united in accepting Blackstone's dictum (*Commentaries on the Laws of England*, 1:135) that "the public good is in nothing more essentially interested, than in the protection of every individual's private rights," the current dispute between those who interpret the Second Amendment in terms of individual rights and those who stress communal duties is an artifact of contemporary scholarship grounded on a dichotomy that would have made little if any sense to anyone in the eighteenth century. The revolutionary generation disliked standing armies and saw them as a threat to liberty. Even when they conceded the necessity of such an army, they wanted to see the individual citizens armed and organized as a militia in such a way as to help provide for the common defense while safeguarding the right to revolution.

10

James Madison's Princes and Peoples

Gary Rosen

Searching for references to Niccolò Machiavelli in the voluminous writings of James Madison is not an especially rewarding exercise. There are precisely three of them, if we are to believe the available indexes, and all are mere notes, acknowledging the authority of the great Florentine but in no way suggesting that he exerted any lasting influence on Madison. Machiavelli first shows up in Madison's adolescent "commonplace" book, where the young Virginian dutifully recorded the opinion of the Cardinal de Retz that most of Machiavelli's readers did not understand him and that others took him "to be a great Politician for no other reason but for having been Wicked" (*PJM* 1:13). Machiavelli next appears years later, as one of many distinguished writers whose works Madison recommended to the Continental Congress for purchase in 1783 (*PJM* 6:84). Finally, among the notes that Madison prepared during the controversy over the Bank of the United States in the early 1790s, we find "Machiavel" declaring that the Bank of St. George at Genoa would gradually gain possession of that commercial republic (*PJM* 13:365). That is the sum of it – hardly the makings of a distinctive Machiavellian interpretation of Madison.

Evidence of direct influence aside, however, there are certain obvious affinities between the two thinkers. Madison is perhaps the outstanding representative in the founding generation of that species of realism and prudence that Machiavelli so signally introduced into political philosophy. The views for which Madison is celebrated – that government necessarily involves the spirit of faction and party, that neither moral nor religious motives can be relied on to control factious oppression, that a free constitution requires both the vigilance of the people and the mutual suspicion of the ambitious (*Fed.* 10, 51) – are like so many maxims culled from the pages of *The Prince* or the *Discourses on Livy*. They are Americanized expressions of what Machiavelli called the "effectual

Parts of this chapter were first published in Gary Rosen, *American Compact: James Madison and the Problem of Founding* (Lawrence, KS: University Press of Kansas, 1999), and are reprinted here with permission.

truth" of politics: that in order to avoid their "ruin" and achieve their "preservation," men should govern themselves in accordance with how they *do* behave rather than in the distorting light of how they *ought* to (*P* 15). Though the extent of Madison's sympathy with this view is somewhat controversial, the basic fact of it is not.[1]

That said, one does not associate Madison's thought with Machiavelli in the first instance. Madison's Machiavellianism, such as it is, appears to have come through other thinkers, men who themselves were disciples in one way or another of the seductive Florentine. It is their particular imprint that we detect in Madison. Thus, a number of scholars have rightly credited David Hume with shaping Madison's ideas on faction and the extended sphere,[2] and it is impossible to miss the influence of Montesquieu in the Virginian's many discussions of the separation of powers.[3] We see the hand of still others in Madison's first principles. As he told Jefferson late in life, describing the essential elements of a political education for the University of Virginia, right-thinking in such matters began with John Locke, Algernon Sidney, and the Declaration of Independence – sources sure to persuade young minds of the truth of the social compact (*MF* 349).[4] With all these thinkers one can make a case for a Machiavellian substratum, for a shared recognition of human vulnerability and selfishness and of the power of self-preservation as a political motive. But each responds to this characteristically modern doctrine in a particular way, and it is this variety that we see reflected and reformulated in Madison.

There is one crucial dimension of Madison's thought, however, where Machiavelli remains the most useful guide. Like Machiavelli, and unlike the Anglo American social compact tradition as a whole, Madison discerns a fundamental divide among human beings, one with far-reaching implications for political life. For Madison, it is not enough to say that human beings are equal by right,

[1] For Madison as a benign, moralizing realist, see William Lee Miller, *The Business of May Next: James Madison and the Founding* (Charlottesville, VA: University Press of Virginia, 1992), 30–2. For Madison as a cold and calculating "constant liberal prince," see Richard K. Matthews, *If Men Were Angels: James Madison and the Heartless Empire of Reason* (Lawrence, KS: University Press of Kansas, 1995), 1–25.

[2] See Douglass Adair, "'That Politics May Be Reduced to a Science': David Hume, James Madison, and the Tenth *Federalist*," in *Fame and the Founding Fathers*, ed. Trevor Colbourn (New York: W. W. Norton, 1974), 93–106; Garry Wills, *Explaining America: The Federalist* (London: Athlone Press, 1981), 179–264. For useful correctives to the more extreme claims of Adair and Wills, see Theodore Draper, "Hume & Madison: The Secrets of Federalist Paper No. 10," *Encounter* 58 (February 1982): 34–47; Edmund S. Morgan, "Safety in Numbers: Madison, Hume and the Tenth *Federalist*," *Huntington Library Quarterly* 49:1 (1986): 95–112. See also Chapter 4 of this book.

[3] See his Notes for a Speech Favoring Revision of the Virginia Constitution of 1776, 14 or 21 June 1784, *PJM* 8:78; Speech on the Term of the Executive, 17 July 1787, *PJM*, 10:103–4; *Fed.* 47. See also James W. Muller, "The American Framers' Debt to Montesquieu," in *The Revival of Constitutionalism*, ed. James W. Muller (Lincoln, NE: University of Nebraska Press, 1988), 87–102. See also Chapter 5 of this book.

[4] For a general discussion of the social compact's place in Madison's political thought, see Rosen, *American Compact*, passim. See also Chapters 2 and 3 of this book.

with none enjoying a natural title to rule.[5] This familiar doctrine provides a necessary moral standard, but it fails to make the all-important practical distinction between the few and the many, the great and the common, princes and peoples .

Machiavelli was well versed in the ways of both classes. In fact, as Markus Fischer makes clear in the prologue to this book, the Florentine's account of these "two diverse humors," which he found in every regime, whether republican or princely, forms the very foundation of his political science. On its face, the distinction points back to the concerns of Aristotelian political science, as some indeed have argued.[6] But Machiavelli's project is hardly classical. Divesting the few and the many of the claims to justice that distinguish them in the classical view, he instead describes each class in terms of its peculiar sort of selfishness and the political function that it is particularly well suited to perform. The great – *grandi* – "desire to command and oppress," delighting in their domination of the people. Their aim is glory, and their virtuosity lies in the founding of regimes. By contrast, the people – *popolo* – "desire neither to be commanded nor oppressed," hoping for little more than to be left alone. Their aim is the secure enjoyment of their modest goods, and their political capacities, such as they are, find their highest expression in the maintenance of regimes. Neither side fully pursues the common good, but together, in more or less open conflict with one another, they are capable of achieving it (*P* 9; *D* 1.4, 9, 16, 58).[7]

As we shall see, such princes and peoples inhabit Madison's political thought as well, though several degrees removed from Machiavelli's somewhat overdrawn portraits. Madison presents the act of founding as a rare feat, one properly belonging to a select few and well outside the ken of the social compact's popular sovereign. But his founders are considerably more public-spirited than Machiavelli's – at least insofar as the act of founding itself is concerned. When it comes to the maintenance of the Constitution, with its carefully enumerated and balanced powers, Madison turns expectantly to the people, the conservative element in the American regime. At the same time, he begins to cast a suspicious eye on the continuing intervention of the few. In his effort to establish the Republican Party in opposition to the policies and principles of Alexander Hamilton, he thus becomes a more consistent student of Machiavelli, trying to give the people the resources they need to resist a proto-aristocracy. His aim remains peculiarly Madisonian, however. Invoking the forms of the Constitution, he attempts to arouse the people's pride as sovereign and to demonstrate how the social compact can be used to transcend the conflict between the many and the few and to establish a regime that is at once moderate and truly popular.

---

[5] Cf. Hobbes, *Leviathan* I.xiii.1–2, xv.23–5; Locke, *TTG* 2.2.4; Sidney, *DCG* 1.10.

[6] See, in particular, J. G. A. Pocock, *The Machiavellian Moment: Florentine Political Thought and the Atlantic Republican Tradition* (Princeton, NJ: Princeton University Press, 1975).

[7] See also Leo Strauss, *Thoughts on Machiavelli* (Chicago: University of Chicago Press, 1958), 127–31, 249–52.

Founding and the Few

As Thomas Jefferson was composing his *Notes on the State of Virginia* in the early 1780s, he could write that most of the American states "were of the opinion, that to render a form of government unalterable by ordinary acts of assembly, the people must delegate persons with special powers. They have accordingly chosen special conventions to form and fix their governments" (*NSV* 13.125). Jefferson had been among the first, in fact, to see conventions, long a part of British and revolutionary American political practice, as something more than an informal (or even illegal) supplement to constituted authority. They were the vehicle through which the sovereign people could exercise the powers to which the social compact entitled them. In 1776, this view had prevailed in most of the states, but not in Virginia. At that time, Jefferson had been alone among the leading men of the commonwealth in opposing the assumption of constituent powers by an assembly elected for other purposes.[8] As the war against Great Britain drew to a close several years later, Virginia's frame of government, established under such dubious authority in Jefferson's eyes, had yet to be put on a satisfactory footing. His *Notes* were, among other things, a call to reform. He urged the meeting of a convention that might place the "ordinance of government" on "a bottom that none will dispute" (*NSV* 13.125).

Distracted by the death of his wife and then called away by national office, Jefferson was unable to press his scheme in the Virginia General Assembly. That duty fell to Madison, who returned from service in the Continental Congress at the end of 1783 with no less of a desire to see the Virginia constitution of 1776 revised. The one surviving document from Madison's ultimately unsuccessful effort at revision shows that the constituent authority of the people was among his chief concerns. For Madison, the "Nature of a Constitution," strictly understood, required the popular election of representatives whose exclusive task was the establishment of a constitution. At a minimum, the people should know that the representatives they chose, whatever their other duties, were to have constituent powers. Even by this lesser standard, the Virginia constitution of 1776 fell short. Under it, as Madison twice noted, "power from [the] people [is] no where pretended." Madison suggested that the people were entitled not only to consent to the government under which they live but also to deliberate over its forms. If consent alone were necessary, the "acquiescence" on which the current Virginia constitution rested would be enough, but he called this a "dangerous basis." The social compact would seem to require the election of representatives *by* the people and *for* the express purpose of designing a constitution in accord with their wishes (*PJM* 8:77–8).

Understood in this way, the Constitutional Convention answered a clear need in the received versions of the social compact: It described a fairly precise

[8] Gordon S. Wood, *The Creation of the American Republic, 1776–1787* (New York: W. W. Norton, 1972), 307, 310–19.

mechanism for founding, for constitution-making. Madison and Jefferson were not the first to identify this need. Jean-Jacques Rousseau and David Hume had also objected to the social compact's account of government's origin, but rather than suggest that the people's role be formalized, they had instead ridiculed the notion of a founderless founding, making it a leading point in their criticisms of the social compact proposed, with important variations, by both Hobbes and Locke. For Rousseau, the great problem of these modern proponents of natural law was that they had to make every participant in the social compact "a great reasoner and a profound metaphysician," capable of devising "a system of legislation." For Hume, too, popular deliberation on forms of government was nothing less than "chimerical." Both writers reverted to a seemingly classical solution, looking to a legislator or founder to do the work of constitution-making.[9] But their true teacher in this regard was Machiavelli, and Madison eventually joined them at the Florentine's knee.

Though Madison had settled again in Virginia by the beginning of 1784, the worsening national situation under the Articles of Confederation was never far from his mind. Among his first achievements upon taking a seat in the General Assembly was to persuade that body to comply with federal requisitions for funds and to instruct its delegates in Congress to support coercive action against non-complying states. But Madison knew that these were little more than temporizing measures. His primary goal remained the vesting of further taxing and commercial powers in the Confederation. To that end, he would go on to promote two state-sponsored gatherings intended to solve the chronic trade problems of the union, first at Mount Vernon in 1785 and then at Annapolis in 1786. As the history books tell us, these two related meetings led to a third, the Federal Convention, making Mount Vernon "a sort of preliminary to the preliminary."[10]

These three gatherings represented a growing conviction on Madison's part that the required reforms could not take place within the context of ordinary politics. Having failed repeatedly in his attempts to amend the Articles of Confederation by the prescribed means – his proposals to secure a reliable source of revenue for the national government had foundered each time on the Confederation's requirement of unanimity[11] – Madison came to see a convention as a necessary alternative, an opportunity for those like himself to circumvent popular forms, however temporarily, in order to better secure popular rule. While a convention began in ordinary politics – it had to be called and

---

[9] Jean-Jacques Rousseau, *Discourse on the Origin and Foundations of Inequality Among Men*, pref., in *The First and Second Discourses*, ed. Roger D. Masters (New York: St. Martin's Press, 1964), 94, and *On the Social Contract*, ed. Roger D. Masters (New York: St. Martin's Press, 1978), 67–70; Hume, "Of the Original Contract," in *EMPL* 472–3.

[10] See Clinton Rossiter, *1787: The Grand Convention* (New York: W. W. Norton, 1966), 54.

[11] See Ralph Ketcham, *James Madison: A Biography* (Charlottesville, VA: University Press of Virginia, 1971), 112–20; Jack N. Rakove, *The Beginnings of National Politics: An Interpretive History of the Continental Congress* (Baltimore, MD: Johns Hopkins University Press, 1979), 282–96, 313–16, 337–9.

convened – the irregularity of its authority and its ultimate lack of responsibility gave it extraordinary latitude. This was a far cry from the standard
described in his speech on revising the Virginia constitution. Indeed, with each
step toward the Federal Convention, the people's place in constitution-making
became more problematic for Madison; his previous insistence on their selection
of constituent representatives – that is, on the people's substantive contribution
to establishing particular constitutional forms – gave way to mere after-the-fact
consent. For him, as we shall see, the possibility of popular reason receded and
was replaced by a reliance on popular feeling.

For Madison, the prepolitical situation was not a condition of anarchy or
constant anxiety, as the standard accounts of the social compact would have it.
Rather it was the absence of necessary political forms at some level of society,
a serious constitutional shortcoming of some sort. The difficulty was that such
a threat was often removed several times from actual arbitrariness or disorder.
It could be *discerned* by a few long before it was *felt* by all. However menacing
a feckless Confederation might be to Madison, it did not trouble the average
American until a Daniel Shays appeared on the scene or trade wars broke out
between the states. Even then, as Madison saw it, a consensus for reform was
unlikely. Simple aversion lacked remedies, knowing what it disliked but not
how to fix it. Those few who were capable of anticipating constitutional crises
differed from their fellow citizens in this regard as well: They could devise
and execute schemes of reform in the face of present or prospective troubles.
Though given their opportunity by the more common reaction of mere fear and
anxiety, they moved decisively beyond it.

For Machiavelli, these were among the defining differences between princes
and peoples. The perfected prince acted with a full knowledge of necessity's
requirements, even during those times when necessity was least insistent. This
was the essence of Machiavelli's most notorious teaching: not that a prince must
be sly and wicked in all that he does, but that he must always be prepared to call
on his slyness and wickedness, to use his ability "not to be good . . . according
to necessity." Such foresight and flexibility made for princely virtue, or *virtù*
(*P* 15, 18). By contrast, the people were naive about necessity, recognizing
neither its omnipresence nor the attitude dictated by the need to manage and
subdue it. This explained their attachment to virtue in its more traditional sense
(*P* 9; *D* 1.55, 58, 3.20). As we shall see, Madison was far indeed from sharing
this moral dichotomy – at least initially – but he did reach a similar practical
conclusion. As Machiavelli put it, with typical starkness, a people that found
itself without an adequate regime was like a domesticated animal "left free in
a field to its fate," incapable of caring for itself. Its desperation exposed its
dependence on the services and know-how of a prince (*D* 1.16).

Late in 1784, Richard Henry Lee, then serving in the Virginia delegation
in Philadelphia, wrote to Madison about the possibility of bringing together
the states to revise the Confederation. In his reply, his earliest statement on
a national convention, Madison did not pretend to have any affection for the
Confederation, but he was reluctant nonetheless to endorse reform. He claimed

ignorance of the delicate political calculus on which such an effort would hinge. On the one hand, there was the "temper" of the people of the different states. Though his fellow Virginians seemed well enough disposed to the Confederation, he could not speak for the other states. On the other hand, there were the state officeholders, the medium through which such popular dispositions would have to be expressed. Among the members of Virginia's General Assembly, he expected the usual "prejudices & jealousies" against innovation, particularly such innovation as would "derogate from their own power & importance." In summarizing the matter to Lee, Madison suggested that more attention would have to be given both to the people's readiness to consider reform and to the particular method, especially in relation to the state governments, to be used in proposing it. "The question," he wrote, was "in what mode & at what moment the experiment for supplying the defects ought to be made" (*PJM* 8:151, 201).

In his concern for the interaction of popular sentiment and official pride and self-regard, Madison might well have been following the advice of Machiavelli. Those intent on putting themselves "at the head of introducing new orders," Machiavelli warned, had two chief difficulties to overcome: the lukewarmness of those who might benefit from the new order and the enmity of those who benefited from the present one. The former were likely to hesitate out of respect for the law and their disbelief in distant, promised goods; the latter could be counted on to resist mightily in defense of their privileges (*P* 6). In Madison's case, it was the people, the potential friends of reform, who mattered most in achieving constitutional change. As he and Machiavelli both realized, popular support gave the founder of new orders a degree of security in the face of opposition from other princely types (*P* 9).

Madison considered talk of a national convention premature in 1784. A second proposal for a national impost was still pending, and the states themselves were beginning to recognize the self-destructive effects of their unregulated and often predatory commerce with one another. He continued to believe that such problems might yet provide a basis for strengthening the Confederation. In the summer of 1784, he persuaded the Virginia legislature to appoint commissioners, himself included, to resolve lingering disputes with Maryland over the use and navigation of the Potomac. Madison thought that such benign cooperation between two states might serve as a reminder of the benefits of union. The forum, one entirely of the states' own making, was significant too. Here sensitive questions of sovereignty could be dealt with narrowly, in the tempering light of interest, and away from threatening national institutions. The resulting conference, held at Mount Vernon in March 1785, took place without Madison – he was notified of it only after the fact – but managed to resolve most of the major issues between Virginia and Maryland and, furthermore, recommended a broader scheme of regional cooperation.

On its face, such an agreement, with its seeming assertion of sectional independence, served only to erode further the authority of the Confederation, the

terms of which it certainly violated in spirit, if not in fact.[12] But Madison did
not view the Mount Vernon meeting in this way. He considered it an "apt
and forceable...illustration of the necessity of uniformity throughout all the
States," as he wrote years later (*RFC* 3:544–55), and hoped that it would bolster his own long-standing efforts to give Congress wider commercial powers.
When the compact between the two states came up for ratification in the following session of the Virginia legislature, he attempted to turn it to his own
purposes, suggesting that it be submitted to Congress "for their sanction, as
being within the word *Treaty* used in the Confederation." When this measure
failed, he asked that Congress might at least be formally notified of the agreement. This too fell by a large majority.[13] During the same session, Madison
suffered a still more serious setback, seeing his proposal for an explicit grant
to Congress of modest commercial powers – "such direct power only as would
not alarm" – slowly emasculated. It was in the context of this "extremity," he
told Jefferson, that he finally lent his support to a resolution by John Tyler that
sought "a general meeting of [commissioners] from the States to consider and
recommend a foederal plan for regulating Commerce" (*PJM* 8:476–7). This
meeting, held some eight months later, was the Annapolis Convention.

Sympathetic historians and biographers have long wished to credit Madison
with the idea of the Annapolis Convention, thus giving the appearance of design
in the successive conventions, from Mount Vernon in 1785 to Philadelphia in
1787. They have gone so far as to suggest that Tyler was little more than a
convenient front for the proposal.[14] More convincing are the critics of this
view, who point out that Madison never claimed authorship of the convention
and, moreover, that he and Tyler were antagonists in the debate over commercial powers. They argue that Virginia's support for the Annapolis Convention,
which was called without reference to Congress, represented a victory for those
opposed to increasing national power.[15]

While this revisionist account is persuasive as to the facts, it fails to explain
Madison's embrace of so seemingly antinational a proposal. The case against
his having been the mastermind of the Annapolis Convention would seem to
apply with no less force to his eventually supporting it. The solution lies in a

---

[12] See Forrest McDonald, *E Pluribus Unum: The Formation of the American Republic, 1776–1790*,
2nd edition (Indianapolis, IN: Liberty Fund, 1979), 235–7; Ketcham, *James Madison*, 169.

[13] JM to James Monroe, 30 December 1785, *PJM* 8:466, 467, n. 3. See also the editorial note: 391.

[14] See Irving Brant, *James Madison* (Indianapolis, IN: Bobbs-Merrill, 1941–61), 2:375–87;
Ketcham, *James Madison*, 169–70.

[15] See editorial note, *PTJ* 9:204–8, and editorial note, *PJM* 9:115–17. The Annapolis Convention
was embarrassed, in fact, by the refusal of its host state, Maryland, to send delegates out of
concern for the prerogatives of the national legislature: "The measure appear'd to the Senate
[of Maryland], tho' undoubtedly adopted by y[ou]r Assembly with the best intentions, to have
a tendency to weaken the authority of Congress, on which the Union, and consequently the
Liberty, and Safety of all the States depend....I shall only observe, that sound policy, if not
the Spirit of the Confederation dictates, that all matters of a general tendency, shou'd be in the
representative Body of the whole, or under its authority." Daniel Carroll to JM, 13 March 1786,
PJM 8:496.

certain shared formal aim of both Tyler and Madison: Both saw the proposal for a convention as an opportunity to escape the influence of a distrusted institution. For Tyler, it was the Continental Congress, whose prior approval of amendments was required under the Articles of Confederation; for Madison, it was the state legislatures themselves, whose participation in the convention would be restricted to the choice of delegates. As the Mount Vernon meeting had shown, the states were willing to cede some of their authority in this limited way. The Tyler proposal, Madison told Washington, seemed "naturally to grow out of" the Mount Vernon meeting and would have "fewer enemies" than his own measures (*PJM* 8:439). What had been intended as an affirmation of state sovereignty became for Madison a relatively untrammeled opportunity to pursue national goals.

In justifying the Annapolis Convention, Madison relied explicitly on the analysis that I have sketched briefly here, emphasizing the interplay of popular sentiment and official reaction. Each presented a discrete obstacle to reform. "If all on whom the correction of these vices depends were well informed and well disposed," he wrote to Monroe, "the mode would be of little moment. But as we have both ignorance and iniquity to control, we must defeat the designs of the latter by humouring the prejudices of the former." As before, Madison took the people's disposition toward constitutional change to be fundamental; it determined all else. If their "ignorance" could be overcome, the "iniquity" of their elected representatives would be of less consequence. Enlightenment would come from the "defects" of the Confederation, which would "force themselves on the public attention" and prepare "the public mind" for change (*PJM* 8:505). The experience of hardship could educate the people, freeing them from their attachment to existing forms. Madison thus trusted to "experience and even distress...for an adequate remedy," and saw the "present crisis" as an auspicious time for the Annapolis Convention, finding in it a concurrence of circumstances likely to produce the needed "unanimity."[16]

Such calculations point to Machiavelli, who also understood popular distress as the necessary opportunity for founding. As he put it, such a situation enabled a prince to introduce a "form" into otherwise recalcitrant human "matter." It was essential to Moses' success that he found the Israelites "enslaved and oppressed by the Egyptians, so that they would be disposed to follow him." The accomplishments of Cyrus depended on his finding the Persians "malcontent with the empire of the Medes," just as the achievements of Theseus depended on the Athenians being "dispersed." Excellent though these princes were, their *virtù* would have remained untested if not for the troubles of their peoples: "such opportunities...made these men successful" (*P* 6). For a founder to succeed, necessity had to intrude with great force on popular complacency.

Madison later confessed that, by the time of the Annapolis Convention, public sentiment had become the only meaningful limit on reform. As he saw it,

---

[16] JM to GW, 9 December 1785; to James Monroe, 14 March 1786; and to TJ, 18 March 1786, in *PJM* 8:438, 498, 503.

the public's approval – or presumed approval – had given reformers a wide berth, allowing them to set aside the limits placed on their activities by formal, representative institutions, whether the state governments or the Confederation. With the help of "further experience" of reform's "necessity" in the months leading up to the meeting (*RFC* 3:545),[17] the Annapolis Convention had brought about two key developments. In the first place, "public opinion" had advanced "in the desired direction." The "general attention" had been turned "to the Critical State of things," preparing "the public mind" for "a salutary Reform of the pol[itical] System" (*RFC* 3:545, 547).[18] In the second place, the convention had called forth "the sentiments and the exertions of the most enlightened & influencial patriots," most notably the twelve men (including Madison and Hamilton) who had gathered at Annapolis.

As Madison made clear in explaining the activities of the convention, this first development was the permissive condition for the fullest expression of the second: "such had been the advance of public opinion...that the Convention...*did not scruple to decline the limited task assigned to it*, and to recommend to the States a Convention with powers adequate to the occasion" (*RFC* 3:545, emphasis added).[19] In this way, the Annapolis Convention set a series of important precedents: It violated the forms under which it met, it did so in the name of a public opinion that had not been articulated in any politically authoritative way, and it assigned to itself on this basis a wide discretion in making recommendations for constitutional reform. The act of constitution-making – if not the final establishment of a constitution – had been removed from the ambit of popular politics. It was now in the hands of the "most enlightened and influencial patriots."

This peculiar relationship between the people and their constitution-makers is even more prominent in Madison's account of the Federal Convention. Public crisis was again the necessary backdrop for constitutional reform. Thus, even as Madison lamented the deteriorating national situation in 1786–7, he could take satisfaction in its salutary effects. In Virginia, he wrote to Thomas Jefferson, "the experience of one year" since the calling of the Annapolis Convention had brought about a "revolution of sentiment." The "evidence of dangerous defects in the Confederation" had "proselyted the most obstinate adversaries of reform" (*PJM* 9:189). If the Federal Convention were to succeed, the crisis

---

[17] Trade wars between the states had continued to escalate, Virginia alone had complied with the most recent federal requisition, a bitter sectional dispute over navigation of the Mississippi had flared up in Congress, and, finally, the New York legislature had killed the second impost proposal, the last hope for anything like federal self-sufficiency in revenue. See Brant, *James Madison*, 2:382–3; McDonald, *E Pluribus Unum*, 239–44.

[18] Madison used similar language immediately after the Federal Convention, writing of the "uneasiness" that had "prepared the public mind for a general reform." JM to TJ, 24 October 1787, *PJM* 10:212.

[19] Cf. *Fed.* 40, where Madison used still stronger language, describing the Annapolis Convention as an instance of "a *very few* deputies, from a *very few* States," assuming the liberty of "recommending a great and critical object, wholly foreign to their commission."

in national affairs would need to work the same transformation throughout the union. Considering "the probable diversity of opinions and prejudices, and of supposed or real interests among the States," Madison wrote a month before delegates began arriving in Philadelphia, the "existing embarrassments and *mortal* diseases of the Confederacy form the only ground of hope" (*PJM* 9:359).

Madison saw the danger of the national situation as an opportunity for the members of the Federal Convention. The people, vulnerable and anxious, would allow these delegates a latitude unknown to ordinary representatives. Early in the proceedings of the convention, Madison urged his colleagues to ignore the fleeting, ill-informed opinions of the people and to focus instead on their permanent needs. He observed

that if the opinions of the people were to be our guide, it w[oul]d be difficult to say what course we ought to take. No member of the Convention could say what the opinions of his Constituents were at this time; much less could he say what they would think if possessed of the information & lights possessed by the members here; & still less what would be their way of thinking 6 or 12 months hence. We ought to consider what was right & necessary in itself for the attainment of a proper Government. (*PJM* 10:49)

If the convention succeeded in this task, its indifference to instruction from the people would be forgotten. The people's relief would overcome their pride. "My own idea," he told Jefferson at the convention's conclusion, "is that the public mind will now or in a very little time receive any thing that promises stability to the public Councils & security to private rights, and that no regard ought to be had to local prejudices or temporary considerations" (*PJM* 10:163).

In *The Federalist*, Madison equivocated to some extent but was fairly forthright in the end about the convention's having gone well beyond its mandate, both in substance and in form. It had designed a national rather than a federal government, in defiance of the principles of the Articles of Confederation and what many of the delegates knew to be the states' wishes. Furthermore, in allowing the assent of popular conventions in nine states to be sufficient for ratifying the Constitution, it had openly flouted the Confederation's provisions for amendment, which assigned a formal role only to the Congress and to the state legislatures, whose approval had to be unanimous (*Fed.* 40).[20] In justifying these "*informal and unauthorized propositions*," Madison drew an important contrast: between the American people, on the one hand, and the small group of "patriotic and respectable" citizens who had assembled in Philadelphia, on

---

[20] Some scholars, motivated perhaps by a desire to find an unassailable legitimacy in the founding, have maintained that there was nothing irregular in the activities of the convention. See Forrest McDonald, *Novus Ordo Seclorum: The Intellectual Origins of the Constitution* (Lawrence, KS: University Press of Kansas, 1985), 279; John P. Roche, "The Founding Fathers: A Reform Caucus in Action," *APSR* 55:4 (December 1961): 799–800. At the time, however, it was something of a commonplace that the convention had gone beyond the limits of its authority, and most students of the period have agreed. See Stanley Elkins and Eric McKitrick, "The Founding Fathers: Young Men of the Revolution," *Political Science Quarterly* 76:2 (June 1961): 209–10; Rossiter, *1787: The Grand Convention*, 262–3; Herbert J. Storing, *What the Anti-Federalists Were For* (Chicago: University of Chicago Press, 1981), 7.

the other. Because the people were incapable of moving "spontaneously and universally ... towards their object," the delegates to the Federal Convention had been compelled to take matters into their own hands, to exercise an "irregular and assumed privilege." Acting on the people's behalf if not precisely with their consent, *they* had vindicated the rights described by the Declaration of Independence (*Fed.* 40).[21] As he summarized the matter in a private letter written at the same time, "there are subjects to which the capacities of the bulk of mankind are unequal," and judging constitutions was chief among them.[22]

This low estimate of popular prudence was evident even in Madison's insistence that the new constitution be ratified by the people. One might expect here some kind of concession to popular judgment, but he invariably cast his argument strictly in terms of authority: Ratification by the people was the only way to ensure that the Constitution would be paramount to the states.[23] He offered no special expression of confidence in the ability of the people to recognize the merits of the instrument. On what, then, would their ratification or rejection be based? Again, on the exertions of the few. A small class would ultimately decide the fate of the Constitution. Madison went so far as to tell the members of the convention that this group was their primary constituency:

> We ought to consider what was right & necessary in itself for the attainment of a proper Governm[en]t. A plan adjusted to this idea will recommend itself.... [A]ll the most enlightened and respectable citizens will be its advocates. Should we fall short of the necessary and proper point, this influential class of citizens will be turned against the plan, and little support in opposition to them can be gained to it from the unreflecting multitude.   (*PJM* 10:49)

Because the people's opinions would be formed by such men, the Constitution could be safely entrusted to popular ratification. Judgment would be supplied by the few, but the rights of all would be honored.

Disturbing as this assessment might be when judged in light of the principles of the Declaration of Independence, it is saved from its most sinister Machiavellian implications by Madison's fundamental agreement with George Washington about the sort of men best suited to lead a republic.[24] The profile he sketched of his princely types, of the few, was quite different from Machiavelli's. They were not amoral seekers of glory and dominion, indifferent to the needs and claims of the many. In the country at large, they represented "the enlightened and impartial part of America," those who possessed "a rational, intelligent,

---

[21] For a more complete analysis of this essay, see Gary Rosen, "James Madison and the Problem of Founding," *RP* 58:3 (Summer 1996): 561–95.

[22] JM to Edmund Randolph, 10 January 1788, in *PJM* 10:355. *Federalist* 40 first appeared on 18 January 1788.

[23] See JM to TJ, 19 March 1787, and to Edmund Pendleton, 22 April 1787; and Speech in the Federal Convention, 5 June 1787, in *PJM* 9:318, 395, 10:27.

[24] See Chapter 7 of this book.

and unbiassed mind."[25] As for the convention itself, its members were, in several instances, "the most respectable characters in the U.S.," and "the best contribution of talents the States could make for the occasion." Selected from "the most experienced & highest standing Citizens," they were "pure in their motives" and "anxiously devoted to the object committed to them."[26] Most important of all, Madison's princes were patriotic in the widest and most principled sense. They were, he told Edmund Pendleton, "real friends of the Revolution," determined both to "perpetuate the Union" *and* to "redeem the honor of the Republican name" (*PJM* 9:295). Though they knew the people's limits, they were committed to the project of popular rule.

Madison never spelled out the reasons for this commitment on the part of his princes, but a range of motives suggest themselves. The lowest of these might be simple pride in their cause, an unwillingness to see their political edifice overturned, their boasts made empty. For most members of the Federal Convention, their names – and their fame – were inextricably linked to the American experiment.[27] Expedience in the face of republican expectations is also a possibility: America had a republican "genius" and, as a practical matter, it had to be accommodated (*Fed.* 39). This suggests founders who were more politic than principled, reminding us of their eminent practicality. At the same time, we should not rule out more aristocratic motives. As Madison's own anguished reflections imply, part of the attraction of the republican project was its difficulty, its lack of precedent. A grand experiment in self-government was a worthy aspiration for supremely able men, even if it would result in a certain injustice to themselves and those like them. Finally, there was the rightness of the cause, the basic (though not unqualified) truth of human equality. With this thought, a gentleman-founder might pause, recognizing that his class could not be relied on to act as a permanent guardian of the people's rights and congratulating himself for assenting to a principle that denied his own pretensions.

These various motives not only made the convention a safe forum for republicanism, they also made the convention possible in the most fundamental sense. Without such genuine devotion to popular rule, the gentlemanly class would have received neither the confidence and respect of the public nor, more importantly, the discretion that came with these attitudes. The convention's patriotic bona fides raised it above suspicion and gave it a uniquely broad, if temporary, authority. The presence of George Washington – who arrived in Philadelphia "amidst the acclamations of the people, as well as more sober marks of the affection and veneration which continue to be felt for his character" (*PJM* 9:415),

[25] See Speech in the Federal Convention, 5 July 1787, and Speech in the Virginia Ratifying Convention, 7 June 1788, in *PJM* 10:93, 11:95

[26] See JM to William Short, 6 June 1787, in *PJM* 10:31; "Preface to Debates in the Convention of 1787," in *RFC* 3:546, 551.

[27] See Douglass Adair's reflections on the importance of fame to men like Washington and Hamilton: Adair, "Fame and the Founding Fathers," in *Fame and the Founding Fathers*, 3–26.

as Madison told Jefferson – and that of lesser figures of impeccable republican credentials allowed the convention to rebut the charge of being an aristocratic conspiracy while conferring on it the opportunity to behave like one.[28]

On this subject, Machiavelli was and remains the great authority, having devoted so many valuable passages, with characteristic evenhandedness, to both the execution and the foiling of conspiracies. Indeed, Madison relied on a certain Machiavellian logic. For the great Florentine, a prince was most secure against subversion by the few when he possessed the favor of the many: He "should take little account of conspiracies if the people show good will to him" (*P* 19). For Madison, the lesson here was for the conspirators: If they possessed the confidence of the people, their schemes, however offensive to the sensibilities of a popular regime, had a reasonable chance of success. This was especially the case, he believed, with the convention, whose aims were limited and whose ultimate intent was popular. To Madison's chagrin, however, this was not the end of the conspiracy. It endured long after the convention, became considerably more ambitious, and ultimately confirmed much of the Machiavellian view of princely types.

Maintenance and the Many

For Madison, the fact that the members of the convention were, by and large, long-standing partisans of republicanism was more than a convenient cover for founding. It was also a strong indication of the role that such men would play in the new regime: However necessary their intervention in the decisive instance of constitution-making, they would not dominate everyday politics in the same fashion. The Constitution would be "wholly popular" (*Fed.* 14). This interpretation of Madison's aims is not universally accepted, of course. Several influential students of the period see an important similarity between the movement for the Constitution, with its aristocratic distance from the people, and Madison's account of representation under the new regime. With regard to both, they argue, it was his intention that virtuous, disinterested gentlemen would prevail over their popular inferiors, who, as he insists, would be totally excluded *"in their collective capacity"* from the conduct of government (*Fed.* 63).[29]

---

[28] Cf. Elkins and McKitrick, "The Founding Fathers: Young Men of the Revolution," 206–7: "Various writers [Beard, Jensen, and Parrington] have said that the activities of the Federalists during this period had in them a clear element of the conspiratorial.... Though it would be wrong to think of the Constitution as something that had to be carried in the face of deep and basic popular opposition, it certainly required a series of brilliant maneuvers to escape the deadening clutch of particularism and inertia.... [The Federalists] cannot be said to have circumvented the popular will, [but they] did have to use techniques which in their sustained drive, tactical mobility, and risk-taking smacked more than a little of the revolutionary."

[29] See Wood, *The Creation of the American Republic*, 471–518, and "Democracy and the Constitution," in *How Democratic Is the Constitution?* ed. Robert A. Goldwin and William A. Schambra (Washington, DC: American Enterprise Institute, 1980), 1–17; Wills, *Explaining America*, 179–264.

But such arguments have it only half right. Their great failing is to misread *Federalist* 10. There Madison indeed expresses the hope that the new Constitution might encourage the election of the wise and the virtuous, but he also explicitly declares that the chief bulwark against factious oppression will be the extended sphere, with its great variety of parties, interests, and sects. As he observes in dismissing as insufficient the aristocratic alternative, "Enlightened statesmen will not always be at the helm" (*Fed.* 10).[30] Though Madison hardly expected the princely few to disappear from the American political scene – they would be especially attracted to the more select offices – he did not suggest that they were critical to the new regime: A constitution designed to honor the claims of the people while muting the destructive effects of their passions and interests.[31]

With the Constitution established, Madison's deepest concern was that the people perform their part according to the Machiavellian model: They had been given a good regime – with their active consent – and it was now their job to see that it endured. As Machiavelli summarized this conservative task within the political division of labor:

> If one individual is capable of ordering, the thing itself is ordered to last long not if it remains on the shoulders of one individual but rather if it remains in the care of many and its maintenance stays with many. For as many are not capable of ordering a thing because they do not know its good . . . so when they have come to know it, they do not agree to abandon it. (D 1.9; see also 1.58)

Madison's solution was a certain sort of constitutional passion, an unthinking attachment to the Constitution as an end in itself. He briefly mentioned such a possibility in his critique of Jefferson's famous proposal that constitutions, like ordinary laws, lapse with each sovereign generation. With the Constitution itself having been in operation less than a year, Madison wrote to his friend of the "share of prejudice" that was "a salutary aid" even to the most rational of governments (cf. *PTJ* 15:392–97 with *PJM* 13:22). A fuller statement of this view had come in *Federalist* 49, the location of another notable public disagreement with Jefferson. Here Madison replied to a more limited application of Jefferson's notion of popular sovereignty, a proposal to resolve disputes over constitutional matters – particularly separation of powers – by referring them to the people as a whole, acting through conventions. Even in this diluted form,

---

[30] For an overview of this question and a summary of the case against Wood and Wills, see Alan Gibson, "Impartial Representation and the Extended Republic: Towards a Comprehensive and Balanced Treatment of the Tenth *Federalist* Paper," *HPT* 12:2 (Summer 1991): 263–304; Paul A. Rahe, *Republics Ancient and Modern: Classical Republicanism and the American Revolution* (Chapel Hill, NC: University of North Carolina Press, 1992), 586–7, 1056–7, n. 60. Madison is far blunter about his expectations for representatives in the "Vices of the Political System of the United States," April 1787, in *PJM* 9:354: "Representative appointments are sought from 3 motives. 1. ambition. 2. personal interest. 3. public good. Unhappily the two first are proved by experience to be the most prevalent."

[31] See Martin Diamond, "Democracy and The Federalist: A Reconsideration of the Framers' Intent," *APSR* 53:1 (March 1959): 52–68.

Jefferson's resort to the people posed a threat to the political sentiments that Madison wished to cultivate: It would deprive the government of "veneration" and undermine a proper "reverence for the laws" (*Fed.* 49).

It is little wonder that these brief statements – with their appeals to "prejudice," "veneration," and "reverence" – have led so many commentators to describe Madison as a conservative of Humean or even Burkean stripe, as a thinker who recommended an attitude of quiet respect, if not outright submission, on the part of the people.[32] There was indeed a moderating project at work in these passages, but it remained very much within the radical premises of the social compact. For Madison, the people retained their "transcendent and precious right" to alter and abolish governments (*Fed.* 40), but they were not to exercise it precipitously, in disregard of their own manifest shortcomings as founders and their rare good fortune at having received the Constitution.

In this, Madison parted company with his philosophical compatriots, most of whom were far readier to see established regimes challenged and recast. As Markus Fischer notes in the prologue to this book, Machiavelli endorsed the notion of perpetual refounding, praising Rome's succession of kings and nobles, with their ever-new modes and orders. What is more, he celebrated the fact that a considerable share in governance was assigned to the people in their collective capacity. In the constant popular tumults that typified the early republic, as well as in the institution of the tribuneship, Machiavelli saw political vigor and a check on the oppressive sway of the few (*D* 1.2–5). As other contributors to this book have observed,[33] Marchamont Nedham, Algernon Sidney, John Locke, and the authors of *Cato's Letters*, though operating within a rather different modern political idiom, retained this reliance on popular discontent as a palpable, even menacing check on tyranny; governors must recognize, as Locke asserts, that a people *"generally ill treated"* will be "ready upon any occasion to ease themselves of a burden that sits heavy upon them" (*TTG* 2.19.211–42, esp. 224).[34] Finally, as Paul Rahe emphasizes in the ninth chapter of this book, we see these notions of popular vigilance and revolution combined in the eclectic thought of Jefferson, who seemed to embrace Machiavellian tumults and Lockean natural rights with equal enthusiasm.[35]

---

[32] Adrienne Koch, *Jefferson and Madison: The Great Collaboration* (New York: Knopf, 1950), 88–91, suggested the comparison (but did not make it herself) by contrasting the views of Jefferson (and Paine) on the question of generational obligation to those of Burke. For more explicit presentations of Madison as a conservative, see Wills, *Explaining America*, 24–33; Drew McCoy, *The Last of the Fathers: James Madison and the Republican Legacy* (Cambridge, UK: Cambridge University Press, 1989), 39–64; Charles A. Miller, *Jefferson and Nature: An Interpretation* (Baltimore, MD: Johns Hopkins University Press, 1988), 162.

[33] See Chapters 1–3 of this book.

[34] For a discussion of the centrality of the right of popular resistance in Locke's political thought, see Thomas L. Pangle, *The Spirit of Modern Republicanism: The Moral Vision of the American Founders and the Philosophy of Locke* (Chicago: University of Chicago Press, 1988), 257–61.

[35] For Jefferson's approval of popular tumults, see Chapter 9 of this book; for his invocation of natural rights, see, of course, the Declaration of Independence but also, among many other

While Madison recognized that such extraconstitutional claims were necessary in some circumstances, he was anxious to give the people a less extreme option. A frequent resort to first principles might indeed prevent serious abuses by a government that had somehow forgotten its republican dependence on the people, but it was also likely to dissipate the veneration that the people themselves would have to feel for the Constitution if it were to restrain *their* excesses. Madison thus aimed to attach the people less to their natural claims than to their conventional ones, to remind them that they, ultimately, were the creators of the forms and limits of the Constitution. This sovereign pride, derived from the social compact, made it possible to *constitutionalize* claims that might otherwise have meant the destruction of the regime.[36]

This Madisonian refinement of popular vigilance did not spring fully formed from the pages of *The Federalist*. There Madison presented "veneration" and "reverence" as mere accretions, accomplished by little more than the passage of time. Motive was lacking for the people's energetic superintendence of their regime. It had been generated to some extent in the debate over ratification, where anxious Anti-Federalists had encouraged popular fear and jealousy by charging that the Constitution would be usurped by a glory-seeking few, bent on national grandeur. At the time, Madison had assured them – and perhaps himself – that such suspicions were groundless, an insult to the people and their patriotic leaders.[37] Several years into the new regime, he was far less sure, and he too would come to rely on this powerful Machiavellian dynamic, prompted by the early republic's most brilliant aspiring prince, Alexander Hamilton.

Though Hamilton had made known his distaste for republican government at the Federal Convention (*RFC* 1:282–93, 424–5),[38] his subsequent role in securing ratification of the Constitution had gone a long way toward allaying whatever fears might have lingered about his loyalty to so popular a regime. For his part, Madison welcomed the participation of Hamilton in the administration that took office in 1789, showing appreciation for the secretary of the treasury's talents even as he disagreed with many of his early financial measures.[39] It is important to note the fairly amicable tone of these disagreements over the purely economic part of Hamilton's program. Though Madison thought Hamilton

---

examples, TJ to JM, 6 September 1789, in *PTJ* 15:392–7; The Kentucky Resolutions, October 1798, in *WrTJ* (ed. Peterson) 449–56.

[36] One might consider this the popular counterpart to the constitutionalizing of executive power that Harvey C. Mansfield, describes in *Taming the Prince: The Ambivalence of Modern Executive Power* (Baltimore, MD: Johns Hopkins University Press, 1989).

[37] See Lance Banning, *The Sacred Fire of Liberty: James Madison and the Founding of the Federal Republic* (Ithaca, NY: Cornell University Press, 1995), 243–53.

[38] Though Hamilton's own plan of government, described in the first of these speeches, was indeed republican in the strictest sense, it clearly revealed his distrust of the people, his designs on the state governments, and his great affection for monarchy. For a helpful discussion of Hamilton's plan and its reception at the Federal Convention, see John C. Miller, *Alexander Hamilton: Portrait in Paradox* (New York: Harper and Row, 1959), 163–73.

[39] See Speech on Assumption of the State Debts, 2 March 1790; JM to Edmund Pendleton, 4 March 1790; and JM to Henry Lee, 13 April 1790, in *PJM* 13:80, 85, 147.

wrong in, for example, failing to compensate the deserving original holders of the national debt, he did not consider this a breach of fundamental principle. Only with Hamilton's attempt to create a national bank – and what it revealed about his understanding of the Constitution – did Madison's opposition begin to turn partisan.[40]

By 1791 he had concluded that it was Hamilton's intention to continue to exercise the latitude assumed by the Federal Convention, to make founding an ongoing part of the regime by attempting to "administer the Government . . . into what he thought it ought to be" (*RFC* 3:534). As Hamilton himself admitted privately, it was his aim to bring about a more adequate Constitution, even if it was not the one ratified by the people.[41] Madison could be blamed, of course, for helping to give a certain legitimacy to such prudential claims. One can certainly imagine the arguments of *Federalist* 40 echoing in Hamilton's ears: If a select number of patriotic and enlightened citizens were indeed the necessary agents of constitutional change, why must they *ever* wait for the people ? If substance mattered more than forms, if the common good took precedence over procedural and interpretive niceties, why should *this* Constitution receive any more deference than the Articles of Confederation (*Fed.* 40)?

Experience would teach Madison a lesson that he might have learned more directly from Machiavelli, who had warned the "prudent orderer of a republic" about the precedent that he set. Though his own "extraordinary" deeds might be excused by their good effects and his devotion to fatherland, he must not pass on to another "the authority that he took": ". . . since men are more prone to evil than to good, his successor could use ambitiously that which had been used virtuously by him." Moreover, and here Machiavelli completed the equation, such singular authority was only best at "ordering"; the conservative task of maintaining a republican regime was better placed "in the care of many" (*D* 1.9).

Hamilton imbibed Machiavellian lessons of his own, not the least of which was the need to retain, for the sake of popular approval, at least the appearance

---

[40] In his desire to save some part of Madison's legacy for broad construction of the Constitution, Brant, *James Madison*, 2:217, reverses these priorities, arguing that disagreement with Hamilton "on social and economic matters . . . grew until it produced a change in Madison's political and constitutional views." Drew R. McCoy, *The Elusive Republic: Political Economy in Jeffersonian America* (New York: W. W. Norton, 1980), 136–65, also reduces the Madison–Hamilton dispute to questions of political economy, though with the rather different intent of claiming Madison for the eighteenth-century English "country" party.

[41] See the personal memorandum written by Hamilton as the Federal Convention drew to a close (Conjectures about the New Constitution, 17–30 September 1787, in *PAH* 4:276): "If the government is adopted, it is probable general Washington will be the President of the United States. This will insure a wise choice of men to administer the government and a good administration. A good administration will conciliate the confidence and affection of the people and perhaps enable the government to acquire more consistency than the proposed constitution seems to promise for so great a Country. It may then triumph altogether over the state governments and reduce them to an intire subordination, dividing the larger states into smaller districts."

of abiding by the established "modes" that he meant to replace (*D* 1.25). This would not be so much of an issue with the scheme of separated and balanced powers described by the Constitution. Though Hamilton had assigned a much more limited role to the people in the plan that he proposed at the Federal Convention, he too had wished to put the departments of the national government on a footing that would encourage their independence and the vigorous defense of their own prerogatives. In fact, such a regime – soundly partitioned and operating through the rule of law – was his definition of a "free" government. As he saw it, the primary purpose of a constitution was not to decide what powers were necessary for the security and prosperity of the people but to see that necessary powers were not used arbitrarily.[42] The choice of means and of objects (in all but the very broadest sense) belonged to the government – which is to say, to the governors. In this respect, his own plan of government had radically differed from the Constitution: He had wished to see a national government with plenary powers of legislation. In his eyes, the Constitution's enumeration of powers was among its chief defects. It was an obstacle for the reform-minded prince to overcome, but this had to be done, as Hamilton knew and as Machiavelli counseled, while "retaining at least the shadow" of the Constitution's forms (*D* 1.25).

We can detect a certain progression in Hamilton's approach to this problem, or at least in his exposition of it. In proposing the first Bank of the United States in early 1791, he did not pretend that the power of incorporation – the specific power in question – was among those listed in the Constitution. Instead he classed it among "implied" as opposed to "express" powers. It was simply an "*instrument*" or "*mean*" for carrying into effect powers that were indisputably granted to the national government (in this case, borrowing money and laying and collecting taxes). To the objection that such a measure could not be described as "necessary" (as used in the "necessary and proper" clause of Article I, Section 8), Hamilton replied that "necessary" in this instance was not to be taken in a restrictive sense, "as if the word *absolutely* or *indispensably* had been prefixed to it," but rather in its more common usage, as meaning "*needful, requisite, incidental, useful*, or *conducive to*" (*PAH* 8:100, 102–3, 105–6). On this view, the urgent needs of the nation could be met within the powers of the Constitution, provided that those powers were understood to include a wide array of means.

A secondary theme of Hamilton's defense of the bank bill was more troubling, however. At points, he suggested that the power in question belonged to the national government not because of its relationship to a specific constitutional provision but because it was necessary to achieve the broad ends of civil society. A liberal construction of the Constitution was not just meant to give

---

[42] See Harvey Flaumenhaft, *The Effective Republic: Administration and Constitution in the Thought of Alexander Hamilton* (Durham, NC: Duke University Press, 1992), 61–5; Gerald Stourzh, *Alexander Hamilton and the Idea of Republican Government* (Stanford, CA: Stanford University Press, 1970), 40–4, 56–63.

operational energy to enumerated powers; it also provided a license of sorts for the "general administration of the affairs of the country" – "its finances, trade, defence, etc." – to be directed in such a way as to bring about the "advancement of the public good." As Hamilton said in a telling passage, "This rule does not depend on the particular form of government or on the particular demarkation of the boundaries of its powers, but on the nature and objects of government itself." He placed no special emphasis on the restrictive meaning of granted constitutional powers (*PAH* 8:105).[43]

As Hamilton tried to expand his program, he was compelled to rely more heavily on this second argument. The liberal construction of specified powers would no longer do. It was necessary to state more forthrightly what he had only implied in his defense of the bank bill: that the sole general limit on the powers of the national government was the public good. This principle first emerged in his famous "Report on Manufactures" (5 December 1791). The power in question on this occasion was the establishment of bounties to encourage particular industries – again, a power not found in the Constitution's enumeration. Hamilton asserted that the objects for which the public monies could be appropriated were "no less comprehensive . . . than the payment of the public debts and the providing for the common defence and '*general Welfare.*'" Whereas before he had relied on the "necessary and proper" clause for an expansive reading of the national government's *powers*, now he turned to the "general welfare" clause to go still further, to give it a wide authority to determine its own *objects*:

> The terms "*general Welfare*" were doubtless intended to signify more than was expressed or imported in those which Preceded; otherwise numerous exigencies incident to the affairs of a Nation would have been left without a provision. The phrase is as comprehensive as any that could have been used; because it was not fit that the constitutional authority of the Union, to appropriate its revenues shou'd have been restricted within narrower limits than the "General Welfare" and because this necessarily embraces a vast variety of particulars, which are susceptible neither of specification nor of definition. . . . It is therefore of necessity left to the discretion of the National Legislature, to pronounce, upon the objects, which concern the general Welfare, and for which under that description, an appropriation of money is requisite and proper.   (*PAH* 10:302–3)

With this formulation, Hamilton could finally leave behind the constitutional constraints that interfered with a vigorous prosecution of the public good. So ample a "discretion" for the national legislature meant latitude for the government as a whole, and not least of all for an ambitious republican prince prepared to endow it with energy, purpose, and a general bearing different from that which was intended by its architects and ratifiers.

---

[43] Cf. *Fed.* 78, where Hamilton spoke of a "limited constitution" as one that contained "certain specified exceptions to the legislative authority." On this view, acts were unconstitutional not when they extended beyond enumerated powers but when they were contrary to the "tenor" – that is, the *general* meaning and intent – of the Constitution.

Whatever his final opinion of Hamilton's motives, Madison initially treated the constitutional doctrines of the secretary of the treasury and his allies as mistaken rather than sinister. In opposing the bank bill on the floor of the House in early February 1791, Madison did not even begin with the question of authority, instead briefly citing his objections on policy grounds. His primary concerns were constitutional, however, and he matched the emphases in Hamilton's own argument. On the matter of how to interpret the Constitution's enumerated powers, Madison agreed that a narrow literalism would render the government inoperable. The "necessary and proper" clause *was* intended to give the Congress a certain latitude – but only in the execution of its specified powers. In place of the "diffuse and ductile" terms favored by friends of the bill as synonyms for "necessary," he suggested that only "direct and incidental" means were available under the Constitution. Without such a rule of construction, the "essential characteristic of the government, as composed of limited and enumerated powers, would be destroyed":

Mark the reasoning on which the validity of the bill depends. To borrow money is made the *end* and the accumulation of capitals, *implied* as the *means*. The accumulation of capitals is then the *end*, and a bank *implied* as the *means*. The bank is then the *end*, and a charter of incorporation, a monopoly, capital punishments, & c. *implied* as the *means*. . . . If implications, thus remote and multiplied, can be linked together, a chain may be formed that will reach every object of legislation, every object within the whole compass of political economy.

The danger of such reasoning was forcefully illustrated by the particular power in question. Not only was a right to grant charters of incorporation not included in the Constitution but, Madison declared, it had been explicitly proposed and rejected at the Federal Convention – a point that he must have recollected with some irony, since he had been the leading proponent of the power in Philadelphia (*PJM* 13:373–8).[44]

Madison did not devote much time to rebutting the more ambitious (but less prominent) argument of Hamilton and his supporters – that such a power belonged to government as such and was inseparable from its capacity to secure the public good. But he did show an awareness of this argument's great potential for mischief. While certain lesser instrumental powers could be deduced from those enumerated in the Constitution, no additional powers "could be inferred from the general nature of government." It was the "peculiar nature" of the national government that its authority was expressly described, no matter how crucial certain absent powers might appear to be. Thus, if "the power of making treaties, for example, [had] been omitted . . . the defect could only have been lamented, or supplied by an amendment of the constitution" (*PJM* 13:379–80). He was willing to accept the view that "government necessarily possesses every power." But it was true only "in theory" and did not

---

[44] For Madison's effort to include a power of incorporation in the Constitution, see his speeches of 18 August and 14 September 1787, in *PJM* 13:477–8, 638.

apply to the government of the United States (*PJM* 13:384). The most obvious reason for confining the national government in this way was to accommodate the pretensions of the states, but it had other grounds as well. So distant an authority could be superintended by the people only if its powers were both strictly enumerated *and* popularly held to be such.

Whatever the rationale for the latitude of interpretation assumed by the sponsors of the bank bill, Madison insisted that it would confirm the worst fears of the Constitution's opponents. Advocates of the Constitution had at first opposed a bill of rights because, they claimed, "powers not given were retained" and "those given were not to be extended by remote implications." This was certainly the belief that had prevailed in the state ratifying conventions, and it had been reiterated in the "explanatory amendments" – what would become the ninth and tenth amendments to the Constitution – proposed by Congress itself. Now, Madison argued, the Congress was giving serious thought to overthrowing these common understandings. Drawing a parallel to the Federal Convention, he suggested that the bank bill was an attempt to extend the process of constitution-making beyond its legitimate term:

With all this evidence of the sense in which the constitution was understood and adopted, will it not be said, if the bill should pass, that its adoption was brought by one set of arguments, and that it is now administered under the influence of another set; and this reproach will have the keener sting, because it is applicable to so many individuals concerned in both the adoption and the administration.

At this point, Madison was not prepared to say that such principles of administration represented an actual conspiracy against the Constitution. But he did emphasize that they would be seen in this light by those distrustful of the princely few. Out of "respect for ourselves," he told his colleagues, we should "shun the appearance of precipitancy and ambition" (*PJM* 13:380–1). If they failed to do so, they would threaten "the principles on which . . . this government ought to be administered": " . . . the enlightened opinion and affection of the people" (*PJM* 13:386–7).

These themes would assume a special prominence as Madison's struggle against Hamilton intensified, leading him to conclude finally that the secretary of the treasury was, in fact, the head of an aristocratic conspiracy to undo the Constitution ratified by the people. The precipitating event for Madison was Hamilton's outright endorsement, in his "Report on Manufactures," of the view that the "general welfare" was the only meaningful constraint on national power. As Madison observed to Henry Lee not long after the report's promulgation, "The federal Gov[ernmen]t has been hitherto limited to the Specified powers, by the greatest Champions for Latitude in expounding those powers. If not only the *means*, but the *objects* are unlimited, the parchment had better be thrown into the fire at once" (*PJM* 14:180). Should such a "usurpation" succeed, "the fundamental and characteristic principle of the Gov[ernmen]t" would be "subverted" (*PJM* 14:193). With this, Madison's opposition, which had previously been confined to the particular measures of Hamilton's program, turned to the administration itself. The republican cause was transformed into the Republican Party, with the political demise of Hamilton and his principles as its end.[45]

The clearest sign of this change can be found in a series of anonymous essays that Madison wrote shortly thereafter for the *National Gazette*. In late September 1792, in an essay entitled "A Candid State of Parties," Madison located the origin of the "anti-republican" party in the movement for the Constitution or, more precisely, in a minority of it: among those few individuals "who were openly or secretly attached to monarchy and aristocracy" and "hoped to make the Constitution a cradle for these hereditary establishments." Even in the heat of partisan rhetoric, Madison recognized that this minority was not merely self-seeking, but that it acted on a public principle. It was persuaded that "mankind are incapable of governing themselves," and had, accordingly, adopted a plan of administration under which the government "may by degrees be narrowed into fewer hands, and approximated to an hereditary form." The "Republican Party" – this being Madison's first recorded use of the term – sought to disprove these views. It regarded such principles as "an insult to the reason and an outrage to the rights of man," maintaining that public measures ought to appeal "both to the understanding and to the general interest of the community." Nor was this simply a matter of republican pride. However convinced the enemies of republicanism might be that the people did not know how to serve their own broad interests, they themselves had proven to be imperfectly attentive to the public good. In their efforts to bring about a more oligarchical regime, they had found it necessary to "strengthen themselves with the men of influence, particularly of moneyed, which is the most active and insinuating influence." In practice, this had meant not a government more capable of pursuing the general welfare but one whose measures were pointed "less to the interest of the many than of the few" (*MF* 189–90).

The seriousness of this threat is a common thread in the party press essays. For Madison, such "corruption" did not represent a general moral decay or an assault on the personal identity of citizens, as some contemporary scholars interpret this important term in eighteenth-century "country" ideology.[46] It was a concrete political problem, a deliberate challenge to constitutional government on the part of "interested partisans" who sought to establish – and here the class divisions of the Machiavellian model emerged in all their harshness – "a real domination of the few" in the midst of "an apparent liberty of the many," as Madison wrote in "Spirit of Governments" (*MF* 183–4). The danger was

---

[45] See Colleen A. Sheehan, "Madison's Party Press Essays," *Interpretation* 17:3 (Spring 1990): 360–3.

[46] According to Bernard Bailyn, *The Ideological Origins of the American Revolution* (Cambridge, MA: Harvard University Press, 1967), 51, English radicals understood corruption generally "as the self-indulgence, effeminizing luxury, and gluttonous pursuit of gain of a generation sunk in new and unaccustomed wealth." For J. G. A. Pocock, *The Machiavellian Moment*, 507–8, corruption reached still deeper, leading those confronted by it "to conclude that malign agencies [were] conspiring against the inner citadels of their personalities."

not just of one-sidedness in administration and policy, he added in "Consolidation." It was that the government, drawing an ever greater number of public responsibilities to the center, might soon overwhelm the people's capacity for informed legislative "control," which was "essential to a faithful discharge of its trust." Under such "universal silence and insensibility," the government would soon be left to a *"self directed course"* (MF 181–2).

And how was this counterrevolutionary movement to be resisted? In his essay "Government of the United States," Madison exploited the logic of the social compact, trumpeting its proud claims of popular self-sufficiency in the hope of creating a strong attachment to the Constitution's forms and limits. As he would have it, the people had to think of their regime much as they did their property, as a thing of their own making that required jealous and energetic protection:

> In bestowing the eulogies due to the partitions and internal checks of power, it ought not the less to be remembered, that they are neither the sole nor the chief palladium of constitutional liberty. The people who are the authors of this blessing, must also be its guardians. Their eyes must be ever ready to mark, their voice to pronounce, and their arm to repel or repair aggressions on the authority of their constitutions; the highest authority next to their own, because the immediate work of their own, and the most sacred part of their property, as recognising and recording the title of every other.
>
> (*PJM* 14:218)

Far from being a machine that might run on its own, the Constitution assumed a certain disposition among its citizens. Recalling the language of *Federalist* 49 and his exchange with Jefferson over intergenerational obligation, Madison wrote in an essay entitled "Charters" of the need for "a more than common reverence for the authority which is to preserve order thro' the whole." This was a species of opinion peculiar to a regime of the American type and crucial to its ultimate success: "How devoutly is it to be wished...that the public opinion of the United States should be enlightened; that it should attach itself to their governments as delineated in the *great charters*, derived not from the usurped power of kings, but from the legitimate authority of the people; and that it should guarantee, with a holy zeal, these political scriptures from every attempt to add to or to diminish from them" (*PJM* 14:192).

Though Madison spoke metaphorically in these passages – his most developed account of constitutional opinion and its origins – his tropes were not accidental. Expressions like "blessing," "sacred," "reverence," "devoutly," "holy zeal," and "political scriptures" pointed to the very heart of his intention. It is no exaggeration to say that his answer to Hamilton was a kind of God-less civil religion, with the Constitution serving as an altar on which the people might proudly declare the sanctity of their natural rights. One might also consider this Madison's answer to Machiavelli, who openly wondered if a republican regime could endure the resignation and otherworldliness of Christianity. For Machiavelli, a proper civil religion required fear as its engine and political success as its end (*D* 2.2, 11–15). Madison too wished to promote an unreflective popular passion for the American regime, but he drew on the resources of the social compact rather than of militant Rome; he invoked the mundane rather than the divine, attempting to invigorate republican citizenship with sovereign pride rather than mortal fear.

The most immediate purpose of such a faith was to rebuke the aristocratic pretensions of Hamilton and his followers. The people, for all of their faults, remained the surest guardians of their own legitimate rights and interests. Whatever the requirements of founding, with its necessary distance from popular views, it was unsafe for government to ask "nothing but obedience" from the people while "leaving the care of their liberties to their wiser rulers" (*PJM* 14:426). Instead, the people owed obedience to the Constitution and thus, indirectly, to themselves. In this regard, it is important to note that, even while resisting Hamilton in the name of the people, Madison did not lose sight of the possibility of popular wrongdoing. For all of the energy that he devoted to combating a minority faction – no small irony in light of his analysis in *Federalist* 10 – he understood that the majority was the abiding threat. Here too he expected veneration to serve as a constraint, directing popular passions and interests into constitutional channels. By "establishing permanent and constitutional maxims of conduct," "the will of the society" could be subjected to "the reason of the society." In this way, the Constitution might prevail over the people's "occasional impressions" and "inconsiderate pursuits" (*MF* 192–3).

In the end, it is this confidence in the possibility of a truly popular regime that most distinguishes Madison's account of princes and peoples from Machiavelli's. Though Madison was willing to supplement the social compact with the agency for founding that it lacked in the standard accounts, he did not follow his great Florentine predecessor in believing that the few governed everywhere, regardless of regime. Even before Madison discovered the danger of relying on princely types in his falling out with Hamilton and the Federalist cause, he had expressed his confidence in a republican experiment that genuinely drew its energy and direction from the people – guided, to be sure, by the Constitution. He saw in the people a potential that went well beyond mere constancy or the desire to escape oppression. If Machiavelli's profile adequately described the first and most elemental of the people's political sentiments, it failed to capture the highest of them: a spirited – one might even say a princely – determination to govern themselves.

11

Was Alexander Hamilton a Machiavellian Statesman?

Karl-Friedrich Walling

Many modern scholars of weight and stature seem to think so, as did a number of his contemporaries in the most heated debates of the founding era. Gerald Stourzh suggests that Hamilton followed Machiavelli in stressing the primacy of foreign over domestic policy. Both J. G. A. Pocock and Stourzh see Hamilton as an advocate of a military and commercial empire whose dynamic *virtù* posed a severe threat to republican virtue. Isaac Kramnick links Hamilton to the language of state-centered power (of *imperium, potestas, gubernaculum*, prerogative, and sovereignty) implicit in Machiavelli's *Prince* (but oddly enough, Kramnick says, not in the *Discourses*). Most recently, John Lamberton Harper has compared Hamilton's and Machiavelli's views on foreign policy more systematically than any scholar thus far. While the high degree of overlapping views between them justifies stressing Hamilton's kinship with the Florentine realist, Harper's omission of the liberal principles that also make Hamilton an anti-Machiavellian statesman is a common fault that this essay seeks to correct. In this book, Gary Rosen has suggested that Hamilton was a "republican prince" who tried to transform the new government under the Constitution of 1787 into what he thought it should be, thus allowing the end of the public good to triumph over the means of constitutional forms. Whereas Rosen leaves out the possibility that Hamilton's broad construction of the Constitution was the only practical means of preserving constitutional government under the stresses especially posed by the necessities and fortunes of war, Harvey C. Mansfield,

This essay is adapted from Karl Walling, "Was Hamilton a Machiavellian Statesman?" *RP* 57:3 (Summer 1995): 419–47, and is reprinted with permission. Lieutenant Colonel Delane Clark and Professors Nathan Tarcov, Harvey C. Mansfield, Forrest McDonald, Robert Scigliano, Ralph Lerner, Jean Yarbrough, Colleen Sheehan, Lance Banning, Carey McWilliams, Paul A. Rahe, and Michael and Catherine Zuckert supplied much needed advice for revising this essay. The Earhart Foundation and the John M. Olin Foundation supplied generous financial assistance. A fuller and more complete statement of the author's views of Alexander Hamilton's similarities with and differences from Machiavelli can be found in Karl-Friedrich Walling, *Republican Empire: Alexander Hamilton on War and Free Government* (Lawrence, KS: University Press of Kansas, 1999).

suggests more accurately that (as Publius) Hamilton partook in the modern effort to tame Machiavelli's prince without declawing him. For Mansfield, Hamilton domesticated Machiavelli's prince to make him safe and useful to American freedom.[1]

For all that has been said or implied about Hamilton's Machiavellianism, however, Hamilton's collected papers include only two references to Machiavelli. Each is quite critical of some of the imperialistic and duplicitous politics commonly associated with the Machiavellian politics that Hamilton believed were put into practice by the revolutionary republic in France and its ministers in America.[2] This fact calls for greater attention to Hamilton's ambiguous relation to Machiavelli than has appeared so far. Did he learn something, however indirectly, from Machiavelli? Or was there something about Machiavelli's general approach to politics that justifies understanding him as an American Machiavellian? How do we account for the times when Hamilton expressed direct opposition to policies that he understood as Machiavellian?

Perhaps no other political figure in Western history paid more attention than Machiavelli to the challenge of waging war effectively and remaining free at the same time. Hamilton was arguably more like Machiavelli than any of the other American founders because he devoted most of his career to addressing this fundamental problem of political theory and practice. Like Machiavelli, he recognized that durable liberty required the kind of republic that could adapt to the changing necessities and fortunes of war. Energy, the central concept in Hamilton's political thought, was his means of endowing the American republic with some of the dynamic Machiavellian *virtù* that even republics require in time of war.

This does not mean that Hamilton was a student of Machiavelli. Instead, his general approach to politics, like Machiavelli's, was based on "long experience of modern things and a continuous reading of ancient ones" (*P* Ep. Ded.). When Hamilton sounded like Machiavelli, it may well be because both Machiavelli and Hamilton often sounded like Livy, the great historian of ancient Rome from whom both drew important lessons about war and free government.[3]

---

[1] Gerald Stourzh, *Alexander Hamilton and the Idea of Republican Government* (Stanford, CA: Stanford University Press, 1970), 132–45; J. G. A. Pocock, *The Machiavellian Moment: Florentine Political Thought and the Atlantic Republican Tradition* (Princeton, NJ: Princeton University Press, 1975), 528–33; Isaac Kramnick, "The 'Great National Discussion': The Discourse of Politics in 1787," *WMQ* 45:1 (January 1988): 24; John Lamberton Harper, *American Machiavelli: Alexander Hamilton and the Origins of U.S. Foreign Policy* (New York: Cambridge University Press, 2004); Harvey C. Mansfield, *Taming the Prince: The Ambivalence of Modern Executive Power* (New York: Free Press, 1989), 247–78; Chapter 10 of this book.

[2] See *Relations with France*, 1795–1796; *The Stand*, No. 1, *New York Commercial Advertiser*, 30 March 1798; Rufus King to AH, 14 July 1798, n. 2, in *PAH* 19:523–4, 21:382, 22:1–2.

[3] Cf. Hamilton's references to Livy in his discussions of the folly of halfway measures in dispensing punishments and of fear and love as the effectual foundations of popular loyalty, in AH to the New York Committee on Correspondence, 20–27 April 1777; to William Livingston, 29 April 1777; and *Letters of Phocion*, nos. 1 and 2, 1–27 January 1784 and April 1784, in *PAH* 2:233, 237, 243, 3:485–6, 534–5, 557, with Livy 8.13, 21, 9.4. As Julius Goebel first observed, Machiavelli

Hamilton also sounded like Machiavelli because he learned much about war and free government from modern political theorists (especially David Hume) who read Machiavelli carefully, in a fashion documented in the earlier chapters of this book.[4] Hamilton then began to combine the modern doctrine of universal liberty with an energetic *virtù* of his own. At the dawn of the age of modern warfare, however, he also discovered something completely new: the necessity of subjecting modern wars of ideology to liberal principles of just war. Otherwise, modern warfare would rapidly surpass the ferocity and cruelty of the ancients, as in fact it has in the past hundred years.

If Hamilton was an American Machiavellian, then he was a highly paradoxical one: a liberal Machiavellian who meant to enable his republic to wage war effectively without sacrificing its liberty. In the first section of this chapter, I suggest that Hamilton was most like Machiavelli in calling for a strong national government headed by an energetic executive who could enable Americans to depend upon their own arms and virtue in time of war. In the second section, I suggest that Hamilton surpassed Machiavelli in addressing the difficulty of waging war and remaining free at the same time. His new modes and orders called for financing war without crime and waging war without transforming America into a garrison state ready to conquer the world. In that respect, his vision of an American republican empire was meant to be the antithesis of the rapacious republicanism that Markus Fischer, quite correctly, sees at the core of Machiavelli's political teaching.[5] Contemporary scholars, ranging from Pocock at one extreme through Stourzh, Harper, and Rosen at the other have sometimes portrayed America as some kind of Machiavellian republic and Hamilton as some kind of Machiavellian prince. In contrast, in the third section of this chapter, I reveal that Hamilton's new order of the ages was designed to supply an effectual moral alternative to the Machiavellian practices of the Old World, and the much more authentic Machiavellian republic that arose from the ruins of the old regime in revolutionary France.

By Our Own Arms and Virtue

To understand Hamilton as he understood himself, one must begin at General Washington's field headquarters during the War for Independence in

---

himself employed similar examples from Livy to argue against halfway measures and to develop a political psychology centered on the passions of love, fear, and hate. See Goebel, *The Law Practice of Alexander Hamilton* (New York: Columbia University Press, 1964), 1:211, and note NM, *D* 1.26, 45, 2.23; *P* 8, 18, 20. Though Hamilton was never as extreme as Machiavelli, he too seems to have made fear and love (of power, honor, and wealth) the fundamental passions of his political psychology. See, for example, his discussion of founding effective government on interest, ambition, attachment, coercion, and influence in Madison's version of his great speech at the Federal Convention, 18 June 1787, in *PAH* 4:188–9.

[4] See Chapters 1 through 6 of this book. For a useful discussion of the founders' indirect debt to Machiavelli, see Thomas L. Pangle, *The Spirit of Modern Republicanism: The Moral Vision of the American Founders and the Philosophy of John Locke* (Chicago: University of Chicago Press, 1988), 30, 52, 64, 66, 110, 168–9, 260, 300 n. 13.

[5] See the prologue of this book.

September 1780, when Hamilton was his principal confidential aide and a lieutenant colonel at the ripe old age of twenty-three. Hamilton was frequently responsible for communicating on Washington's behalf with the state governments and the Continental Congress. A letter that the young colonel wrote on 3 September 1780 from Washington's headquarters to James Duane, a friend who was serving in Congress, is nothing less than a military briefing on the necessity of immediate constitutional and administrative reform to win the war (*PAH* 2:400–18, esp. 401). It addresses all the military-political "defects of our present system, and the measures necessary to save us from ruin." Edmund Cody Burnett, one of the first great historians of the Continental Congress, observed that "It was a long way from 1780 to 1787, but it would seem to have been directly, perhaps chiefly, from this implantation by Hamilton that the Federal Convention of 1787 actually grew."[6]

Burnett probably overstates his case; though important, the lessons of the War for Independence were not the only subjects of the convention's deliberations. Nonetheless, our understanding of Hamilton's views on constitutional reform may benefit greatly from examining the early thought of the tough-talking young colonel as he sought to infuse some genuine *virtù* into Congress at a time when independence had not yet been won, and the liberty it was meant to secure was very much in doubt.

To understand the briefing, it is essential to recognize the doubtful character of the American cause. The army was starving – again! Hamilton feared another winter like the one he had experienced with the soldiers at Valley Forge in 1777–8, where they died of disease, hunger, and cold at the rate of over four hundred a month. All told, as many as twenty-five hundred soldiers, or about a fourth of Washington's command, may have perished in the six months that the army spent in the camp. Largely because of its disorganization, Congress had left the post of quartermaster general vacant during the three coldest months of that ordeal. Not surprisingly, the soldiers tended to blame Congress for their accumulated sufferings. There was a grave danger that the soldiers would become "a mob, rather than an army." They were without "clothing, without pay, without provision, without morals, without discipline." The order of terms in this sentence is important. Hamilton progressed from the necessities of soldiers to their virtues, and implied that the latter were succumbing to the former. "We begin to hate our country for its neglect of us," he told the congressman, and "the country begins to hate us for our oppressions of them. Congress has long since been jealous of us; we have lost all confidence in them, and give the worst construction to all they do. Held together by the slenderest of ties we are ripening for a dissolution" (*PAH* 2:406).[7] He warned that without immediate support, a rebellious army might even turn its weapons on Congress. Then, the cause of the war would surely be lost.

---

[6] See Edmund Cody Burnett, *The Continental Congress* (New York: Macmillan, 1941), 487.

[7] See Howard Peckham, *The War for Independence* (Chicago: University of Chicago Press, 1958), 82–5.

American liberty depended on soldiers who were loyal to Congress and willing to fight. Such soldiers are the practical equivalent of Socrates' noble dogs, who are gentle toward their fellow citizens and fierce toward enemies (Pl. *Rep.* 375a). It was "vain to make apologies" to soldiers who had no food, weapons, or shoes. Congress might be forgiven for failing to provide for the army at the beginning of the war, when no one had any experience with this task, but after five years, there was no excuse for neglecting those who had suffered most for American liberty. As Hamilton wrote to his friend Colonel John Laurens, even the officers "were out of humor" with Congress. The "*worst of evils,*" a "*loss of our virtue,*" seemed imminent. Hamilton added bitterly, "I hate Congress – I hate the army – I hate the world – I hate myself." Not only the army's spirit, but his own had reached the bottom of despair (*PAH* 2:348, 428).

We are not accustomed to hearing Hamilton say much about virtue, much less to his calling the loss of virtue the worst of evils. Perhaps this is because in recent years we have been habituated to a simplistic conception of a term that, after all, is one of the most complicated in political and ethical theory.[8] Republican virtue cannot simply mean altruistic sacrifice of private interest, or jealous opposition to power based on ever-vigilant scrutiny of those who possess it, as one might presume if one focused simply on the thought of Hamilton's opponents. In Hamilton's view, they all too frequently elevated jealousy, which is normally considered a vice, into a virtue.[9] Republican virtue must include not only the devotion of Brutus in opposing internal dangers to liberty, but also the stubbornness of the Roman soldiers who opposed Hannibal, the greatest external danger to Roman liberty. If so, republican virtue must also require the *virtù*, or resourcefulness and determination, of Fabius and Scipio, the generals who led Rome's armies to victory in their mortal struggle with Carthage. This was certainly Machiavelli's view. He argued that not only the virtues, but also the "sins of the people are caused by their princes," because, as Lorenzo de Medici said, "'on the ruler all eyes are turned'" (*D* 3.29).

Like Machiavelli, Hamilton blamed the sins of the American people on the sins of their government. Before the Revolution began, he sounded very much like Machiavelli. "Contests for liberty," he declared, "have ever been found the most bloody, implacable and obstinate. The disciplined troops Great Britain could send against us are but few. Our superiority in number would overbalance our inferiority in discipline. It would be a hard, if not an impracticable task to subjugate us by force." Experience would soon teach Hamilton that he had overestimated America's actual strength. The advantages of spirit and numbers do not count for much unless a nation has the kind of government that can draw on them and employ them with effect, and if it lacks such a

---

[8] See, for example, Gordon S. Wood, *The Creation of the American Republic, 1776–1787* (New York: W. W. Norton, 1969), 65–70.

[9] Cf. TJ's praise of jealousy in his Kentucky Resolutions, in *WrTJ* (ed. Peterson) 449–56, with Hamilton's discussion of jealousy as a vice in *Fed.* 1, and see Chapter 9 of this book.

government, it may not be able to sustain such spirit. After five years of war, Great Britain had managed to keep the odds at least even with "little more than fourteen thousand effective men." Nothing but a "GENERAL DISAFFECTION of the PEOPLE, or MISMANAGEMENT in their RULERS" could account for the inability of the confederation to win the war. Hamilton dared not admit the former alternative, at least not in public, and therefore stressed the sins of the rulers as the cause of growing disaffection among the people.[10] To be sure, Hamilton had a very low tolerance for platitudinous assertions that disinterested virtue was the foundation of republican government. Nonetheless, he meant to build public-spirited virtue on the solid, not necessarily low, but certainly effective grounds of public confidence and private interest.

Like Machiavelli, Hamilton deplored depending on the uncertain arms and virtue of others, including the states. Such dependence undermined confidence in the ability of Congress and the army to support themselves and to take the initiative against the enemy. Hamilton stressed a decline of confidence in Congress within the army, among investors (whose support was necessary to finance the war), and among the people at large. There was a "universal sentiment," he told Duane, that the existing government was a "bad one," and incapable of waging the war effectively. Something had to be done to "revive the hopes of the people, and give a new direction to their passions" (cf. *PAH* 2:417 with NM, *D* 3.33). No one would risk as much as might be necessary to win the war unless Congress proved it was worthy of the enormous trust that had been placed in it. This would never be possible if Congress continued to rely upon the states to support the army. The "source of all our military misfortunes," Hamilton declared, was the "fluctuating state of our army." Nothing contributed to the ebb and flow of recruiting and retention more than dependence upon the states for supplies, revenue, and troops. This was "too precarious a dependence because the states," particularly those situated in a calm theater of the war, "will never be sufficiently impressed by our necessities." Experience revealed that "[e]ach will make its own ease a primary object, the supply of the army a secondary one." The colonel spoke for the whole army when he claimed that "we feel the insufficiency of this plan, and have reason to dread under it a ruinous extremity of want" (cf. *PAH* 2:406 and *Fed.* 15 with NM, *P* 1, 24, *D* 3.11).

Hamilton wrote his briefing before the Articles of Confederation had been accepted by all the states. The pre-Confederation Congress never had "any definite power granted them and of course could exercise none." It lacked the legitimacy that arises from a formal delegation of powers and "could do nothing more than recommend," but after years of frustration, the colonel found this common explanation for delay and stagnation inexcusable. "The manner in which Congress was appointed," in an extraconstitutional emergency

---

[10] Cf. *A Full Vindication*, December, 1774; *The Farmer Refuted*, February 1775; *Continentalist* no. 3, 9 August 1781, in *PAH* 1:54, 155–6, 2:662–3, with *D* 2.2, 16, *P* 5. In private, Hamilton sometimes displayed grave doubts about popular attachment to the Revolution; see, for example, AH to Colonel John Laurens, 30 June 1780, in *PAH* 2:347.

when American liberty was at stake, "and the public good required" that Congress should have done what the Romans did when they appointed a dictator: Congress should have considered itself "vested with full power to *preserve the republic from harm.*" Congress had already acted according to this principle by declaring independence, forming an army and a navy, establishing diplomatic relations and alliances, and so on. All these "implications of complete sovereignty were never disputed" and should therefore have served as the "standard of the whole conduct of the Administration." Until the Articles of Confederation were drafted and accepted, all of Congress's powers were "discretionary powers, limited only by the object for which they were given. . . . in the present case, the independence and freedom of America." After its first moments of boldness, however, Congress had grown accustomed to what both Hamilton and Machiavelli considered the vice of "doing right by halves, and spoiling a good intention in the execution." Since Congress had already acted on the assumption of complete sovereignty, it had to resume its discretionary powers and assert control over every power necessary to support the war.[11]

Yet this plan might have been "thought too bold by the generality of Congress" to be practical at this stage of the war. Moreover, although the Articles of Confederation formalized some of the necessary war powers, the Articles themselves were half measures that did not rise to the necessities implied in declaring independence. They might even provide additional excuses for doing nothing, as in fact they would for the rest of the war. Perhaps worst of all, the half measures might force Congress to choose between violating the Articles to avoid defeat or risking defeat to remain faithful to the constitutional rule of law. Both Hamilton and Machiavelli believed well-founded republics should avoid this dilemma as much as possible because it tends to undermine the rule of law itself. To avoid this dilemma, nothing was more important than a constitutional convention with plenipotentiary authority to grant Congress "complete sovereignty in all that relates to war, peace, trade, finance, and the management of foreign affairs." It was essential to make the resumption of sovereign powers unambiguously legitimate by constitutionalizing it (cf. *Fed.* 25 with NM, *D* 1.34, 45).[12]

Just as Hamilton criticized Congress for depending on the uncertain arms and virtue of the states, he also criticized it for depending too much on foreign allies. "Too sanguine expectations from Europe have unintentionally relaxed our efforts, by diverting a sense of danger, and begetting an opinion that the inequality in the contest would make every campaign the last," he wrote in early August 1781 in the third number of *The Continentalist.* Congress ignored the energy that both Hamilton and Machiavelli believed belonged to a single state,

---

[11] Consider AH to James Duane, 3 September 1780; to Marquis de Barbe-Marbois, 7 February 1781; "Unsubmitted Resolution Calling for a Constitutional Convention," July 1783, in *PAH* 2:400–18 (at 401, 406–7), 554, 3:421, in light of Burnett, *The Continental Congress*, 452–6, 484–5, and see NM, *D* 1.27, 34, 2.15, 3.24.

[12] See Mansfield, *Taming the Prince*, 255–7.

like England, with a unified command against many allied states. Moreover, every rumor of a foreign loan, a secret arms shipment, or the influence of the European powers in seeking a negotiated settlement diminished the incentives in Congress to procure supplies from domestic sources. "Finding the rest of Europe either friendly or pacific, [Congress] never calculated the contingencies which might alter that disposition." For example, both America and France were bound by treaty not to make a separate peace, but for all the influence of the philosophes, France was in the war to hurt England and help itself. During the decisive campaign of the war, the siege of Yorktown, the French army was actually larger than the force of Continentals that Washington managed to mobilize for the siege. The siege succeeded only because of the help of the French navy. Precisely because victory depended on the French, the costs of betrayal could have been catastrophic for the Revolution. If Congress did not wish to risk such a disaster, then Hamilton argued there was only one viable strategy. Congress would need to prepare for a long war that might have to be fought without any allies, or even against former allies. It would have to rely on its own arms and *virtù*. As Machiavelli said in explaining why the princes of Italy had lost their states, "one should never fall in the belief you can find someone to pick you up. Whether it does not happen or happens, it is not security for you because the defense was base and did not depend on you. And those defenses are good, are certain, and are lasting, that depend on you yourself and your virtue" (cf. *PAH* 2:663–4 with NM, *P* 24; *D* 2.4).

Yet self-reliance in Congress would not be sufficient to restore public confidence. The wartime government had no separation of powers, and this fact had much strategic and moral importance. Congress ran every aspect of the war, but Congress was "properly a deliberative corps and it forgets itself when it tries to play the executive." Hamilton both exalted and criticized Congress when he said this. It was responsible to deliberate upon policy, which is perhaps the highest task of government, but incapable of executing policy against an enemy able to oppose its resolutions. Its members did not serve long enough to learn how to run a nation at war. Frequent rotation made it extremely difficult for anyone to assume responsibility for the overall conduct of any part of the war effort. Consequently, Congress could never convince the people that it had the *virtù* to dominate the enemy.[13]

Hamilton believed that the only way to resurrect public confidence was to form regular executive departments headed by individuals who could supply method and system to the war effort. He did not yet advocate a unitary executive substantially independent of Congress, but he was well on the way to one. In a lengthy letter written to Robert Morris on 30 April 1781, shortly after Morris had been appointed superintendent of finance, Hamilton argued that "an administration by single men" was the "only resource we have to extricate ourselves from the distresses, which threaten the subversion of our

---

[13] Consider AH to George Clinton, 13 February 1778, and to James Duane, 3 September 1780, in *PAH* 1:425, 2:403–4, in light of Burnett, *The Continental Congress*, 317, 503, 592, 605, 607.

cause.... It is palpable that the people have lost all confidence in our public councils." Moreover, friends in Europe shared the "same disposition." Neither the people at home nor allies abroad would give "half the succors to this country while Congress holds the reins of administration" as they would grant if administration were "entrusted to individuals of established reputation and conspicuous for probity, abilities, and fortune" (*PAH* 2:604–35, at 604–5). As Hamilton had explained to James Duane, winning the war required an effort to "blend the advantages of monarchy and a republic in our constitution" (*PAH* 2:405).

Hamilton's controversial speech of 18 June 1787 should be interpreted in light of these remarks. In the letter that he addressed to Duane, Hamilton was not talking about instituting a monarchy, and certainly not a hereditary one. Instead, he was discussing the different advantages enjoyed by monarchies and republics in time of war. According to Montesquieu, combining the strategic advantages of large monarchies (strength and numbers) with the political advantages of small republics (liberty and spirit) is the fundamental objective of all republican federations (*EL* 2.9.1). Hamilton was therefore exploring how to make federal theory work in practice. The problem with federal theory, at least as developed by Montesquieu, however, is that it never explained how federations can have the advantages of monarchy, which literally means the rule of one, without one person actually governing with respect to those matters where one executes policy best. "Of all the cares and concerns of government," Hamilton would later argue, "the direction of war most peculiarly demands those qualities which distinguish the exercise of power by a single hand. The direction of war implies the direction of the common strength; and the power of directing and employing the common strength, forms an usual and essential part in the definition of executive authority" (*Fed.* 74). The absence of a unitary executive goes far to explain why federations never lived up to Montesquieu's expectations. As Machiavelli explained, they were far too slow and indecisive to compete against large unitary states under the direction of one person – unless of course they fell under the hegemony of a dominant republic, as happened when Rome transformed the Latin confederation into an empire subject to its will. When this happens, however, the means by which republics seek to prepare for war become the instrument of their own enslavement (*D* 2.6).

Hamilton understood this great dilemma of republican federations better than any of the founders, but like Machiavelli, he also understood the moral and strategic advantages of republics in a manner that is frequently ignored. He did not mean to sacrifice the advantages of republics to acquire those of monarchy, but to combine the advantages of both forms of government. In an effort to persuade Duane to lobby for a congressional power to tax to support the war, Hamilton asserted that "Where the public good is evidently the object, more can be expected in governments like ours than in any other. The obedience of a free people to general laws however hard they bear is ever more perfect than that of slaves subject to the arbitrary will of a prince" (*PAH* 2:413). Later, at the Federal Convention, he claimed that one reason a "free government is to be preferred to an absolute monarchy" is the "tendency of the Free Government to interest the passions of the community in its favor," and to "beget public spirit and public confidence" (*PAH* 4:163, 218). Both Machiavelli and Hamilton understood that a free people sacrifice for their country, as Alexis de Tocqueville would later say about public spirit in America, almost out of greed. The difference is that Hamilton and Machiavelli suggested that this patriotic greed was directed at least as much by the ambitions republican citizens have for their children as those they have for themselves. Consistent with Tocqueville and Abraham Lincoln, however, they would probably agree that the spirit of republicans arises much less from reverence for the past than from hopes for the future.[14]

Yet if the citizens are to fight, they must believe that victory is possible. To Morris again, Hamilton argued that there was "so rooted a diffidence of the government, that if we could be assured the measures of Congress would be dictated by the most perfect wisdom and public spirit, there would still be a necessity of change in the forms of administration to give a new spring and current to the passions and hopes of the people" (*PAH* 2:605). Winning the war, he insisted in his letters to Duane and Morris both, required a separation of powers with an executive capable of preparing for the predictable necessities and responding to the unpredictable fortunes of war (*PAH* 2:404, 605).

At the beginning of the war, Hamilton copied a maxim from Demosthenes on the back pages of his military pay book. The statement explains precisely what he wanted in a wartime executive: "'As a general marches at the head of his troops,'" Demosthenes advised, "'so too ought wise politicians, if I dare use the expression, to march at the head of events; insomuch as they ought not to await the *event* to know the measures to take; but the measures which they have taken ought to produce the event.'" Next to this maxim, Hamilton copied another from Longinus: "'Where attack him it will be said? Ah Athenians, war, war itself will discover you his weak sides if you seek them.'" Hamilton added his own appreciation, "[s]ublimely simple," to these ancient precepts of military wisdom (*PAH* 1:390). Their advice was broadly consistent with Machiavelli's. Especially in time of war, *Fortuna* favors the bold and impetuous who subject her to overwhelming necessities that prevent any effectual resistance (NM, *P* 25; *AW* 7.154–5, 157, 159). Hamilton understood that no republic can dominate *Fortuna* or generate public-spirited citizens without unity and a substantial degree of independence in the executive, the prerequisites of *virtù* in that office.[15]

---

[14] Cf. "Remarks at the New York Ratifying Convention," 28 June 1788, in *PAH* 5:125, with NM, *D* 2.2; Alexis de Tocqueville, *Democracy in America*, tr. George Lawrence (New York: Harper, 1966), 1:237; Lincoln's speech to the 166th Ohio Regiment, 22 August 1864, in *The Political Thought of Abraham Lincoln*, ed. Richard N. Current (New York: Bobbs-Merrill, 1967), 330.

[15] See also Carl von Clausewitz, *On War*, ed. Anatol Rapoport (New York: Penguin, 1985), 3.6, 259.

Hamilton's stress on assuming the responsibility to preserve the republic from harm has significant implications for understanding his later quarrel with Jefferson. If Paul Rahe is right to suggest in the ninth chapter of this book that Jeffersonian vigilance owes much to Machiavelli's suspicions of men in power, then Hamilton and Jefferson emphasized different dimensions of Machiavelli's teaching: Jefferson, one that had become old and conventional in the writings of Marchamont Nedham, John Locke, Algernon Sidney, *Cato's Letters*, and the like[16]; Hamilton, one which seemed novel, if not even heretical, only because radical Whig political thought emphasized popular vigilance much more than statesmanlike responsibility. Machiavelli, however, is famous for arguing that not only princes but also republics must change their virtues according to the qualities of the times. Sometimes vigilance is more important than responsibility, and vice versa. For this reason, the survival of the American republic may owe much more than we understand to the original opposition between Hamilton and Jefferson. Though envisioned by none of the founders, party conflict usually makes those in opposition more vigilant and the necessities of governing often make those in power more responsible. Party conflict also helps modern republicans choose the right statesmen for the times, a capacity that Machiavelli considered one of the great advantages of republics. (NM, *P* 25; *D* 3.9).[17]

Waging War and Sustaining Liberty

If executive departments were established, they would be essential to two of Hamilton's extremely innovative plans for winning the war: founding a national bank and reorganizing the army. Though neither plan developed as Hamilton wished during the war, both became central elements in his strategy for waging war effectively and remaining free at the same time as the de facto prime minister of the Washington administration and inspector general of the army in the administration of John Adams. Like Machiavelli, Hamilton meant to restore the public spirit required for victory during the War for Independence, but unlike Machiavelli, he meant to fund the war without crime and support the army without terrorizing the people or turning America into a garrison state bent on world conquest.

By the time Hamilton wrote his briefing, the continental currency had collapsed. Congress printed money to pay the army and its creditors, and then hoped the states and foreign loans would supply the hard cash to back up its paper. The hopes never materialized enough to prevent the depreciation of the currency and the consequent stagnation of the economy. Substantial portions of America were even reduced to a barter economy.[18] With a worthless currency,

---

[16] See Chapters 1–3 of this book.

[17] See Walling, *Republican Empire*, passim, esp. 10, 279–89.

[18] See Burnett, *The Continental Congress*, 419, 426–7; Donald F. Swanson, *The Origins of Hamilton's Fiscal Policies* (Gainesville, FL: University of Florida Press, 1963), 35–7.

Hamilton knew it was virtually impossible to produce the goods or raise the revenue necessary to prosecute the war with vigor. In contrast to Hamilton, Machiavelli denied that gold, or wealth in general, comprises the "sinews of war; for gold is not enough to find good soldiers, but good soldiers are quite enough to find gold." Yet Machiavelli meant that good arms can always get gold by exacting tribute from foreign neighbors, that is, by stealing it from the enemy. He was well aware that nothing undermines public spirit more than a government obliged to rob its own citizens. Likewise, both Hamilton and Washington deplored the desperate occasions when they were obliged to confiscate private property for military use. They knew that their tactical expedients often contradicted their strategic necessities; every horse and shoe they took cost the army the support of citizens deprived of their property. Yet their objections to confiscating property were not confined to its tendency to undermine public spirit. The Revolution, after all, was being waged to secure American rights, including the right to property. The tactical expedients of the army were therefore in grave tension with the moral objectives of the Revolution.[19]

To deserve victory, Congress needed to find a way to raise money without stealing it. Both liberal principle and the Machiavellian necessity to hold the support of the people therefore required Hamilton to pay attention to the "revolution in the system of war" produced by the "science of finance" (cf. *Fed.* 8 with NM, *D* 1.37; 2.2; *P* 19, 21). Washington's Fabian strategy simply could not succeed without coming to terms with that science. "'Tis by introducing order into our finances – by restoring public credit – not by gaining battles that we are to attain our object," Hamilton wrote to the like-minded Robert Morris in April 1781. "'Tis by putting ourselves in the position to continue the war, not by temporary, violent and unnatural efforts to bring it to a decisive issue, that we shall in reality bring it to a speedy and successful one" (*PAH* 2:606). Yet the strategic advantage of effective finance was also a moral advantage, and one that did not require superhuman sacrifices for the public good. The "signal merit of a vigorous system of national credit," Hamilton would later argue, is that it "enables a government to support war without violating property, destroying industry, or interfering unreasonably with individual enjoyments." Without effective finance, a nation becomes prey to "every enterprising invader" or must resort to "oppression of the citizens" through high taxes and confiscatory policies. By means of sound credit, however, war "becomes less a scourge" and "loses a great portion of its calamity," at least for the citizens who must ultimately pay for it. Sound credit, backed by provisions for funding the national debt, would enable the present to borrow from the future in time of danger in order to secure the liberty of posterity without robbing the present of its rights (*PAH* 19:53–4).[20]

---

[19] See AH to Major General John Sullivan, 7 July 1777, and to Colonel Clement Biddle, 20 August 1780, in *PAH* 1:284, 2:380. See also NM *D* 2.10.

[20] See also Harvey Flaumenhaft, *The Effective Republic, Administration and Constitution in the Thought of Alexander Hamilton* (Durham, NC: Duke University Press, 1992), 19.

Contrary to those who suggest that Hamilton sacrificed public-spirited virtue to *virtù*,[21] Hamilton's credit policies were also designed to produce public-spirited citizens who would risk their lives and their property on behalf of their liberty. In his letter to Duane, Hamilton claimed it was the business of the government to inspire "confidence by adopting the measures I have recommended." Under a "good plan of executive administration" capable of putting his proposals in a "train of vigorous execution," there would be a "new spring to our affairs; government would recover its respectability," and "individuals would renounce their diffidence" (*PAH* 2:414). "All we have to fear," Hamilton claimed, is what Franklin Delano Roosevelt later called fear itself: "a general disgust and alarm" that could lead the army to disband, or the people to clamor "for peace on any terms," including the loss of their liberty in the struggle with England. If Morris proposed and Congress adopted a national bank offering investors a significant return for their risk, then Hamilton believed public and private credit could be united and multiplied. In a crisis, Congress might borrow from the bank to help pay for the war, as the British did from the Bank of England and as all successful modern republics had done from the time of Renaissance Venice (*PAH* 2:604–5, 631).[22] Nonetheless, the fundamental purpose of the bank was not to fund the war, at least not directly. Like the notes Hamilton would later issue to fund the national debt as secretary of the treasury, the bank notes would supply a substitute for money, which could be traded and used to spur industry. By supplying a trustworthy medium of exchange, the notes would resurrect public confidence, help investors to produce the material necessary for a war economy, and produce profits that Congress could tax to fund the war and the confederation's enormous debts (*PAH* 2:414, 604–5, 631).

The dependence of public spirit on effective finance was virtually unknown to Americans of Hamilton's time, and most contemporary scholars of the founders therefore pay little attention to it. Yet Hamilton was not the only innovative statesman of his time to understand how the daring and resourceful *virtù* of a finance minister might influence the morals – or more accurately, the morale – of his people. Jacques Necker, the minister of finance in France during the

---

[21] See footnote 1.

[22] In this respect, Hamilton differed significantly from one of his greatest teachers, David Hume, who acknowledged that, historically, credit had increased the power of the state (especially for defense), but worried, along lines soon to be taken up by Hamilton's adversaries, that too much debt would be an oppressive burden to posterity. The debate continues to the present, with Hamiltonians arguing that, provided a modern economy continues to grow, public debt is not necessarily a curse. If it is converted to capital, it may well be a blessing, which indeed it was while Hamilton was secretary of the treasury, both because of the industry it fostered and because of its tendency to consolidate monied men (or what Machiavelli termed "the great") in support of the perpetuation of the Union. This tendency was the goose that laid the golden egg for monied men – and through them it helped make the American union more durable. See Hume, "Of Public Credit," in *EMPL* 349–65.

war, argued that a finance minister must "above all, by active and continual anxiety, excite confidence, that precious sentiment which unites the future to the present.... and lays the foundation of the happiness of the people. Then everyone will look on the contributions which are demanded of him, as a just assistance afforded to the exigencies of the state, and as the price of the good order which surrounds him, and the security which he enjoys." By such means, the minister may recall the "ideas of justice and patriotism" among the people, but if they lose their confidence, "private interest will be everywhere opposed to the public welfare." A "skillful administration," he claimed, has the "effect of putting in action those it persuades, of strengthening the moral ideas, of rousing the imagination, and of joining together the opinions and sentiments of men by the confidence it produces." For this reason, it could have the "greatest influence over the social virtues and morals." Necker therefore claimed it is the "fault of the administration," and especially its finance minister, "if these natural dispositions, so adapted to PATRIOTISM," are not produced by and attached to the government.[23]

According to Machiavelli, those who mean to remodel a republic must keep up at least the semblance of old forms (*P* 18; *D* 1.25).[24] Hamilton put this insight into practice in all his fiscal and monetary policies. On the one hand, those policies founded public spirit on the politically practicable basis of public confidence; on the other hand, they made fanatical devotion to a republic less necessary by establishing the economic foundations of overwhelming military power. The fundamental cause of the Continental Congress's difficulties in funding the war had been the lack of specie in America, he explained in the *First Report on Public Credit* (9 January 1790) that he issued as secretary of the treasury. There had not been enough specie to back Congress's paper. The specie supply would not increase simply because the new federal Congress established a bank. Yet if the notes were backed by a foreign loan and denominated in the old forms of pounds and shillings rather than worthless dollars, the people might believe the specie in the bank was as available as specie in the Bank of England. Then, the "illusion" of solidity would produce confidence in the bank notes (*PAH* 6:69).[25] In time, perhaps, the credit bubble would burst, especially if someone without Hamilton's administrative skills managed it, but if it lasted long enough to fund the war, he explained to Morris, Americans would be free. This by itself would justify the risk. Yet Hamilton understood that the "real wealth" of a nation is not its specie, but its "labor and commodities."

[23] See Jacques Necker, *A Treatise on the Finances of France*, tr. Thomas Mortimer (London: Logographic Press, 1787), 1:ix–xiii, xxii–xxiii, xciv; Donald F. Swanson and Andrew P. Trout, "Alexander Hamilton, 'the Celebrated Mr. Necker,' and Public Credit," *WMQ* 47:3 (July 1990): 424–30; Forrest McDonald, *Alexander Hamilton: A Biography* (New York: W. W. Norton, 1979), 135–6, 164–71.
[24] Cf. Locke, *TTG* 2.19.225; Hume, *EMPL* 32.
[25] See McDonald, *Alexander Hamilton*, 171.

If the bubble could last beyond the end of the war, resuscitated credit could promote a new kind of economy of industrious increase, which is now the most important foundation of modern military power (cf. *PAH* 2:616–20, 624, with NM, *D* 1.25, 47). Indeed, though it is often forgotten, Hamilton's famous *Report on Manufactures* was a response to a request from Congress (which was perhaps planted by friends of Hamilton) to make America self-sufficient in the industrial foundations of modern warfare.[26]

The second part of Hamilton's strategy to win the war was an effort to make America's potential energy kinetic. He meant to mobilize an entire nation for war in a manner that prefigured the nation at arms of the French Revolution, and Clausewitz's understanding of the strategic revolution produced by that political revolution. As with the Constitution that Hamilton would later defend in 1787, the strategy was meant to endure for ages.[27] The first step was to replace the cumbersome method of gaining recruits through bounties for short-term service with a draft for three years. This would not only increase the numbers of the army, but also give veterans time to train recruits to be effective soldiers. The second step was to establish a pension plan of half pay for life for the officers corps. Although some in Congress feared pensions would corrupt the army by making it dependent on Congress rather than the states, Hamilton looked at such "corruption" as the foundation of national loyalty (and thus virtue) in the army. The pension would secure the "attachment of the army to Congress.... We should then have discipline, an army in reality, as well as in name." Without such attachment, Hamilton was well aware that the army would be neither effective in the field nor safe to the liberties of the American people.[28]

---

[26] One can trace the relation between the modern economy of increase through trade and credit and the economic foundations of modern military power from Machiavelli (NM, *P* 16, 21) to Locke (*TTG* 2.5.43) and beyond: See Hume, "Of Commerce," in *EMPL*, 258–63; Adam Smith, *Wealth of Nations*, ed. R. H. Campbell, et al. (Indianapolis, IN: Liberty Classics, 1979), 1:463–4, 2:705–9, 781–8; *Report on Manufactures*, 5 December 1791, and *Defense of the Funding System*, July 1795, in *PAH* 10:230, 254–56, 259, 262–3, 291, 19:53–4 – with an eye to Edward Meade Earle's classic, "Adam Smith, Alexander Hamilton, and Friedrich List: The Economic Foundations of Military Power," in *Makers of Modern Strategy: From Machiavelli to the Nuclear Age*, ed. Peter Paret (Princeton, NJ: Princeton University Press, 1986), 217–61.

[27] Consider Clausewitz, *On War*, 8.3, in light of Peter Paret, "Clausewitz," in *Makers of Modern Strategy*, 186–213; Earle, "Adam Smith, Alexander Hamilton, and Friedrich List," 217–61; Russell F. Weigley, *Towards an American Army: Military Thought from Washington to Marshall* (New York: Columbia University Press, 1962), 10–29; Samuel P. Huntington, *The Soldier and the State: The Theory and Practice of Civil–Military Relations* (Cambridge, MA: Harvard University Press, 1957), 193–221; John Fiske, *The Critical Period in American History* (Boston: Riverside Press, 1899), 101–3.

[28] Hamilton also wanted to rid the army of foreign officers whose presence tended to undermine the morale of American officers, but it was difficult to cashier them without offending American allies. Sometimes, it seems, the only way to follow Machiavelli's famous advice to get rid of mercenaries is to pension them. Cf. AH to William Duer, 6 May 1777; to George Clinton, 13 February 1778; and to James Duane, 3 September 1780, in *PAH* 1:247, 425, 2:409–10, with NM, *P* 12; and see Burnett, *The Continental Congress*, 312–13, 393, 444.

The third step was the most revolutionary. Hamilton planned to enlist slaves in the South, and promise them their freedom with their muskets. As he put it to John Jay in mid-March 1779, freedom would "secure their fidelity, animate their courage," and have a "good influence" on those who remained in bondage by "opening the door to emancipation." Their habits of obedience coupled with their new spirit of liberty might make them the most loyal and courageous soldiers that America could produce. As the South became the primary theater of the war in the last years of the Revolution, such soldiers were at a premium because there were extremely few whites who could be pressed into service. Hamilton claimed that emancipation followed from both "the dictates of humanity and true policy." Together with Jay, Hamilton founded the New York Society for Manumission of the Slaves in 1787, and he remained on its board for the rest of his life. During the War for Independence, it had "no small weight" to Hamilton that employing this "unfortunate class of men" might open the door to freedom for all. He may therefore have disguised humanity as good policy. Speaking very soberly – or, rather, in a manner calculated to inspire terror in the hearts of all slaveowners – he argued that if the southerners did not emancipate and arm their slaves, the "enemy probably" would. The "best way to counteract the temptations they hold," he declared, would "be to offer them ourselves" (*PAH* 2:17–19).

Support in Congress for some version of this plan was so strong that Hamilton's best friend, Colonel John Laurens, was sent to South Carolina to lobby the legislature to enlist the slaves, but Laurens was never able to convince more than a fifth of the state legislators to support the plan, and it does not appear to have had significant support anywhere else in the South.[29] Nonetheless, the plan was consistent with Machiavelli's advice and prefigures the many social revolutions caused by war in American history. Just as the Romans found it necessary to grant greater freedom to the people in order to use them in their armies, Americans and all modern nations have found it impossible to wage war effectively without granting ever more freedom to the lowest orders of society. Modern revolutions made modern democratic (or mass) wars possible, but modern democratic warfare made modern mass democracy ever more necessary, if not even inevitable. The great question was whether the new form of democracy produced by the simultaneous revolutions in war and politics would produce freedom or despotism.[30]

Hamilton's end-of-the-war report on a military peace establishment was a remarkably far-sighted effort to ensure that the new mode of warfare remained compatible with free government. Both economy and prejudice seemed to favor a military organization based on citizen-soldiers in the militia, who appeared to be less expensive and more effective and loyal than their presumed alternative, a standing army of mercenary soldiers who fought for pay. Hamilton, however,

---

[29] See Paul A. Rahe, *Republics Ancient and Modern: Classical Republicanism and the American Revolution* (Chapel Hill, NC: University of North Carolina Press, 1992), 621–2.

[30] Cf. NM, *D* 1.6, with Tocqueville, *Democracy in America*, 1:57, 2:705.

denied that a militia is less expensive than a small well-trained force because modern military power requires a productive economy, and thus a division of labor between soldiers and civilians. Training the militia to be effective would require great amounts of money and also decrease industry while the militia trained. Since wealth was the principal source of military power, the decrease in industry would ultimately make America less fit for war than would reliance on professionals. On the basis of solid experience, Hamilton doubted that many citizens would be willing to train enough to merit the title of a well-regulated militia. In a nation devoted to the pursuit of happiness, the "militia would not long, if at all, submit to be dragged from their homes and families to perform the most disagreeable duty in time of profound peace." The effectual truth of modern commercial republics is that they require professional, reasonably well-paid soldiers because no one else in such republics is willing to spend a lifetime preparing for war.[31]

In contrast to Hamilton, Machiavelli stressed reliance on a popular militia drawn from among the citizens and their subjects in Florence's *contado*, as we have seen,[32] but the moral significance of this difference has not yet been explored. As Machiavelli knew (because he was in charge of raising the Florentine militia), a militia composed of farmers and shopkeepers was unreliable. In 1512, five thousand experienced (and starving) Spanish mercenaries met four thousand Florentine militiamen who had been trained (but were not led) by Machiavelli in a garrison at Prato, ten miles northwest of Florence. Six thousand other militiamen guarded Florence. The militiamen at Prato panicked and laid down their arms in the face of the more disciplined Spanish force. In the next three weeks, as many as five thousand militiamen and citizens at Prato fell victim to "the Spanish fury." The massacre destroyed the resolve of the Florentines, who quickly surrendered, and Florence was restored to the Medici. Reliance on the militia cost Florence its liberty, and Machiavelli his job in the Florentine Chancery and Council of Ten for War. Since he was tortured soon after losing his job, Machiavelli certainly had good reason to regret relying on the militia.[33]

Machiavelli had something very Roman in mind when, instead of the Florentine militia, he called for an army drawn from among the commune's citizens and subjects. In the *Art of War*, Machiavelli's interlocutor, Fabrizio, observed that Rome's armies, "thanks to continual wars," were a "mixture of veterans and new men." Although there were always raw recruits in the army there were also so many veterans, that the "new and old mixed together" made a "united and good body." When the Roman soldiers trained, they were drilled by veterans of previous campaigns, who filled in for the most important element of

[31] See AH to John Dickinson, 25–30 September 1783, in *PAH* 3:454; *Fed.* 8, 24.
[32] See Chapter 1 of this book.
[33] See Victor A. Rudowski, *The Prince, an Historical Critique* (New York: Twayne, 1992), 77–8.

any military organization, the noncommissioned officers. Rome's legions were therefore very close to the functional equivalent of a modern professional army. Machiavelli knew this kind of army must live by theft and therefore conquest and tribute because too few civilians were left at home to support them. If a modern Philip of Macedon adopted his proposals, Fabrizio then claimed, his state might grow "so powerful" that he could conquer them all (and unite Italy) in a few years. Then, his son, a new Alexander, might become "prince of all the world" (*AW* 1.199–218, 8.243).[34]

Hamilton did not believe Rome was an appropriate model for America. "All her maxims and habits were military, her government was constituted for war," he wrote in *The Federalist*. "Ours is unfit for it, and our situation [as a modern, free, commercial people] still less than our constitution, invites us to emulate the conduct of Rome, or to attempt to display an unprofitable heroism." In this context, Hamilton was trying to dissuade his fellow New Yorkers from imitating the Romans by conquering Vermont, which had seceded from the empire state. He was well aware that the heroic virtues of antiquity were dependent on some miserable vices that do not fit well in a society based on universal natural rights. Sparta, he later claimed, was little more than an "armed camp," and Rome was "never sated of carnage and conquest" (*Fed.* 8).[35]

Any attempt to replicate the effectiveness of ancient citizen armies would require imitating their ferocious imperialism or transforming America into an armed camp, or both, but how could America wage war effectively without risking these dangers? Hamilton's proposal was a peacetime military establishment of a little over three thousand officers and men. Unlike the militia, the professionals would have the time to train to become effective soldiers; unlike mercenaries, the professionals would be local people with a stake in their country's safety and well-being. As Machiavelli himself argued, such a stake would go far to secure their loyalty to the republic (*D* 1.43). Hamilton was among the first to propose founding a military academy to train future officers in a rigorous program of science, technology, and the principles of war. Career officers would also be cycled through the military academy quite frequently for refresher and enhancement training. Except during an emergency, however, the professional's primary mission was not to wage war. Instead, it was to teach other citizens to wage war. If the army were capable of almost infinite expansion, citizens could be classified and serve in various kinds of reserve and militia units, which Hamilton aimed to maintain at at least four different levels of readiness. Then, only the professionals and those in an elite reserve corps, called "train bands," would spend much time in service, but all could be mobilized, processed, and trained very quickly according to the degree and kind of military threat. For

[34] Note AH to William Loughton Smith, 10 April 1797, and to Theodore Sedgewick, 2 February, 1799, in *PAH* 21:40, 22:453. See also Weigley, *Towards an American Army*, 25.

[35] See *Remarks on an Act Acknowledging the Independence of Vermont*, 28 March 1787, in *PAH* 4:140, and Flaumenhaft, *The Effective Republic*, 19.

this reason, Hamilton paid almost as much attention to non-commissioned officers (NCOs) as to commissioned officers. He "always" wanted to have enough professional NCOs on hand to train a reserve force of fifty thousand men – that is, a force sixteen times as large as the professional army! As storm clouds gathered, more civilians could be drawn into service; as they dissipated, the non-professionals could be released from duty. Expenses could be kept low, but only if the professionals were kept at the highest level of training and readiness. Americans might then combine the skill of professionals with the numbers and spirit of republican citizens without impoverishing themselves or producing a military despotism.[36]

Hamilton thought a great deal about the dangers that war poses to free government, and especially to the spirit of liberty in the people. Indeed, his defense of an energetic union in *The Federalist* was predicated partly on the premise that some kinds of military power are much safer for liberty than others. "Safety from external danger," Hamilton claimed, "is the most powerful director of national conduct. Even the ardent love of liberty will, after a time, give way to its dictates." The casualties of war are not limited to the battlefield. "The violent destruction of life and property incident to war – the continual effort and alarm attendant on a state of continual danger, will compel nations most attached to liberty, to resort for repose and security, to institutions, which have a tendency to destroy their civil and political rights." To some extent, this insight simply describes the movement from the state of nature or war into civil society, but the problem is that necessity may panic the people, or their representatives, to such an extent that they do not stop at a point safe to their civil and political rights. "To be more safe, they, at length, become willing to run the risk of being less free" (cf. *Fed*.8 with NM, *D* 1.3, 2.25, 3.1).

To avoid this danger, Hamilton proposed a firm union and reliance on naval power. Hamilton assumed that without an energetic government, the American union would collapse. The states would then become a variety of more or less hostile land powers. The "perpetual menacings of danger" would oblige each state to be "always prepared to repel" invasion from its neighbors with armies numerous enough for instant defense. The result would be not only an arms race, but a race toward despotism. "The continual necessity for their services" would elevate the "importance of the soldier" and degrade the "condition of the citizen." Especially on the borders, citizens would grow accustomed to "frequent infringements on their rights" by the military that would "serve to weaken their sense of those rights." In time their free spirit would become slavish as they were "brought to consider the soldiery not only as their protectors, but as their superiors." Quite tragically, Americans would then "in a little time see established in every part of this country, the same engines of despotism which have been the scourge of the old world!" (*Fed*. 8).

---

[36] See AH's draft of Washington's "Speech to Congress," 10 November 1796; *Report on a Military Peace Establishment*; and various proposals for reorganizing the military during the Quasi-War, in *PAH* 3:391–2, 20:384–5, 21:83, 342–3, 362, 486, 22:389–90, 24:70, 310.

There was one important exception to this Old World pattern: namely, Great Britain, the greatest sea power of the eighteenth century. America was not England, but until England united, it was wracked by civil war, lived in constant danger of invasion, and had not yet produced the free spirit that insisted on the constitutional rule of law. If Americans were united under an energetic government with a powerful navy to keep danger at a distance, they could be at least as exceptional as England. Most citizens would feel safe from the perils of foreign and civil war. Then, there could rarely be a "pretext" for the large standing armies on their own territory that were necessary for land powers surrounded by hostile neighbors. The people would be in "no danger of being broken to military subordination." Because the laws would not relax to face military exigencies, the "civil state" could remain in "full vigor, neither corrupted nor confounded with the principles or propensities of the other state." The citizens would not be "habituated to look up to the military power for protection, or to submit to its oppressions." They would therefore "neither love nor fear the soldiery." As has been common in American history, the people would look at the military in a "spirit of jealous acquiescence in a necessary evil." When the power necessary to protect them from external danger was "exerted to the prejudice of their rights," they would "stand ready to resist it." Or perhaps better, since wars tend to panic most governments and peoples, the odds in favor of steady nerves and avoiding a military despotism were greatest if America became a great sea power able to project power abroad and avoided the necessity of large land forces on its own territory as much as possible. The foundation of American freedom would be the vigilant spirit of the people, but that spirit would arise from the security supplied by the energy and foresight of their government (*Fed.* 8).[37]

At least as much as ideology, this strategy of projecting naval power abroad may explain why the great sea powers of our century – the United States and England – remained free while great land powers surrounded by hostile neighbors – such as Germany, Russia, and China – never gained or soon lost their liberty. Machiavelli understood this strategy very well. The Italian cities that came closest to England's naval mastery were commercial Venice and Genoa. "Since [the Venetians] did not possess much territory on land, they employed their strength chiefly at sea, where they carried on their wars with great spirit, and made considerable acquisitions." Republican Venice and Genoa had done "wonderful things" with their commercial, maritime empires, and they were not confined simply to waging war. Why did Venice remain free for so long? Because commerce had destroyed the foundations of the agrarian feudal aristocracy. Venetian gentlemen were gentlemen "rather in name than

---

[37] For an alternative view, which ignores the evidence cited in this essay and treats Hamilton as the leader of a militarist conspiracy, see Richard H. Kohn, *The Eagle and the Sword: The Federalists and the Creation of the Military Establishment in America, 1783–1802* (New York: Free Press, 1975), 252, 272–3, 284–6. Stanley Elkins and Eric McKitrick offer a slightly more balanced account in *The Age of Federalism* (Oxford, UK: Oxford University Press, 1993), 715–19.

in fact." They did not have "great incomes from landed possessions." Their riches were "based on trade and moveable property," and "none of them" had fortified castles to resist the republic. None had any independent "jurisdiction over men," and thus none was able to develop an army of personal dependents. Citizens were thus able to defend themselves against the *grandi*. Machiavelli thus appears to have had a "Janus-face" that looked in two directions: one toward ancient Rome, and the other toward the proto-modern commercial republics of Italy. While some who followed the Florentine seized on the Roman model of combining military power and freedom, others would develop the Venetian model much further than Machiavelli and lay the foundations of modern universal liberty (*P* 21; *D* 1.55; *AW* 1.162–92).[38]

Hamilton's Anti-Machiavellian Republic

Near the end of President Washington's second term, in May 1796, when many thought war with republican France was possible, Hamilton sketched a design for a Great Seal of the United States. The seal was to be a globe depicting Europe and a part of Africa, America, and the Atlantic Ocean. In the Old World, a "Colossus," representing the French Directory, had one foot in Europe and another extending partly across the Atlantic towards America. It had a quintuple crown and a broken iron scepter in its right hand. It wore a pileus, or cap of liberty, but significantly, the cap was on backward. A snake had wrapped itself around the staff of the scepter, as if it were in the act of strangling a label upon which was written "Rights of Man." In the New World was Pallas Athena, representing the "Genius [or spirit] of America." She bore a "firm and composed countenance" and an "attitude of defiance." With a gold breast plate, a shield in one hand, and a spear in the other, she was capable of both offense and defense. Yet her genius was not the same as that of antiquity. Instead of the customary terrifying Medusa's head, her shield was engraved with the "scales of Justice" and her helmet encircled with olive wreaths. She also wore a radiated crown of glory, or halo, as a sign of providential interposition on behalf of America in its quarrel with the Jacobins. The allegory was meant to show that "though loving peace," the genius of America was "yet guided by *Wisdom*, or an enlightened sense of her own rights and interests." She was determined to exert her "*valor*, in breaking the scepter of the Tyrant." Hamilton believed it would improve the allegory to "represent the Ocean in a Tempest & Neptune striking with his Trident the projected leg of the Colossus." Yet he also wondered if this addition would render the allegory too "complicated" to be readily understandable in America. It implied that sometimes Americans

---

[38] See J. G. A. Pocock, *The Machiavellian Moment: Florentine Political Thought and the Atlantic Republican Tradition* (Princeton, NJ: Princeton University Press, 1975), 210, 423, 495; cf. Locke, *TTG* 2.5.42; Hume, "Of Refinement in the Arts," in *EMPL* 277–8; Smith, *The Wealth of Nations* 1:401–2, 412; New York Ratifying Convention, 27 June 1788, and *Report on Manufactures*, 5 December 1791, in *PAH* 5:101, 10:253–4.

might have to cooperate with a less dangerous tyrant, like England, in order to deter or defeat a more dangerous one, like France (*PAH* 20:208–9).[39]

Much can be learned about Hamilton's relation to Machiavelli from this seal, especially if one concentrates on its images of the Old World, the New World, and the Brave New World ushered in by the French Revolution. In 1776, Americans declared their independence from the tyrant of the sea, but how did the tyrannies of the Old World acquire their dominions? Hamilton had a very Machiavellian answer. Politically as well as geographically, the world could be divided into four parts: Europe, Asia, Africa, and America. "Unhappily for the other three, Europe, by her arms and by her negotiations, by [Machiavellian] force and by [Machiavellian] fraud," had in "different degrees extended her dominion over them all." Yet Athena was the patron goddess of the world's most famous democracy. Her scales of justice therefore had to be rooted in principles of human equality, which were in tension with the "superiority" that Europe had long maintained over its dominions. That superiority "tempted her to plume herself the mistress of the world, and to consider the rest of mankind as created for her benefit." Facts had too long supported the "arrogant pretensions of the European." It belonged to the United States "to vindicate the honor" not simply of America but of the "human race" itself. If Americans disdained to be "the instruments of European greatness," then they would have to confront the Machiavellian princes of Europe with overwhelming power. They would have to bind themselves together in a "strict and indissoluble Union," and also erect a "great American system," which would presumably include the rest of the Western Hemisphere after it had revolted against its masters. Led by the United States, that system would be "superior to the control of all transatlantic force or influence and able to dictate the terms of the connection between the old and the new world!" The seeds of the Monroe Doctrine are clearly latent in this passage, which calls for vindicating the doctrine of equal natural rights by resisting the Machiavellian imperialism of the Old World (*Fed.* 11).[40]

The harshness of Old World practices, both domestically and within the European empires, made it difficult for most Americans not to be sympathetic

---

[39] Hamilton spent the last years of his career as an American Churchill, warning of a gathering storm in Europe that might soon cross the sea to America. His warnings were not often taken seriously, in part because the French claimed to fight for liberty, and Hamilton's party committed many excesses (which Hamilton often sought to prevent) in dealing with suspected Jacobins in America. Moreover, the French invasion did not materialize, at least not during Hamilton's watch. Yet Hamilton's fears were not without foundation. Napoleon did in fact try to send two different military expeditions to New Orleans via Haiti in the administration of Thomas Jefferson, who dismantled the forces Hamilton had built to confront the best troops of Europe. Fortunately, the courage of rebellious slaves and the persistence of malaria-carrying mosquitoes in Haiti inflicted so many casualties on the French expeditions that Jefferson was able to avoid the necessity of relying on his own arms. See Forrest McDonald, *The Presidency of Thomas Jefferson* (Lawrence, KS: University Press of Kansas, 1976), 62–4.

[40] See also David Epstein, *The Political Theory of the Federalist* (Chicago: University Press of Chicago, 1984), 11–34.

toward the revolution in France. Hamilton shared those sympathies, but resisting an old tyranny is not the same as establishing a new free government. Sooner than most of his countrymen, Hamilton came to think that Americans and the French did not share the same principles. Indeed, their principles were diametrically opposed. In his sketch of the American seal, France wore the cap of liberty backwards, as if it had perverted its original cause by conquering and exploiting much of Europe under the pretext of setting it free. The conduct of France was inconsistent with modern liberty, which is meant to be universal rather than the mere privilege of the strong. For Hamilton at least, the universalization of liberty – that is, the doctrine of the rights of man – is virtually unthinkable without the preceding universal teaching of Christianity, which deliberately sought to limit wars of conquest and "rights" of the strong. "The praise of a civilized world," Hamilton declared at the height of the French Revolution, "is justly due to Christianity. War, by the humane principles of that religion," which established the doctrine of just war, has "been stripped of half its horrors." When the French made war on Christianity itself, they allowed these horrors to return. Their republican revolution inspired religious passion without religion, or what we today would call patriotic and ideological fanaticism, a modern development that is not all that far from what Machiavelli intended when he sought to render religion more civil and patriotic. Whereas Machiavelli deplored Christianity for making us soft and dividing our loyalties between church and state, Hamilton defended it because it subjected the state to some law superior to the general will. Without some form of that subordination, the only law was the will of the strong. When the French "renounce[d] Christianity," they imitated the "same spirit of dominion which governed the ancient Romans," who believed they "had a right to be Masters of the World and to treat the rest of Mankind as their vassals." They relapsed into "Barbarism" and war resumed the "hideous and savage form which it wore in the ages of *Roman* and Gothic violence." Hamilton therefore argued that "[i]f there be anything solid in virtue," a time would come when it would be considered a "disgrace" for any partisan of the rights of man "to have advocated the Revolution in France in its later stages."[41]

Like Machiavelli, Hamilton was aware that throughout most of human history the moral price of liberty for some has been their dominion over others. In

---

[41] See "The Cause of France," 1794; "The French Revolution," 1794; and "The War in Europe," September–December 1796, in *PAH* 17:585–8, 20:339–40. Largely because modern ideological warfare does inspire passions rivaling religious fanaticism, Hamilton did not think it would be possible to combat the French effectively without attaching the passions of religion to constitutional government in America. He proposed forming a Christian Constitutional Society, which might have been a more dynamic alternative to the moribund Federalist Party and have become an American version of the Christian Democrat parties of Europe. Constitutional government would thus have become a kind of Machiavellian civil religion, but for the purposes of combating the much uglier, atheistic civil religion of republican France. See AH to Timothy Pickering, 22 March 1797, and to James Bayard, 16–21 April 1802, in *PAH* 20:545, 25:606; and note NM, *D* 1.15, 2.2.

his first political pamphlet, Hamilton quoted David Hume, who was paraphrasing Machiavelli, in order to argue that free governments that are also mighty empires, such as England in 1775 and Rome before it, make the cruelest tyrants over their conquered provinces, which they exploit for their own benefit. Yet strategic necessity required Americans to unite and form their own empire to oppose the great empires of the old and new regimes of Europe. Could America be both a mighty empire and a new kind of republic that secured the rights of all members of the empire at the same time? Hamilton was not sure, but following Hume again, he had some hope, a vision of a perfect commonwealth, or what Machiavelli might call an imaginary republic, a political "PRODIGY" of "reflection and choice" that could combine strength and size with the legitimacy that arises from the consent of the governed. An empire might also be a "representative democracy," a term Hamilton may well have coined. This term, and the determination to found a government on consent rather than crime, distinguish the principles (if not always the practice) of modern liberal from ancient or Machiavellian republics very well. The latter accept tyranny in their empires to secure the liberty of the stronger; the former aim to extend liberty throughout their empires in order to make them legitimate. To give Machiavelli his due, perhaps all government is some mixture of force, fraud, and consent, but so far as possible, Hamilton sought to render the American empire legitimate by founding it on consent. "The fabric of the American empire," he claimed, "ought to rest on the solid basis of the consent of the people. The streams of national power ought to flow immediately from that pure, original fountain of all legitimate authority." For Hamilton at least, the only legitimate and effectual alternative to the Machiavellian politics of the ancient and new regimes of Europe was to republicanize the American empire. In principle at least, Hamilton's republican empire would therefore be the moral antithesis of the imperious republics championed by Machiavelli.[42]

To return to the original question, was Alexander Hamilton a Machiavellian statesman ? Of necessity, the answer depends on the perspective employed. Fearing Machiavellian princes, Hamilton's opponents often wondered whether he gave enough due to consent and republican government. Fearing Machiavellian republics and empires, Hamilton often wondered if his opponents gave enough due to the necessity of energy even (or especially) in a republic.[43] Hamilton paid at least as much attention as Machiavelli to the necessity of strength in government and energy in the executive. He had a subtle understanding of the relation between *virtù* and virtue – between effective, confidence-inspiring government and the public spirit of free citizens. Yet he also moralized Machiavelli's

---

[42] Cf. *The Farmer Refuted*, February 1775; AH to Gouveneur Morris, 19 May 1777; *The Stand*, no. 3, *New York Commercial Advertiser*, 7 April 1798, in *PAH* 1:86–7, 255, 21:408, and *Fed.* 1, 22, 85, with NM, *P* 15, 21; *D* 1.pref., 2.2; and Hume, "Of the Original Contract" and "An Idea for a Perfect Commonwealth," in *EMPL*, 21, 471, 525.

[43] See Speech of 18 June 1787 and "Conversation with Thomas Jefferson," 13 August 1791, in *PAH* 4:193, 9:33–4.

teaching by proposing a national bank, a professional citizen army, and a powerful commercial, maritime empire as ways to avoid the crime, despotism, and militarization of society (and virtue) that Machiavelli seemed to consider inseparable from republican warfare. Like Machiavelli, he sought to found a mighty empire, but unlike Machiavelli, he also sought to make it legitimate by constitutionalizing and republicanizing it. When it comes to waging war and remaining free at the same time, the American republican empire has been both more successful and more deserving of success than any other nation in history. The chief credit for this remarkable accomplishment belongs to Alexander Hamilton.

Index